SONDHEIM

SONDHEIM

His Life, His Shows, His Legacy

STEPHEN M. SILVERMAN

BLACK DOG
& LEVENTHAL
PUBLISHERS
NEW YORK

Cover design by Katie Benezra
Cover copyright © 2023 by Hachette Book Group, Inc.

Front cover photograph © Janette Pellegrini/Getty Images. Back cover photographs (left to right): Van Williams/Photofest; Carlos Barria/REUTERS/Alamy; © Entertainment Pictures/Entertainment Pictures/Alamy

Black Dog & Leventhal Publishers
Hachette Book Group
1290 Avenue of the Americas
New York, NY 10104

www.hachettebookgroup.com
www.blackdogandleventhal.com

First Edition: October 2023

Black Dog & Leventhal Publishers is an imprint of Perseus Books, LLC, a subsidiary of Hachette Book Group, Inc. The Black Dog & Leventhal Publishers name and logo are trademarks of Hachette Book Group, Inc.

The publisher is not responsible for websites (or their content) that are not owned by the publisher.

The Hachette Speakers Bureau provides a wide range of authors for speaking events.
To find out more, go to www.HachetteSpeakersBureau.com or email HachetteSpeakers@hbgusa.com.

Black Dog & Leventhal books may be purchased in bulk for business, educational, or promotional use.
For more information, please contact your local bookseller or the Hachette Book Group Special Markets Department at Special.Markets@hbgusa.com.

Print book interior design by Katie Benezra

Additional copyright/credits information is on page 293.

Library of Congress Cataloging-in-Publication Data
Names: Silverman, Stephen M., author.
Title: Sondheim : his life, his shows, his legacy / Stephen M. Silverman.
Description: First edition. | New York, NY : Black Dog & Leventhal, 2023. | Includes bibliographical references and index.
Summary: "An illustrated celebration of the output and impact of the legendary Stephen Sondheim. Organized by work, with sidebars throughout, this book is filled with quotes from collaborators, mentors, students, and devotees, all profusely illustrated with original photographs, programs, scenery, costume, and poster art, and more"—Provided by publisher.
Identifiers: LCCN 2022038782 (print) | LCCN 2022038783 (ebook) | ISBN 9780762482351 (hardcover) | ISBN 9780762482368 (ebook)
Subjects: LCSH: Sondheim, Stephen. | Composers—United States—Biography. | Lyricists—United States—Biography.
Classification: LCC ML410.S6872 S55 2023 (print) | LCC ML410.S6872 (ebook) | DDC 782.1/4092 [B]—dc23/eng/20220817
LC record available at https://lccn.loc.gov/2022038782
LC ebook record available at https://lccn.loc.gov/2022038783

ISBNs: 978-0-7624-8235-1 (hardcover), 978-0-7624-8236-8 (ebook)

Printed in China

1010

10 9 8 7 6 5 4 3 2 1

For my agent,
Martha Kaplan,
who is always the voice of reason.

But I like her just the same.

He exploded our notions of what a musical could be or be about, and while the press and public came to cheer or sneer, he was already inventing the next one.

—ANGELA LANSBURY, IN 1993, ON THE OCCASION OF STEPHEN SONDHEIM RECEIVING HIS KENNEDY CENTER HONOR

CONTENTS

Though he was not particularly tall or imposing, Stephen Sondheim (circa 1976) nonetheless
projected a tremendous presence, especially when he took his seat in a theatre.

TUNING UP

"I'm interested in the theatre because I'm interested in communication with audiences," the Broadway composer-lyricist Stephen Sondheim said. "Otherwise, I would be in concert music. I'd be in another kind of profession. I love the theatre as much as music, and the whole idea of getting across to an audience and making them laugh, making them cry—just making them feel—is paramount to me."

With a legacy of sixteen musical scores and lyrics to three more shows, Sondheim made audiences *feel*.

"I don't think the theatre is about converting people to new ideas," he said. "I think it's about confirming ideas you have by dramatizing them and making them human."

Who but Sondheim could express the conviction, complexity, and pain of a cannibalistic mass murderer as he did, meticulously, with *Sweeney Todd: The Demon Barber of Fleet Street*? Or dare even attempt to find humanity inside the lethal protagonists of the disquieting *Assassins*?

After his twin successes writing lyrics for the classics *West Side Story* and *Gypsy* while barely on the cusp of thirty, Sondheim, at forty, created *Company*, setting to music and words urban anxieties and the riddles of relationships. He followed with *Follies*, stitching together a frayed tapestry about love and desire, and then *A Little Night Music*, placing human foibles and foolish memories before audiences in three-quarter time. His *Pacific Overtures* told of the desecration of an empire; *Merrily We Roll Along*, the

wounding effects of straying from one's ambitions; *Sunday in the Park with George*, that it might be better to create your own world than occupy this one.

Did someone say iconoclastic?

That's before taking into consideration the various pleasures and lessons to be gleaned from *A Funny Thing Happened on the Way to the Forum*, *Anyone Can Whistle*, *Into the Woods*, and the alternately titled *Wise Guys*, *Bounce*, and *Road Show*.

"Writers write what they want to see on a stage," Sondheim said in 1994, as *Passion*, his chamber musical about obsession, was set to premiere on Broadway. The show, he said, "is about how the force of somebody's feelings for you can crack you open, and how it is the life force in a deadened world."

Taken collectively, Sondheim and his musicals changed the game, by redefining the genre, aligning life's misfortunes to melody, and making the art of making art inclusive to outsiders.

And all in rhyme.

His body of work advanced both the soundtrack of people's lives and the manner of the American musical—where traditional song-and-dance shows had not only shied away from issues but generally acted as a buffer against life's inauspiciousness, which Sondheim's works took as their focal point.

"If I consciously sat down to write something that would send people out of the theatre really happy," Sondheim said, "I wouldn't know how to do it."

Unpredictability was his calling and his path. This was apparent from youth, which he spent as a protégé of Oscar Hammerstein II. "Write what you believe, and you'll be ninety-nine percent ahead of the game," Hammerstein told him. "As soon as he put it into those competitive terms," said Sondheim, "I never used his kind of imagery again."

As history bore out, Sondheim's nonconformity was worn as a badge of honor; witness his professional collaborations with Jerome Robbins, Leonard Bernstein, Hal Prince, James Lapine, and others.

"Modern literature is full of difficult, challenging artists who toiled in obscurity until the public caught up with them and made them famous," contemporary literary critic Adam Kirsch observed. "Sondheim presents the much rarer case of an artist who started out at the heart of the establishment and moved away from it as his work became more ambitious and complex."

Like a Shakespeare sonnet, a Sondheim lyric is knotty and dense, even if Sondheim shook off any suggestion that he was a poet. "A poem you can read at your own speed," he would counter. "You can't do that with a song. A song exists in time."

Similarly, he shunned classifying *Sweeney Todd* as an opera, despite its being sung through: "Opera is designed to show off the human voice," he said, "but *Sweeney* is about telling a story and telling it as swiftly as possible."

Granted, upon first exposure, critics often did not know what to make of his work.

"I try not to read my reviews," he said, "but there's always some friend who'll come along and, under the guise of trying to comfort you, let you know that you've been speared."

The public wasn't particularly certain of what to make of his shows, either, sometimes finding them esoteric or beyond their grasp.

"Order out of chaos" was a recurrent theme of Sondheim's. "That's why I like crossword puzzles—order out of chaos," he told NPR's Terry Gross. "I think that's what art's about anyway. I think that's why people make art."

On the patio of his New York City townhouse, in 1972, his working tools: a well-worn Clement Wood rhyming dictionary; *Roget's Thesaurus* (1946 edition); yellow legal pads with a precise line count of thirty-two; a shot glass (with vodka, later wine); and the same soft-lead Eberhard Faber Blackwing No. 602 pencils favored by Frank Lloyd Wright.

"I've never thought for one minute: 'Oh, this line, oh, this dissonance is going to turn this audience off. I'd better change it.' Not once. That's a fool's game. To try to prejudge while you're writing is a waste of time."

Both critics and the public did catch up with him, however, mostly through later revivals, reimaginings, and revues.

In contrast to his leading lady, Desirée, in *A Little Night Music*, Sondheim did not risk losing his timing late in his career.

If anything, contrarian that he was, he did the opposite.

—

Baby Boomers, whether they knew it or not, were first influenced by Sondheim with the Oscar-winning 1961 movie *West Side Story*, which spawned cover versions of "Tonight" by such chart-toppers as Johnny Mathis, Eddie Fisher, the Four Lads, Jackie Wilson, Bobby Rydell, and Andy Williams.

Sondheim got his next big radio hit in 1973 with "Send in the Clowns," Desirée's delicate lament of lost love from *A Little Night Music*. The ballad, an international sensation after Judy Collins, Frank Sinatra, and others recorded it, quelled arguments that a Sondheim song could only exist within the framework of its show (although that was never a putdown), and the even louder claim that he was incapable of writing melody (which *was* a putdown).

Skip to 1985, and Barbra Streisand's *The Broadway Album*. With the exception of its standards by Frank Loesser, Rodgers and Hammerstein, Jerome Kern, DuBose Heyward, and the Gershwins, her recording disproportionately consisted of Sondheim: "Putting It Together" from *Sunday in the Park with George*; "Something's Coming" from *West Side Story*; "Not While I'm Around" from *Sweeney Todd*; "Being Alive" from *Company*; "Send in the Clowns" (with an added verse Streisand requested from Sondheim); "Pretty Women" from *Sweeney Todd*; "The Ladies Who Lunch" from *Company*; and "Somewhere" from *West Side Story*.

Uncertain of the project's commercial potential, given its reliance on a songwriter whose fan base was regarded as a small cadre of musical elitists at best, Columbia Records "wouldn't even, at that time, pay me until it sold two and a half million copies," said Streisand, despite her having a history with the label that went back nearly a quarter century.

The album sold more than four million copies.

Sondheim's profile was raised beyond Broadway.

—

The gateway to Sondheim for Generations X, Y, and Z tends to be the 1987 *Into the Woods*, an inventive show that gives modern voice to the Brothers Grimm and ample roles for youngsters cast in school and summer-camp productions.

"It's a show with no four-letter words in it, so nobody gets offended," said Sondheim, who also happened to mention it was one of the most popular titles with the Music Theatre International licensing agency.

Attention must likewise be paid to *Original Cast Album: Company*, a 1970 documentary that kept the Sondheim flame burning for more than half a century. Cinema verité filmmaker D. A. Pennebaker spent one fifteen-hour day—plus overtime to catch prickly actor Elaine Stritch's retake of "The Ladies Who Lunch"—inside Manhattan's CBS Thirtieth Street Studio as cast, creators, and recording crew committed the audacious new stage musical to vinyl.

Regarded by some as the most faithful screen adaptation of any Sondheim show—Sondheim himself likened it to a newsreel—Pennebaker's fifty-three-minute feature first aired on PBS in the early '70s and was subsequently shown at colleges and film festivals, until it slipped from sight—only to resurface in poorly duped prints that still drew devotion from video bootleggers and Sondheim cultists.

Finally, in 2021, Criterion released a 4K digital restoration on Blu-ray and added the title to its streaming service—crowning what, by then, had become a full-fledged Sondheim renaissance.

"I'm deeply embarrassed. I'm thrilled, but deeply embarrassed," Sondheim said when a theatre was named for him in Times Square to mark his eightieth birthday, in 2010. "I've always hated my last name," he added. "It just doesn't sing."

—

"In 2019 alone," Sondheim biographer David Benedict tabulated, "Adam Driver sang 'Being Alive,' [Sondheim's] anthem of hope from *Company*, in the film *Marriage Story*; Daniel Craig hummed a few bars of his *Follies* torch song 'Losing My Mind' in *Knives Out*; [and] his biggest, Grammy-winning hit 'Send in the Clowns' appeared to ironic effect sung by the ringleader of Joaquin Phoenix's attackers in *Joker*."

RIBBING IN RHYME

How recognizable a pop-culture figure was Stephen Sondheim?

Well enough to be spoofed. John Mulaney and Seth Meyers set up the theatre titan with their 2019 mockumentary, *Original Cast Album: Co-Op*, which mimics down to the turtle-necks D. A. Pennebaker's *Original Cast Album: Company*.

The show within the movie, the fictive Broadway musical Co-Op, is as much a love-hate letter to New York as the Sondheim–George Furth–Hal Prince prototype.

Richard Kind stars as a typically Sondheimian—which is to

Comedian John Mulaney, who played a neurotic composer in the spoof *Original Cast Album: Co-Op* (here, with Renée Elise Goldsberry), believed Sondheim lied in interviews: "He's like, 'I write lying down with pencils, and I like to have a drink before I do.'" This way, Mulaney reasoned, those following Sondheim's example would fall asleep, "so he would be the best."

say, highly strung—doorman of the co-op, although the scene-stealer is Paula Pell.

In her pert little hat and Peter Pan collar, the comedic actor (*30 Rock, Parks and Recreation*) and writer (*Saturday Night Live*) spews her eleven o'clock number, "I Gotta Go"—which she literally has to, for an ophthalmologist appointment—exhuming the spirit of Elaine Stritch from Pennebaker's film and all but eviscerating it.

A bleary-eyed, disheveled Mulaney weaves in and out as a composer-lyricist named Simon Sawyer—note the alliterative initials—callously slipping notes to a worn-out acting ensemble just informed that their Broadway show had closed the night before (shades of *Anyone Can Whistle* and *Merrily We Roll Along*, which recorded their cast albums a day after their closures).

Of Co-op's six song spoofs with their '70s sense and sensibility—lyrics by Meyers and Mulaney and music by Eli Bolin, aping *Assassins, Sweeney Todd, Little Shop of Horrors*, and *Working*—Sondheim opined, "The lyrics are crowded."

Jennifer Aniston and Billy Crudup, as rival network stars, also let fly with a sardonic "Not While I'm Around" from *Sweeney Todd* on the Apple TV+ *The Morning Show*, while late in 2019 came the promise that Dominic Cooke, director of London's National Theatre production of *Follies* with Imelda Staunton, would take charge of a screen version of that 1971 favorite for Heyday Films, best known for the *Harry Potter* series. "I'm more than delighted," said Sondheim, "I'm thrilled."

That news arrived on the heels of director Richard Linklater having already begun principal photography on *Merrily We Roll Along*, with Paul Mescal as Frank,

OPPOSITE: With pen and ink, Broadway's definitive caricaturist Al Hirschfeld (1903–2003) vividly encapsulated composer-lyricist Sondheim and producer-director Hal Prince's "series of landmark musicals that set the high-water mark for what the musical theater could achieve," Al Hirschfeld Foundation creative director David Leopold wrote in the 2015 *The Hirschfeld Century*. The artist also rendered solo portraits of a pensive Sondheim in 1977 and again (as seen here) in 1999.

RIGHT: In preparation for her 1985 *The Broadway Album*, Barbra Streisand "called up Steve and said I was interested in doing some of his songs," she told Stephen Holden of the *New York Times*. "We hardly knew each other." In fact, the only Sondheim she ever had recorded was "There Won't Be Trumpets," which, she said, "ended up not being released."

a composer; Beanie Feldstein as Mary, a budding novelist; and Ben Platt as Charley, Frank's writing partner. As the story covers a twenty-year time span, which Linklater scheduled to film at intervals over two decades, the movie's premiere is not expected until 2040.

Meanwhile, the Sondheim net continued to be cast even wider thanks to production revivals, with the momentum only expected to accelerate in 2020, given the arrival of the master's ninetieth birthday. Then came the pandemic.

Three high-profile productions—director Marianne Elliott's Broadway-bound London import of *Company* fueled by Patti LuPone's "The Ladies Who Lunch" and, with Sondheim's blessing, a gender swap of some roles; a Classic Stage Company Off-Broadway revival of *Assassins*, directed by the group's artistic director, John Doyle; and Steven Spielberg's $100 million cinematic reboot of *West Side Story*—were put on hold until 2021.

In 2000, Queen Elizabeth II greeted Sondheim at a Buckingham Palace reception to honor winners of the Praemium Imperiale Award, presented by the Imperial Family of Japan and the Japan Art Association in recognition of outstanding achievement in the arts.

Then, on Friday, November 26, 2021, the day after Thanksgiving, global tributes began pouring in from the moment news broke that Stephen Sondheim had died.

Fans lit candles and laid bouquets at the stage door of the Bernard B. Jacobs Theatre, where the new *Company* had begun performances only eleven days before.

"We have lost the Shakespeare of musical theatre," its director, Elliott, said in a statement before that evening's curtain.

Paul McCartney tweeted, "We have lost a great talent, but his music will live long and prosper."

The following Sunday, Lin-Manuel Miranda, surrounded by several Sondheim stars and casts representing every show on Broadway, stood in New York's Duffy Square and, choking up, read from Sondheim's book, *Look, I Made a Hat.*

Then the crowd sang "Sunday."

—

In 2020, when Sondheim turned seventy, he assessed the current Broadway landscape and told critic and essayist Frank Rich in a story titled, simply, "Conversations with Sondheim" (afterward, the two took their discussion on a tour of several states): "You have two kinds of shows on Broadway—revivals and the same kind of musicals over and over again, all spectacles."

Gone, he said, was the invigorating world in which he had grown up, when "the kind of shows I liked were still viable: those that developed stories through song in which the songs had individual voices."

And yet, the inveterate risk-taker invariably found novel ways of forging ahead.

SINGING HIS PRIZES

"As a composer and a lyricist, and a genre unto himself, Sondheim challenges his audiences," President Barack Obama said at a White House ceremony in November 2015, when he awarded Sondheim the Presidential Medal of Freedom. "His greatest hits aren't tunes you can hum, they're reflections on roads we didn't take and wishes gone wrong, relationships so frayed and fractured there's nothing left to do but 'Send in the Clowns.'"

Sondheim maintained that "the only awards that have any significant value are the ones that come with cash."

His proof: One prize, around 1990, allowed him to buy a Hamburg Steinway, which can cost at least $100,000.*

Over time, Sondheim was the recipient of a Pulitzer Prize, a Kennedy Center Honor, a National Medal of Arts Award, the Presidential Medal of Freedom, eight Tonys, eight Grammys, five Olivier Awards, an Academy Award, and an appointment to the American Academy of Arts and Letters, as well as a Visiting Professorship of Contemporary Theatre at Oxford University.

He also had two theatres named for him, one on Broadway and the other in London's West End.

Even more daunting, the vaunted status was achieved within his lifetime.

Richard Rodgers, with forty-three shows and more than nine hundred songs to his credit, was gone eleven years before a Broadway house was named for him.

For George Gershwin, the wait took forty-six years.

---

* As it turned out, the Hamburg Steinway sound was not to Sondheim's liking.

Through a college friend, twenty-three-year-old Sondheim (standing, with hands in pockets) landed a job on director John Huston's *Beat the Devil*. In foreground, from left: Peter Lorre, Humphrey Bogart, dialogue coach Hazel Meadows, and Gina Lollobrigida. Bogart and Sondheim bonded over chess—and would call out moves to each other even when a board was not available.

SPIRITUAL PRESENCE

I.

As first professional writing gigs go, Stephen Sondheim's was enviable, and nationally televised.

He was twenty-three.

The vehicle was *Topper*, a weekly half-hour situation comedy based on 1926 and 1932 novels by Thorne Smith, a *New Yorker* writer who was often as inebriated as his Prohibition-era characters. Cary Grant and Constance Bennett starred in a 1937 movie adaptation that spawned two sequels in 1938 and 1941.

Just like in the three movies, the CBS-TV incarnation, which first ran from 1953 to 1955, involved stuffed-shirt banker Cosmo Topper* and his haunting by two high-living ghosts who formerly resided in his suburban home, George and Marion Kerby. Exclusive to the TV version was their martini-loving St. Bernard, Neil, also deceased.

The novelty was, only Topper—and the TV audience—could see and hear George and Marion "constantly screw up his life," as Sondheim put it. This left Cosmo's already high-strung wife, Henrietta, all the more befuddled.

Out of seventy-eight *Topper* episodes produced, the actual number to which Sondheim contributed has been estimated as anywhere from a likely eleven to as many as twenty-nine, according to his senior writing partner on the show, who tended to exaggerate. Equally conflicting are stories of how Sondheim's participation even came about, other than it began when his surrogate parents, Dorothy and Oscar Hammerstein, took him to a dinner party.

Sondheim chronicler and later producer Craig Zadan reported that the auspicious meal took place at the Bucks County, Pennsylvania, home of the Hammersteins' neighbors, the actor Dorothy Stickney and her husband, the actor-playwright-producer Howard Lindsay. Sondheim biographer Meryle Secrest said dinner was served in a Clinton, New

---

* British actor Leo G. Carroll, a six-time collaborator with Alfred Hitchcock, played Topper; real-life spouses Anne Jeffreys and Robert Sterling played the Kerbys; and Lee Patrick, Humphrey Bogart's office-assistant-character Effie in *The Maltese Falcon*, played Henrietta.

OPPOSITE: A forerunner of *Bewitched* and *I Dream of Jeannie*, *Topper* was minimalized by Sondheim. Even so, series star Anne Jeffreys (here with Robert Serling, left, and Leo G. Carroll) remembered that at the premiere of *Company*, Sondheim approached her and said, "You don't even remember me, [but] I was one of the writers for *Topper*."

RIGHT: Stephen's mother, Etta Janet "Foxy" Sondheim, with her only child, Stephen, circa 1931.

FAR RIGHT: Sondheim taught himself to read by studying the labels in his parents' record collection. The first was "Ain't Misbehavin'"; after that, he graduated to reading the *New York Times*.

Jersey, country house belonging to longtime Hammerstein friends Donald and Pat Klopfer, he of the publishing business and she from a Broadway theatre-owning family.

Wherever the location, the young Sondheim, fresh from working with Humphrey Bogart on the Amalfi-coast film location of director John Huston's *Beat the Devil*,* was handily rubbing shoulders within a clique of celebrated achievers in their respective fields.

This would lead to his first writing job.

—

An only child of absentee working parents of German and Lithuanian Jewish background, Stephen Joshua Sondheim was born March 22, 1930, in New York City, and looked after by the family's household staff in the newly opened luxury San Remo apartment building on Central Park West.

"We lived very nicely," the adult Sondheim recalled, "but at the back of the building. After my father remarried, he moved to Fifth Avenue, still at the back of the building. From him I get my tendency to pessimism. He always looked at the black side, imagined the worst that could happen."

Verbally precocious and able to read from an early age, a practice he picked up by studying old 78 record labels on the family Capehart phonograph player, Sondheim was educated at the private preparatory Ethical Culture School. "One of my showings-off was that I would read the *New York Times* to my first-grade class aloud—and I didn't understand half the words I was reading—but I could read it."

He took "the obligatory two years of piano lessons" between ages six and seven, "which is what every nice, upper-middle-class kid on the Upper West Side did." When company arrived, the pajama-clad Sondheim "would be trotted out at the end of the day to play 'Flight of the Bumblebee,' or something like that, and then trotted back to my bedroom." Sondheim said in the 2010 Broadway revue *Sondheim on Sondheim* that his first experience on the piano was when he was very young and sat next to his father, who couldn't read music but liked to plunk out show tunes. Stephen would place his hand over his father's and follow along.

Atypical for the Upper West Side, Hebrew lessons and Sunday school were not part of Stephen's curriculum; as the son of nonobservant parents, he was never bar mitzvahed.

---

* Sondheim served as a clapper boy.

Also not in the picture was a sense of continuity, a general pattern throughout most of his childhood.

His homelife became strained in 1940 when Stephen was ten. His father, Herbert Sondheim, a successful dress manufacturer on Seventh Avenue, left Stephen's mother, Etta Janet "Foxy" Sondheim (her maiden name was Fox), for another woman, the Cuban-born Alicia Babé, a manager of fashion promotion at Macy's department store and, according to the adult Stephen, "a nice lady."

"I liked my father a lot, he was a swell fellow, but I didn't see him very often because my mother was bitter about him," said Sondheim, who went "many days, and weeks, and months when I didn't see my own father."

Foxy, a graduate of the Parsons School of Design and a stylist for the firm that bore her husband's name, never forgave Herbert.

"She would have members of her family follow me to see if I met him in secret," Foxy's by-then celebrated son told *Time* magazine in 1987. "She would telephone his

"You might have thought him the head of a major Wall Street bank or law firm," author John Steele Gordon said of his uncle, Oscar Hammerstein II, who "dressed conservatively (except for an occasional weakness for the boldly patterned bow ties then in fashion) but always with unconscious elegance." Sondheim seconded the elegance, "which may surprise those who associate him with the homespun quality of his work."

apartment to see if I answered, then hang up. I was a substitute for him, and she took out all her anger and craziness on me. From her I get my tendency to hysteria."

Nevertheless, Foxy knew how to sound maternal when the occasion demanded. At the time her son's *Follies* was generating attention, in 1971, *Time* reported that she "fondly" recalled for its interviewer, "Steve always wanted to be the American Noël Coward."

"My mother was supportive of me once she found out that I was now hobnobbing with Leonard Bernstein," Sondheim said. She "was only interested in success and fame. So, she liked what I did when it got good reviews, and not when it didn't. She was entirely a creature of public opinion."

As a result of the divorce, Stephen was sent to boarding school at the New York Military Academy at Cornwall on Hudson, where he skipped seventh grade and found, to his liking, "a kind of orderly discipline that helped counteract the chaos of home."

On campus, he was captivated by the school's pipe organ, which sparked an interest in music and satisfied his fascination with gadgets. "I took one look at those manuals [the hand keyboard] and took a year of organ there."

It was while he was an academy student that Foxy bought a summerhouse in Doylestown, Pennsylvania, the seat of tony Bucks County, sixty-five miles southwest from Manhattan and a haven for New York's literary and theatre set.

Among them were the Oscar Hammersteins.

—

Shortly before Foxy and Stephen arrived in Doylestown, Oscar Hammerstein, called "Ockie" by all, was licking his wounds over the disappointing reception accorded his last Broadway collaboration with composer Jerome Kern, 1939's *Very Warm for May*.

Not disappointed, however, was one enthusiastic nine-year-old in Manhattan.

"The curtain went up and revealed a piano," remembered Sondheim, whose father had taken him to the show, which featured a wafer-thin plot about a summer stock troupe. "A butler took a duster and brushed it up, tinkling the keys. I thought that was thrilling."

Very Warm for May also contained what Sondheim ranked "one of the most gorgeous, free-flowing melodies ever written." The song, "All the Things You Are," was the lone standard to come out of the show.

"Some of Kern's forms are extraordinary, and that may be the only song in which the tonic* is never stated until the last chord," Sondheim said, praising Kern for keeping the harmony "so subtle. If you study 'All the Things You Are,' it starts in the relative minor, and it ends up in the major, but it *never* states the tonic."

Despite this song, and a cast that included a wise-cracking Eve Arden, a dancing Vera-Ellen, and direction by a rookie named Vincente Minnelli, *Very Warm for May* was an unmistakable setback for Kern and Hammerstein, who, twelve years earlier, in 1927, had given cultural heft to the Broadway musical by adapting Edna Ferber's 1926 novel *Show Boat*.

The sprawling production—Ferber's 341-page book was even more sprawling—told the backstage stories of three generations aboard a Mississippi theatre steamboat, the *Cotton Blossom*.

"What Oscar clearly did" with *Show Boat*, Sondheim said, "not so much as a pioneer but as a synthesizer, was to take operetta principles and wed them to American musical comedy . . . song and dialogue intermixed that would tell a story and tell a story of some emotional truth and reality."

At the same time, "He made musicals more difficult to write, because suddenly you had the task of telling a story as well as writing songs."

---

* The tonic is the first-scale degree that provides the tonal center; one explanation is that it's the "do" in "do-re-mi."

TOP: Jerome Kern and Oscar Hammerstein's 1939 Broadway musical *Very Warm for May* failed with critics and audiences, but not with nine-year-old Stephen Sondheim. The cast included June Allyson, Jack Whiting, Vera-Ellen, and, far right, Eve Arden.

ABOVE: "Musical numbers should carry the action of the play and should be representative of the personalities of the characters who sing them," said Jerome Kern (here in 1934).

"No two productions are alike," Sondheim, a certifiable polymath, said of the 1927 *Show Boat* (original Ziegfeld Theatre production here). The first preview ran four and a half hours; opening night ran three. In the intervening years, revisions ran rampant, and even the movie versions, in 1929, 1936, and 1951, vary in story line, let alone (in the two sound versions) musical score.

PLATINUM PADDLE WHEELER

Around the end of World War I, during what has been called Broadway's Silver Age, musicals bothered little with plots, so long as ample opportunity existed for a procession of kicking chorus girls and a hook on which to hang songs that could translate into sheet music and recording sales.

Then, along came *Show Boat*, grounded in serious issues of misfocused love, family vs. career, gambling, alcoholism, and racism, and performed by a diverse cast, daring on its own terms, even with the show's stereotypical characters.

Kern and Hammerstein's songs helped develop the story, rather than stop it dead for old-hat specialty numbers. And what songs: "Ol' Man River," "Can't Help Lovin' Dat Man," "Make Believe," "You Are Love."

So palpable an advancement was *Show Boat* that its producer, Florenz Ziegfeld, flirted with the notion of mounting a twin production in a second Broadway house.

From Sondheim's perspective, however, *Show Boat* proved a disappointment in one regard: Its success failed to embolden musical writers of the time into abandoning their stale formulas in favor of seeking out new vistas.

FAR LEFT: "I must say that I object vigorously to your reprinting my juvenilia," Sondheim wrote to *Sondheim Review* editor Paul Salsini after the quarterly reported on his student shows. (Here, his Williams College musical *Phinney's Rainbow*, with twenty of his songs.) "Not only is it embarrassing, but I feel you are nibbling me to death." Even after the admonishment, the *Review* gamely continued its examinations of Sondheim's early efforts.

LEFT: Sondheim was editor of his Doylestown prep school's yearbook, which captioned his photo: "Do you need information about the theatre? Perhaps you require an intellectual giant to aid you in schoolwork, or maybe you'd like to hear some really masterful piano playing. Anyway, Steve's your man . . . George School's own Rachmaninoff."

Through a mutual friend, in 1939, Foxy Sondheim had lunch in Manhattan with Dorothy Hammerstein, who up until a year before had run her own successful interior design business, catering to well-heeled clients on both coasts. After showing Dorothy her Central Park West apartment, Foxy went on about how she and Herbert frequently entertained, wondering if Dorothy might consider coming out of retirement and freshening up the Sondheim residence.

Task in hand, and with Oscar's permission—now in his late forties, the theatre man was genuinely concerned his career had stalled—Dorothy Hammerstein was back in business, to the extent that she lived in Manhattan the better part of the week while Oscar stayed in Bucks County.

When Foxy and Stephen settled in Doylestown, "she sort of foisted me" on the Hammersteins, said Sondheim, who, according to Oscar's granddaughter-in-law, had his own room in the family manse. "By Christmas," said Jamie Hammerstein, Dorothy and Oscar's elder son, born exactly a year and a day after Stephen, "Stephen was more a Hammerstein than a Sondheim." Jamie also remembered, "I loved him as a brother, but Steve was not warm."

Accounts, some by Sondheim himself, reveal that Hammerstein clearly saw promise in the young Sondheim that he did not outwardly express about his own children, of which he had three: William and Alice by his first wife, Myra Finn, and James, or Jamie, by Dorothy. Dorothy also had two children, Henry and Susan, from her previous husband, diamond merchant Henry Jacobson.

"He and my father shared something, I think," Sondheim said of Hammerstein, "which is that they were not good parents until you were at a rational age." The problem that presented, he later discerned, having entered psychoanalysis when he was twenty-eight, was that "by the time you are a rational age, a number of wounds have been inflicted."

At the time Sondheim became a familiar figure in the Hammerstein home,* Oscar, after various Hollywood propositions had failed to materialize, was circling around a new project with a new collaborator. Composer Richard Rodgers was having

---

* The Sondheim house was three miles from the Hammerstein estate, which was humbly known as the Farm. Oscar's grandson, Oscar "Andy" Hammerstein III, said there were so many children running around the place that Oscar II devised a flag system; if a black flag was flying, it meant he was not to be disturbed. If red, he wanted a tennis partner.

June Walker as Laurey
Williams, Helen Westley
as Aunt Eller Murphy,
and Franchot Tone as
Curly McClain in the
original 1931 Broadway
production of *Green
Grow the Lilacs;* twelve
years later, Richard
Rodgers and Oscar
Hammerstein II turned
it into their first triumph
together, *Oklahoma!*

professional problems of his own; his creative partner, lyricist Lorenz Hart, suffered from chronic alcoholism.

Rodgers was leaning toward musicalizing a property sent by the Theatre Guild,* which wanted a Rodgers and Hart score and a Hammerstein libretto based on a not-quite successful play the Guild had produced ten years before, 1931's *Green Grow the Lilacs,* by Lynn Riggs.

Riggs, a gay Oklahoman of Cherokee descent, also wrote poems, novels, and screenplays, including those for David O. Selznick's *The Garden of Allah* and Cecil B. DeMille's *The Plainsman,* both produced in 1936.

Unbeknownst to Rodgers, Hammerstein had received his own copy of the Riggs play from the Guild and was himself keen on the property, hoping to supply both lyrics and libretto, but after meeting with Rodgers, he was willing to step back for Hart's sake. Moreover, Hammerstein told Rodgers, "If you and Larry are in the middle of a job and he can't finish it, I'll finish it for him, and nobody but the two of us ever need know."

"I really don't think *Green Grow the Lilacs* can be turned into a good musical. I think you're making a mistake," Rodgers claimed Hart said to him.

Rodgers and Hammerstein set about writing together, fashioning the songs, the book, even the dances to impel the story forward. They initially titled their show *Away We Go!,* which was how the marquees read during previews in New Haven and Boston. For most of the birth period, Hammerstein wrote his lyrics before Rodgers set them to music, merely one of the departures from the norm in what was taking shape. (Larry Hart needed the music before he could be corralled into setting lyrics to paper.)

---

* In 1925, for the *Garrick Gaieties* revue, Rodgers and Hart had supplied the Guild with a great success and the new writing team its first hit: the song "Manhattan."

There was no chorus line, per se. There was no "musical comedy" subtitle; this would be a "musical play." There were barely any sets, owing to the budget constraints of the Guild, just basic painted backdrops. The costumes weren't much, either, though they were brightly colored. There was also poor word of mouth from the usual Broadway naysayers, with Rodgers himself fretting that Oscar "had not had a solid Broadway success in almost ten years."

Until opening night.

Of Hammerstein's accomplishment, Sondheim said, "He took a play that was about homosexuality in the West and turned it into a sunny musical. Because he saw something in it that was beyond what Lynn Riggs had written, about the opening of territories, the promise of America. He saw that which anybody else reading that play would not have seen."

And that was *Oklahoma!*

—

"It wasn't the story. I mean, which boy is the girl going to take to the picnic? What could be more ridiculous?" Agnes de Mille, the choreographer of *Oklahoma!*, said in 1979, days before the opening of a splashy Broadway revival. She was explaining why the original show was such a success. The girl was homesteader Laurey Williams; the boys, local cowboy Curly McLain and Laurey's hired farmhand, Jud Fry.

"If you look on paper, 'Oh, What a Beautiful Mornin',' it doesn't look like much," Sondheim said about Curly's plain and simple entrance number. But Hammerstein "understood that what happens when music is applied to words, that the words explode—they have their own rainbows, they have their own magic."

Making the distinction between Oscar's lyrics and his own, Sondheim said, "I write a lot of conversational lyrics. They read well. Oscar's do not read very well,

"Look," choreographer Agnes de Mille said about the success of *Oklahoma!* (original production seen here), "it was wartime, 1943, and New York was where all the soldiers were brought before they were shipped overseas. And at the back of the theatre every night, there was a triple row of uniforms, standing, and the men were crying their hearts out, watching this jolly show, where the jokes are American, the songs are American— they're about corn, aren't they?—and here was something about everything they were going over to fight for."

LOVE'S BITTERSWEET SONGS

Mandy Patinkin, on the cover of his 1995 album *Oscar & Steve*, brought out the warmth in Sondheim and the wit in Hammerstein.

Mandy Patinkin, for his 1995 CD *Oscar & Steve*, juxtaposed *Carousel*'s "If I Loved You" with "Loving You," from Sondheim's *Passion*. In concerts, he combined the two.

Surmising that Sondheim's childhood likely provided the source of the pain he expressed in his lyrics, Patinkin, the original star of *Sunday in the Park with George*, submitted that the composer used "the canvas of the music paper as the battlefield for his emotions."

Despite Hammerstein's influence on the young Sondheim, the intrinsically disparate styles of the two writers, optimistic as opposed to skeptical, bucolic in contrast to urbane, are all the more evident when the two songs are heard side by side.

Both, in their own ways, touch a raw nerve while they uncover the sorrows that can arise out of romance.*

Sondheim's conditional love song, melodically on a par with Rodgers's and one of his most beautiful compositions, wrenches the gut more forcibly than Hammerstein's tender lyrics furnish—and yet, both songs poetically deliver their messages and stunningly service the shows they inhabit.

---

* Describing the precarious position a songwriter finds himself in when expressing such statements, musician Paul Simon, reviewing Sondheim's 2010 memoir and lyrics compendium *Finishing the Hat*, wrote, "If a writer composes a lyric with a complex thought or vivid image and fails to say it well, then the lines seem pretentious. If the songwriter goes for the heart and misses, then it's sentimental."

because they need music, and it's because of the super simplicity of the language—and it's precisely *that* that gives them such force."

Oklahoma! had force. "It was received in 1943 the way *Hamilton* is received today, as something really radically new in the theater," said Todd S. Purdum, author of *Something Wonderful*, on the changes Rodgers and Hammerstein brought to the medium.

Oklahoma! launched the Golden Age of the Broadway Musical, established a benchmark for long-running musicals (2,212 performances), initiated the marketing concept of the original cast record, and was of such renown that, starting seven months into its Broadway run, ten million people went to see its 250-city national tour between October 1943 and April 1954.

The following year, the movie version, in the newly introduced Todd-AO 70mm widescreen process, with six-track stereophonic sound, also set an example in technology and exhibition, opening in limited, big-city, reserved-seat engagements before a general release to neighborhood theatres in the more adaptable CinemaScope.

Rodgers and Hammerstein had become an institution.

Sondheim was thirteen when Oscar Hammerstein took him to see *Oklahoma!*, although the adolescent had been around the Hammerstein home during a major part of the show's development.

"What I learned from him was how to tell a story," Sondheim said. "Because of the success of *Oklahoma!* and subsequent shows, most musical theater now tells stories through songs." That had not been the case until *Oklahoma!*. "So, he was teaching me that. But he also taught me how to structure a song. He taught me the use of a rhyme, and oh, *everything*."

Under Hammerstein's guidance, Sondheim learned to develop character, steer clear of inconsistencies, and embrace concision. "His creative imagination was far more sophisticated than the work itself," Sondheim said of Hammerstein, whom he compared to Eugene O'Neill in terms of his willingness to experiment.

Contrary to common belief, however, *Oklahoma!* was *not* the first-ever book musical,* "but it was the first in which dancing actually bridges the plot. The story had huge gaps," said Agnes de Mille, whose dances brought new dimension to Broadway—compared to numbers choreographer George Balanchine had done in such shows as Rodgers and Hart's 1936 *On Your Toes*, which were viewed more as musical interludes.

"It had also been Oscar's intention to close Act I of *Oklahoma!* with a circus ballet," said de Mille. "He came to me and wanted to know how I liked his idea, and I said, 'That might be good. It might also be boring.'"

Rodgers and Hammerstein approached de Mille in the first place because, in 1942, she had created, choreographed, and danced the lead in a debut piece for the Ballet Russes de Monte Carlo. With music by Aaron Copland, and the first ballet to include tap-dancing, *Rodeo* was a love story set on a ranch in the American Southwest, so de Mille knew the territory. She had also received twenty-two curtain calls and a standing ovation at *Rodeo*'s Metropolitan Opera House premiere.

---

* Antecedents include *Show Boat*, *Pal Joey*, and *Lady in the Dark*.

SPINNING MAGIC

"I was drawn to Oscar, much more than to his work," Sondheim told Library of Congress music specialist Mark Eden Horowitz. Sondheim found there were times that Hammerstein relied too heavily on pretty, poetic-sounding words, rather than on strong images that a listener could quickly absorb and visualize before moving on.

Still, the opinion hardly negated Sondheim's strongly held belief that the "bench scene" in Rodgers and Hammerstein's *Carousel*, the duo's successor to *Oklahoma!*, is "probably the singular most important moment in the evolution of contemporary musicals."

In the course of the sequence's twelve minutes, the two protagonists, idealistic New England millworker Julie Jordan and street-tough carousel barker Billy Bigelow, socially distance on a park bench and literally shoot the breeze, puncturing the still night air with pointed self-confessions that flow like the petals off the overhead tree. The entire time, they are subtly underscored by musical themes, some apprehensive, even ominous, that foretell their fates—that both their lives are about to be transformed, and not for the better.

Total strangers at the start, they close the scene as ill-fated lovers and segue into the gold standard of conditional love songs, "If I Loved You"—the condition being that the two insist they are *not* in love with one another, even if that's not true.

Hammerstein took the words directly from a conversation in *Carousel*'s source, the 1909 Ferenc Molnár Hungarian stage drama *Liliom*.

"But you wouldn't marry a rough guy like me—that is, eh—if you loved me," Liliom, a Budapest amusement park barker, says to Julie, a servant girl he has just encountered.

"I'm a great audience," said Sondheim. "I cry very easily." He was fifteen when he saw *Carousel* on opening night, April 19, 1945. (Here, Jan Clayton and John Raitt as Julie and Billy, in the "bench scene.") By final curtain, his tears had permanently stained the "lucky" fur stole Dorothy Hammerstein traditionally wore to her husband's openings.

Oklahoma!'s seventeen-minute Dream Ballet climaxes, not with a typically upbeat tease that sends its audience out for a drink at intermission, but with a menacing Jud—one modern Jungian dream analyst compared him to Lucifer, or Darth Vader—leading a frightened Laurey away by the hand, as "Curly stands alone, puzzled, dejected, and defeated, as the curtain falls," Hammerstein wrote.

II.

"I, of course, had been brought up to think of music as inspirational, as the kind of thing when you're staring out of your New York penthouse, you look over the city, and suddenly a little birdie comes to your shoulder and goes 'bah-duh-duh-duh,'" Sondheim, now shaking his head in jest, told Omar Sangare, chairman and professor of theatre at Sondheim's alma mater, Williams College, in 2021.

In the fall of 1946, sixteen-year-old Sondheim, feeling confined in Pennsylvania, enrolled in the small, liberal arts college Williams, in Massachusetts, on the advice of his counselor at his preparatory George School, a Quaker institution near Doylestown. Although his heart was in mathematics, he was inspired—the shadow of Oscar Hammerstein looming large—to major in music after taking an elective with his first teacher on the subject, "a man named Robert Barrow," Sondheim recounted another time.

Barrow began teaching at Williams in 1939, "and everybody hated him because he was very dry . . . and I thought he was wonderful because he was very dry." Barrow also had a reputation for being the finest Common Practice Harmony* instructor in the nation. He would instill in Sondheim the realization that art isn't easy.

"Robert Barrow said music is about scale, and then he went into tonal music, and grammatic music, and it just opened my eyes—that's what an education should do—and I learned how music works." By graduation, "I no longer thought of [music] as some kind of airy inspirational divine gift. I thought of it as a science, as a way of organizing sound, which, of course, is exactly what it is."

Sondheim likened this discovery to "the skies opening up," then told himself, "'Well, I can do that.' Because you just don't know. You think it's a talent, you think you're born with this thing. What I've found, and what I believe, is that everybody is talented. It's just that some people get it developed and some don't."

TOP: After graduation from the George School, Sondheim entered Williams College: "I had to fight my way to get permission to do a musical there," he recalled nearly sixty years later. "They thought that was . . . not within academic standards."

ABOVE: "I was so taken with the music professor," Sondheim said of Robert Barrow, "that I decided to major in music and to write as much as I could."

* Common Practice is the general term for the start of Western Harmony, which grew out of liturgical and secular music during the Renaissance and is divided into three periods: Baroque (1600–1750), Classical (1750–1820), and Romantic (1810–1920).

THE GILDED STAGE

"The architecture of musicals dates back to Broadway's Golden Age, the dates of which can be agreed upon by no one," the producer Jack Viertel wrote in his essential *The Secret Life of the American Musical*. "My opinion is that it begins on the opening night of *Oklahoma!* (March 31, 1943) and ends on the opening night of *A Chorus Line* (July 25, 1975)."

Some historians see the Golden Age as folding its tent by the mid-'60s, when rock was monopolizing the airwaves, theatre audiences were growing older, and crime was overtaking the Times Square Theatre District.

Before the downturn, the Golden

Ethel Merman and her *Annie Get Your Gun* producers, Richard Rodgers (left) and Oscar Hammerstein, in 1946, during the Golden Age of the Broadway Musical. The three would each play a role in Sondheim's life—and he in theirs.

Age engendered shows still being revived today. New practitioners, as well as those whose operettas had defined the Silver Age, picked up on the R&H formula, or at least waved their batons in that direction.*

These included Irving Berlin (*Annie Get Your Gun*), Cole Porter (*Kiss Me, Kate*), E. Y. "Yip" Harburg and Burton Lane (*Finian's Rainbow*), Frank Loesser (*Guys and Dolls*, *How to Succeed in Business Without Really Trying*), Johnny Mercer and Harold Arlen (*St. Louis Woman*), Betty Comden, Adolph Green, and Leonard Bernstein (*On the Town*, *Wonderful Town*), Comden and Green and Jule Styne (*Bells Are Ringing*), Alan Jay Lerner and Frederick Loewe (*Brigadoon*, *Paint Your Wagon*, *My Fair Lady*, *Camelot*), Richard Adler and Jerry Ross (*The Pajama Game*, *Damn Yankees*), Meredith Willson (*The Music Man*), Jerry Bock and Sheldon Harnick (*Fiorello!*, *She Loves Me*, *Fiddler on the Roof*), Charles Strouse and Lee Adams (*Bye Bye Birdie*), Jerry Herman (*Hello, Dolly!*, *Mame*), Jule Styne and Bob Merrill (*Funny Girl*), John Kander and Fred Ebb (*Cabaret*, *Chicago*), Mitch Leigh and Joe Darion (*Man of La Mancha*), and Cy Coleman with Dorothy Fields (*Sweet Charity*), a favorite of Sondheim's for her effortless-seeming lyrics and use of her own vernacular.

Sondheim joined the integrated-book tradition in 1957, with his lyrics for *West Side Story* and, two years later, with *Gypsy*—although by the early 1960s, he was telegraphing a new message.

"People are still writing Rodgers and Hammerstein musicals. I find that a rut," he said. "Instead of writing what Rodgers and Hammerstein had to offer, and inventing on top of it, and adding to it, and expanding it, they have been copying, and that seems to be a great mistake, a waste of time, and unlikely to be successful."

---

* One exception was *Hair*, "The American Tribal Love-Rock Musical," with its scattershot but winning music, book, and lyrics by Gerome Ragni and James Rado, and music by Galt MacDermot. It opened in the tumultuous year of 1968 and was a phenomenon. As for its influence, its spiritual descendant would not come to Broadway for another twenty-eight years, Jonathan Larson's *Rent*.

At Williams, Sondheim wrote twenty songs for a show about the college, *Phinney's Rainbow*, whose title was a double play on the names *Finian's Rainbow* (1947) and the then president of the college, James "Phinney" Baxter III. *Phinney's* was the first musical ever produced by the school's theatre group. Sondheim's second campus musical was *All That Glitters*, based on George S. Kaufman and Marc Connelly's strange and seldom performed stream-of-consciousness play titled *Beggar on Horseback*, about a composer who struggles between composing popular or serious music. Sondheim chose the 1924 Expressionist drama—it contains an extended dream sequence that depicts a murder—as part of a four-pronged informal exercise Oscar Hammerstein assigned back when Stephen was still a student in Doylestown, to help him find his own voice.

Music professor Milton Babbitt, with whom Sondheim studied for two years, advocated "advanced music"—and offered no apologies if audiences found it too difficult to understand.

According to the Hammerstein syllabus, Sondheim's first musical should be based on a play he admired (ergo, *Beggar on Horseback*); the second, a play he liked but thought flawed (Maxwell Anderson's *1936 High Tor*); the third, an existing but not previously dramatized novel or short story (*Mary Poppins*); and the fourth, an original (which Sondheim titled *Climb High*).

When it came to P. L. Travers's flying nanny, Sondheim began the project before leaving Williams, wrote about two-thirds, called it, or at least one of its songs, *Bad Tuesday*, but could never find a satisfactory way of linking the tales into one coherent story.

Speaking of the effort decades later, Sondheim said, dryly, his version was "fairly different from the film" made by Walt Disney.

———

After graduating magna cum laude from Williams, and at Robert Barrow's encouragement, Sondheim applied for and won the Hubbard Hutchinson Memorial Fellowship, named for a Williams graduate who went on to become a musician and music writer for the *New York Times*.

The Hutchinson honor, which Sondheim received two years in a row, brought two annual grants of $3,000 (adjusted for inflation, $35,000 a year today), so graduating students could continue their pursuit of the creative arts.

As Sondheim budgeted the prize, it was enough to live well in New York, provided he paid no rent. So, setting up a cot in the dining room, he moved in with his father, stepmother, and their two sons, Herbert Jr. and Walter. Then, four hours once a week, in the instructor's downtown studio, he studied compositional technique with Princeton professor Milton Babbitt, a highly engaging, highly intellectual, high-modernist composer with a love of show tunes.

"We would spend the first hour analyzing songs by Jerome Kern or by [Buddy G.] DeSylva, [Lew] Brown and [Ray] Henderson—the classic songs of the American theater and American movies," said Sondheim, remembering Babbitt's encyclopedic knowledge and perfect recall. This would be followed by "three hours on Beethoven and Bach, and it was all about essentially compositional analysis."

Babbitt believed that formulas, rather than spontaneous choices, led to variables of pitch and volume. He also taught advanced mathematics, pioneered synthesized music with the aid of humongous mainframe computers (in 1957), and composed seminal avant-gardist works—performed to mostly confounded audiences. It was said, just as it later was of Sondheim, that Babbitt's "difficult music" required repeated listenings before it could be appreciated, even comprehended.*

To counter the criticism, no matter how many times the issue was raised, Babbitt tendered the rich melodies he composed for a stage musical about Helen of Troy he was developing in the late 1940s for Broadway star Mary Martin.

Disappointingly for Babbitt, she went off and played Nellie Forbush in Rodgers and Hammerstein's *South Pacific* instead.

Babbitt, in 1982, received a Special Citation "for his life's work as a distinguished and seminal American composer" from the Pulitzer Committee, which cited his friendships with Arnold Schoenberg and Edgard Varèse, his influence on "a generation of European composers, including Pierre Boulez and Karlheinz Stockhausen," and the fact that Babbitt "even trained Stephen Sondheim in a private tutorial."

Under Babbitt's instruction, Sondheim learned "to analyze the music, look at what it is. How do you sustain something, hold a piece together for forty-five minutes, if it's a symphony, or three minutes, if it's a song? How do you manage time? That's what he taught me." Sondheim further credited Babbitt with "the utilization of themes over and over again, but developed, not repeating." Sondheim said that helps tighten the music and make for a better experience, and was something he did in abundance for *Sweeney Todd*.

"What it amounts to is, music exists in time, so how do you make it cohere?"

What Babbitt didn't teach Sondheim was atonal music. "He said, 'There's no point until you've exhausted tonal resources for yourself. You haven't, have you?'"

Recalling Babbitt as another rigorous and inspirational teacher after Hammerstein and Barrow, Sondheim listed his personal musical influences as Ravel, Britten, Rachmaninoff, and Stravinsky.** "They show up all the time in my stuff," said Sondheim.

As for Babbitt's memory of his Broadway-bound pupil, whom the tutor painted as a quick study but a slow worker, on account of his steadily searching to satisfy himself, Sondheim, said Babbitt, "was also constantly being diverted with parties."

Still, "no one could have been more serious about his music than Steve, and he wanted to improve himself in every conceivable way. He wanted his music to be as sophisticated and as knowing within the obvious constraints of a Broadway musical."

---

* Which might explain the line in *Merrily We Roll Along*, when the producer tells the crestfallen theatre hopefuls, "It's not a tune you can hum."

** That last composer is also mentioned in *Merrily* as a composer whose work one can't hum.

The music of French impressionist composer Maurice Ravel (1875–1937, here in 1925), strongly influenced Sondheim throughout the Broadway composer's life, beginning in his teen years.

Going back to that 1953 dinner party hosted by either Dorothy Stickney and Howard Lindsay or the Klopfers, in addition to Dorothy and Oscar Hammerstein and Sondheim, another guest was a fellow graduate of Williams College, George Oppenheimer.

Thirty years Sondheim's senior, Oppenheimer, a cofounder of the book-publishing company Viking Press and onetime screenwriter for MGM (*Libeled Lady*, *A Day at the Races*), had studied playwriting under the pathbreaking Harvard professor George Pierce Baker, whose students included Eugene O'Neill, Philip Barry, Sidney Howard, Thomas Wolfe, John Dos Passos, and Elia Kazan. (When Harvard's board balked at Baker's proposal that the university should establish a School of Drama, he took his idea to Yale, which made good of it.)

Oppenheimer's first Broadway play, *Here Today*, was produced in 1932, starred Ruth Gordon, and was based on an imagined Caribbean beach party made up of thinly disguised versions of writers Robert Benchley, Donald Ogden Stewart, and Dorothy Parker, who later said after a loud crash interrupted one of her cocktail parties, "Pay no attention. It's only George Oppenheimer dropping a name."

Commissioned in 1951 to bring *Topper* to the small screen, Oppenheimer ground out a pilot episode and, assuming the project would never materialize, was surprised more than a year later when the series was greenlit, forcing him, he recalled, "to prepare the first group of half-hour episodes in a period usually allocated for the creation of a sonnet."

For good measure, he was told to find an assistant to accompany him to Hollywood "all in a matter of days," an exigency brought up in conversation at dinner with the Hammersteins—and which Oscar immediately remedied, according to Oppenheimer. "He had a young protégé, Stephen Sondheim by name."

Once Oppenheimer reviewed Sondheim's writing samples, they agreed to collaborate for half a year, with Sondheim receiving a weekly stipend of $300, the equivalent of $3,150 today.

Plot points on the Oppenheimer-Sondheim *Topper* episodes, inclusive of disruptions from the Kerbys, dealt with hiring a housekeeper (the expressive character actress Kathleen Freeman); nabbing a burglar (George and Marion's butting in all but gets Cosmo indicted); and wife Henrietta's composing an advertising jingle to win a trip to Europe (her cringeworthy attempts at rhyming the product's name, "Individual Oats," with "like music with beautiful notes" and "the cereal everyone votes—for" bear a fairly recognizable Sondheim imprint).

"We alternated writing scripts," Sondheim said in 2005. He credited the repetition of writing the episodes with instilling a discipline for structuring the arc of a story and framing scenes within the severe time restrictions of the allotted twenty-two minutes, with breaks for the requisite commercials.

This coalesced with a creative instruction from Hammerstein: "A song, like a play, should have a beginning, a middle, and an end. It should have an idea, state the idea, and then build the idea and develop it, and finish. And in the end, you should be in a place different from where you began."

After six months, the TV grind proved enough for Sondheim, and the situation was further worsened by the arrival of his mother. Then there was Oppenheimer. He revealed himself to be bipolar, so he left *Topper* to become drama critic for Long Island's *Newsday*.

While still in California, Sondheim pitched various scripts for radio and TV, among them two based on another Cary Grant movie, *Mr. Blandings Builds His Dream House*, as well as a teleplay, "Teddy and the Magician," for an unrealized series called *Kodak Family Adventure*. He and his future *A Funny Thing Happened on the Way to the Forum* collaborator Larry Gelbart also submitted a dramatic treatment called *The King of Diamonds*, about an industrial spy with epilepsy.

"The company whose secrets were being rifled had a lower-case 'i' in its name," remembered Gelbart, "and the dot over the 'I' at the reception desk contained the wall safe works that our spy hero was able to crack."

None of these sold.

Sondheim's answer was to return to his native New York City, set up his own first apartment there, and strive to break into theatre.

"There are two lyrics in this show I liked then and I still like," Sondheim said of *West Side Story*'s first two songs: "Jet Song" and "Something's Coming." "They have a kind of angry, inner drive that comes from feeling and passion, rather than from an author putting down words on paper."

STREET
FIGHTERS

As a favor, in 1954 George Oppenheimer introduced Sondheim to
a pair of Broadway producers: actor-producer Martin Gabel, who had
begun with Orson Welles's Mercury Theatre and was married to actress
and broadcast personality Arlene Francis, and Henry Margolis, whose
investments included the French restaurant La Côte Basque,
home to the highest echelon of the ladies who lunched.

Gabel and Margolis "were going to do a musical version of James M. Cain's novel *Serenade*," said Sondheim.

The violent romance, from 1937, told of opera star John Howard Sharp, whose voice goes dry after succumbing to the sexual advances of a wealthy male patron. Sharp's crisis lands him in Mexico, where he meets Juana Montes, "a three-peso whore," who believes he'd make the perfect mentor and pimp. After physically consummating their relationship in Acapulco, which gives John his voice back, he and Juana go to Hollywood, where he becomes a musical star, only to recognize his true love: opera. Things grow complicated, and bloody, in New York once his former patron reenters the picture.

Composer Leonard Bernstein, playwright-scenarist Arthur Laurents, and choreographer-director Jerome Robbins were attached to *Serenade*, although Robbins was pushing for another idea—a modern retelling of *Romeo and Juliet*—while Laurents flat-out told Bernstein that *Serenade* was trash.

"I don't know who was going to do the lyrics," Sondheim said, "but Bernstein and Robbins had dropped out, so they were looking for a composer." Sondheim auditioned, "but then the project was dropped about two months later, because Warner Bros. had announced that they were going to do a film of *Serenade*."*

———

* Sanitizing Cain's novel, Warners' 1956 *Serenade*, starring lirico-spinto-tenor-cum-actor Mario Lanza and Joan Fontaine as part of his love triangle—the other was Spanish actress Sarita Montiel as Juana, not as a prostitute but a bullfighter's daughter—packaged familiar arias, a couple of new songs by Nicholas Brodsky and Sammy Cahn, and an implausible happy ending.

"Depends who you ask" was Sondheim's standard reply about the origin of *West Side Story*.

The easy answer was a 1590s play by William Shakespeare, although Sondheim would allude to Jerome Robbins's coaching the actor Montgomery Clift on how he might "find" the role of Romeo. The year was 1947, the site was the newly founded Actors Studio in New York, where Robbins—already established as a star dancer-choreographer with his ballet *Fancy Free*, as well as a much-in-demand choreographer on Broadway after the hit musicals *On the Town* and *High Button Shoes*—was getting a feel for the school's Method approach.

When Clift hit a wall regarding the schism between the Montagues and the Capulets, "Robbins put it in modern terms and suggested that it was 'as if' there was a feud between two ghetto street gangs in New York," wrote Patricia Bosworth, a Clift biographer, providing as good a synopsis of *West Side Story* as any—although, at this juncture, the show was still ten years away and its lyricist a student at Williams.

"This part seems very passive," Robbins quoted Montgomery Clift as saying. "Would you tell me what you think I should do with it."

Once Robbins thought to bring the story up to date, "I wrote a very brief outline and started looking for a producer and collaborators who'd be interested." Producers weren't. "Arthur and Lenny were."

Jerome Robbins conceived, choreographed, and performed the 1944 ballet *Fancy Free* to music by Leonard Bernstein. From left: Robbins, John Kriza, Harold Lang, Janet Reed, and Muriel Bentley.

TOP: Arthur Laurents, circa 1946.

ABOVE: Leonard Bernstein, 1945.

Arthur was the writer Arthur Laurents, who, by 1947, had a Broadway credit (*Home of the Brave*) and was about to gain one in Hollywood (Alfred Hitchcock's *Rope*). Born Arthur Levine, Laurents grew up in Brooklyn's Bushwick neighborhood, where bare-knuckle knockdowns between Irish and Jewish kids were commonplace. Laurents pursued writing at New York University and sold a play to CBS Radio before being drafted into World War II. A member of the Army Pictorial Service stationed in Astoria, Queens, New York, he wrote training films and radio propaganda—a scene he re-created for the opening of his most famous screenplay, *The Way We Were*. He also imbued the movie's Barbra Streisand character, Katie Morosky, with many of his own personality traits and political ideals. Although not a Communist, he had studied with a Marxist group and was blacklisted for a time.

Lenny, meanwhile, was Leonard Bernstein, with whom Robbins already had a history, as composer of the music to Robbins's breakthrough *Fancy Free*. Five months before the ballet's premiere, November 14, 1943, Bernstein, only twenty-five, stepped in at the last minute for an ailing New York Philharmonic conductor Bruno Walter and confidently led the evening's concert. CBS-Radio carried the Carnegie Hall event live, and the next morning's *New York Times* front *and* editorial pages trumpeted the triumph. Bernstein was an overnight sensation.

Fancy Free, about three sailors and their girls, was based on three of Paul Cadmus's homoerotic paintings: *The Fleet's In*, *Shore Leave*, and *Sailors and Floozies*. Robbins, like Bernstein, the son of Old World parents, sought to perform something definitively New World, *American*. When their one-act ballet premiered at the Metropolitan Opera House April 14, 1944, Robbins and Bernstein captured the same lightning in a bottle Agnes de Mille had with Aaron Copland and *Rodeo* two years earlier. And, like de Mille, who transitioned to Broadway but still kept a foothold in ballet, both men extended their reach into theatre while also remaining rooted in their respective worlds of classical music and modern dance.

Hoping to create something serious with their next endeavor, Robbins and Bernstein instead followed set designer Oliver Smith's suggestion that they expand *Fancy Free* into a full-blown musical. Joining them were director George Abbott, and friends of Bernstein's, sketch-revue writers Betty Comden and Adolph Green, for the book and lyrics; except for Abbott, they were all Broadway neophytes.

On the Town, as it was called, also cast Comden and Green in two of the principal roles and opened to supportive reviews on December 28, 1944, establishing—and in Abbott's case, further solidifying—the theatre chops of its creators.

As for Sondheim, at the time Robbins and Montgomery Clift were first delving into Romeo's motivations, the seventeen-year-old was already boasting Broadway-level stage experience: Oscar Hammerstein had hired him during the Williams College summer break to work as a gofer on what would become Rodgers and Hammerstein's fascinating failure, *Allegro*.

———

As the careers of Laurents, Robbins, and Bernstein gained further traction, their on-again, off-again *Romeo and Juliet* venture went through various permutations (feuding Jews and Catholics, whites and Hispanics, whites and blacks), along with titles (*East Side Story*, *Operation Capulet*, *Gangway!*), even settings (downtown Los Angeles, New York's Lower East Side, Harlem). Fellow composer Jack Gottlieb warned his friend Bernstein that the field might already have been tapped out—who needed another musical about a floating crap game?

By 1949, Bernstein had penciled in "An out and out plea for social tolerance" atop his copy of Shakespeare's tragedy. Robbins typed up an outline with handwritten notes indicating where and what the action would be. His six scenes for Act I included a hideout for a fight against Jews, a street festival for "R & J" to meet, a balcony for a "quiet love scene," a drugstore where "R" works, a bridal scene with wedding manne-quins, and a playground for the fatal fight between Tybalt and Mercutio.

Act II, which would conclude with Romeo's death in a cellar, was to open with a Seder and a small ballet, followed by a larger ballet mid-act.

"It's not a dream sequence ballet," Robbins said about the number, in 1980, while overseeing a painstakingly faithful Broadway revival of *West Side Story*. "It's really a longing for where they want to be, and that, under the right circumstances, they are all capable of lyricism and peace."

Sondheim was a seventeen-year-old gofer on Rodgers and Hammerstein's 1947 *Allegro*. Considered the first "concept" musical, the show expressed its theme through its stag-ing and score.

HOW DO YOU SOLVE A PROBLEM LIKE *ALLEGRO*?

Forty-seven years after he fetched coffee and typed scripts in anticipation of *Allegro*'s Boston opening, Stephen Sondheim introduced a 1994 New York City Center *Encores!* revival of the rarely performed curiosity.

He described *Allegro* as nothing short of "remarkable," given concepts Hammerstein put into making it "the first commercial attempt to tell a man's entire life story in a musical" and the first to use "a musical comedy chorus as a Greek chorus" onstage to "explore the inner thoughts of the main characters"—a device that also made its way into Sondheim's *Merrily We Roll Along*.

Allegro begins in 1905 and tells of Joseph Taylor Jr., a small-town doctor who, at the urging of his unloving wife, moves to the big city, only to lose his sense of self. He finds himself, and the right partner, by final curtain.

"It changed the musical theatre," said Sondheim, ever the Hammerstein torchbearer, even when taking swipes at his mentor. He further stated that *Allegro* was the one show Hammerstein had wished to revisit, although "nothing could ever really fix that show."

Hammerstein saw Taylor's story as mirroring his own, in that success—awards, important committees, ceremonies—had lured him away from what he was born to do: write.

In musical terms, *allegro* means "brisk tempo," while here it also stands for the fact that life passes too quickly.

The show certainly did, running only nine months once audiences realized they weren't getting another *Oklahoma!* or *Carousel.*

Rodgers and Hammerstein became victims of their own success.

By "they" he was referring to Tony and Maria, the musical's Romeo and Juliet, although, by the mid-1950s, *West Side Story* had yet to evolve that far, let alone find a final title, which did not materialize until late in the show's 1957 rehearsal period.

On August 25, 1955, when Leonard Bernstein and Arthur Laurents were both working in Hollywood, the two met poolside at the Beverly Hills Hotel and *Romeo and Juliet* again came up for discussion, as did a *Los Angeles Times* article on gang violence in Southern California. By the following year, Laurents had a three-page scene breakdown for what was simply titled *Romeo* and which included characters named by Shakespeare, such as Benvolio, and those by Laurents, Bernardo.

Sondheim, whom Laurents recalled as "unprepossessing, an indoor complexion, droopy clothes," came aboard in the fall of 1955. On October 4, the two spoke in the salon-like living room of the actors Ruth Ford and Zachary Scott in the Dakota apartment building. Sondheim had been brought there by his friend, the writer-director Burt Shevelove.* Knowing that *Serenade* was history, Sondheim inquired what Laurents was working on, then "idly" asked who was writing lyrics for this *Romeo and Juliet* project.

"Oh, I never thought of you," Laurents replied, literally smacking his forehead, according to Sondheim. "We're looking, because Betty and Adolph were supposed

---

* The occasion was the opening night of the English translation of the Ugo Betti play *Island of Goats*, starring Uta Hagen and Laurence Harvey. It lasted seven performances.

to do it, but they can't get out of their Hollywood contract."*

Thanks to Martin Gabel, Laurents had been privy to Sondheim's score to what would have been his first musical, the abandoned *Saturday Night*. Laurents, notoriously caustic, told the twenty-five-year-old** that he "really liked your lyrics," but "I didn't like the music so much."

Sondheim was not interested in being confined to lyric writing, "but I *was* interested in meeting Leonard Bernstein." Through Laurents, and with Robbins also in attendance, he did.

Sondheim auditioned some songs from *Saturday Night*, which was "about a group of kids at the time of the stock market crash. It was a very New York show, all colloquial. Lenny liked to intimidate people. He asked, 'Haven't you got anything poetic?'"

Sondheim explained how that wouldn't be appropriate for the characters, young guys in Brooklyn, "but," Sondheim said, Bernstein "liked what he heard." As Bernstein jotted down at the time, "A young lyricist named Stephen Sondheim came and sang us some of his songs today. What a talent! I think he's ideal for this project, as do we all."

Sondheim, 1957.

"I'm very flattered," Sondheim replied when Bernstein called to say that he was welcome to come aboard. "Let me call you back," Sondheim further responded.

Sondheim immediately phoned Hammerstein, presenting the case that he really wasn't interested in only writing the lyrics.

Hammerstein advised, "I think you should do it, because these are three extremely gifted professionals . . . and you can always write music later."

Besides, Hammerstein said, "It's a job."

---

* The duo were involved in MGM's quasi follow-up to *On the Town*, *It's Always Fair Weather*, again with Gene Kelly, although filming finished in January 1955. In December 1955, Comden and Green plopped a telephone directory on the desk of composer Jule Styne in New York and suggested they do a musical about a phone-answering service for their former revue costar, Judy Holliday. That became *Bells Are Ringing*.

** Laurents was thirty-eight, a year older than both Robbins and Bernstein.

ORIGINALLY announced to open on Broadway in 1955, Sondheim's *Saturday Night* finally made it to Off-Broadway in 2000.

A SPREE GROWS IN BROOKLYN

Off-Broadway critics and fans were kind in 2000 when, forty-five years after its unrealized Broadway premiere, Sondheim's freshman effort, *Saturday Night*, was at last unveiled. In it were portents of what would later flow from his soft-lead pencils.

Kathleen Marshall choreographed and directed for New York's Second Stage following separate productions in London and Chicago; in the intervening years, songs from the score became firmly entrenched on the cabaret circuit: "Saturday Night" (fellas yearning for dates), "Isn't It?" (Junior League poseur seducing the hero), "What More Do I Need?" (love transforming Brooklyn into Shangri-La), and, for lack of a better adjective, the haunting "So Many People" (heroine falling prey to the effects of love). Since 2000, there have been various full revival productions and special concert versions performed.

Based on the play *Front Porch in Flatbush* by twin brothers Julius J. and Philip Epstein (with Howard Koch, they had written Hollywood's *Casablanca*), *Saturday Night* follows girl-crazy pals, in particular Gene, a lowly stock runner on Wall Street and, it turns out, a con man manqué—"mutton dressed up as lamb, as we say Down Under," said Australian actor David Campbell, who played the part at Second Stage.

Julius Epstein alone wrote the musical book; Philip died in 1952, the same year Sondheim and Lemuel Ayres met at the wedding of a mutual friend. Ayres, who designed *Oklahoma!* and designed and produced *Kiss Me, Kate*, held the rights to *Front Porch* and was turned down in the score-writing department by Frank Loesser, leaving the job-door open.

Enter Sondheim, who sealed the deal by selling Ayres three tryout songs at $100 a pop.

After eight backers' auditions, the coffers were only half full when Ayres, having long concealed his diagnosis, died of leukemia at the age of forty. His widow, costume designer Susan Osborne Ayres, sought to move forward, but *Saturday Night* stagnated, although interest was ignited in the wake of the 1959 success of *Gypsy*.

Sondheim's collaborator on that show, composer Jule Styne, set about producing *Saturday Night* for Broadway, with Bob Fosse choreographing and directing.

"Bobby got as far as one day of auditions," Sondheim told arts journalist Barry Singer, "mainly to audition a movie actor named Keefe Brasselle (at [Julius] Epstein's request) for the lead, though Bobby wanted to play it himself. And yes, it was our only (brief) professional relationship."

At the time, Sondheim put his own kibosh on the project, because he "didn't want to revisit old work."

"There's a lot of plot in *West Side Story*, but its scenes are probably the shortest of any book musical that's ever existed," said Sondheim, who, true to Hammerstein's word, was learning on the job. "Not only was I, for the first time, writing lyrics to someone else's music," but "the someone was a legend verging on myth."

Bernstein "liked to work together in a room, and I liked to work separately. So we compromised. We'd separate for two days and then we'd get together on the third day. We talked on the phone a lot."

Sondheim said Laurents shared a lesson that had come into vogue at the Actors Studio in the '50s: subtext, "to make words and intention collide" and create a space that gives an actor room to *act*. Laurents himself "did something very smart," Sondheim added. "He said the trouble with street slang is that it dates. So, he made up a lot of language and has the guys say things like, 'riga-tiga-tum-tum.' It's a sort of Alice in Wonderland language that doesn't date."

Not that Sondheim was lacking for ideas: "I wanted to be the first person to use a four-letter word on Broadway."

The expletive—which, as CBS Records cast-album producer Goddard Lieberson cautioned, could not be used, under fear of bringing obscenity charges once the recording crossed state lines—was to be applied to the bane of the gangs' existence, Officer Krupke. "F—— you!" was euphemistically changed to "Krup you!"

Krupke is the cop on the beat where the all-white Jets brawl to keep their West Side turf. They are threatened by the rival Sharks, young men who have recently arrived from Puerto Rico. These were the contemporary equivalents of the Capulets and the Montagues, at least, in terms of feuding factions.

"We started rehearsals in a place called the Chester Hale Studio, on Fifty-Sixth Street near Carnegie Hall, in a loft above a garage," said Robbins. Peter Gennaro assisted as co-choreographer. "He did most of 'America' and [shown here] the Sharks' dances in the dance hall competition," Robbins acknowledged.

Chita Rivera (center), who played Maria's minder Anita on Broadway, said Robbins was particularly harsh with Michael "Mickey" Calin, who played Riff. "He was perfect for the role—smooth, handsome, and the girls loved him," said Rivera. "One time I walked past Jerry, and he was about to let Mickey have it. I said, 'Please, don't.'"

"We would meet wherever we could, depending on our schedules," Robbins said of *West Side Story*'s thirteen-month prerehearsal period. "Arthur would come in with a scene, the others would say they could do a song on this material, I'd supply, 'How about if we did this as a dance?'"

Robbins was speaking disingenuously; invariably, if not uniformly, he got his way—even if it meant barring Bernstein, Laurents, and Sondheim from rehearsals, which he did. Sondheim, being the kid in the group, often received the least amount of attention.

"They could only come when Robbins invited them, which was rare. He only invited them when he wanted to show them something," Grover Dale, who played one of the Jets, Snowboy, in the original cast, said in 2022.* "So, they were hardly around in those days."

Years later, Sondheim told his collaborator on *Sunday in the Park with George* and *Into the Woods*, James Lapine, "I went into the rehearsal room" when Robbins was working on *West Side Story*. "He immediately turned to me and said, 'Get out.'" It wasn't so much Robbins's words, said Sondheim, but the look on his face. "He was *making*. You don't want to be making something in front of somebody else."

In case any question existed as to who was in charge, Robbins's complete credit on *West Side Story* read, "Entire Original Production Directed and Choreographed by"— which, as contracted, appeared in a special box—as well as "Based on a Conception by Jerome Robbins."

After one particularly fractious rehearsal during tryouts in Washington, DC, Sondheim, whom Dale described as "shy, very quiet and laidback in those days," found

---

* Dale also codirected, with Robbins, the 1989 *Jerome Robbins' Broadway*.

Bernstein in a bar, a row of empty Scotch glasses lined up before him. That was the maestro's self-contained solution to Robbins's entirely autocratic decision to add musical notes to "Somewhere."

Under Robbins's command, *West Side Story* was not only the first musical to introduce its characters through dance—starting with the whistles and finger snaps of the Prologue—but also the first to weave its dance, dialogue, and song sequences together with seamless, cinematic fluidity.

"You came out scarred," Sondheim said of working with Robbins, whom he also tagged as "the only genius" he had ever associated with, "but you came out with good work."

———

Bernstein's melody for "Gee, Officer Krupke" was lifted from his score to *Candide*, which he was writing simultaneously with *West Side Story*. In the musical farce, based on Voltaire, the "Krupke" tune was "Where Does It Get You in the End?" Another grab from *Candide* was "One Hand, One Heart"; originally to be inserted into *West Side Story*'s balcony scene. In the end, it was switched to the bridal shop where Maria worked, so she and Tony could momentarily imagine exchanging marital vows. The replacement for the balcony scene was "Tonight," although Bernstein had his heart set on "Somewhere."

"We argued that a change didn't make logical sense," remembered Sondheim. "Jerry said, 'But it makes theatrical sense,' and he was absolutely right."

Sondheim also learned, years after the fact, that the foot-stomping "America" was not something Bernstein had written on the spur of the moment, despite appearances at the time. "He'd written the tune in his teens for an unproduced ballet called *Conch Town*."

Overlooking the fact they had completely opposing personalities,* Bernstein appreciated that Sondheim knew music, which facilitated the writing. What Sondheim did not appreciate was Bernstein's fancying himself a lyricist.

He "would sketch out something that was purple prose, not poetry. It screamed: 'Look at me! I'm being poetic!'" said Sondheim, taking to heart the Hammerstein rule to underwrite and let the music take care of the rest.

Ever self-critical, Sondheim regretted the lyrics to "Tonight," sung by Tony (Larry Kert) and Maria (Carol Lawrence) in the "balcony scene." A street kid like Tony, Sondheim said, would never have articulated "a phrase that fancy" about how, until that moment, the world was just an address. "I thought, 'Wait a minute. That sure sounds like he's been reading a lot to me.'"

———

* Bernstein the extrovert, Sondheim the introvert.

UNDERGROUND MOVEMENT

The Sharks and Jets aren't the only ones to rumble to Bernstein and Sondheim.

Apparently, so does the No. 2 subway train in Times Square—to the tune of "Somewhere," from *West Side Story*, the *New York Times* uncovered in 2002.

Not the entire song, only Bernstein's first three notes, corresponding to Sondheim's lyrics "There's a place."

The brief recital occurs just as the doors shut and the cars begin screeching out of the station, said riders interviewed, including one clinical psychologist. Another straphanger insisted the sound was the result of an overseas plot to brainwash New Yorkers.

A better theory was that it has something to do with propulsion and the electrical current.

One subway-system executive said he would never pick anything from *West Side Story* because he had once been an usher for a production and was sick of hearing the music. Another more objectively stated, "I don't think it was planned that way."

The newspaper revisited the phenomenon in 2009 and got a chief mechanical officer to admit, "We went out and heard it for ourselves."

Jamie Bernstein, daughter of Leonard, said that once the three notes were first noticed, "people said to each other, 'Did you hear it?'"

Be that as it may, the *Times* concluded, the rhythmic reverberation was a total fluke.

"Afraid of taking a chance on an unknown," said Sondheim, Bernstein picked apart every word, leaving the lyricist "to argue and defend every point." Disagreements, when they arose, were diffused by playing "cut-throat anagrams," said Sondheim, "but by the time we opened in Washington all the lyrics were mine, with some one- or two-line exceptions."

Nevertheless, given the top names attached to the show, on the morning of August 20, 1957, Washington reviewers overlooked one contributor: Stephen Sondheim. Even after what they had been through together, Bernstein "very generously took his name off the lyric writer list."

Broadway contracts of the time called for 6 percent of the gross box office receipts to be divided among the "book, music and lyrics: two, two and two," Sondheim later clarified. "Because Bernstein and Laurents and Robbins had such clout, [theirs] was a slightly larger percentage."

The music and lyrics alone garnered 4 percent. "Lenny was to get three, I was to get one, and Lenny said, 'We'll even out,'" said Sondheim, "and I foolishly said, 'Oh, don't be silly. All I care about is the credit.'

"Somebody should have stuffed a handkerchief in my mouth."

—

Somersaults were performed to find a producer to take on *West Side Story* after the usual suspects passed, George Abbott and Richard Rodgers among them. Rodgers, at least, offered constructive criticism: Maria should not die in the end, just because Shakespeare killed off Juliet. Besides, the loss was redundant; Tony's death effectively extinguished Maria's spirit.

Cheryl Crawford,* whose credits included a successful 1942 *Porgy and Bess* revival and *Brigadoon*, served as producer for a year—until she got cold feet on April 22, 1957, six weeks before the start of July rehearsals. With Bernstein set to take over the New York Philharmonic that October, time was of the essence.

"We have had this whole school of ashcan realism" was Bernstein's recollection of why Crawford stepped away. "She wanted us to explain why these kids were the way they were" was Sondheim's. Laurents: "I have a letter from her saying she wanted to see how the neighborhood changes from immigrant Jew to Puerto Rican and Black." Robbins: "My version of Cheryl's withdrawal is very simple: She couldn't raise the money."

Sondheim called his friend Hal Prince in Boston, where the twenty-nine-year-old producer was grumbling over his troubled tryout of *New Girl in Town*, a musical based on *Anna Christie*.

After hearing out Prince, Sondheim was finally able to voice his own problems. The producer expressed sympathy, said goodbye, then quickly called back. Prince said he and Robert Griffith, his partner on the back-to-back hits *The Pajama Game* and *Damn Yankees*, would like to hear the *West Side Story* score.

By the end of the week, they had. They liked it.

They signed on.

—

"This is the first show whose chorus had individual characterizations," Sondheim said. "Maybe one or two people would be characterized, like Agnes de Mille's the Girl Who Falls Down in *Oklahoma!*, but, in *West Side Story*, each of the members of the chorus had a name and a personality and was cast accordingly."

Over Robbins's mandated eight-week rehearsal period, which Carol Lawrence, cast as Maria, likened to "a battleground," those who didn't measure up to his demands were fired. Affecting his Method approach, Robbins fomented real rumbles between the two gangs, leading to "violence and sexual intimidation, fights and injuries," said Lawrence, "bloody noses, wrenched backs, concussions, broken teeth, torn ligaments, and fractured bones."

The show opened at the Winter Garden Theatre on September 26, 1957. The weather was a dry, pleasant sixty-two degrees at curtain time, but inside the theatre the temperature was impossible to read.

The audience "sat there in dead silence for the first half hour, because the reviews from out of town had made it sound like some kind of masterpiece," Sondheim said.

---

* In what qualified as his first Broadway exposure, Sondheim had written a title song for Crawford's 1956 production of the N. Richard Nash play *The Girls of Summer*, starring Shelley Winters.

MEMORIES ARE MADE OF THIS

Prior to playing Maria, Carol Lawrence (far left) was in the short-lived musical *Shangri-La*, based on the James Hilton novel *Lost Horizon*. In this *West Side Story* publicity photo, Sondheim is at the rehearsal piano with Bernstein at far right.

"When I wrote a piece about the alchemy of auditions for the *New York Times*, I related a story that Carol Lawrence had told me about her auditioning for *West Side Story*," said the actor, singer, recording artist, and writer Melissa Errico, known for her Broadway roles in *My Fair Lady* and *One Touch of Venus* and for her rich interpretations of Sondheim.

Errico's 2019 article quoted Lawrence talking about her record thirteen auditions to play Maria, and how at the last one, Jerome Robbins hid her in the theatre while, onstage, Larry Kert, as Tony, sang "Maria," then had Lawrence surprise him by launching into the balcony scene until they both finished singing "Tonight." Lawrence went on to say that Leonard Bernstein, speaking through tears, called it "the most mesmerizing audition I've ever seen in my life."

After the story appeared, "Sondheim wrote to me, not to the *Times*, protesting Carol's version as inaccurate and typical of a performer's self-centeredness and warning me—an actor!—not to believe anything actors said about getting parts," Errico said.

"It seemed to me, given the power inequality between Steve, the master of the New York stage, and Carol, an elderly woman with little beyond her memories, that he ought to grant her the right to her own story as she chose to narrate it, and I wrote and told him so. Nicely."

According to Errico, Sondheim "came right back: 'Fair enough. You're more generous than I am.'

"Which was itself generous of him."

(*Washington Post* critic Richard L. Coe's opening line had pulled no punches: "'West Side Story' is a work of art") "And so there was virtually no response. They just sat there as at a temple."

The mood lightened with the "America" number. "Chita Rivera lifted her skirts and danced all over the stage, and the audience suddenly were reminded they were at a musical, and from then on they had a very good time."

When it came time for the cast to take its bow, the audience "stared back in deathly silence," remembered Lawrence, fearing the worst. Then they leapt to their feet "and pandemonium erupted—cheers and whistles, thunderous applause punctuated with *bravos*."

"Death is a swell curtain for a story," Sondheim said. "It is, quote, 'the final curtain,' and, so in a way, it's a natural ending, a logical ending to a story."

"I didn't think it would last three months," Laurents said later.

Reviews were respectable, not rapturous, although some critics detected that the theatre had moved forward in terms of choreography conveying a hard-edged story. The mentions Sondheim received included a few backhanded compliments.

The Broadway run was respectable, too, 732 performances, and the show went on a national tour, but it was by no means a smash.

That same season's sunny *The Music Man* went on for 1,375 performances, received nine Tony nominations and won five, including those for Outstanding Musical, Leading Actor Robert Preston, and Featured Actress Barbara Cook.

West Side Story, nominated in six Tony categories, won in only two: Robbins's choreography and Oliver Smith's scenic design.

But the movie was a monster hit.

——

West Side Story was produced on Broadway for about $300,000 ($3 million today), only a shade less than what United Artists, the only studio to bid on the property, paid for the movie rights. Among the Broadway angels were Herbert Sondheim and some of his friends, who ponied up $1,500. "Not many laughs, are there?" was the elder Sondheim's verdict after reading the script. This prompted Stephen to assure his father he didn't have to invest: "But I'm glad he did." As for the reactions of his surrogate parents, Dorothy Hammerstein cried from emotion when Sondheim first played her "Maria."

"I had my reservations about the movie," Jerome Robbins said twenty years after his involvement in the $6.75 million screen version, which he choreographed and codirected with Robert Wise. "I wasn't sure we could capture the lyric and poetic qualities we had onstage. But there were certain things you could do better on film. The 'Cool' number we shot in a garage. You can get a certain tension through cutting that you can't get onstage."

Changes made from stage to screen included extending the Prologue, "Gee, Officer Krupke" and "Cool" exchanging places, adding the Shark men to "America" (onstage it was performed by the women only), and some of Laurents's dialogue, especially ethnic slurs, being removed or watered down by screenwriter Ernest Lehman. The assault on Anita was also tempered. Sondheim's lyric changes were most noticeable in the prelude to "America," which stresses the advantages of living in the U.S. as opposed to Puerto Rico. From there, the song takes on a new edge, with additional lyrics, as the number erupts into a battle of the sexes. Also in the film, "One Hand, One Heart" and the "A Boy Like That"/"I Have a Love" duet were both slightly truncated, with the ensemble "Somewhere" stage ballet—the one Robbins described as showing "where they want to be"—altogether eliminated.

Lehman, who'd seen the show in Chicago with Robert Wise, wanted to be more dramatic than musical with the material. "I was a little astonished that the numbers were quite often in the wrong place. You don't do 'Gee, Officer Krupke' after the rumble," he said in a 1997 Writers Guild Foundation interview. Onstage, "Maria sings 'I Feel Pretty,' after the two bodies are lying on the ground." He moved up Maria's number and "put 'Gee, Officer Krupke' before the war council meeting, where it belongs."

In terms of casting, Elizabeth Taylor's and Harry Belafonte's names were brought up for Maria and Tony, according to producer Walter Mirisch. Robert Wise wanted

Codirectors Jerome Robbins (left) and Robert Wise; "Jerry felt that the prologue should be done on stylized sets," said movie producer Walter Mirisch, "whereas Bob Wise and I didn't want the film to look like a photographed stage play." This became but one point of contention.

Elvis Presley. Russ Tamblyn, who'd had movie experience (*Seven Brides for Seven Brothers*, *Peyton Place*) was eager to play the lead but landed the part of Riff, Tony's Mercutio-like cofounder of the Jets. The 70mm Super Panavision lens did not work to the advantage of original cast members Carol Lawrence and Larry Kert, who were tested. "We felt they were both too old," said Mirisch.*

Other names on the table: Elizabeth Ashley, Warren Beatty, Richard Chamberlain, Bobby Darin, Troy Donahue, Audrey Hepburn, Gary Lockwood, Anthony Perkins, Suzanne Pleshette, Burt Reynolds, and Jill St. John.

Twenty-two-year-old Richard Beymer, an Actors Studio alumnus who lent his boyish presence to *The Diary of Anne Frank*, was cast as Tony, with his singing voice dubbed by vocalist James Howard Bryant.

Natalie Wood, also twenty-two, was cast as Maria because she was the right age and could act, said Mirisch. Wood also had box office appeal. The producer admitted she was not Hispanic, and, despite her wanting to sing her own numbers, Wood's voice was dubbed by Marni Nixon, who also filled in some of the higher octaves for Rita Moreno, as Anita, in "A Boy Like That." Nixon's voice had subbed for Deborah Kerr, in *The King and I*, and would later do the same for Audrey Hepburn, in *My Fair Lady*.

The *West Side Story* soundtrack album spent fifty-four weeks at No. 1 on the *Billboard* sales charts and went triple platinum, vying with Michael Jackson's *Thriller*

* Lawrence was twenty-eight; Kert, twenty-nine.

as one of the top-selling albums of all time—and this after Bernstein accused the movie's musical director, Johnny Green, of sabotaging his and Sondheim's score by over-orchestrating it with too many musicians. *

George Chakiris, in red shirt, played Bernardo, leader of the Sharks, and earned one of *West Side Story*'s ten Academy Awards. The Ohio-born actor-dancer had earlier played Riff in the London stage production of the musical.

—

Red-carpet premieres were held in New York at the Rivoli Theatre on October 18, 1961, and in Hollywood, at Grauman's Chinese Theatre on December 14, with the 70mm prints playing top-priced, reserved-seat engagements in both venues for well over a year. At Grauman's, the picture ran for fifty-seven weeks, six weeks longer than *Star Wars*, which played in the same theatre sixteen years later. *West Side Story* remained in the Rivoli for seventy-seven weeks.

"The movie played the longest in Paris," said Robbins. "It had a terrific impact that has always surprised me. I've been introduced to people who didn't know me from any other work but *West Side Story*."

A slightly bemused look on his face, Robbins added, "I think a lot of my works for the ballet will last longer than *West Side Story*, but it seemed to have a lot of impact on the world."

---

* Green's response, according to his daughter, Kathe Green, in 2022, was that her father, assessing what others had earned in comparison, said, "It's a pity Stephen Sondheim didn't make any money from *West Side Story*."

HOW JEROME ROBBINS LOST HIS "COOL"

West Side Story started filming in August 1960. With Jerome Robbins and Robert Wise codirecting, Robbins choreographing, and Wise also producing, principal photography began on Manhattan's Upper West Side, in an area that was soon to be redeveloped into Lincoln Center.

Forty-five days into shooting, Jerome Robbins, seen here rehearsing part of the opening number, was blamed for the movie being twenty-four days behind schedule. He was fired.

Production then moved to soundstages in Los Angeles.

By April 1961, the film's associate producer, Saul Chaplin,* was baring his soul to Leonard Bernstein about Robbins's misdeeds.

"That's one story," Robbins said, in 1980.

Chaplin's complaints included Robbins's ignoring his own mistakes, losing pace with the music, egging on Natalie Wood to do her own singing, and operating in "his usual vaguely dishonest manner."

After completing four segments—the Prologue, "Cool," "I Feel Pretty," and "America"—Robbins was fired, leaving him, said Mirisch, "hurt, furious, and insulted." He wanted his name removed from the picture.

It was decided to table that decision until after Robbins had seen the finished film.

His credits remained.

The following year, *West Side Story* dominated the Oscars, winning ten, including those for Best Picture, Director (Wise and Robbins), Supporting Actress (Rita Moreno as Anita), Supporting Actor (George Chakiris as Bernardo), and an Honorary Award for Brilliant Achievements in the Art of Choreography on Film, to Jerome Robbins.

---

* Chaplin was Hal Prince's father-in-law, Prince being married to Saul and Ethel Chaplin's daughter, Judy Prince.

LEFT AND OPPOSITE:
Ansel Elgort and
Rachel Zegler as Tony
and Maria in Steven
Spielberg's 2021 *West
Side Story*. Natalie
Wood and Richard
Beymer played the
leads in the 1961 movie
version; in 1980, Jerome
Robbins said he would
still cast the two as the
star-crossed lovers.

Sondheim's verdict?*

"I don't think *West Side Story*'s a good movie at all because it's not a movie. It's a photograph of a stage. When I see a gang of juvenile delinquents dancing down a real street, Broadway, in color-coordinated sneakers, with color-coordinated wash on the line behind them, I'm not scared."

—

"You can't update *West Side Story*," Jerome Robbins maintained—that is, until he tried.

"There was a plan afoot a few years ago," Sondheim said in 1998, the same year Robbins died, "to do *West Side Story* and update it to the '90s, but nothing has come of it. It was something Jerry Robbins was pushing. It would have mostly meant updating the orchestration."

"The show has two aspects in the past," said Robbins, "the time of events in the play itself, and then all the stagecraft. Everything we invented also came out of that time."

What Robbins found ageless was the show's "drive and power and guts and, I hope, vitality"—the reasons, he said, why "most people credit *West Side Story* as an innovative show." He further remarked, "Other shows have evolved from it."

Perhaps none more so than the 1975 *A Chorus Line*, "conceived, directed, and choreographed" by Michael Bennett, who, having auditioned in 1960, age sixteen, had dropped out of high school so he could play *West Side Story*'s Baby John for its domestic and international tours. Bennett's driving ambition, according to one biographer was to "dance Robbins's choreography and to study and dissect how Robbins had achieved the dazzling effects."

---

* Sondheim was answering a query posed by London's National Theatre director, Rufus Norris, in 2016.

West Side Story has been faithfully reexecuted, as well as resurrected and reimagined, in several incarnations since its 1957 debut. The Library of Congress says the show "continues to be mounted regularly in high schools, universities, community, and regional theaters, and in first-class revivals around the world." With more than 250 productions of the show every year, "the libretto has been translated in[to] over twenty-six languages, including Chinese, Hebrew, Dutch, and six separate Spanish translations based on countries and local dialects."

An international company has been touring since 2003, with stops in twenty-eight countries on three continents. The tour retains the original Robbins choreography, and, after pausing for the pandemic, resumed in 2022 under the direction of Lonny Prince, who played Charley in the original Broadway production of *Merrily We Roll Along* before becoming a director.

The Black Lives Matter movement inspired Ivo van Hove's radical *West Side Story* on Broadway in 2019, replacing the considered-sacrosanct Robbins choreography with hip-hop and club styles by Belgium's Anne Teresa De Keersmaeker, whose angular gestures had earlier sparked the moves in Beyoncé's 2011 "Countdown" music video.

In 2021, Justin Peck of the New York City Ballet choreographed Steven Spielberg's cinematic reinterpretation of *West Side Story*, which was grittier and longer—by four minutes—than the 1961 version. Latinx actors played the Sharks. Screenwriter Tony Kushner provided backstories to the main characters; Tony (the Jet, not the screenwriter), played by Ansel Elgort, has served a year's stretch in Sing Sing for nearly killing a man. Rachel Zegler's Maria arrived in America five years after her brother Bernardo, to take care of their father. Rita Moreno, who was Anita in 1961,

LEFT AND BELOW:
"Imagine this little girl in the back seat of a white Ford Focus. When you look into her eyes, you see an openly queer woman of color, an Afro-Latina who found her strength in life through art," Ariana DeBose said when accepting her Oscar for playing Anita in the 2021 *West Side Story*. (The same role for which Rita Moreno, below, won sixty years before.) "So, to anybody who's ever questioned your identity ever, ever, ever, or you find yourself living in the gray spaces, I promise you this: There is indeed a place for us."

took on the Doc character, now renamed Valentina but still steeped in the wisdom of Shakespeare's Friar Laurence, who was Romeo's spiritual advisor.

Kushner said Sondheim provided "tons of notes" for the first two drafts of the screenplay. After all, "He's Stephen Sondheim." The lyricist was also a booster for the film, telling Stephen Colbert's *Late Show* audience three months before the movie's release, "The whole thing has a real sparkle to it and real energy, and it feels fresh." An even bigger booster was Spielberg's fellow director Guillermo del Toro (*Pan's Labyrinth*, *The Shape of Water*, *Nightmare Alley*), who tweeted at length to his two million followers about how Spielberg pulled off "brain-surgery levels of precision."

Despite the enthusiasm, and mostly admiration from critics and a stellar Rotten Tomatoes rating, the film failed to set the box office ablaze.

When Spielberg's *West Side Story* was still in theatres, it was announced that the Long Wharf Theatre in New Haven, Connecticut, had commissioned a sequel to the original stage version.

In its way, Mike Faist's Riff in the 2021 movie brought *West Side Story* full circle: The actor's intensity recalled that of Montgomery Clift's, whose query to Jerome Robbins on how to play Romeo launched the very concept of the musical in the first place.

"What happened to that young woman, Maria, after she walks out of the park after Tony has been murdered?" wondered Steven Sapp, who, writing the musical with his wife, Mildred Ruiz-Sapp, intended to take the grieving protagonist back to her native Puerto Rico, "where she has to take notice of everything that she has lived and everything that has happened to her."

The new story could conceivably address issues that have long dogged *West Side Story*, especially the overly accented and heavily made-up 1961 movie.

"What is our response specifically as artists of color?" Jacob Padrón, artistic director of the Long Wharf and co-founder of the Artists' Anti-Racism Coalition, said, in late 2021. "What is our response to this piece that one could argue has been culturally appropriated?"

As far back as his postmortem discussion with Hammerstein after first meeting Leonard Bernstein, a flippant Sondheim admitted* that he didn't even know any Puerto Ricans *or* poor people.

Meaning no insult—and operating in a don't-rock-the-boat era—the Jewish, liberal, even radical, primarily gay or bisexual, creators "were much less concerned with the sociological aspects of the story than with the theatrical ones," Sondheim, at that juncture the creative team's lone survivor, told Shakespeare scholar Daniel Pollack-Pelzner, in 2020. "The ethnic warfare was merely a vehicle to tell the Romeo and Juliet story. It might just as well have been the Hatfields and the McCoys."

Advancing the sentiment, Tony Kushner said, "The creators believed very deeply that race, hatred, and bigotry and oppression and discrimination are profoundly malevolent aberrations and can lead to cataclysmic consequences."

Concluded Kushner, "It is an anti-racist, democratic musical."

---

* Sondheim shared the same comment with his agent, Flora Roberts, whom James Lapine, in his book *Putting It Together*, described as "a plump woman of a certain age with a gravelly voice and a warm demeanor."

ETHEL MERMAN in **GYPSY** a new musical

"He places value on the music, what kind of word fits each note," Gypsy's veteran composer, Jule Styne, said of Sondheim, the 1959 show's young lyricist. "When you soar musically, he knows he must say something as important as the notes."

GOT IT

"Home was a strange word coming from Mother. I thought of it again and again as I sat at the window in the backseat of the car and watched the frozen miles go by. Home, to us, had always meant the hotel, or the theatre. Now it meant Grandpa's house in Seattle. Or did it?"

It did long enough to set the stage for "Some People," primary character Rose's first number in *Gypsy*, the 1959 Robbins-Laurents-Sondheim alliance with composer Jule Styne. It starred Ethel Merman and came to serve as a bellwether for damn near every show business musical.

The remembrance of Home and Mother sprang from the pages of *Gypsy*, the 1957 autobiography of Gypsy Rose Lee, who Sondheim said "put the tease in striptease." Arthur Laurents, who found Lee "charming and evasive," diplomatically dismissed the memoir as "imaginative,"* while a straight-faced John Steinbeck, for the thirty-five-cent Dell paperback version, contributed the cover blurb, "I found it irresistible. It's quite a performance. I bet some of it is even true."

In actual fact, Carolyn Quinn, author of a 2013 biography of Lee's mother, found that *Gypsy*'s account of her own life hewed closer to the truth than previously suspected, with humor added.

Whatever its veracity, not long after *Gypsy*'s publication, the Broadway producer David Merrick sought the rights to the book with the aim of having Jerome Robbins stage it as a musical.

Simultaneously, Sondheim was setting to music and lyrics some comical adventures first devised by the ancient Roman playwright Titus Maccius Plautus. Abetting him were Burt Shevelove and Larry Gelbart, who gave Robbins a peek at an early draft of the script, which at that point contained three Sondheim songs.

It was called *A Roman Comedy*, and Robbins was impressed.

—

Gypsy Rose Lee had a book to peddle. Born Rose Hovick, in Seattle, in 1911, with a caul, which some interpret to mean the baby will possess psychic ability,** Lee had a survivor's instinct for making the most of herself. Her adoption of the name Gypsy

---

* He subtitled the show on which the book was based "A Musical Fable."

** "Like a gypsy fortune-teller," it was said.

LEFT AND OPPOSITE:
After decades of reveal-
ing almost everything
onstage, Gypsy Rose
Lee (left, circa 1940),
sat down in 1956 (right)
to reveal even more
between the sheets—
of her memoir. The
work inspired the musi-
cal Gypsy.

reputedly took place in 1931, at Toledo, Ohio's Gayety Theater—Lee read tea leaves
like a fortune-teller—and her garter-pulling signature act began around the same
time, soon after radio had buried vaudeville. In truth, Lee's burlesque routine barely
contained any stripping. Audiences came to hear her snappy stage patter more than to
gawk at her body, which, underneath her prefabricated fall-away gowns, was concealed
by flesh-colored bodysuits.

"I wasn't naked," she insisted after one police bust. "I was completely covered by a
blue spotlight."

With a quick wit and flamboyant personality, Lee propelled herself onto pop
culture's radar even before there was radar. Journalist and word scholar H. L. Mencken
coined the word "ecdysiast" for her, and Rodgers and Hart referenced her in their song
"Zip" in *Pal Joey*, a pacesetting musical that happened to feature, in the role of scheming chorine Gladys Bumps, Gypsy's real-life younger sister, the one-time "Baby June,"
June Havoc—who, while her older sister was stripping, was scrambling to establish
a career as an actress. The adult June did not appreciate being simply referred to as
Gypsy Rose Lee's sister.

Grinding out her book in nine months on a rented typewriter, Lee sold her
manuscript to Harper and Brothers, the New York publishing home to Herman

Melville, Mark Twain, and Aldous Huxley.
When Harper's published an excerpt in their
eponymous monthly magazine, the story came to
David Merrick's attention. The former St. Louis
lawyer arrived in New York to make his fortune
producing on Broadway, and he did. He offered
Lee $4,000 ($40,000 today), plus a percentage
of the box office gross, for the theatrical rights.
She accepted, even in the face of a $200,000 deal
from Warner Bros. (the studio would eventually
buy the movie rights for $650,000 against 10 per-
cent of the gross), a sum that was being matched
by the illustrious MGM musical producer Arthur
Freed. Lerner and Loewe, who had just set
Broadway afire with *My Fair Lady*, also wanted
to get their hands on *Gypsy*.

Merrick got the nod because, in the 1940s,
Lee had been personally involved with the showman Mike Todd, and she detected Todd's same
killer instincts in Merrick. She was right. As a
partner, Merrick brought in Leland Hayward, the
gentlemanly über-agent whose clients included
Greta Garbo and Katharine Hepburn (who
wanted to marry him). He had also produced the
hits *South Pacific* and *Mister Roberts*.

Hayward and his then wife, social and fashion icon Slim Keith, were close friends
of Robbins, and over lunch at the Colony restaurant, Hayward hoped to entice Arthur
Laurents into writing *Gypsy*'s book, after he and Merrick had tried, unsuccessfully, to
enlist Betty Comden and Adolph Green.*

At lunch, Laurents stood firm against Hayward's offer; working with Robbins on
West Side Story had been difficult enough. He also did not care to sully his hands writing about a stripper. Hayward, however, was convinced Laurents could be convinced.
What finally wore down the playwright's resistance was a cocktail-party encounter
with a guest who said she had been the lover of Gypsy Rose Lee's mother, Rose
Evangeline Thompson Hovick. The woman spilled the beans on the felonious and
sexual behavior of Mother Rose, who besides shoving a bill-collecting hotel manager
out of a window, allegedly shot a woman in a jealous rage and made the death look like
a suicide.

Laurents now thought a musical about a Lady Macbeth–like character could be
interesting. Daughter Gypsy didn't object; her mother had been dead since 1954. Lee's
only demand was that the show carry the same title as her memoir, *Gypsy*.

Signing on, Laurents brought up the name Stephen Sondheim to do the score—
music and lyrics.

Jerome Robbins also took credit for bringing up Stephen Sondheim, having just
read the ancient Rome script.

He talked up Sondheim's work to Leland Hayward with an eye toward Hayward's
producing *A Roman Comedy* and bringing in Robbins to stage it.

In 1937, Mama Rose Hovick (right) greeted her newlywed daughter Gypsy and third husband, Robert Mizzy, after the couple's transcontinental trailer honeymoon. *Time* magazine reported that Gypsy was twenty-three (she was twenty-six), and Mizzy, twenty-five, was a "wealthy New York dental supply dealer." The marriage lasted four years.

* Comden and Green were already in Hollywood, adapting the Rosalind Russell
Broadway vehicle *Auntie Mame* to the screen.

Attending rehearsals for the show that revisited her youth, Gypsy Rose Lee told Ethel Merman she felt "like a ghost at a banquet." From left: Jerome Robbins, Sondheim, Lee, Arthur Laurents, and Jule Styne.

"Listen to them as soon as you can and have Steve explain the ideas I have," Robbins said of Sondheim's songs.

Almost as an afterthought, Robbins added, "Maybe he would be a good idea for 'Gypsy.'"

—

"Miss Merman can deliberately flat a long note and make it sound brassy and fine, and then she can work up to an exciting finish with a few unexpected bars," *New Yorker* contributor Margaret Case Harriman wrote in the magazine's profile of Cole Porter, in 1940. "He tries, too, to put the words 'very' and 'terrific' in the lyrics he writes for Miss Merman; no one, he says, can sing these words as she can."

Jerome Robbins, embracing his star, Ethel Merman, admitted to not understanding the title of her Act I curtain number, "Everything's Coming Up Roses." "Everything's coming up Rose's *what*?," he asked.

While Sondheim and Laurents often took pleasure in deriding Ethel Merman—"not bright," said Laurents, who got yelled at by some male Merman fans in Greenwich Village when his jab hit print—the celebrated musical star, who would create the role of Rose on Broadway, got along fine with Jerome Robbins. Even in later years, when Merman was in her seventies, Robbins thought she still would be ideal in a revival of *Gypsy*.

Sondheim liked to tell the story about Merman's foul mouth, illustrating with an anecdote that had also been attributed to the actress Maureen Stapleton—that when Merman appeared as a guest on television's *The Loretta Young Show*, Young, a Catholic, kept a glass jar on the set, and anytime anyone used a profanity in her presence, a twenty-five-cent contribution had to be placed into the container. The money

MERMAN CALLED IT "A BLEEPIN' ARIA"

Gypsy's action begins with a song-and-dance talent contest and culminates with Rose's desperate grasp at martyrdom.

That moment takes place in the mesmerizing "Rose's Turn," which has been described as a musical nervous breakdown.

Recalling when the number was first put in, the show's dance arranger, John Kander,* remembered, "I was in a room where he and Jule Styne were doing 'Rose's Turn' and Steve was performing it. It was new [and] breathtaking—still the best performance of that that I've ever seen in my life."

Sondheim said he and Robbins, sans Styne, assembled the showstopper one night by piecing together other songs from the show as pretty much a stop-gap measure once Robbins realized he didn't have time to create what he initially foresaw as a Rose ballet for the spot.

Jule Styne contradicted this account by saying he came in one morning with the number, then played the piano, and Sondheim sang.

Styne also reputedly told Robbins, "You want ballet music? Get Bernstein."

---

* In the next two decades, with his lyricist-collaborator Fred Ebb, composer Kander would make his own Broadway history with *Cabaret* and *Chicago*.

"When I wrote 'Small World,'" said Sondheim, here with Ethel Merman, "Jule Styne, the composer, was very upset because, he said, 'This can only be sung by a woman, and my friend Frank [Sinatra] needs a song.'" Styne's priority was to make a hit record; Sondheim's, to make the song work for the show.

would go to charity. Ethel slipped up three times, costing her seventy-five cents, before finally whipping out a large bill from her purse and telling Loretta what she could go do with herself.

What the working-class Astoria, Queens, native Ethel Agnes Zimmermann might have lacked in polish, she made up for in boldness, brassiness, and box office.

In her less-than-introspective 1978 memoir, for which she collaborated with veteran entertainment journalist George Eells, who filled in the blanks to offer continuity, Merman states that she recognized from an early draft that Laurents's book scenes were strong enough to make the music dispensable.

"*Gypsy*," she said, "was a full-fledged play."

Sondheim came to the same conclusion after his first reading, to which Laurents replied, "You're dead wrong. It's much larger than life. It wouldn't work as a straight play."

—

Sondheim's and Merman's first reactions to Laurents's script, it turned out, were closer to the mark than Robbins's; he envisioned the show as a vaudeville pageant, with jugglers, acrobats, and a dog act. Laurents circulated the rumor that Robbins never got over the fact he could not feel proprietary toward *Gypsy* the way he had toward the dance-oriented *West Side Story*, and the two bickered over that distinction for the rest of their lives.

What Laurents would concede, in his third memoir, was, "Ethel was Jerry's choice; he was determined she would be a winner." Once that decision was made, Merman and Laurents met late one afternoon in Sardi's. He warned her that the role would present a challenge.

"Rose is a monster," he said.

"I'll do anything you want me to," she replied—although, during the Philadelphia tryout, the team, mostly Jerome Robbins, had to coax her into delivering a line for the "Some People" sequence. It did not go as planned.

"Ethel told me her public would be alienated if they heard her tell her father to go to hell," Sondheim said. "So the passage was cut."

"I got sympathy," Merman rationalized. "People cried."

Nevertheless, as Sondheim was aware, Rose's true colors would still seep out. Her first number, "Some People,"* is "a very ugly, bitter, angry song," he said. Its incisive lyrics, about what separates Rose from those she writes off for lacking her ambition, reveal Rose's roster of negative qualities, with the song capped by Rose stealing her father's fifty-year railroad employee plaque off his wall, in order to pawn it.

Pleased that this song is "shocking," Sondheim said, "It's supposed to prepare you for the fact that this woman is not a nice lady."

If "Some People" did not make the point, Rose's next number would. She delivers it to the semi–love interest, Herbie.

"'Small World' is a con song," said Sondheim. Rose "sees a man who's attracted to her." The feeling is not necessarily mutual.

"He's nice and all that, but he *is* an agent, and she needs an agent very badly, so suddenly she starts to find things they have in common."

Her faux interest in the guy is all meant to trap him, said Sondheim.

"And, indeed, by the end of the song he's caught."

—

Sondheim said one of his main attractions to *Gypsy* was that "Rose would offer Ethel and us authors a chance to blindside the audience"—by showing them Merman could *act*.

To guarantee her participation, Merrick and Hayward made the star a business partner. After all, her Broadway track record went back to 1930; at age twenty-two, she stepped onto the stage of the Alvin Theatre in *Girl Crazy*, opened her mouth, and blew the roof off with the Gershwins' "I Got Rhythm." Merman's *Gypsy* contract

---

* In terms of writing for a star, Jule Styne said the release in this song, when Rose sings, "But I-I-I-I," gives the audience what it wants from Merman, a long, loud clarion declaration of "Here I am!"

MOTHER DISCOURAGE

"Many people have difficult relationships with their parents," Sondheim said. Here, his mother, Foxy. "People see Madame Rose in *Gypsy*, and say 'It's your mother,' but it wasn't."

Gypsy's lyricist knew about difficult mothers.

Foxy Sondheim was "quite a remarkable character," her son told literary critic Michiko Kakutani, in 1994.

Having rarely held back on the topic of his mother—triggering a widely held suspicion that Foxy inspired the bitterness unleashed in "The Ladies Who Lunch"—Sondheim reiterated an on-the-record story that would subsequently echo through nearly every Sondheim profile and obituary. It pertained to what he described as a hand-delivered letter from his mother in the 1970s, when he was in his forties.

As Foxy was to be outfitted with a heart pacemaker, a procedure she inflated into a major operation, Sondheim quoted her as writing him, "'The night before I undergo open heart surgery'—underlined three times. Open parenthesis. 'My surgeon's term.' Close parenthesis. 'The only regret I have in life is giving you birth.'"

"She didn't want me on earth," he said in another interview. "I was an inconvenience."

Nearly fifty years after the revelation, Sondheim was able to tell *New Yorker* writer D. T. Max that he was finally able to exorcise his mother's negativity, "because I've told so many people about what a horror she was, and I've told so many funny stories that I laugh at them now."

Sondheim claimed he never spoke to Foxy again and did not attend her funeral. She died in 1992 at ninety-four. (Sondheim's father, Herbert, predeceased Foxy when, at age seventy-one, he died in 1966. "My stepmother and I forced him to retire," Sondheim said, "and I'm sorry to say I think it killed him—he missed the worry.")

Sondheim, however, contradicted himself when, in 2012, he told journalist Tim Teeman for the *Times* of London that he had financially supported Foxy and visited her in a nursing home "the last few years" of her life.

In 2022, it was disclosed that, in 2013, Sondheim had told a close work associate that when it came to the letter-writing incident, "It never happened."

called for 5 percent of the box office take until the show recouped, then 7 percent of the gross going forward, plus living expenses.

For the score, Merrick sought Merman's songwriter on *Annie Get Your Gun* and *Call Me Madam*, Irving Berlin. A show about a stripper? He passed. Hoping to boost the composer's morale, Leland Hayward approached Cole Porter, another pro at creating for Merman, but Porter was too depressed, having recently undergone surgery to remove his right leg, the final insult after his damaging 1937 horse-riding accident.* Cy Coleman and Carolyn Leigh wrote four songs on spec, including the jazzy "Firefly" (which Tony Bennett sent to No. 20 on the *Billboard* chart), but Merrick didn't bite.

Sondheim adhered to the tenet that it was Merman who nixed having an unproven twenty-eight-year-old handle the entire score to *Gypsy*. "First, it had been agreed that I'd write both the music and lyrics," said Sondheim. "The deal with Leland, Merrick, Laurents, and Robbins was firm, I thought."

Laurents suggested Merman's agent was the culpable party. Merman had been stung by the green songwriters behind her most recent show, the unsuc-cessful *Happy Hunting*, which featured songs by Matt Dubey and Harold Karr. Whoever the cause, Sondheim was not approved.

Merrick told Jule Styne to remain patient. "Steve Sondheim wants to do the music and lyrics," the producer said, "but Ethel wants you to do the music. I want you to do the music, and Leland wants you to do the music. But Steve insists that he do both. We're trying to work something out."

Styne pointed out that Sondheim "had collaborated on *West Side Story* with Lenny Bernstein. Why can't he collaborate with me?"

Merrick said Sondheim was "sensitive." Styne said he was, too.

Merrick said to give him a week.

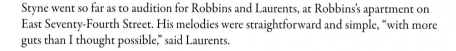

Styne went so far as to audition for Robbins and Laurents, at Robbins's apartment on East Seventy-Fourth Street. His melodies were straightforward and simple, "with more guts than I thought possible," said Laurents.

---

* Once the score was prepared, Merman, Jule Styne, and Sondheim previewed high-lights for Cole Porter in his Waldorf-Astoria residential suite. With Sondheim singing, Styne playing piano, and Merman taking it all in, Porter got a particular kick out of an inner rhyme in "Together, Wherever We Go," when the lyric "amigos" popped up. Too weak to applaud, Styne recalled, Porter tapped his spoon on an ashtray.

"I never had the good fortune of meeting your mother, but she must've been a fabulous per-son," Ethel Merman told Lee on the TV talk show *Gypsy Rose Lee and Her Friends*, in 1967. "She had so much heart, and whatever she did, she did for the girls—all out, for them. They were her life." The star's interpre-tation of Rose didn't jibe with Sondheim's and Laurents's.

THE GREAT COLLABORATOR

After *Gypsy*, Styne (right) wanted Sondheim to collaborate with him on *Funny Girl* as a vehicle for Mary Martin, but Sondheim thought Martin wasn't suited to play Fanny Brice from the Lower East Side. Sondheim passed—as did Mary Martin.

Jule Styne had a remarkable track record: *Gentlemen Prefer Blondes, High Button Shoes, Peter Pan,* and *Bells Are Ringing.*

Besides, he and Merman had worked together in the late 1930s, when she made movies for 20th Century-Fox, where Styne was a vocal coach. He was also a producer on her television starring vehicles earlier in the '50s, including a *Colgate Comedy Hour* presentation of *Anything* Goes.

More important, he knew how to craft songs for a star, such as Carol Channing ("A Little Girl from Little Rock" and "Diamonds Are a Girl's Best Friend," in *Gentlemen Prefer Blondes*) and Judy Holliday ("Just in Time," "The Party's Over," and the bravura comic number "I'm Going Back," in *Bells Are Ringing*).

For Merman in *Gypsy,* he would personify Rose's all-American aspirations with the recurring four notes of "I had a dream" *and* provide Merman with a dream score.

At the time of discussions with David Merrick, Jule—pronounced "Julie," and used in lieu of his birth name, Julius, so as not to confuse him with another showbiz powerhouse, Jules Styne, founder of the Music Corporation of America—had already won an Oscar for composing "Three Coins in the Fountain" and scored several number one hits ("Time After Time," "It's Magic," "Let It Snow"), among his two thousand songs.

Born in London's East End, Jule moved with his family to Chicago when he was eight, mingled with mobsters, was a roué and improvident gambler, and had his own distinctive style of speaking, as if he were backing into his sentences, or else assuming that the listener already knew what he was talking about.

Betty Comden and Adolph Green referred to his rapid-fire delivery as "verbal shorthand," or "Stynese."

Sondheim, already displaying his penchant for complexity, was desperate not to be, in his words, "pigeonholed strictly as a lyric writer."

"The worst thing about being a lyricist is that everyone else is in rehearsal [and] you are back at the hotel, trying to fix those two terrible lines," he said; funnily enough, at the time of their later endeavors, Hal Prince would complain that when their shows went out of town, Sondheim didn't like to go with them.*

"I find lyric writing one of the most unpleasant professions in the world, whereas music is fun—not that it isn't hard, too. You can sweat a lot over music, but it's very fulfilling."

---

* "He hated coming to rehearsals," said the actor Nancy Dussault, who knew Sondheim from the early 1960s. She recalled his lying down on the edge of the stage and resting. In his own defense, Sondheim said, "By the time of rehearsals, I know the book better than the librettist does."

East Forty-Ninth, vintage 1920. The tall façade behind the automobile leads into what Sondheim dubbed "The House That Gypsy Built."

ON THE STREET WHERE HE LIVED

"My guess is that I had two-and-a-quarter, going to two-and-a-half once the show made a profit," Sondheim said, in reference to the royalties he earned on *Gypsy*. In basic terms, for every dollar the production made, Sondheim would have earned roughly 2.25 to 2.5 cents.

"I don't remember what shows grossed in those days, but let's say it was $100,000."

Variety's pre-opening prediction was that *Gypsy* would pull in a more-than-healthy $81,000 a week. The box office reached its all-time peak during January 1960, when the total hit $86,472.26. (The show had closed for Christmas week, as was common practice then.)

Going by Sondheim's $100,000 estimate, "That amounts to $2,500 a week, or $2,250. That was a lot of money for those days, when theatre tickets cost four dollars and ninety cents." He had also made some money on the *West Side Story* soundtrack.

By April 1960, eleven months into *Gypsy*'s run, the production had paid back its investors, who had put up the necessary $420,000.

By that year's summer, however, ticket sales cooled, and the show moved from the nearly 1,800-seat Broadway Theatre, where it had opened, to the 1,400-seat Imperial. Merrick also asked the participants to take a 50 percent reduction in their royalties.

"Mother," Gypsy Rose Lee's son, Erik Lee Preminger, said, "claimed to prefer the intimacy of the smaller theatre. She made no such claim for the smaller royalty checks."

Sondheim's earnings turned out to be enough for him to move from his East Eighties apartment into a townhouse on East Forty-Ninth Street, next door to where Katharine Hepburn had been living since 1936. Their gardens adjoined, along with those of eighteen other houses on the block.

"My father co-signed the loan," said Sondheim, who also remembered that around three o'clock one morning while he was composing *Company*, Hepburn, barefoot and in a babushka, came banging on his door to tell him to stop that racket.*

Although, in 1984, the same year as *Sunday in the Park with George*, Sondheim purchased a second home in Roxbury, Connecticut, he would live and work in the Turtle Bay residence for the rest of his days.

He called it "The House That *Gypsy* Built."

---

* "I did," Hepburn, beaming proudly, confirmed in 1987.

Merman and Sandra Church, who played the overlooked daughter Louise; Jerome Robbins thought she was too young to play a glamorous stripper in Act II and wanted to cast Carol Lawrence. Suzanne Pleshette also auditioned, but Church sang her heart out in a borrowed sexy negligée and sewed up the part.

Sondheim had more to his argument. "Jule's shows had been in a rather traditional mold, what used to be called 'musical comedy.' Songs and block comedy scenes. I didn't know how he'd adapt to another way of thinking, whether he'd be able to keep his eyes and ears on character and story rather than hit songs."

Hammerstein convinced Sondheim to write the lyrics for *Gypsy*. For starters, it would teach him to tailor material for a star. And secondly, because Hammerstein knew Sondheim had his heart set on *A Roman Comedy*, which would become *A Funny Thing Happened on the Way to the Forum*, the *Gypsy* project "goes into rehearsal in six months, so the most it would be is six months out of your life."

—

"*Gypsy* was written in three months," Sondheim told writer and essayist Adam Gopnik, years after the show had made it to practically every list of the Top Ten, even Five, Greatest Musicals of All Time. "That is a very short time. We all understood what it was about. Jule understood what the style of the music should be—because he was brought up in that atmosphere. Vaudeville."

Once Hayward and Merrick, in tandem, personally requested that Sondheim do the lyrics, Sondheim and Styne met and began work in the fall of 1958. "I thought he might hit me over the head," said the composer, aware of Sondheim's desire to have done the music. "He was young, ambitious, and a huge talent. But he was also gentle, and we got along fine."

The usual routine had Laurents presenting Sondheim with a scene, perhaps some dialogue, then Sondheim consulting with Styne, who was practically a songwriting machine—the complete opposite of the style and pace of his young collaborator, who found Styne, out of his three major composing collaborators, "the most flexible I worked with, because he kept referring to himself as a tunesmith rather than a composer."*

"Out of impatience, not ego," said Sondheim, Styne handed him thirteen songs that had been sitting in Jule's trunk, either because they were cut from other projects or intended for shows that never got off the ground. This included, according to Sondheim, "The Cow Song" for June's vaudeville number.

There were more: The melody for "Everything's Coming Up Roses" had been cut from *High Button Shoes*, for which Sammy Cahn had supplied lyrics for something called "I'm Betwixt! I'm Between!" Another Styne-Cahn effort, "Why Did You Have to Wait So Long?" was for an unproduced Marilyn Monroe movie called *Pink Tights*, only to be repurposed for a 1957 TV musical version of *Ruggles of Red Gap* under the name "I'm in Pursuit of Happiness." Sondheim unknowingly turned it into "You'll Never Get Away from Me."

"If he had told me that a completed lyric had been written to it, I would have never agreed to work with that tune," Sondheim said. "I thought we should write everything fresh, for the particular moods and situations of the show. I think Jule was a bit disappointed."

---

* After their Gypsy collaboration, Styne expressed a desire to continue working together, so Sondheim supplied lyrics to two songs Tony Bennett recorded, "Home Is the Place" and "Come Over Here," but Sondheim found he needed the book of a musical to inspire him.

RESOLUTION IN THE KEY OF C MAJOR

For sheer intensity, there's little that can top Gypsy's Act I curtain number, "Everything's Coming Up Roses."

The song unfolds at the exact moment this "very ambitious lady," whose whole life centers around advancing the career of the younger of her two daughters, "suddenly is confronted with disaster," Sondheim said.

Daughter June, the family's breadwinner, has run off and eloped. (Arthur Laurents claimed June Havoc told him she was thirteen when that happened, but he discovered that not to be true.) The chorus boys have left the act to go their separate ways, too.

Amplifying the irony of Rose's having been, in Sondheim's words, "left with her world crashing down around her," the scene strands her in a remote train station, looking all the more abandoned given the backdrop designer Jo Mielziner has placed behind her: a boundless, not particularly welcoming frontier.

For this moment, Sondheim and Styne, whose music and lyrics for Gypsy fit hand to glove, wrote "a very jubilant kind of 'Hallelujah' song," something totally upbeat, Sondheim said, to contrast with the heavy dread of the situation.

As the anthem is heard, Rose's lover, Herbie, and her elder daughter, Louise, are too stunned to move, incredulous that nothing can shake this woman.

Rose, having turned on a dime, decides to refocus her life on her long-overlooked Louise, yet is completely clueless as to just how desperate she appears—or that vaudeville is as dead as her chances.

"The effect, we hope, is equivalent to a horror movie," said Sondheim.

When Gypsy was trying out in Philadelphia, Merman asked costar Jack Klugman what he was doing after the show. "Playing poker," he replied. "It'd be more fun in my hotel room," she said. Sondheim thought the two exuded no sexual chemistry onstage but that didn't detract from the story.

"Little Lamb" also fell into that category, but Sondheim liked the old melody, as did Styne, and the two saw it as a way to define Louise's loneliness. Robbins didn't like it. He thought the number slowed the story, so he cut it in Philadelphia, where the show was running overtime.

For once, the director-choreographer found himself facing the wrath of someone else.

As Laurents—and nearly everyone—told the story, "Jule came on stage, very cool, very calm, and said: 'Mr. Robbins, I have informed my lawyers that if "Little Lamb" is not back in the show tonight, I will withdraw my entire score.'"

Back it went.

—

The reviews were ambrosia, but the Tonys were arsenic. With eight nominations, including for Best Musical, Best Actress in a Musical (Merman), Best Featured Actor in a Musical (Jack Klugman), Best Featured Actress in a Musical (Sandra Church), Best Scenic Design (Oliver Smith), Best Costume Design (Raoul Pène Du Bois), and Best Direction of a Musical (Robbins), Gypsy took home nothing.

Mary Martin was named Best Musical Actress for *The Sound of Music*—"How are you supposed to buck a nun?" was Merman's quotable retort—and the Rodgers and

Hammerstein behemoth* tied with *Fiorello!* for the top musical honor. Jule Styne and Sondheim's dynamic score was not even nominated.

The biggest snub came when Merman was passed over for the movie, which, she said, Hollywood producer-director Mervyn LeRoy had promised her over the course of various visits to the show. Rosalind Russell starred onscreen, with her singing voice enhanced by *Allegro* original cast member Lisa Kirk. (Natalie Wood, as Gypsy, did her own singing.)

Russell, who was married to the movie's producer, Frederick Brisson, had recently delivered two back-to-back winners for Warner Bros., both lifted from Broadway sources: *Auntie Mame*, which proved a smash, and playwright Leonard Spigelgass's *A Majority of One*, directed and produced by Mervyn LeRoy, about a Jewish widow (Russell) and her relationship with a Japanese widower (Alec Guinness), which proved embarrassing but profitable.

LeRoy and Spigelgass retained their collaboration on the movie *Gypsy*, aiming for the spirit but never achieving the verve of the stage original.** The charming "Together, Wherever We Go" number was cut for time, and, while no means an epic, the picture ran a challenging two hours, twenty-three minutes. The train station backdrop for "Everything's Coming Up Roses" looks like what it was: a painted studio backdrop, which comes out cheesy when blown up to widescreen Technirama.

"Merman had starred in the [1953] movie version of her Broadway musical *Call Me Madam*, and the results hadn't come up to the producer's expectations," Rosalind Russell (here with Karl Malden, in the 1962 movie Gypsy) wrote in her autobiography. "I felt she should have gotten the part in Gypsy, it belonged to her. But I'd learned from [MGM star] Myrna Loy early on: 'Grab 'em if they come up.'"

---

* The movie version, directed by Robert Wise and starring Julie Andrews and the Alps, followed and proved a commercial and cultural sensation. Sondheim referred to its score as "plodding."

** Warner Bros. devoted its energy that year to its screen version of *The Music Man*, an Oscar nominee for Best Picture.

Natalie Wood made the cover of *Life* magazine shortly after hitting the jackpot with *West Side Story* and right before the release of *Gypsy*, in which she played Louise.

Sondheim held the finished product in contempt; Laurents outright hated it; Robbins rolled his eyes at its mention; and Styne, a seasoned Hollywood veteran, voiced downright enmity. "The movies destroyed every musical they ever made from the stage," he said.

Still, the picture has its defenders. In 1993, shortly after a TV version of *Gypsy* with Bette Midler as Rose was aired on CBS, the *Los Angeles Times* ran a provocative defense of the 1962 movie. Critic Joe Baltake* praised the film's "fidelity to the play," Russell for fleshing "out the character of Rose as no one else ever has," and Natalie Wood for being "the only actress ever to do anything remotely memorable with the title character."

---

* "If Sondheim wanted to complain," the critic wrote, he should take a look at "the film of *A Little Night Music*, made, ironically, by the very people who presented it on stage."

"When I won," Angela Lansbury said of her 1975 Tony for the role Merman originated in 1959, "I gave her credit. She wrote me a note thanking me. I thought that was very touching."

Shortly before the CBS broadcast, Jule Styne was in his East Side apartment, a preview tape of Midler singing "Small World" resounding through his living room sound system. He was sighing with delight.

"Isn't she wonderful?" he said. "The best Rose ever."

And Merman?

His smile faded. "She scared me."

Arthur Laurents directed stage productions of *Gypsy* starting with a 1973 London premiere starring Angela Lansbury, followed by a 1989 Broadway revival with Tyne Daly, and another still, in 2008, with Patti LuPone.* (In 2003, Sam Mendes directed a Broadway revival starring Bernadette Peters; Laurents went out of his way to bad-mouth the changes Mendes made.)**

For years, Laurents fixated on having a new and reconceived version brought to the screen. From time to time the blogosphere would bubble over with semiconfirmed reports of Barbra Streisand considering a proposal to direct and play Rose, costarring with Lady Gaga as Louise and John Travolta as Herbie. In early 2011, a *New York Times* item quoted Laurents*** suggesting Tom Hanks for Herbie.

"I would be very pleased if we had a different film version for the historical record," the playwright said.

---

* All three actors won Tonys for their performances of Rose.

** In 2015, Imelda Staunton, directed by Jonathan Kent, won an Olivier Award for her performance as Rose in the West End, and Sondheim was very high on her performance.

*** Laurents died May 5, 2011, age ninety-three.

Gypsy's son, Erik Lee Preminger, saw Laura Benanti's Tony-winning Louise in the 2008 revival and told her, "Oh, my God, I'm watching my mother." From left: Boyd Gaines (who played Herbie), Patti LuPone (Rose), Arthur Laurents, and Benanti.

Laurents later retracted the statement. It seems he'd received some advice.

"Sondheim told me something that he got from the British—and it's wonderful. He said, 'You want a record because the theater is ephemeral. But that's wrong. The theater's greatest essence is that it is ephemeral. You don't need a record. The fact that it's ephemeral means you can have different productions, different Roses on into infinity.'"

Laurents concluded, "I don't want a definitive record. I want it to stay alive."

———

The Sound of Music ran for 1,433 performances on Broadway. *Gypsy* ran 702.

"*Gypsy* says something fairly hard to take: that every child eventually has to become responsible for his parents," Sondheim said. He categorized the realization as "something that everybody knows but nobody likes to think about a lot. And that's why *Gypsy*, at base, in spite of the terrific reviews, wasn't a smash hit."

Oscar Hammerstein visited Philly when his protégé's show was trying out. "He had a couple things to say about song placement, not about rewriting a song. He never said, 'Gee, I think that song is wrong,' or, 'I wish that lyric were more graceful,'" said Sondheim. "He probably restrained himself from that purposefully. I wasn't calling him down to say, 'Is this line a good line?' I sought his advice as a Grand Master of Musical Theater."

August 23, 1960, fifteen months after the opening of *Gypsy*, at age sixty-five, Oscar Hammerstein II died of stomach cancer.

"I don't really remember talking to Oscar about my music very much," Sondheim said in 2001. "He never heard any of the so-called 'mature scores.' All he heard was *Saturday Night* . . . I think he certainly encouraged me, but he died before *Forum*."

That was his professional remembrance.

Personally, Sondheim said, "He saved my life with his counsel and his presence."

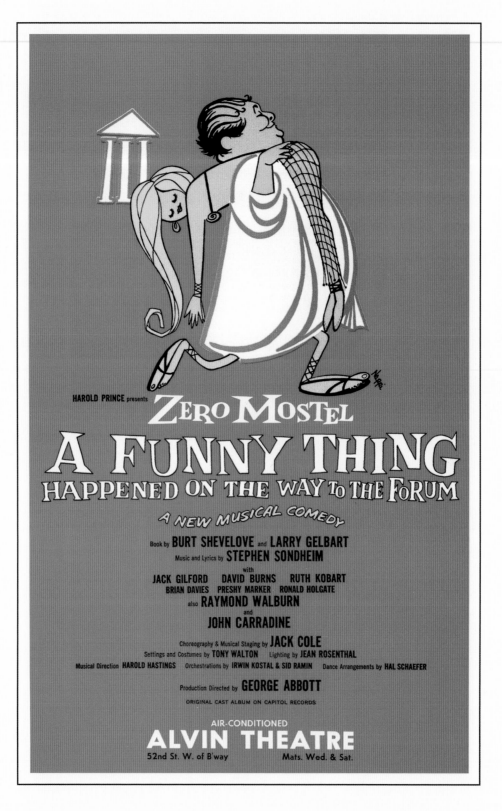

When Burt Shevelove first broached the subject of adapting the works of Ancient Roman playwright Plautus into a musical, "the plays [were] still funny," said Sondheim. "I couldn't figure out why I was still laughing."

TOGA PARTY

Nineteen months before the opening night of his next show—which took place on May 8, 1962—Stephen Sondheim told a rapt audience of New York City high school students, "The show that's almost completed now I've been working on for almost three years with my collaborators is a show called *A Funny Thing Happened on the Way to the Forum*."

Motivated by the audience's lively response to the title, Sondheim, in his *Mad Men*–era sports coat and narrow necktie, quipped, "This is the year for long titles of musicals," a nod to that season's *How to Succeed in Business Without Really Trying*.

"Anyway, this is a show from an idea from a man named Burt Shevelove, who is one of the authors of the book. He's writing it—they're just finishing it now—with Larry Gelbart, and it's based on the plays of Plautus, who is a two-thousand-year-old situation comedy writer."

The audience found that funny. Sondheim reacted with a small grin.

"Plautus wrote a large number of short plays, each of which has been rewritten many, many times, not knowingly, right up through Desi and Lucy* and Sergeant Bilko,** whose prototype is to be found in the plays of Plautus. And we've taken about nine of his plays and made an amalgam of them into one evening of musical theatre in the Roman style"—meaning distinct separations of tragedy and comedy—"but with a group of comics instead of a group of so-called actors and performers of anything but of a comic nature."

Without pause,*** he went on, "The show's to star Milton Berle, it's being directed by George Abbott, and produced by Hal Prince, who also produced *West Side*. And the evening is sort of a celebration of comedy. There isn't a serious moment in the whole show. We hope maybe there'll be a couple of charming ones, but it's mostly comic from beginning

---

* Desi Arnaz and Lucille Ball; Sondheim was referring to *I Love Lucy*.

** The lead character on what has been called one of the funniest TV sitcoms of all time, the 1955–1959 *You'll Never Get Rich*, or *The Phil Silvers Show*. The star character and his platoon were more interested in poker games than army drills.

*** Sondheim tended to think even faster than he could talk, and he talked fast.

to end, and the use of songs in it, I hope, will be different from the so-called 'integrated musical' where the songs and the story constantly flow in and out of each other that have been going on for so many years now. I think, a rather tired formula that—"

And with that, the host leapt in to ask Sondheim what was going to happen when the lyricist got "terribly annoyed with the composer."

Forum marked Sondheim's Broadway debut as both lyricist and composer.

—

Sondheim's detailed description ended up being wrong on at least two counts. It took five years, not three, and ten drafts to complete *Forum*. And Milton Berle didn't make it to showtime.

The first hitch developed when Robbins, who three years earlier had shown Leland Hayward fragments of what was then called *A Roman Play*, jumped ship upon learning David Merrick was now producing *Forum*. The go-round with the mercurial maniac on *Gypsy* had been more than enough for Robbins.

Sondheim and his collaborators bought back the option on their *A Funny Thing Happened on the Way to the Forum* from the notoriously difficult producer David Merrick (above), hoping they could convince Jerome Robbins to join them.

Sondheim, Shevelove, and Gelbart did some backtracking of their own; for $4,000, they bought back the rights from Merrick, hoping they could return Robbins to the fold. They were successful, but then Robbins abruptly backed out again. His resignation was "sent in the form of a message conveyed to us through a third party," said Gelbart. "It was a shot between the eyes."

Fortunately, the three men had a strong enough working relationship that they were able to withstand the impediments associated with mounting a major new Broadway musical. Another significant influence on Sondheim, Shevelove (pronounced "Shev-vel-love"), was fifteen years Sondheim's elder, and, according to Sondheim, he stressed "clarity of language, as well as clarity of thought." Another Shevelove rule: "The best art always seems effortless—maybe not true of something like *Guernica*, but true of lyric writing."

When Shevelove, Gelbart, and Sondheim started work on *Forum* in 1958, Shevelove followed his own advice and pushed for making the show as funny as possible, especially given the sudden lack of actual comedy in musical comedies on Broadway—as witnessed by *West Side Story* and soon enough, the darker undertones of *Gypsy*. He did not want the songs to advance the plot, Hammerstein style, but to allow the audience time to collect themselves between jokes. Another tip from Shevelove: "Never sacrifice smoothness for cleverness. Better dull than clumsy."

Shevelove's interest in Plautus began in 1942, when as a graduate student at Yale he wrote lyrics and book for a campus musical he called *When in Rome* that he adapted from the ancient playwright's *Miles Gloriosus*, about a swaggering Greek soldier, and *Pseudolus*, about a scheming slave. A seed was planted.

Larry Gelbart, whose impressive CV would include writing (in addition to developing and producing) the Emmy-winning TV series *M*A*S*H*, the Oscar-winning

The *Forum* team, from left: lyricist-composer Sondheim, book writers Larry Gelbart and Burt Shevelove, and director George Abbott. Shevelove did not want the songs to advance the plot but instead to serve as respites from the relentless barrage of gags.

screenplay for *Tootsie*, and the Tony-winning book for *City of Angels*, got his showbiz start from then–radio comedian Danny Thomas, who played a daydreaming mailman on Fanny Brice's *The Baby Snooks Show*. Thomas hired the teenaged Larry after he read some of Larry's jokes given to the entertainer by his barber, Harry Gelbart, who was Larry's father.

Working with Sondheim "was not smooth sailing," Gelbart admitted. "We were forever asking Steve—and later George Abbott was asking him—to write songs not for Lenny Bernstein in the third row but for the audience." Reminded once too often, Sondheim shot back, "You want those kinds of songs? Call Jule Styne."

In fact, Bernstein, after Sondheim had previewed the *Forum* score for him, did not wholly approve of Sondheim's compositions. "There's a good deal in *Forum* of what Lenny called my wrong-note music, the dissonances," Sondheim said of the style he was then developing. "I suppose you could say it started with *Forum*." Regarding lyrics, Sondheim also admitted that, with this show, he had found his personal voice: "I recognized that I was being clever in my own way, not in a Cole Porter way, not in a Frank Loesser way."

George Abbott, at the ripe age of seventy-five,* came into the picture when the creative team passed on producer-director Joshua Logan, who requested rewrites entailing "more naked boys and things like that," said Sondheim. He also thought

* Abbott died in 1995 at the even riper age of 106.

75

Abbott was "completely humorless," but the director, who was also a notable play doctor—meaning he would come in and help fix struggling new works—had a reputation for keeping a plot moving.

To interest Abbott in directing *Forum*, producer Prince, who stepped in after Merrick's forced abdication, arranged an audition one Friday morning. Sondheim played piano and sang. Shevelove and Gelbart read their book aloud. None of the physical comedy was performed, and Abbott, pronouncing the work "sophomoric," fled after two hours. The team had barely cracked Act II.

"There's a point at which disappointment becomes part of the game," Gelbart philosophized.

Prince, refusing to surrender, messengered the script to Abbott at his Catskills weekend home, asking "Mr. Abbott"—as he was always addressed—to read it with an open mind. Abbott did just that and was big enough to admit he was wrong.

With Abbott officially on board to direct, the creative team now turned their eye to casting. The show was originally fashioned to fit the talents of Sergeant Bilko himself, Phil Silvers, who was meant to star as the slave Pseudolus, who plots his way through a maze of obstacles in order to gain his freedom. (Make that *plotz*; the show

Director George Abbott grew alarmed during rehearsals because Zero Mostel (far left, as Pseudolus) "would begin to act before I had finished saying something." Admonishing the actor, Abbott told him, "Zero, you don't listen," to which Mostel replied, "My wife has been telling me that for years."

owes more to the post-war Borscht Belt than Plautian Rome.*) At the end of the day, Silvers didn't understand the material and in another blow to the project, he bowed out.

Berle, nicknamed "Mr. Television" because his weekly program, *Texaco Star Theatre*, popularized the new medium and spurred the sales of TV sets, was throwing his still-considerable weight around, and eventually went too far. He demanded a financial slice of *Forum*, including international rights. "More important," said Hal Prince, "he was asserting his opinion in respect to casting, choice of choreographer, scenic and costume design, and even theatre." The team and Berle parted ways.

With Silvers and Berle gone, Shevelove and Gelbart thought of casting the comedian Red Buttons, with whom they had both worked in early 1950s TV (just as they had with Sid Caesar and Bob Hope), while Hal Prince thought of the artist-performer Zero Mostel. Shevelove, Gelbart, and Sondheim objected; Mostel had a reputation for going off script and pandering to the audience.

"The trouble with Zero is he didn't know a fart from a bon mot," Gelbart said.

What Prince and Abbott didn't know was that, independently, the others were auditioning Red Buttons, a situation that found its way into the newspapers.

Mostel, who at the very same time was being wooed by Prince and Abbott, chose to overlook the writers' vote of no confidence.

Mostel let Prince and Abbott continue to woo.

Then Mostel's wife, Kathryn, said, "If you don't take it, I'm going to stab you in the balls."

Citing Dramatists Guild rules guarding authors' rights of approval, the writers threatened to withdraw their play.

If that weren't enough, Prince's partner, Bobby Griffiths, dropped dead of a heart attack shortly after the two agreed to produce *Forum*.

"I like to think there was no connection between events," said Gelbart.

—

"The book has this elegant low-comedy style," Sondheim said, "and the songs are sort of salon songs. That's an exaggeration, but there's a disparity between the score and the book."

That the two were incompatible was a theory first advanced by Sondheim's playwright pal James Goldman, who would go on to write the books for *Evening Primrose* and *Follies*. Once he heard the opinion, Sondheim could never let go of it. In one of his final interviews, Sondheim reasserted that Goldman was correct, and said, "The worst mistake you can make, in a collaboration, is writing different musicals."

Early previews were far from promising. "It was a disaster out of town,"** said Sondheim. For one thing, *Forum* was too long. "Some of the best jokes were cut, such as, when they're passing the wine around, 'Ah, Two . . . that was a good year,' and 'Pseudolus, you're stupid . . . S-T-V-P-I-D. Stupid.'"

---

* With some *Mad* magazine tossed in for good measure.

** Larry Gelbart's much-quoted "If Hitler's still alive, I hope he's out of town with a musical," pertained to his show a year before *Forum*, *The Conquering Hero*, an adaptation of the Preston Sturges screen comedy *Hail the Conquering Hero*. (It lasted eight performances on Broadway.) Gelbart made the remark upon hearing that Israeli agents in Argentina had finally caught elusive Nazi war criminal Adolf Eichmann.

Forum co-author Larry Gelbart recalled with chagrin that Zero Mostel, here in his Alvin Theatre dressing room, would break character during performances to announce the day's baseball scores. "His fans were so worshipful," said Gelbart, "he took advantage of that."

He and Abbott would stand in the back of the theatre so they could read the audience. "You can tell from silences, from restlessness, sometimes from coughing. Sometimes from the quality of the applause," Sondheim said. "The key is not to rush into a response. It's a great mistake just to go home and rewrite. Or just fire an actor. To zero in on what's wrong immediately is always wrong. You gotta let it play."

Meanwhile, members of the audience were walking out. "We thought that what we were seeing was terrific. Finally, one evening George [Abbott, attempting a joke,] said, 'I don't know what to do. You'd better call in George Abbott.'"

As every theatre buff knows—and can all but recite—Jerome Robbins saved *A Funny Thing Happened on the Way to the Forum* after Sondheim pressed Hal Prince to call him in when the show was in Washington, DC. The request, however, was not without its complications; nine years earlier, a very unfunny thing had happened with Robbins in the nation's capital.

On May 5, 1953, Robbins named names before the House Un-American Activities Committee. His appearance had been spurred by a threat from newspaper columnist and TV host Ed Sullivan, who said that unless the choreographer-director faced the interrogators on the Committee, Sullivan would expose Robbins's leftist sympathies and sexual orientation. Protecting his own hide, Robbins named eight people, tossing them onto the blacklist of unemployable actors, writers, directors, and artists.

Among those Robbins named was Madeline Lee Gilford, the actor wife of comic actor Jack Gilford. Mostel was also blacklisted. Both Mostel and Jack Gilford were in *Forum*, Mostel as the star, after Sondheim, Gelbart, and Shevelove had reluctantly agreed to his being cast.*

---

* Abbott and Prince persisted that Mostel be hired, and Shevelove, Gelbart, and Sondheim relented. News clippings from mid-March 1962 confirm the decision.

Sondheim wrote the foot-stomping "Comedy Tonight" on the orders of Jerome Robbins, after *Forum*'s previous opening numbers left the audience without a clue as to what the show was about.

Just as *Washington Post* critic Richard Coe's review of *Forum* was published underneath the headline, "Mr. Abbott: Close It!," Jerome Robbins was in Southern California collecting his Oscars for *West Side Story*.

The show was three weeks away from opening on Broadway. Prince put in a call. Robbins agreed to devote ten days to fixing *Forum*.*

For the first previews, Sondheim said, he "had written two opening numbers—I wrote one number that was probably just right for the score, but George Abbott said that he couldn't hum it. So that was the end of that."

The opener, "Invocation," was more of a preface and spelled out rules for the audience. In 1974, Sondheim and Shevelove would repurpose the number, altering it slightly, for a new endeavor called *The Frogs*, which was based on the play by Aristophanes.

---

* For which he would receive 0.5 percent of ticket sales.

Forum's clown quartet mugging their way through "Everybody Ought to Have a Maid"; from left: John Carradine as Marcus Lycus, Jack Gilford as Hysterium, David Burns as Senex, and Mostel as Pseudolus.

For his second try, Sondheim composed "Love Is in the Air," which he determined was "lighthearted, airy, and filled with little puns, and chock with charm."* Robbins determined that it confused the audience.

"He said, 'It's the opening number that's killing it. It's not telling them what the show's about. You've got to write a baggy-pants number,'" recalled Sondheim. "So I wrote this song called 'Comedy Tonight.' Jerry insisted, though, 'I don't want you to tell any jokes, let me tell the jokes.' Very smart of him. That's why the lyric is so bland and dull—it's background for Jerry's pyrotechnics. It may be the best opening number ever put on the stage. The audience was so satisfied at the end of it that we thought, 'Let's not do the rest of the show.'"

Robbins did major patchwork, altering designer Tony Walton's sets so they would not distract from the stage action and sidelining the show's credited choreographer, the underrated Jack Cole. Later, Cole referenced the title of the recently published novel *The Agony and the Ecstasy* to describe what it felt like to work with Robbins and Sondheim.

Cole was "not Stephen's style," George Martin, an experienced Broadway dancer and the choreographer's assistant on *Forum*, recalled in 2003. "He didn't discuss intellectually his choreography or his work."

Prince said Abbott accepted Robbins's takeover with his usual stoicism.

As for Robbins's reception by the cast, Jack Gilford threatened to quit, until his wife Madeline said, "Why should you blacklist yourself?" Mostel told Hal Prince, "I don't have to have lunch with him, do I?," then greeted Robbins with "Hi, there, blabbermouth." (Another version had Mostel calling Robbins "Loose Lips.") The remark

---

* Robin Williams and Christine Baranski sing it in the 1996 Mike Nichols film *The Birdcage*.

reputedly got a laugh and broke the ice, although it was said Mostel never spoke to Robbins again—or, at least, not pleasantly.* Three years later, the two constantly clashed but ultimately succeeded in working together on *Fiddler on the Roof*.

Robbins fed Sondheim the lines for the socko "Comedy Tonight"—Sondheim's calling the lyric bland and dull is meant to refute the Hammerstein dictum of letting the music work its magic, which "Comedy Tonight" does in spades—then polished the second-act dance number Chase of the Three Virgins (the show has a definite *Playboy* Party Jokes vibe) and staged six numbers: "I'm Calm," "Impossible," "Lovely" (including Gilford's drag version performed in character as Hysterium, the chief eunuch), "Pretty Little Picture," "That'll Show 'Em," and the "Comedy Tonight" reprise for the finale.

"The first song is what makes or breaks the show. You start off with the right opening, and you can ride for forty-five minutes on the telephone book," said Sondheim.

"On the other hand, if you start off with the wrong one, it's an uphill fight all the way."

—

A Funny Thing Happened on the Way to the Forum was Stephen Sondheim's longest-running Broadway show, with 964 performances in total. In 1963, a London West End production starring Frankie Howerd left such an impression that, in 1969, Howerd resumed the toga and starred in *Up Pompeii!,* a BBC sitcom that veered so closely to *Forum* that the network's legal department warned the show's creators to proceed with caution.

In 1966, Richard Lester, who directed the Beatles in the Marx Brothers–like *A Hard Day's Night* and *Help!*, shot the movie version of *Forum* in Spain, with Mostel and Gilford reprising their stage roles. Phil Silvers appeared as Marcus Lycus, keeper of the brothel, and, in his final role, Buster Keaton played Erronius, a near-sighted old man looking for his two children after they were cradle-robbed by pirates.

Save for "Comedy Tonight," "Lovely,"** "Everybody Ought to Have a Maid," and "Bring Me My Bride," the movie is long on slapstick and short on musical numbers, with frenetic editing that presaged TikTok. Sondheim professed to like the screen version, if only because Lester made a movie and not a filmed play.

In 1972, Phil Silvers at last played Pseudolus in a Broadway revival directed by Shevelove that, either because it was too soon after the original or the movie, failed to run for as long as Clive Barnes's rave review in the *New York Times* augured. Still, Silvers won a Tony for the role.*** The star then took the show to London but suffered a stroke, which necessitated the early closing of the production.

---

* Unlike Gelbart, Robbins admired Mostel, albeit begrudgingly; when the performer died, Robbins wrote in his journal that it was hard to think of "that gargantuan man" no longer being around.

** A wispy Michael Crawford, eleven years before he donned the mask and cape for the London premiere of *The Phantom of the Opera*, played *Forum*'s onscreen romantic lead, Hero. Australian actor Annette Andre played his love interest, Philia.

*** As did Larry Blyden, as Hysterium.

CREATING A SPLASH

A funny thing happened on the way to Hades.

In 405 BC, only months after the death of the tragedian playwright Euripides, the farceur Aristophanes came up with *The Frogs*, a comedy about journeying into the underworld with a drunken Dionysus, his hayseed servant Xanthias, and Dionysus's half brother, the hopelessly oafish but heroically muscled Heracles.

Reaching their destination calls for crossing the River Styx, protected by the singing amphibians of the title.

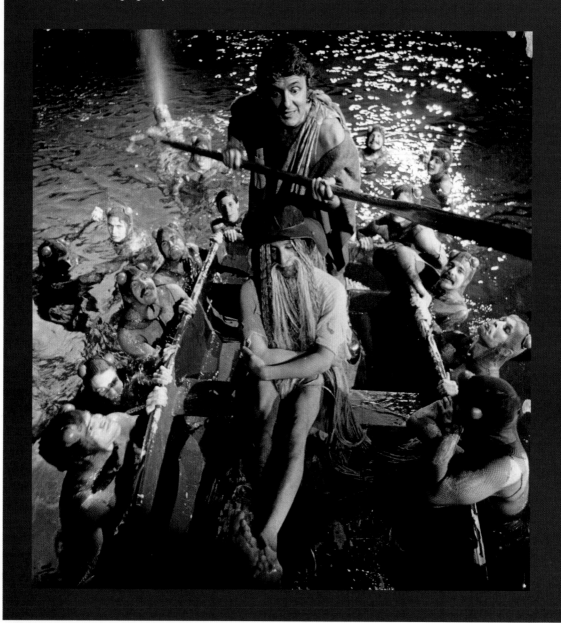

OPPOSITE AND ABOVE: Burt Shevelove staged Aristophanes's *The Frogs* in the Yale swimming pool in 1941 (above), then revisited the satire in 1974 (left), asking Sondheim to supply incidental music. In 2004, Nathan Lane expanded the script and starred in a production at Lincoln Center. "We tried," said Lane. "And we failed. *But* we got six fabulous new Sondheim songs. You're welcome."

Without revealing too much—the play is strong on dialogue, weak on structure—Euripides and his great predecessor, Aeschylus, engage in a poetry contest that the latter wins, securing him a place on Earth to help Athens out of her woes. (The city-state is currently battling Sparta; this *is* the Peloponnesian War, after all.)

Just as he tackled ancient Rome, Burt Shevelove set his sights on ancient Greece when he was a Yale drama student, and in 1941 he wrote and directed his version of *The Frogs*. Filling in for the River Styx was the university's Exhibition Pool in the Payne Whitney Gymnasium.

Revisiting the idea in 1974, Shevelove made some changes, swapping the tragedian poets of the original with George Bernard Shaw and William Shakespeare.

Sondheim, accepting Shevelove's invitation to supply incidental music, remained faithful to the style of a Greek chorus. There was also an aquatic ballet.

The production was staged at the same site of Shevelove's 1941 effort, this time with a twenty-one-man chorus clad in green Speedos, and a sixty-eight-member ensemble. Among them were Yale School of Drama students Meryl Streep, Sigourney Weaver, and Christopher Durang.

Sondheim was less than pleased with the outcome, even though his stalwart musical director Paul Gemignani and orchestrator Jonathan Tunick both lent a helping hand.

"If you're writing for a chorus in a swimming pool," Sondheim said, "you've got to thin out the harmonies." The gym's acoustics were so poor, he grumbled, "it was like putting on a show in a men's urinal."

After a rushed rehearsal, *The Frogs* ran for a week at Yale, as scheduled, but, to Sondheim's dismay, the New York critics showed up. Sondheim, after all, was riding high from his three-in-a-row hits: *Company, Follies,* and *A Little Night Music,* so any fresh effort was newsworthy.

The *New York Times,* while generally applauding "the theatrical event," hinted that Sondheim could have used more time.

Movie director Richard Lester's 1966 *A Funny Thing Happened on the Way to the Forum* managed to transform a sumptuous Roman banquet into leftover stew; here, Zero Mostel as Pseudolus and Michael Crawford as Hero.

Nathan Lane slipped on a pair of sandals for a 1996 revival directed by Jerry Zaks and choreographed by Rob Marshall. It ran 715 performances and won Lane his first Tony.

"His material was challenging and complex to learn and perform," Lane said of Sondheim, "but once you got it into your head, it never left you because it was just so brilliantly written."

When Lane stepped out of the role, Whoopi Goldberg stepped in. Sondheim rewrote some of the lyrics in the song "Free" for her, the tour-de-force number that deftly encapsulates Pseudolus's life goal. The character also no longer fixated on Gymnasia, one of Lycus's courtesans.

Not that Goldberg's tenure was completely free from strife.

"That damn toga," she said. "You can't look cute in a toga."

—

While *Forum* was still being polished, Sondheim, Shevelove, and Gelbart nurtured the notion of "doing a show about a team of collaborators who had written a hit and, a year later, wanted to work together again," Gelbart remembered in 2009. "Only, by that time, they weren't talking to one another."

Sondheim was stung by his lack of a Tony nomination and, at the awards ceremony, not one of his Tony-accepting colleagues so much as mentioned his name. The winners were Mostel (Leading Actor in a Musical), Abbott (Direction of a Musical), Prince (Producer of a Musical), Gelbart and Shevelove (Best Authors), Ruth Kobart (Best Featured Actress), and Jack Gilford (Best Featured Actor).

There were likely other bumps along the way.

As Gelbart said about the unrealized next project, "We had somehow managed to live out our premise instead of writing it."

GETTING STUCK ON SONDHEIM

A funny thing happened on the way to the emporium.

The older Sondheim's richly etched face made its way to retail, adorning contemporary paintings, placards, playbills, banners, badges, even body tattoos. (Seriously, check out Pinterest.)

As with Albert Einstein and Mickey Mouse, and, for that matter, Ludwig van Beethoven, Sondheim's thoughtful visage has appeared on a variety of merchandise, ranging from modish T-shirts to decorative coffee mugs—albeit, in keeping with the man's reserved nature, in strictly limited editions.

In 2016, a millennial web developer named Tyson Armstrong was scrolling through Etsy from the comfort of his home in Melbourne, Australia, when he ran across an enamel pin featuring Angela Lansbury's face during her *Murder, She Wrote* period. He bought it, along with a Masters of the Universe He-Man pin.

"Then I thought, well, if no one else is doing it, I'll give it a go." His pin subject was Stephen Sondheim. "I worked out a design and found a manufacturing factory in China."

Armstrong placed a first order for one hundred Sondheim pins, fifty being the factory's minimum. He figured, at worst, he'd be stuck with one hundred pins.

After the $10 finished product was posted on Twitter, "within twenty-four hours, they completely sold out." Nearly 40 percent of the orders came from New York, and the rest from throughout the world.

"Some from lonely outposts," Armstrong said. "Thailand. Missouri."

Since then, besides becoming a permanent U.S. resident, the entrepreneur has added a star-studded lineup to the inventory on his BroadwayPins.com website, including Audra McDonald, Sutton Foster, Lin-Manuel Miranda, Patti LuPone, and Elaine Stritch, "who's very popular," Armstrong said, "although no one is as popular as Sondheim."

"Whether you're in the park with George, heading into the woods, or visiting Japan for the first time, take Sondheim with you to guide you through any tricky internal rhymes you might encounter," Broadway Pins entrepreneur Tyson Armstrong posted on his e-commerce site, where the merchandise also includes small likenesses of Audra McDonald, Bernadette Peters, Elaine Stritch, and others.

Kermit Bloomgarden & Diana Krasny present
Lee Remick   Angela Lansbury
Harry Guardino
in a wild new musical by
Arthur Laurents & Stephen Sondheim

Anyone Can Whistle

MAJESTIC THEATRE
44th St. West of Broadway   Matinees Wed & Sat

"It was way ahead of its time, in that it was experimental," Sondheim said of *Anyone Can Whistle*. "Essentially, the show is about, on one level, nonconformity and conformity in contemporary society, which is not particularly interesting."`

NEVER DO ANYTHING TWICE

I.

"I like to change styles," Sondheim said in 2008, having exercised that prerogative his entire life; Hammerstein had, after all, sent him off in four different directions.

"One of the things that appeals to me about a story is if I've never done anything like it before. It has to be some unknown territory. It's got to make you nervous."

If it doesn't, Sondheim said, "then you're going to write the same thing you wrote before."

Dispirited after his treatment by Tony nominators and his *Forum* collaborators, Sondheim recalled twenty years afterward, in 1982, "I just remember thinking, 'Okay, let's go on.' That's when I went to Arthur [Laurents] and said I wanted to do something with really a lot of music in it and really weird."

Truer words could not have been said. His next project, *Anyone Can Whistle*, takes place in a financially strapped small American town, where the venal mayor, Cora Hoover Hooper, conceives of a miraculous water-spouting rock to attract pious tourists. The town's only other economic resource is a sanitarium known as the Cookie Jar, which houses patients called Cookies. When the Cookies get loose and mingle with the visiting religious pilgrims, no one can tell who's who, or even if the audience watching

the production are themselves a bunch of Cookies. Head Cookie Jar nurse Fay Apple is ordered to round up the Cookies, but instead she retaliates and threatens to expose the miracle rock for the fake that it is. (No, it's not yet intermission.) Facing arrest, Apple seeks her own miracle, who arrives in the person of the handsome J. Bowden Hapgood, who is possibly a doctor but ultimately a Cookie. If this were not enough to digest, Apple also has a hidden identity of her own: She can only let down her guard when taking on the persona of an "ooh-la-la" French "Lady from Lourdes." In the end, Apple and Hapgood face an uncertain future together, and the rock actually does spurt miracle water.

That was the plot—although it was not so much a plot as a plot device from which to launch an assault on conformity. And greed. And religion. And government interference. And totalitarianism. And so much else.

Anyone Can Whistle "was about so many things," said Sondheim, that he and Laurents, who was directing in addition to penning the book, "weren't able to

establish in the first few minutes exactly what it *was* about." He also admitted that the tone of the show was a turnoff; he and Laurents treated the audience with condescension bordering on contempt.

Originally, Laurents conceived of *Anyone Can Whistle** as two different plays, which might explain the unalloyed mix of surrealism and musical comedy that appears in the final product—and the length of the book: three acts. Sondheim joined the project in 1962, charged with coming up with three different numbers for three opening acts and an elongated "Cookie Chase" that would be tied to a string of individual songs and dances.

Sondheim sensed a risk in having two intermissions: "Once you've broken the mood, people go out onto the street and see the neon lights and are smoking their cigarettes, and you hear chatter about, 'Well, are we going to get back home in time for the babysitter?' It's very hard to get back in the mood."

Equally troublesome was Laurents's failure to focus the book, an ongoing concern for the producer Kermit Bloomgarden, whose Broadway hits included plays by Lillian Hellman, including *The Little Foxes*, as well as *Death of a Salesman*, *The Diary of Anne Frank*, and *The Music Man*. Laurents's original story became a particular cause for alarm. "Too far out," one *Anyone Can Whistle* investor expressed to Bloomgarden, as other money people chimed in with similar sentiments. Sondheim was forced to agree that his and Laurents's effort was "not a coherent success."

Laurents and Sondheim had spent two years just looking for a producer, and once they found theirs, thirty-three backers' auditions and 115 investors were required to

Arthur Laurents and Sondheim in the recording studio for the *Anyone Can Whistle* cast album, which was committed to vinyl the day after the show's brief Broadway run.

---

* There were also various titles along the way: *The Nut Show*, *The Natives Are Restless*, and *Side Show*.

REVIVALIST MOVEMENT

"What keeps the theater alive is reinterpretation," Sondheim told *60 Minutes* in 2020, when avant-gardist director Ivo van Hove was assembling his deconstructed *West Side Story* for Broadway.

Citing malleability as a positive force that differentiates theatre from movies and television, Sondheim said, "Each generation brings new ways of looking at a play."

West Side Story might be one thing—iconic—but what about *Anyone Can Whistle*?

So few people saw it in 1964. (It has been joked that if as many people had actually seen the original *Anyone Can Whistle* as claimed they had seen it, the production would have run longer than *Cats*.) And yet, it is its very underdog status that helped elevate the show to its cult standing among Sondheim fanatics. That and the Sondheim score.

Varied as the numbers are, "I don't really see anything going on among the songs that has any consistency," Sondheim told music specialist Mark Eden Horowitz. "And the fact is, a number of numbers were replaced, so I don't think it was very much of a conceived score."

Still, there are gems to be admired. Among them: Cora's bluesy "Me and My Town," in the manner of onetime MGM vocal coach Kay Thompson and her sophisticated, midcentury nightclub act (theatrical to the hilt, a signal that Cora is all artifice); the revivalist pastiche "Miracle Song"; Fay's determined "There Won't Be Trumpets" (cut before opening, when fifteen minutes needed to be sheared; it lingered long enough to become a cabaret staple); the ensemble's Act I curtain number "Simple," an ironically (given the title) intricate sorting out of the Cookies.

"If you listen to the music," Sondheim said, in what smacks of a rare self-compliment, "it really doesn't sound like anybody else who was writing at the time."

meet the not immodest $350,000 budget ($3.2 million today).

And yet, whether out of goodwill or genuine enthusiasm, the show's investing angels included Irving Berlin ($7,000; or, $64,000 today), Richard Rodgers ($3,500; $32,000 today), and Stephen's father, Herbert Sondheim ($1,750; $16,000 today).

The show turned out to be Sondheim's *Allegro*—heavily flawed, financially unfortunate, but of lingering fascination.

—

Angela Lansbury, who auditioned to play Mayor Cora after Laurents had written her a personal letter saying he and Sondheim would like to hear her sing, won the role. Admittedly, she was "unable to make head or tail" of the script, but figured, "It must be good, because these guys wrote it." This would be her first Broadway musical in what would lead to a long line of successes and Tony Awards, for *Mame*, *Dear World*, *Gypsy* (revival), *Sweeney Todd*, *Blithe Spirit*,* and a 2022 Special Tony for Lifetime Achievement in the Theatre.

"The rehearsals of *Anyone Can Whistle* were fraught with disagreement, upsets, drama—everybody was going crazy, running up and down" the aisles of the theatre, the London-born, MGM-trained actress said. "It wasn't my style at all, because I have always been a rather quiet person."

She harbored fears that Laurents was making Cora "repugnant" by the direction he was taking her, and her song, "A Parade in Town?," she said, "nearly ruined my voice." Furthermore, Lansbury heard rumblings that she was to be replaced by Nancy Walker.

Adding to the pressures of what was already a physically challenging role, there was to be "this wonderful ballet sequence" staged by the choreographer Herbert Ross. (Ross, whose dances are remembered for providing the humor that the book lacked, would receive the show's only Tony nomination.)

---

* A 2009 revival, and not a musical.

"I remember screaming my ass off at Stephen," Lansbury said. "What the hell do you want me to do?'" His response offered no comfort. "Steve wasn't easy. He was a fence-sitter."

She then realized Sondheim's ongoing attempts to placate everyone weren't the problem. It was the book.

"We were on the road," Lansbury said. "The audience wasn't liking what they were seeing. They were almost throwing tomatoes at the stage."

She acknowledged that Laurents, whom she "found difficult,"* was "fighting with his own book and trying to make it work."

That didn't stop preview crowds from being "very verbal and noisy, screaming and shouting" at the stage, Lansbury remembered.

"That's tough to swallow for the author."

---

* Lansbury's comments were made long after her experiences on both the 1964 *Anyone Can Whistle* and the 1974 *Gypsy*, for which Laurents sought her out for the lead and then praised her performance, especially the dimension she brought to "Rose's Turn."

OPPOSITE: *Anyone Can Whistle*'s musical director, Herb Greene (far right), "had a very strong way of dealing with singers who were new to the game and didn't know what they were doing," said Angela Lansbury. Greene put his hands around actors' throats and nearly strangled them. "Most extraordinary," Lansbury said. The cast was on a rehearsal break; from left: Lee Remick, Lansbury, and Harry Guardino.

RIGHT: Lee Remick (left) and Angela Lansbury both made their Broadway musical debuts in 1964's *Anyone Can Whistle* and over the years would continue their professional relationships with Sondheim despite the rockiness of their initial project together.

Oscar nominee (*The Days of Wine and Roses*) Lee Remick also made her Broadway musical debut in the role of Nurse Apple, and stage and screen actor Harry Guardino was hired as Hapgood. Together, they shared the reflective "With So Little to Be Sure Of," while Remick rendered the title tune, with its theme of self-discovery. Guardino's Act II solo was the message song "Everybody Says Don't."

Remick "was going out with Steve at the time. He was tremendously taken with her," Sondheim biographer Meryle Secrest told classical music writer and author Norman Lebrecht. In turn, it was widely said that Remick was taken with Sondheim, just as it was widely known that Sondheim was gay. Their relationship took place in an era when coming out publicly was not an established norm; nonetheless, it appears Sondheim and Remick were strongly attracted to one another, and theirs was an enduring friendship.

"Arthur said the song 'Anyone Can Whistle' would be Steve's epitaph," Secrest said. "It's about Steve—a person who is out of touch with feelings."

The Fay Apple role originally had been written for Barbra Streisand—the character was named Fay Cohen when the call first went out to her—but Streisand opted to do *Funny Girl* instead.

"She made the right choice," Sondheim said.

Anyone Can Whistle opened at the Majestic Theatre April 4, 1964, and closed April 11, after twelve previews and nine performances. Reviews were dispiriting. George Oppenheimer, writing in *Newsday*, called the show "less way out than way off."

The original cast recording took place on Sunday, April 12, under the supervision of Columbia Records president Goddard Lieberson. Sondheim was so grateful to Lieberson for preserving the piece, even though the LP could contain only a portion of what had been written and performed, that he dedicated the score to the record producer.

"Why did it crash? Most of the fault was mine," said Laurents. "I was both writer and director. I needed someone to tell me that you go blind if you do both."

"I don't mind putting my name on a flop, as long as we've done something that hasn't been tried before," Sondheim said, going on to admit that he wasn't depressed over the show's closing, but that he wished more of his friends had been able to see it.

MANY A *WHISTLE* STOP

Donna Murphy in a 2010 concert presentation of *Anyone Can Whistle*.

Sondheim and Laurents told Casey Nicholaw, the director of a fun-filled 2010 concert version of *Anyone Can Whistle*, that when they first wrote the piece, "they were coming from a place of 'We're smart kids' and 'We're touching every button,'" said Donna Murphy, who played Mayor Cora. "At the same time, they wanted a lyrical, unexpected love story at the center."

Throughout the years, revivals, concerts, and charity performances have shown you can't keep a cult musical down.

Angela Lansbury narrated a 1995 *Anyone Can Whistle* Carnegie Hall benefit for the Gay Men's Health Crisis, with Madeline Kahn as Cora, Bernadette Peters as Fay, and Scott Bakula as Hapgood.

A decade later, those roles, respectively, went to Patti LuPone, Audra McDonald, and Michael Cerveris. The venue was the Ravinia Festival in Highland Park, Illinois.

Encores! brought an all-star slimmed-down yet faithful version to New York's City Center in 2010, with the score played up and the book judiciously pruned. Casey Nicholaw directed Donna Murphy as Cora, Sutton Foster as Fay, and Raúl Esparza as Hapgood.

That same year in London, at the Jermyn Street Theatre (where *Saturday Night* had its 2009 West End premiere), director Tom Littler set *Whistle* in 1930s Germany, which still didn't bring many new fans to the book.

After twenty-three years in the making, in 2020, British label Jay Records released a nearly two-hour first complete studio recording, longueurs included. Laurents narrated; Julia McKenzie was Cora; Maria Friedman, Fay; and John Barrowman, Hapgood.

As if to underscore how times and tastes had changed, because the basic material had not, a small-scale but fully staged *Anyone Can Whistle* was mounted in 2022 at London's Southwark Playhouse, with director Georgie Rankcom allowing that "gender norms" and "political ideas," which might have been "too radical" when the show opened on Broadway in 1964, could "feel quite current and easy to express now."

The effort got attention.

The headline on the *Guardian* review: "Sondheim Flop Gets a Blazing Revival."

"One of the first things you have to decide with a musical is, why should there be songs?" said Sondheim. "You can put songs in any story, but what I think you have to look for is, why are songs necessary to the story? If it is unnecessary, the show turns out to be not very good."

That, in a nutshell, was Sondheim's summation of his lone collaboration with Richard Rodgers, *Do I Hear a Waltz?*—although the show that opened March 18, 1965, and ran 220 performances at the Forty-Sixth Street Theatre* could honestly be classified as better than "not very good."

Sondheim held firm that the production was done for all the wrong reasons.

Director John Dexter's staging of the 1965 production of *Do I Hear a Waltz?* was so inert that choreographer Herbert Ross was brought in during Boston tryouts to provide movement. This improved the title number, so named because the main character, Leona, an American tourist visiting Venice, believed she would hear a waltz the moment she fell in love.

The show was based on *The Time of the Cuckoo*, a 1952 play by Arthur Laurents, starring Shirley Booth as Leona Samish, "a sort of forty-year-old secretary going to Venice for the first time and being flirted with across the Piazza San Marco and reacting to it in the most enthusiastic way, and then leaving because it was totally impractical," said Katharine Hepburn, who played the role in British director David Lean's 1955 movie adaptation, retitled *Summertime* and filmed entirely in Venice.

Leona catches the eye of a local shopkeeper, Renato Di Rossi, who happens to be married—which may work fine in Italy, but not among Puritanical Americans.

Thanks to an introduction by Sondheim, Laurents approached Rodgers and Hammerstein in 1958 with a request that they adapt the play into an intimate musical, but Oscar thought it too soon after the Booth and Hepburn versions. Rodgers thought the plot was too thin. The request resurfaced after Hammerstein's death,

* In 1990, it was renamed the Richard Rodgers Theatre.

Elizabeth Allen, who played Leona, lacked the vulnerability needed for her role, while Sergio Franchi, who played her married lover, Renato, possessed a mellifluous singing voice but little acting skill. Laurents wanted Mary Martin for the lead, but Richard Rodgers thought she was too old. Sondheim wanted Phyllis Newman. Other possibilities included Barbara Cook, Florence Henderson, Anne Bancroft, and perennial Laurents favorite, Barbra Streisand.

From left: Richard Rodgers, Sondheim, the back of director John Dexter's head, and Arthur Laurents. Sondheim said, "I regret spending a year of my life on *Do I Hear a Waltz?*. In Mary Rodgers's view, its songs were superfluous. "It was a terrible, terrible experience," said Sondheim.

when Rodgers's collaboration with Alan Jay Lerner on a musical about a young woman with ESP* had crumbled over Lerner's lackadaisical work ethic.

Mary Rodgers, Richard's daughter, appealed to Sondheim, her friend since the 1940s, and asked him to intervene. Richard Rodgers suffered frequent bouts of depression, which Mary was convinced could be alleviated if he would just get back to work. There was also the persuasive Laurents factor, and one even weightier: Sondheim had promised a dying Oscar Hammerstein that he would consider working with his mentor's longtime partner.

It proved not a good match, given the contrasting styles and sensibilities of Stephen and Richard. "You've got to do it as a semi-opera," Sondheim advised Rodgers, but "Dick thought in terms of songs."

"My father was not an intellectual writer," said Mary Rodgers. "He had gone to Juilliard, and he knew plenty. But he didn't sit down and figure out intellectually where a song should go or how it should be constructed."

One might have assumed he could have been handed that lesson by Hammerstein, although, according to Sondheim, Oscar had "conflicted feelings about his collaborator," and it was said the two legends never successfully communicated on a personal level.

---

* This would become the 1965 *On a Clear Day You Can See Forever*, by Lerner and Burton Lane, starring Barbara Harris.

Sondheim was anything but conflicted about Rodgers. The thorny new partnership flew in the face of his vow not to provide lyrics alone. Rodgers also wielded an imbalance of power; he was serving as the show's producer. There was also a generation gap; Rodgers was sixty-two to Sondheim's thirty-four.

"He felt the well had run dry," said Sondheim. "I couldn't get him to rewrite." Rodgers also drank heavily and fell asleep at a meeting with Franco Zeffirelli where they were supposed to discuss the La Scala opera director's helming *Do I Hear a Waltz?*

Exit Zeffirelli.

Although Sondheim and Rodgers both agreed to sidestep tarantellas or any music that might be expected, Rodgers took issue with some of the lyrics. The breaking point came when Rodgers dressed down Sondheim in front of the company over some lyrics. Whether or not these were for the song "We're Gonna Be All Right" has been debated; what is known is that Rodgers objected to a line about a honeymoon couple's potential extramarital dalliances, and the husband's singing that sometimes he might be homosexual. The line was excised.*

For Sondheim, the insult severed the partnership; when the two were interviewed together by a *New York Times* reporter in advance of the opening of *Do I Hear a Waltz?*, Sondheim "barely reacted" when Rodgers remarked, "I watched him grow from an attractive little boy to a monster."

In her posthumously published 2022 memoir,** *Shy: The Alarmingly Outspoken Memoirs of Mary Rodgers*, for which she collaborated with critic Jesse Green, Rodgers wrote of having had an unrequited crush on Sondheim from the time she first met him at the Hammersteins' when she was thirteen (Sondheim was fourteen), and how her father "hated Steve," not only because she was talking constantly about him, but because he was both "brilliant" *and* Oscar's protégé. (In the early 1960s, she and Sondheim also embarked on a trial marriage of sorts, in which they shared a bed in his house but no intimacy, a complicated situation she labeled "wildly uncomfortable." The relationship quickly dissolved, but evidently the friendship and her love for him did not.)

Sondheim likened *Do I Hear a Waltz?* to "a plane that doesn't take off." Certainly, the Sondheim wit is not on full display, although his lyrics earned him his first Tony nomination. (Jerry Bock won the award, for *Fiddler on the Roof*, which was that year's Tony favorite and also beloved by the public.)

Six years later, Rodgers wrote Sondheim a gracious and congratulatory letter when *Company* opened, and Sondheim cordially thanked him, replying that the words meant all the more because they were coming from him.

The pleasantries came to an abrupt halt in 1973, when Sondheim was memorably quoted in *Newsweek* saying that Oscar Hammerstein was a man of limited talent but infinite soul, while Richard Rodgers was a man of infinite talent but limited soul.

Sondheim and Rodgers never spoke to each other again.***

---

* Only to be reinstated in subsequent productions, starting in 1973, when the full, unexpurgated version debuted at an all-star *Sondheim: A Musical Tribute* at the Shubert Theatre.

** Mary Rodgers died in 2014, age eighty-three.

*** Richard Rodgers died December 30, 1979, age seventy-seven.

A SONDHEIM PRIMER

"I must've told this story five thousand times," Sondheim said of a tale from his adolescence when he had written a script about his school and given it to Oscar Hammerstein, with every expectation that Hammerstein would make Sondheim the first fifteen-year-old in history to have a musical produced on Broadway.

Instead, Hammerstein asked if he could be honest, Sondheim acceded, and the master told the pupil, "In that case, it's the worst thing I've ever read."

Oscar quickly assured Stephen that the work wasn't without talent, and then he proceeded to analyze every line page by page, creating a primer for writing musicals that Sondheim essentially relied upon thereafter. Sondheim also passed this rubric on to others, especially when, in 1990, he was made the first Cameron Mackintosh Visiting Professor of Contemporary Theatre at St. Catherine's College in Oxford, under an endowment established by the theatrical producer.

Adam Guettel, a double Tony winner as composer and orchestrator of the 2005 *The Light in the Piazza*, which followed his much-lauded Off-Broadway production *Floyd Collins*, tells a similar story about Sondheim.

"I had brought him my first batch of music when I was fifteen, which I thought he would just be bowled over by," Guettel recalled forty-three years later, in 2022. "I don't know what I had called it, but probably something rather self-aggrandizing, giving it airs that it didn't deserve, and he quickly set me straight."

Afterward, Guettel "wrote him a passive-aggressive letter to say I was deflated. I was grateful for his time, but I felt he was not very encouraging."

"I had every bit the amount of time with him as anyone serious about this business would have, in terms of studying his lyrics and music and listening to them over and over," composer-lyricist Adam Guettel (left, with Sondheim in his Manhattan townhouse, in 2009) said in 2022. Chief among the lessons learned, Guettel said, were the Sondheim rules: "At the top of every page, whether it's written down or there in just a tacit way, is the word 'clarity.' And that God is in the details. Specificity is universality. Brevity. And the notion that lyrics go by very quickly, so keep them simple, keep them specific enough so that they are instantly meaningful. No poetry. Nothing opaque." He added, "Those are the things I learned from Steve and hold by and appreciate him for."

Sondheim responded. (Guettel keeps a copy of the letter on his phone.) "Dear Adam, Thanks for the letter, but I didn't mean to be 'not very encouraging.' In fact, I hoped I was being quite the reverse. For me, true encouragement consists not so much of burbling as a detailed attention. In any event, be assured I think you're serious, literate, intelligent, and talented, and, surprisingly, the last is the least, because it means little without the others."

Sondheim told Guettel to "keep writing, because that's what we all do," and signed it, "Love, Steve."

Guettel had known Sondheim his entire life. Guettel's mother, Mary Rodgers Guettel, was a friend of Sondheim's from the time the two were interns at Connecticut's Westport Playhouse. She and Sondheim collaborated on the 1966 Off-Broadway *The Mad Show*, inspired by *Mad* magazine (their song, the tongue-twisting "The Boy from . . . " spoofed the bossa-nova hit "The Girl from Ipanema"), and Rodgers composed the music for Broadway's 1959 *Once Upon a Mattress*, starring a young Carol Burnett. Mary's father, and Adam's grandfather, was Richard Rodgers.

"People think of him as a mentor," Guettel said of Sondheim, "and I do, too, but not in a normal sense. I had two sessions with him that were actually focused on my work—in my entire life. People think, 'Oh, you must've been at his place all the time, or you would just pick up the phone and say, "What do you think of this?"' Only twice I went to him with specific things. The rest of the time, when he was over at our house, I would listen to him and absorb, that great privilege of just being around him when he was speaking to my mom, listening to them squabble, or just listening to them laugh."

Guettel particularly recalled Sondheim "being around the dinner table, when my parents would have people over like Marshall Barer, who wrote the lyrics to *Once Upon a Mattress* and a number of other great things. He wrote a quatrain that went, 'I lie with my arms about you / Within you, and yet without you / Within you I can't contain you / Without you I can't continue,' and Steve said"—at this point, Guettel mimics Sondheim's bewilderment—"which speaks volumes of Steve's methodology, 'Marshall, how did you arrive at that?' And Marshall said, blithely, 'I didn't. It just arrived.' On to the next conversation."

Another attribute of their relationship, Guettel said, "was that when he was angry with me, which he was occasionally, he was quick about it."

As an example, Guettel cited an incident in 2001, when plans were afoot to produce a studio recording of *Evening Primrose*. "I was supposed to sing the lead. It was when I was in my thirties and had really gotten going on *The Light in the Piazza*. I knew that it was going well. Bells were ringing, and things were coming out of me—it didn't feel like homework. If it feels like homework, it's going to feel like homework to the person listening to it."

Nevertheless, the *Evening Primrose* recording date loomed.

"At the time, I'd already been associated with Steve for other reasons, singing his work in public and other, different things. The combination of writing *A Light in the Piazza* and getting it to the next step, and knowing that I was being associated with him and the nepotism thing, I called Tommy Krasker, the [*Primrose* recording] producer, six weeks or two months ahead of time, and said, 'Tommy, I'm not quitting or anything, but I just want to ask you: How attached is Steve to my singing this? Because I'm really into doing *Piazza*, and I just need to make sure that I am able to craft a career of my own.'"

Krasker replied, "Adam, Steve doesn't even know that you're doing it. He doesn't even really know the record is being made, he's so busy."

"And I said, 'Really? Well, what do you think would happen if I were to step aside?'"

Krasker told Guettel, "Well, first of all, he wouldn't care. He doesn't even know. But also, we have Neil Patrick Harris in the wings, waiting, and, frankly, he'll sell more records, so we'd be thrilled."

Guettel withdrew.

"Five days later," Guettel said, "I opened my mailbox, and there's one of those little letters . . . the cotton [stationery], the courier-typeface address on the back. And I'm like, 'I've seen these letters before.'"

Guettel opened the envelope while still in his lobby and can still recite the message inside: "Adam, If you're wondering whether I'm sore about your dumping 'Evening Primrose'—don't. Steve."

"Withering," said Guettel. "But quick. And over. I shook for days. Then, the next time, fine."

ABC Stage 67
will captivate you tonight.
Anthony Perkins stars
in a musical play about
a mystical night society.

THE PEOPLE ARE GONE. The doors are locked, darkness descends inside a department store. Fleeing from the pressures of the outside world, an unhappy poet is at last alone. But not quite. In his newfound sanctuary, he suddenly comes across a group of hermits who've been hiding there for years. Amongst them, a young girl with whom he falls in love.

Tonight, ABC Stage 67 presents "Evening Primrose," an eerie yet charming story with music and lyrics by the noted "West Side Story" lyricist, Stephen Sondheim. Included in the cast are Dorothy Stickney, Larry Gates and lovely newcomer, Charmian Carr.

abc In color at 10:00 pm on ⑦

III.

Hell is not inhabited by Shaw and Shakespeare, no matter what *The Frogs* might say. It is inhabited by starchy busybodies, or so Sondheim and playwright James Goldman led TV audiences to believe with their macabre TV musical drama, *Evening Primrose*.

Airing in 1966, Sondheim's only musical for television, *Evening Primrose*, contained five songs and a book by James Goldman, who would go on to write *Follies*.

The one-night-only event aired November 16, 1966, as an episode of the weekly *ABC Stage 67*, an experimental anthology series overseen on the network level by "an old friend of the family, a fellow named Hubbell Robinson," Sondheim said. "I had the nerve to call Hubbell and say, 'Would you give Jim Goldman and me a chance to write an hour-long musical?'"

In fact, according to Anthony Perkins, who starred in *Evening Primrose*, Robinson had dated Foxy Sondheim. Robinson's career had been spent mostly at CBS, where as head of programming he was instrumental in the development of the Walter Cronkite–hosted *Twentieth Century*, Broadway showcases *Playhouse 90* and *Studio One*, and wildly popular fare like *I Love Lucy*, *The Phil Silvers Show*, and *Gunsmoke*.

Robinson gave the go-ahead to Sondheim and Goldman, who for the past year had been toiling on a murder mystery set against a reunion of *Follies* showgirls, called *The Girls Upstairs* (sans murder, this would eventually become *Follies*). The timing of the ABC deal was fortuitous; Sondheim even told Robinson that the Goldmans, who were expecting a child, needed the next month's rent.* They got it, and then some; according to notes in Paley Center files, the two writers split $301,000 ($2.6 million today). They were also set to receive another $90,000 for a first repeat broadcast and $70,000 for a second, if there had been any.

ABC Stage 67 was not a success.

The week *Evening Primrose* was broadcast, the Nielsen Ratings crown was worn by *Bonanza*, *The Lucy Show*, and a CBS special titled *Clown Alley*.

—

* In early 1966, Goldman's play, *The Lion in Winter*, a domestic drama between Henry II of England and Eleanor of Aquitaine, had a brief Broadway run. Two years later the movie version, with Peter O'Toole and Katharine Hepburn, was nominated for Best Picture and would bring Goldman an Oscar for Best Screenplay.

Television musicals until this time had been largely scaled-down adaptations of Broadway classics. One month before *Evening Primrose* aired, ABC presented *Brigadoon*, starring Robert Goulet; before that the telemusical tradition stretched back into the 1950s, with Ethel Merman, Frank Sinatra, and Bert Lahr in *Anything Goes* (1954), Mary Martin and John Raitt in *Annie Get Your Gun* (1957), and original Broadway stars Alfred Drake and Patricia Morrison in *Kiss Me, Kate* (1958).

For several years, Martin's 1955 *Peter Pan* was a small-screen annual, just like MGM's *The Wizard of Oz*, although the Seabiscuit of all TV musicals was Rodgers and Hammerstein's 1957 written-for-television *Cinderella*, starring Julie Andrews. It commanded a staggering 107 million viewers.*

Evening Primrose was a different animal altogether. Sondheim and Goldman assembled their surreal scenario from a short story by frequent *New Yorker* writer John Collier, whose own scripts included a 1935 box office flop that then became a cult classic, *Sylvia Scarlett,* starring Katharine Hepburn as a con artist who goes on the lam by dressing as a man. The eccentric characters in *Evening Primrose*, like the plant from which the story takes its title, only flower at sunset.

As the plot goes, poet Charles Snell hides out in a department store** after closing time, only to discover a group of people who have been living in the store for years, and who only come out at night. At the beck and call of this nocturnal group are a band of marauding mortician-taxidermists who—spoiler alert—kill anyone who tries to leave the store, thereby threatening to expose the hideout. The corpses are then disposed of by morphing them into mannequins and setting them in the store's display windows.

Anthony Perkins, known to movie audiences as the emotionally conflicted son John in *Friendly Persuasion* and the ultimate mama's boy in *Psycho*, played the alienated Charles Snell, who arrives with no inkling that others have already pioneered his idea to lock down inside this commodious domain.

In his opening solo on the escalator, Charles identifies as a behind-on-his-rent poet of dubious talent but strong conviction. His song, "If You Can Find Me, I'm Here," declares his intention to stay on in the department store with all the goods freely at his disposal, from light refreshment to entire wardrobes and, ironically, outdoor goods. The idealist is relieved to leave behind awful neighbors downing their "pretzels and beer."

Besides portending an oft-quoted line from *Follies'* "I'm Still Here," the song works as a kind of "Oh, What a Beautiful Mornin'" in reverse, because it honestly doesn't sound like anything is going to go this guy's way.

Of the four musical numbers in the show—the others are "I Remember," "When," and "Take Me to the World"—"If You Can Find Me, I'm Here" was one that displeased Sondheim. "Everything in the store should have had a price tag on it," he said, referring to the background props—his way of a joke. Sondheim also admitted that during filming, it was he who told Perkins not to look directly at the camera

---

* The 2012 *The Sound of Music Live*, starring Carrie Underwood, drew nearly twenty-two million viewers through various platforms, while subsequent live telecasts of Broadway musicals have seen audience numbers significantly shrink.

** Interior and exterior location filming took place on a Sunday morning at the Stern Brothers department store, once a fixture at Sixth Avenue and Forty-Second Street. Macy's at first welcomed the TV crew but then withdrew approval; perhaps company executives didn't want to encourage people to come live in their store.

OPPOSITE: After *The Sound of Music* and *Evening Primrose*, twenty-three-year-old Charmian Carr left show business. 'Was it something we did?,' her costar Anthony Perkins quoted Sondheim as saying. "You know," said Perkins, "working with Robert Wise when they were doing *The Sound of Music*, probably perfecting every detail, which was certainly more than we had a chance to do . . . we rushed her. Maybe that was it."

but at his surroundings instead, only the advice backfired. Perkins and his character "seem unfocused."

Once ensconced, Charles meets and falls in love with the disenchanted nineteen-year-old Ella (as in Cinder-), who had been separated from her mother in the store's hat department when she was six. Ever since, she has been maid to the demanding doyenne Mrs. Monday, who calls the shots for all those hiding in the secret world. Monday's message is clear: Attempt to leave, and thereby threaten to expose her cloistered retinue, and you shall be punished.

In a 180-degree turn from her role as eldest daughter Liesl von Trapp in the previous year's blockbuster film production of the family-friendly *The Sound of Music*, Charmian Carr played the damaged Ella. Ella begs Charles to get her out of the store. She sings "Take Me to the World." Charles surrenders to her wish, and that seals the eventual demise of both characters.

Despite the depressing context, "Take Me to the World" proved a Sondheim evergreen, a standard that has been covered by everyone from Barbra Streisand with Antonio Banderas to Bernadette Peters, Mandy Patinkin, Judy Collins, Sutton Foster, Neil Patrick Harris (as Charles in a 2001 studio recording of the full score), and Barbara Cook, in the 2010 Broadway revue *Sondheim on Sondheim*.

"I Remember," recorded by Streisand, Peters, Collins, Cleo Laine, Melissa Errico, John Pizzarelli, Liz Callaway, Betty Buckley, Sarah Brightman, and others, also has a following, and a backstory. Sondheim lifted it practically verbatim from a monologue Goldman had written for Ella.

"Jim started out with this lovely phrase, 'I remember snow,' and I kept trying to work with it, and I knew that at the end I wanted to use the word 'die.' After some hours, the light went on; I thought, 'It's called 'I Remember Sky,' then I can repeat it at the end and rhyme it with 'die,'" said Sondheim. "The light flashed on, and I was able to go ahead with it."

On another occasion, Sondheim said he asked Goldman to write the monologue starting with the desired phrase. "I find it useful to work closely with every book writer. I think that's necessary if you want to write a piece that holds together. It's also fun."

Because of the tight schedule, seasoned TV director Paul Bogart filmed most of the dialogue scenes in one take. "It has a vaguely amateur feeling, which I like," Sondheim said of the finished product, which, while often compared to a Rod Serling *Twilight Zone* episode, also smacked of the old *Playhouse 90*.

Seventy-year-old Dorothy Stickney, best known to theatre audiences of a certain era for her role as the mother in her husband Howard Lindsay's unprecedented Broadway hit *Life with Father*—and possibly Sondheim's host in 1953 when he connected with George Oppenheimer—played the persnickety Mrs. Monday.*

Speaking about *Evening Primrose* in 1989, Tony Perkins said it was Sondheim and Goldman's idea to cast "a number of old-time theatre stars [and] give them this opportunity to appear as what they were—relics, almost unliving relics."

Perkins thought their presentation "was done with a great deal of dignity, but the stars didn't see it that way." In fact, they felt insulted.

When asked about the score, the actor acknowledged "the songs are beautiful. It's impossible for Steve to treat anything lightly or trivially." He also said of his close friend, "Steve had a sort of sardonic manner in those days"—Perkins additionally tossed in the adjectives "mercurial," "sometimes melancholy," and "compulsive neatnik"—but "when it came to writing these songs, Steve gave it as much as he

OPPOSITE (TOP):
Originally shot in color, *Evening Primrose* was long believed to be a lost film, and today it exists only in black-and-white. Long after the original telecast, a live, staged version ran for three weeks in London, in 2005.

OPPOSITE (BOTTOM):
Five years later in New York, Tony Walton directed and designed a production at John Jay College. Candice Bergen played the snooty Mrs. Monday, who in the original production had been played by Dorothy Stickney (seen here in a confrontation with Anthony Perkins as Charmian Carr looks on in horror).

---

* Stickney played the Queen in Rodgers and Hammerstein's 1957 TV *Cinderella*.

would have *Follies* or *Company*, which is just the way he works."

That wasn't the only way he worked. For years there was no extant copy of *Evening Primrose*, which was originally filmed and broadcast in color. There still is no available color version, but in 2010, forty-four years after its TV debut, a pristine 16mm black-and-white print of *Evening Primrose* was tracked down by Paley Center historian Jane Klain and released commercially on a legally licensed DVD.

Until then, there had only been illegal videos.

"Most of the bootleg copies are out there," Sondheim confided, "because I lent it to people."

Creative standards established by Rodgers and Hammerstein held reign on Broadway for nearly thirty years, Sondheim acknowledged in 1977, while also admitting that he too had paddled "in that stream, even though I've consciously been doing shows that have cut into that stream—you know, story-less musicals, for example, like *Company*." That, he said, was "in seemingly direct contrast to what Hammerstein did."

PRINCELY ACTS

I.

Alan Jay Lerner came home from the opening night of *Company*,
in 1970, and started to cry, his then wife, Karen Lerner,
remembered. "He said, 'My way of writing musicals is over.'"

Company—score by Sondheim, book by George Furth, produced and directed by Hal Prince, choreographed by Michael Bennett, sets by Boris Aronson—opened during the war in Vietnam. Divides within the country were deep, generational, and ideological. From that perspective, the Golden Age of Broadway was not only tarnished but deemed counterproductive.

"*Company* both reflects that war and goes beyond it," musical comedy tracker Sylvia Fine said in 1979. The sexual revolution and the Age of Analysis also landed squarely on the timeline; culturally, Mike Nichols's *The Graduate* and Philip Roth's *Portnoy's Complaint* had turned the status quo on its ear.

Fine, who wrote stage and screen patter songs* for her husband Danny Kaye in the 1940s, praised Sondheim as "the *wunderkind* of the '70s" and his *Company* score as "contemporary as rock." Eschewing both story line and chronology, *Company* delivered a "sharp, cynical," and "cold, fisheye look" at five couples celebrating the thirty-fifth birthday of their intolerably single friend, Robert.

"If you asked Hal Prince to state what *Company* is about in less than one sentence and asked George Furth and asked me, we would probably come up with different sentences," Sondheim said. "But we all know about the underlying metaphor of Manhattan, which is, after all, the handiest locale for the inhumanity of contemporary living and the difficulties of making relationships."

"I had thought we were doing these seven one-act plays of mine that Hal had optioned," said Furth, "but out of those seven, only one and a half ended up as *Company*. I had no idea I was writing a whole new Broadway show."

---

* Although few so fast as *Company*'s "Getting Married Today."

"We wanted a show where the audience would sit for two hours screaming their heads off with laughter, and then go home and not be able to sleep," said Sondheim.

"We did not want to follow where the audience took us," said Hal Prince.

"We wanted to take the audience where we wanted to go."

George Furth (left) with Sondheim, who claimed that the *Company* librettist was so unmusical that he did not so much as own a record player.

—

Sondheim and George Furth met in 1963, when Furth, a character actor recognizable to movie audiences as hapless railroad employee Woodcock in *Butch Cassidy and the Sundance Kid*, and as one of the loudmouth townsfolk in *Blazing Saddles*, was appearing in the cast of *Hot Spot*, an ill-fated Judy Holliday Broadway-bound musical about a blundering Peace Corps volunteer. Mary Rodgers composed the music; among the show doctors, after Bob Fosse and Jerome Robbins had separately lent their hands, was Arthur Laurents, who called in Sondheim to work on two numbers.

Cut to a few years later. Furth's analyst suggested writing as a form of therapy, and Furth fashioned several unconnected short plays set in California, each about different couples he knew. One of the women, hard-living and hard-drinking, was based on the actor Elaine Stritch, who had romances over the years with Ben Gazzara, Gig Young, and Rock Hudson (or, at least, an extended flirtation).

Furth secured Kim Stanley to play all of the women in the playlets, with the men's roles divided between Ron Liebman and John McMartin. What Furth couldn't secure was financing, leading him to seek advice from Sondheim, who read the script, titled *Company*, and pronounced it "terrific, the dialogue the best since Albee."

The script went to Hal Prince, who thought that Kim Stanley "had all the chops to accomplish" the separate plays, "but I could not get out of my head the image of her changing full costumes, wigs, and makeup furiously offstage. In fact, that's all I could see."

His conclusion: "Why don't we make a musical out of this?"

Sondheim's response: "My God, what an odd idea."

No one was more surprised than Furth, who was already rehearsing on the Paramount lot to play the fiancé of Barbra Streisand's clairvoyant character in *On a Clear Day You Can See Forever*. The studio subsequently replaced Furth with Larry Blyden.

Prince put Furth up in a midtown hotel so the creative team could meet in Prince's Rockefeller Center office. In short order, the title *Company* was changed to *Threes* (it would change back again). According to Sondheim, he, Furth, Prince, and, eventually, choreographer Michael Bennett "talked for weeks, and finally came up with the notion of a third person, an observer of these marriages who would put them in focus."

Sondheim christened the character Robert, or Bobby, "so he could be referred to differently by each of his friends," said Prince.

—

"George started rewriting," Sondheim said, "and when I'd put the work off as long as humanly possible, I started the songs."

Sondheim's procrastination partially had to do with the project he and James Goldman had been working on for the past five years, *The Girls Upstairs*. Rewrites were still required, but that would conflict with the demands for time on *Company*. The dilemma forced Prince, who saw no sense in Sondheim and Goldman investing six more months on a project that had yet to gel after five years of work, to hold Sondheim contractually bound to making sure *Company* was ready for rehearsals by February 1970.

"I knew from the beginning the score would have to be quite strange. I was also pretty sure I could do something fresh with it," said Sondheim.

One holdup: What did he know about marriage? George Furth, another gay single man, could offer few pointers. Mary Rodgers, who had just begun a second marriage, could. She and Sondheim shared two lengthy conversations in his townhouse, and he took notes. Sondheim considered her contribution payback for her having gotten him involved in *Do I Hear a Waltz?*

Asked in 2014 to recall what she said, Rodgers answered, "Well, it's all in the songs, especially 'Someone Is Waiting' and 'Being Alive.' Marriage has wonderful moments and terrible moments. I can't do better in explaining it than the lyrics can."

"It was a natural thing for Mom to talk to him," Rodgers's son, Adam Guettel, said in 2022, "because she was very good and deft, and brief, in her insights into marriage. Of course, the score is the very machine in terms of composition and use of music in storytelling. I think that's why the show works so beautifully."

Guettel said Sondheim was such a frequent guest in his parents' home, including at the large annual Christmas parties, "that there were marriages around him, so *Company* could have been fermenting in his mind." Being single, "he must have thought himself partly beneath it, and partly above it, but certainly outside of it. Also,

MANHATTAN MELODY

"In every show, there should be a secret metaphor that nobody knows except the authors," said Sondheim. "If you find the underlying metaphor and then *don't* state it, it helps shape the whole work."

For *Company*, that metaphor was Manhattan, which was

As noted by educator and historian Jeffrey Rubel, Boris Aronson's "set of skeletonized Plexiglas and steel" for *Company* "brought the oppressive urban environment into the theatre." Sondheim said the design helped him focus on what the show was about.

why Prince had Furth abandon the original California setting. This show and its characters needed to be representational of New York's particular brand of angst and alienation.

"In *Company*," said Sondheim, "we were making a comparison between contemporary marriage and the island of Manhattan." At the time, both institutions were cracking around the edges.

"Robert bears little resemblance to me in my bachelor days," Hal Prince said while the show was running. "I was never a third man in social relationships. But it does speak to me in its examination of certain marriages and more particularly in its examination of what it's like to live in New York."

Complementing the Manhattan metaphor was Boris Aronson's Constructivist set, a multi-level "urban jungle gym" of Plexiglas and chrome that took its inspiration from Irish-born British artist Francis Bacon's experiments with lights and mirrors. The compartmentalized *Company* set featured two elevators, interior spatial units, and background photographic slides of the cityscape that were altered in image and tone to set the mood of each song number.

"Married life in New York City isn't rocking the afternoon away on a front porch," Aronson said. "In New York, people sit stacked up on top of each other in transparent cages."

Sondheim said it wasn't until he had seen the scale model of Aronson's set in Hal Prince's office that he was able to imagine the *Company* score.

So vital a character was the set that when the elevators were removed for the scaled-down bus-and-truck tour, "the audience had no clue as to what they were watching," said Michael Bennett's associate, Bob Avian.

"They only saw a show about marriage in the abstract and knew it was not to their liking."

if you look at *Company*, there's a very loving component, the examination of marriage from so many points of view suggests a lot of love around it."

And yet, Guettel said, "the principal character is lonely, and isn't married, so there is also forgiveness and love.

"These are universal points of view."

—

"The first choral stuff I ever wrote was the opening to *Company*," said Sondheim. "I had canonic entrances,* and it had choral bits. To my surprise, [conductor Hal Hastings] said: 'No, most of it works very well.'"

The stage voices were enhanced by four unseen female singers in the orchestra pit—they were dubbed "The Vocal Minority," as opposed to Richard Nixon's "The Silent Majority"—a device put to use before *Company* in the Burt Bacharach–Hal David musical *Promises, Promises*,** which was orchestrated by Jonathan Tunick and choreographed by Michael Bennett. Both would work with Sondheim for the first time on *Company*; in Tunick's case, the professional alliance lasted their entire careers.

Another *Company* advancement came in the form of an electric piano called a Rock-Si-Chord, which provided the telephone's oscillating busy signal at the opening of the show—the music doesn't kick in until after a long stretch of mostly voiceover dialogue about Robert's birthday—and it was repeated as the action of the show moved along.

"The function of the songs is unlike anything I've ever done before, or anything most people have done," Sondheim told critic Kevin Kelly when the show was trying out in Boston. "The songs are never integrated in the Rodgers and Hammerstein sense. People sing for the most unconventional reasons. The songs essentially are sub-text, and/or comments on what's going on. Some songs even occur between scenes, in limbo. Some, smack in the middle of a scene."

The Manhattan metaphor justified the presence of "Another Hundred People," "the *only* song that doesn't deal with one-to-one relationships," said Sondheim. The number was inserted after Pamela Myers, fresh from the Cincinnati Conservatory of Music, auditioned for the role of Marta and sang a moving rendition of "Little Green Apples," followed by a hilarious version of "Shy," from *Once Upon a Mattress*.

At the conclusion of Myers's performance, Sondheim, Prince, and Furth exchanged glances; Furth started to tailor the part of Marta to Myers; and Sondheim wrote her the song—which ended up being cut in Boston. It somehow brought Act II to a halt.

Sondheim was impressed by how well Myers took the disappointing news and promised he'd find another spot for the number.

"Another Hundred People"—think of a conveyor belt delivering new inhabitants to New York City every minute of every day—was then finessed into Act I, while Robert sits on a park bench talking to various girlfriends as Marta observes. It worked.

"Another Hundred People" didn't stop the act.

It stopped the show.

---

* The introduction of an initial melody that is then imitated, after specific time intervals, at either the same or a different pitch.

** *Promises, Promises*, an adaptation of Billy Wilder's *The Apartment*, offered another portrait of late '60s Manhattan, but its depiction was far glossier than *Company*'s.

"WHY IS EVERYONE PICKING ON BOBBY?"

Tiffany Babb is a poet, cultural critic, and a writer of comics who runs a Sondheim page on Facebook titled "Good Thing Going: A Group for Kind Sondheim Fans."

Mid-2021, around the time she launched the page, Babb manufactured a "Sondheim Fan Club" badge with Sondheim's likeness. Its image came from an acrylic painting she did, and, through Etsy, she sells the button and others like it, including one with the phrase from the Sondheim book title, "Look, I Made a Hat."

"He's my biggest inspiration," said Babb, who has a master of arts degree in American Studies from Columbia. She first saw a production of *Company* at Princeton, her sister's university.

"I was hooked," she says.

Babb found her view of the show changing over the years. "As a teenager, I thought, 'Why is everyone picking on Bobby? His life seems ideal.' As I got older, I developed a deeper understanding of the joys and sacrifices of sharing your life."

The show's one constant for her is "Sorry-Grateful," for its "incredible nuance" and purposeful paradoxes about what it says about coupling.

"Sondheim's ability to express this complexity, his refusal to land on a simple answer even at the end of the song, makes 'Sorry-Grateful' read as if it contains all truth about marriage and relationships and, simultaneously, none of them at all," Babb wrote in an essay.

"'Sorry-Grateful' carries many different meanings, most of them contradictory, but what it argues, in its form, is that something like marriage can rarely be boiled down into straightforward answers because it is experienced daily.

"It grows and changes, it is not stagnant, it is not still, it cannot be solidified."

—

Robert, or Bobby, or any of the other derivations his pals call him, was written with Anthony Perkins in mind, but Perkins was looking to direct, and so he attached himself to Bruce Jay Friedman's 1970 Off-Broadway comedy *Steambath*.

"Tony thought the character of Bobby was the cipher at the center of *Company* and would be very difficult to act," said Sondheim. "It's true. He's onstage the whole time and just reacts. It's a passive figure. That's the way Tony explained it to me, and it was difficult to play a passive part. Everybody else has all the colors."

Instead, boyishly handsome Dean Jones, a stage and TV actor and onetime Disney star who appeared in *That Darn Cat!* and *The Love Bug*, was signed on to play Robert for a year.

Because his own divorce was looming, Dean Jones (forefront) wanted to leave *Company* while the show was trying out in Boston. Nearly a quarter century later, he voiced regret "that I didn't realize there was a larger issue—my responsibility to my fellow performers and to the people who came to see the show."

"I liked the whole experience," Jones recalled thirty years later, in 2000, for a symposium on Sondheim at the Paley Center in Los Angeles. He blamed his brief time with the production on an unfortunate matter of timing; after Boston, the show opened at Broadway's Alvin Theatre on April 26, 1970, and on May 28, Jones was permanently replaced by his standby, Larry Kert. As the show was getting on its feet, Jones's marriage to his wife of sixteen years, Mae Entwisle, landed on the rocks. It was also said that New York City and Broadway were not his scene, although the official word, in press releases, was that Jones had contracted hepatitis, which was not true.

Jones's situation was further exacerbated by his eleven o'clock number, "Happily Ever After," in which Sondheim painted a bleak portrait of marriage.

"When I got the chance to tell all of the people in the Boston audience that if they thought that they were going to live happily ever after in a marriage, then they were sadly mistaken," said Jones. He admitted he may have put "too much of an edge" on his delivery.

"I remember breaking the fourth wall and looking right into the faces of these poor people and saying, 'happily ever after in hell.' I remember the look in their eyes to this day." What their look told him, Jones said, was, "Why is this man so angry?"

111

"I came offstage and said to Steve, 'They hate us.' And he said, 'You'll have another song in two days.'"

The alternatives were "Marry Me a Little" and "Multitudes of Amys." But Sondheim finally settled upon "Being Alive."

That didn't solve the actor's personal dilemma.

Prince, weighing the burden on the actor and how his departure might also affect the show's box office results, convinced Jones to stay at least through the New York opening and the recording of

Robert (Dean Jones), center, with two of his married friends: Sarah (Barbara Barrie), who is hypercritical, tends to overreact, and knows karate, and her recovering alcoholic husband Harry (Charles Kimbrough), who is more grateful to be married than he is sorry—at least, he thinks.

the cast album. His "Being Alive," which was the replacement for "Happily Ever After," is one of the highlights of the D. A. Pennebaker documentary, *Original Cast Album: Company*. In 2000, Jones could still remember the pressures involved.

We "had not had a day off in, literally, a month, so when I recorded 'Being Alive,' it was four a.m., and we had been recording since nine the preceding morning. So, there was a certain level of"—he forced a laugh—"resentment and anger."

"Dean was something of a diva," said Sondheim, simultaneously acknowledging that "the best 'Being Alive' he ever did is on this recording . . . because he was trying so hard, and he didn't have confidence in his voice." Sondheim said the effort is noticeable in the Pennebaker film. "There's a close-up of him, and he's practically sweating the notes out."

Besides being impressed by the speed at which Sondheim came up with a new song, Jones said he was grateful "Happily Ever After" was replaced because "Being Alive," with its "classic cry for companionship, even though it's going to cause pain [is] meaningful to so many people, including myself."

———

By 1970, the dream-sequence ballet had gone the way of the twenty-cent subway fare. As if to hammer home this message, *Company* was cast with practically no trained dancers, except for Donna McKechnie, who, under choreographer Michael Bennett's guidance, executed the one dance solo in the show.

Bennett and Sondheim worked closely together, which Sondheim found vital. He had learned from Jerome Robbins that it was necessary to give the director and/ or choreographer enough music and suggestions for action that would allow a number to be properly staged. Sondheim considered this a working blueprint, and when he offered it to Bennett, the choreographer was both grateful and surprised.

"I'm a lot like Robert," Larry Kert, who succeeded Dean Jones, said in 1970. "I'm not committed to anyone, and yet I don't look forward to being alone for the rest of my life. That's why I'm in analysis . . . to find out why I'm so afraid of emotional commitment to another human being."

"He'd always had to invent out of nowhere," said Sondheim, who, for the opening of *Company*, had asked Boris Aronson how long it would take for the elevator to move from top to bottom. This way, Sondheim could provide Bennett with enough music to develop the right finish to the number.

Bennett associate Bob Avian said, given the cast's lack of dance experience, Bennett determined that the "Side by Side" number for the opening of Act II should be performed as if it were a suburban PTA talent show. Elaine Stritch's demand was that she not be given the same steps and gestures as anyone else in the lineup.

The orchestral number "Tick Tock," arranged by David Shire, allowed Bennett a chance to let McKechnie shine. She played Kathy, one of Robert's single hookups to whom he won't commit; in fact, Kathy has left Manhattan for Vermont. As Robert and a flighty flight attendant, April, heat up his mattress while their lovemaking comments are heard in voice-over, Kathy executes a dizzyingly erotic dance to music that sounds like a kitchen timer about to go off.

Once climax is reached and the two bedmates arouse themselves the next morning, they sing "Barcelona"—which itself climaxes with Robert's sober realization that, despite his pillow-talk pleas, he really doesn't want April to stay.

Later productions of *Company* cut "Tick Tock," not only because few dancers could measure up to McKechnie, but, as Avian witnessed in an out-of-town production, "Tick Tock" was performed as if it were being done in a roadside lap-dance bar.

That would change with British director Marianne Elliott's 2018 reimagining of *Company*.

"Tick Tock" did not come back as a dream-sequence ballet, but it did become a dream sequence.

A TOAST TO ELAINE STRITCH

She did more than lunch.

Elaine Stritch was a showbiz survivor who, a quarter of a century after her career-defining role as Joanne in *Company*, became a household name in her eighties when she played Colleen, the harridan mother of the Alec Baldwin character on TV's *30 Rock*.

In 2003, the New York Landmarks Conservancy declared her a Living Landmark. She and Sondheim had first met while traversing the same theatrical circles in the mid-1950s and, on one occasion, talking into the wee hours at Donohue's Steak House on Lexington Avenue. She later said she hoped for more than just talk between them but came to realize that was never going to happen.

Like New York and her *Company* character Joanne, Stritch was every bit as individualistic and unrelenting. Professionally, she was nearly as famous for the roles she didn't land as the ones she did.

Stritch was the first Trixie when Jackie Gleason's *The Honeymooners* was set to launch, in 1955, until Gleason fired her before airtime. "The problem is, Stritch, you're as good as me in drag," Gleason said. "And there ain't room for both of us."

Years later she claimed, in her 2003 one-woman Broadway show, *Elaine Stritch at Liberty*, that she blew her audition for a 1980s NBC sitcom by dropping an expletive. The role of Dorothy Zbornak instead went to Beatrice Arthur. The show was *Golden Girls*.

With a voice once compared to a car shifting gears without the clutch—and a presence, both onstage and off, likened to Godzilla in a stalled elevator—Stritch may have been an unlikely Broadway musical star, yet early in her career she understudied for Ethel Merman in 1950's *Call Me Madam*.

In her own right—admittedly, there were dry spells—she starred in a 1952 revival of *Pal Joey* and Noël Coward's 1961 *Sail Away*. Then came *Company*, which introduced her signature musical declaration, Sondheim's paean to Manhattan's jaded upper crust, "The Ladies Who Lunch." She copped a nomination but not the Tony.*

In an early draft, before there was a song in the spot, Furth suggested Joanne was Mrs. Robinson to Bobby's Benjamin Braddock, from *The Graduate*.

---

* The award went to Helen Gallagher for her role as Lucille Early in Burt Shevelove's revised retake of the 1925 musical *No, No, Nanette*.

"She was a convent girl," Hal Prince said of Elaine Stritch. "She was just as clueless as she was sophisticated." The two were part of the marathon recording session of *Company*, although the smiles faded fast. Stritch finished singing "The Ladies Who Lunch" for posterity a couple days later.

A strict Catholic, Stritch spent twelve years at the Sacred Heart Catholic Girls School, and when she first came to New York, in 1944, she lived in a convent while taking drama classes.

"Let me tell you about those convents," she said in 1988. "Convent schools teach you to play against everything, which is what I'm still doing."

As the years progressed, she adopted another Sondheim song as her signature, and, to little surprise, sang the hell out of it.

"I'm Still Here."

—

"Don't ask me how, but a friend and I wrangled an invitation to the last gypsy run-through* of *Company*," said pianist and singer Steve Ross, who, as an interpreter of the Great American songbook, was a fixture in the Algonquin Hotel's Oak Room for the better part of two decades. The time he's discussing here is early 1970.

"We'd heard rumblings about some sort of urban vibe to the show, and that it was something rather new."

By the time the curtain came down at the Alvin Theatre, Ross said, "I told my friend, 'Well, whatever *it* was, it's changed.' 'Moon' and 'June' would always rhyme, but now we had a whole new language on Broadway."

Chief theatre critic Clive Barnes was equivocal, bordering on discouraging, in his *New York Times* review ("Mr. Sondheim's lyrics are way above the rest of the show") and particularly voiced reservations about the "trivial, shallow, worthless, and horrid" characters, although he found some value to the flight attendant. Second-string critic Mel Gussow came in to review Larry Kert's performance, which he found more

Mimicking the Andrews Sisters for "You Could Drive a Person Crazy" are, from left, Susan Browning, Donna McKechnie, and Pamela Myers. McKechnie's Act II solo dance, "Tick Tock," took place as Robert and the flight attendant April (played by Browning) frolic in bed. The number was devised specifically for McKechnie by the show's choreographer, Michael Bennett.

* A by-invitation-only preview performance with no sets and costumes, and only a piano accompaniment; Broadway dancers who went from show to show were previously known as gypsies, until the term came to be considered derogatory.

moving than Dean Jones's, and, admiring the show, described it as "an original, unconventional work, which may be why some in the audience seemed restless."

The *Times* also sat down to interview Sondheim. Addressing those who found the musical's perspective to be antimarriage, he said, "I do *not* understand that, because it's the most pro-marriage show in the world. It says, very clearly, that to be emotionally committed to somebody is very difficult, but to be alone is impossible; to commit is to live, and not to commit is to be dead." He insisted that anyone who missed that message "was just not listening very carefully."

Company was nominated for a then-record fourteen Tony Awards, and won six, including Best Musical and Direction (both to Prince), Scenic Design (Aronson), Book (Furth), and Music and Lyrics, which back then were in two separate categories.

"I never thought highly of awards, but I must say, it's awfully nice to win one," Sondheim said upon accepting his first Tony for music, after his name was announced by presenter Angela Lansbury. On his second call to the stage, this time by Carol Channing, he said, "It's even nicer to win two."

Succinct as he might have been, the two awards, and what they represented, spoke volumes. The theatre establishment not only recognized Sondheim, now clearly a lyricist *and* composer, but did so by honoring a show that didn't play by the old rules, or any rules—essentially thumbing its nose at the old school of musical theatre. Ironically, *Company*'s chief competition at the Tonys that year turned out to be a gussied-up revival of the 1925 *No, No, Nanette*, a commercial hit riding the crest of a nostalgia wave sweeping the older generation. That was fine; Prince and Sondheim would confront nostalgia on their own terms with their next venture, *Follies.*

"*Company* is doing all right," Prince said as the show approached its first anniversary. "It's open and it's going to stay open. It's soon to be staged in Europe. Maybe it was ahead of its time. I don't think so: maybe it just speaks to a smaller audience."

He added, "*West Side Story* had a similar history: acceptance from a few at first; resistance from the many. And then it caught on and seems destined for the ranks of the classics."

In the end, "*Company* never played a sold-out week," Prince wrote in a 2017 memoir, revealing that the original production, which ran 705 performances before closing on January 1, 1972,* often played to only 60 percent capacity, "but it paid off and showed a profit."

In respect to *Company*'s effect on its composer, Mary Rodgers said, "My only expectation, and it was shared by all his close friends, was that Steve would have to make it, because if he didn't, he would die."

—

That most vituperative of critics, *New York* magazine's John Simon, admitted in the summer of 2002, albeit thirty-two years late, "I may have originally underrated *Company* because of its book by George Furth."

In something of a mea culpa, Simon, reviewing a Sondheim festival at Washington's Kennedy Center that offered *Company* and *Sunday in the Park with*

---

* The national tour, which played eight weeks in Los Angeles and seven in San Francisco, starred George Chakiris and Elaine Stritch, opened on May 20, 1971, and ran for a year; the London production, with Larry Kert and Stritch, opened in January 1972 shortly after the Broadway version closed and ran for 344 performances.

George, concluded, "Seeing his works together reminds us how high a bar he set for his unlucky collaborators."

Sondheim never bought into that argument, no matter how many times it was raised, and he went to great lengths to say that he would have been lost without his collaborators. "I've only been a collaborative animal," Sondheim said. "I love collaboration. I like the exchange of ideas, I like somebody to call on when I'm stuck, and I like the family feeling of it."

As the years passed, with new opportunities to assess most of Sondheim's shows, *Company* is the one that has received the lion's share of reevaluation. In May 2022, pegged to the Marianne Elliott reimagining of the show that was about to appear on Broadway, PBS's *Great Performances* devoted ninety minutes to a documentary on the importance of *Company*—and Bobby, and Sondheim.

"I think he's in everything he did, some more explicitly than others," *New Yorker* critic Hilton Als said. "I mean, it's sort of like trying to separate Tennessee Williams from Blanche DuBois. I'm not saying [Williams] is Blanche DuBois, but his understanding of Blanche DuBois is quite phenomenal."

In 1995, "Marry Me a Little" made it back into the show as the closer to Act I. Scott Ellis directed the revival and Boyd Gaines was Bobby, who, in fresh dialogue supplied by Furth, is asked by another character (male) if he's ever had a same-sex experience (he has). The "Tick Tock" number was dropped from the production. In "You Could Drive a Person Crazy," still delivered as an Andrews Sisters–style* pastiche, Sondheim jettisoned the word *fag*.

That same year, Sam Mendes directed a London Donmar Warehouse production of *Company* that transferred to the Albery Theatre with even further updates approved by Sondheim and Furth. Adrian Lester played Bobby, the first Black actor on either side of the Atlantic to take on the role, and BBC 2 broadcast a taped version in 1997.

Director-choreographer John Doyle's pared-down version, with all the actors playing their own musical instruments except for Raúl Esparza's Bobby, transferred from Cincinnati's Playhouse in the Park to Broadway's Ethel Barrymore Theatre, in 2006. It won the Tony for Best Revival, and was aired on PBS's *Great Performances* in 2007, then released on DVD the following year.

Paul Gemignani conducted thirty-five-pieces in orchestrations faithful to the original for an April 2011 staged concert at Lincoln Center directed by Lonny Price and starring Neil Patrick Harris as Bobby, Stephen Colbert as Harry, Craig Bierko as Peter, Jon Cryer as David, Katie Finneran as Amy, Christina Hendricks as April, Aaron Lazar as Paul, Jill Paice as Susan, Martha Plimpton as Sarah, Anika Noni Rose as Marta, Jennifer Laura Thompson as Jenny, Jim Walton (the original Frank in *Merrily We Roll Along*) as Larry, Chryssie Whitehead as Kathy, and Patti LuPone as

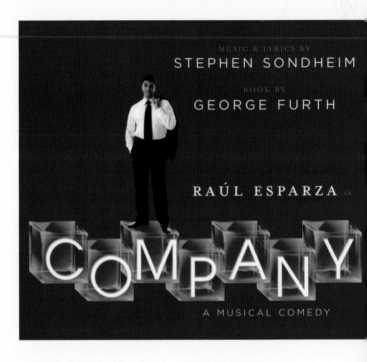

MUSIC & LYRICS BY
STEPHEN SONDHEIM

BOOK BY
GEORGE FURTH

RAÚL ESPARZA IN

COMPANY

A MUSICAL COMEDY

ACROSS SPREAD: "It's very tricky, intellectually precise writing—very demanding and almost mathematical," veteran Sondheim performer Raúl Esparza (above) said of singing Sondheim. "There's so much heart there, complemented by the complexities. I think the complexities bring it out." The complexities do not act as a barrier, either; *Company* productions have played in 2011, with Neil Patrick Harris and Christina Hendricks (opposite, top left, as Bobby and April) and the New York Philharmonic; in the Philippines, in 2019 (opposite, top right); and with Antonio Banderas as Roberto at the actor's eight-hundred-seat Soho Theater in Málaga, Spain, in 2022 (opposite, bottom).

---

* The Andrews Sisters were three Minneapolis-born siblings who harmonized and had major song hits in the 1940s.

Joanne, following her taking command of "The Ladies Who Lunch" at Sondheim's eightieth birthday concert at Avery Fisher Hall, in 2010. When she reached the line about anyone still wearing a hat, LuPone shot a look to Elaine Stritch, who was sitting on the stage, awaiting her turn to sing "I'm Still Here." Stritch was wearing a hat.

Numerous international productions have been mounted since 1997 in most every corner of the world, from the Philippines to Peru, from Singapore to Slovenia.

Few productions, however, set off an adrenaline rush—or number of social media postings, or TV interviews by cast members—like the 2018 gender-swap edition directed by Marianne Elliott, whom Sondheim had admired for her stagings of *War Horse* and *The Curious Incident of the Dog in the Night-Time*, as well as her 2008 *Saint Joan* at Britain's National Theatre.

Various alterations to the show had been suggested previously, the loudest rumble surrounding a potential all-male version, which after all these years could finally put to rest any suspicion about Bobby's sexuality, but Sondheim and the Furth estate (he died in 2008) nixed the plan—despite all best efforts and talents, including those of *Harry Potter and the Cursed Child* director John Tiffany. "It just felt forced," said Sondheim, reiterating what Hal and his wife, Judy Prince, had long said about the specificity of Furth's dialogue: "He's J. D. Salinger."

Once director Elliott and her producing partner, Chris Harper, examined *Company*, which Elliott had been aware of since childhood when two family friends played show tunes, she thought, "It feels so relevant and contemporary to make it about a woman because a woman is still struggling with those issues in a way that only men were in 1969."

Elliott decided not to treat this as an old play needing revision, but a new project all its own—and thus began months' worth of contact between Sondheim and Elliott in the form of phone calls and emails, some of which were published on Deadline.com on June 8, 2022, four days before the season's Tonys. (Her *Company* received a record nine nominations, more than any revival in the Tonys' history. It won five, including those for Elliott's direction, featured performances by Patti LuPone and Matt Doyle, and Best Revival of a Musical. Elliott thanked Sondheim "for trusting me to tell his story in a different way and putting a woman front and center." Despite all the attention, the $13 million production closed after only three hundred performances on Broadway. A national tour was planned afterward.)

Among early points of discussion was Sondheim's aversion to the main character's having a gay couple as friends, although Elliott pointed out that this would be the case for many single women in New York. The emails Elliott released reveal Sondheim wanted no reference to homosexuality in the show at all.* Sondheim said that ever since the original production, people had thought *Company* was about homosexuality, and that was never his or George Furth's intention.

His attitude changed, however, showing just how open he was to new opinions.

Elliott sent Sondheim an email telling him to sit down, grab a glass of wine, and hear her out. She had taped the actor Jonathan Bailey—who would soon set hearts

Patti LuPone (left) won an Olivier Award for her performance as Joanne in the London cast of Marianne Elliott's 2018 gender-swapped *Company*, with Rosalie Craig as Bobbie. LuPone won a Tony when she reprised the role in 2021 for a New York production starring Katrina Lenk (right) as Bobbie.

---

* Another revelation: Furth based the pot-smoking couple on the movie star Jennifer Jones and her producer-husband David O. Selznick, with whom he had shared a joint.

In 2013, Sondheim nixed an all-male *Company* proposed by director John Tiffany. Marianne Elliot later suggested some different twists, and Jonathan Bailey won an Olivier for his Jamie (formerly Amy).

aflutter as the season-two hunk on Netflix's *Bridgerton*—delivering the song that had previously been sung by Amy, the skittish bride-to-be, the rapid-fire "Getting Married Today."*

Once Sondheim received the video, he emailed back and told Elliott to sit down and grab a glass of wine. "This is not what you're expecting to hear," he said. "I love the idea."

Bobby became Bobbie, played by Rosalie Craig in London and Katrina Lenk in New York. Other amendments: couples' dialogue was inverted (with women delivering lines said by men in 1970, and vice versa), the ditzy stewardess of 1970 was now a muscle-bound flight attendant, but still ditzy, and other knowing tweaks were also made. Any changes or addenda came directly from Furth's original drafts of *Company*.

"Tick Tock" now took place inside Bobbie's bedroom and bathroom, and it became a perpetual-motion routine letting her imagine what life would be like if she settled down with Andy the flight attendant. In her imagining, it would be very routine indeed, all while her biological clock was ticking, fortissimo.

Patti LuPone played Joanne on both sides of the Atlantic and observed why *Company 2.0* was perhaps more relevant than the original.

"I think it's more poignant to have a woman," the star told Maureen Dowd (LuPone shared the same opinion on television's *The View*), "because we get asked that question, 'When are you going to get married? The clock is ticking. Eggs are getting old.'

"Boys don't get asked that question, especially when they're thirty-five, boinking beautiful women."

___

* Amy would become Jamie, played by Jonathan Bailey in the West End and Matt Doyle on Broadway.

II.

If Jerome Robbins's intention with *Gypsy* was to create a vaude-ville pageant, then Hal Prince's intention with *Follies* was to re-create the era of Ziegfeld.

Follies, with its cast of fifty, one hundred fifty costumes, and nearly thirty musicians in the pit, achieved this goal both in terms of the mythic, last-of-its-kind stature that still surrounds the original 1971 production, and the Ziegfeld-like profligacy of its production expenses: $800,000, or $5.6 million today, which boosted the weekly operating expenses (called a "nut") to such a high level as to short-circuit the original run after 522 performances.

But Broadway was not alone in misjudging the market. Hollywood at the time was also forced to ring down the curtain on the lavish screen musical. Twentieth Century-Fox, after hitting paydirt with *The Sound of Music* in 1965, ended up in the red four years later with the costliest adaptation of all time, the $25 million (nearly $195 million today) *Hello, Dolly!**

"It is also very important that you make the distinction between 'success and failure' and 'hit and flop,'" Prince said in 2007, perhaps trying to draw a distinction between prestige hit and commercial flop. "*Follies* was a huge success that lost all of its investment money. Hits are shows that do well at the box office, and some of them I wouldn't want my name on."

Six years before *Follies* opened at the Winter Garden Theatre to reviews so divided they would have required a United Nations mediator to deliver a consensus, Sondheim asked the playwright James Goldman if he had an idea for a musical. Sondheim admired Goldman's 1961 London play *They Might Be Giants*, in which a judge imagines himself to be Sherlock Holmes. He comes under the psychiatric care of a Dr. Watson, and together they track the criminal Moriarty. It was said that Goldman

"I was much influenced in those days by the movies of Alain Resnais, and I think *Follies* was probably more influenced by *Last Year at Marienbad* than anything else," Sondheim said, referring to the French filmmaker who used a nonlinear approach to narrative. "It had to do with time."

---

* Some movie industry estimates still list *Dolly!* as the high-spending champ, although combined with its worldwide marketing campaign, Disney's 2017 live-action *Beauty and the Beast* is believed to have cost $300 million. Broadway's most expensive production was the ill-fated 2011 *Spider-Man: Turn Off the Dark*, at $75 million.

blocked any American production of his work because he was not pleased with the London version, although there was a charmingly oddball movie adaptation made in 1971, starring George C. Scott and Joanne Woodward. It essentially sank without a trace.

Goldman suggested to Sondheim a piece about a reunion, possibly of Vassar women, until he came across a news article about a gathering of former Ziegfeld show-girls. Thus began the first of what is believed to be nineteen drafts of what would evolve into the *Follies* script. Their working title was *The Girls Upstairs*, suggesting stage-door Johnnys showing up after the show to woo chorus girls, still in various states of deshabille in their upstairs dressing rooms.

As Sondheim remembered, it "started out as a sort of 'who'll do it,' not a 'whodunit,' in which we brought four characters together to a party who'd had a complicated relationship in the past, and their old angers and insecurities and passions are reignited at this reunion."

It was estimated that book writer James Goldman did nineteen drafts before a final *Follies* libretto was ready to open on Broadway; since the show's 1971 premiere, several more versions of the book have been fashioned.

At the end of the first act, "they each had a reason to wish one of the others was dead. So, the so-called suspense was: Who's going to attempt to kill whom?"

"It was extremely well-written," recalled Hal Prince, "and I didn't like it."

—

When he first read the script, Prince was simply reacting as a friend. *The Girls Upstairs* had been optioned by David Merrick and Leland Hayward, then picked up by Stuart Ostrow. Ostrow, who had worked with Frank Loesser at the composer's Frank Music Corporation and Frank Productions, would later produce the Broadway hits *1776*, *Pippin*, and *M. Butterfly*. But six weeks before production was to start, he let his option on *The Girls Upstairs* lapse.

As he had done thirteen years before, when Cheryl Crawford withdrew from *West Side Story*, Sondheim went to Prince, who made him an offer: Finish the show about marriage with George Furth, and Prince would produce *The Girls Upstairs*. The producer-director was not particularly interested in a "straight-on realistic musical," which, to him, seemed "a contradiction in terms." He shot down the murder mystery aspect entirely. "I wasn't remotely interested until I started to wonder about where these characters came from," Prince said. "I asked for young counterparts to these middle-aged couples."

In initial drafts, the couples simply remembered their pasts through dialogue rather than reliving their pasts through action. Prince wanted something more abstract, to give the show "a gauzy feeling." Prince's creativity kicked up a notch when he glimpsed a 1960 *Life* magazine photo by Eliot Elisofon on the last page of a coffee-table book titled *The Best Remaining Seats: The Story of the Golden Age of the Movie Palace*. A study in contrasts, there stood silent screen star Gloria Swanson, dressed to the nines and surrounded by the wreckage of the Cathedral of the Motion Picture, New York's Roxy Theatre, which had just gotten the first hit of the wrecker's ball. Swanson's feature film, *The Love of Sunya*, had opened the 5,920-seat landmark in 1930 in a ceremony grand enough to bring out Mayor Jimmy Walker.

Prince now knew the visual theme he would seek. He also chose the name *Follies*, to suggest Ziegfeld, but also the British expression for foolishness and the French word for madness (*folie*).

"James and I had limited theatrical imagination," said Sondheim. "We were afraid of flashbacks because of the scenery suddenly coming on and all. Hal said there's no need. He said, 'I would like to stage it with just light, like a ballet, so you can have simultaneous scenes going on.' That meant that we could have figures from the past that we had dealt with in another way, on the stage simultaneously."

When *Follies* was still a murder mystery with music called *The Girls Upstairs*, "Sally tries to kill Ben, although he can't even see that she has a gun because he doesn't have his glasses on," Sondheim said at a Dramatists Guild special project, in 1978. "She missed, and then they all went home, unhappy."

Hal Prince's inspiration for the look and theme of *Follies* came from this Eliot Elisofon photograph of 1920s screen star Gloria Swanson. Elisofon photographed Swanson, who had been dressed by Jean Louis and was sporting $170,000 worth of jewels, during the demolition of the Cathedral of the Motion Picture—New York City's Roxy Theatre, in 1960.

This gave way to a memory play, one with decidedly bitter memories. "In the thirty years since they've seen each other," Sondheim said of the main characters, "their lives have fallen apart, just as the Follies have, just as the country has."

Sondheim said Goldman began constructing a very "schizophrenic script," with the middle-aged characters' action and dialogue set along the right side of the page, and the younger ones' on the left. Prince finally told them to stop worrying where things would take place because "Hal wanted the challenge" of making everything work onstage.

Highly attuned to the musical needs, Sondheim delved into the past "with affection, respect, and delight. In no way am I pointing out how silly the songs were because I don't think they're silly. What they are is innocent." America in 1971, he acknowledged, would no longer accept the frivolous revue material and patriotic tableaux of the past. By writing pastiche, Sondheim could take from the musical cream of the bygone era and embellish from his own perspective.

"It seems to me *Follies* is about eight different characters," he said, referring to Benjamin Stone, Wall Street brahmin (John McMartin); Phyllis Rogers Stone, Ben's society wife (Alexis Smith); Buddy Plummer, Ben's friend and a Phoenix-based traveling salesman (Gene Nelson); and Sally Durant Plummer (Dorothy Collins), Buddy's ignored wife who imagines herself to be still in love with Ben; and their four younger, idealistic selves.

"Buddy and Sally and Phyllis and Ben sing about three songs apiece, but everybody else gets to sing one song." Sondheim estimated that there were twenty-two songs in the original production, and subsequent collections have included as many as thirty-three. By that very calculation, Sondheim said, *Follies* is "a scrapbook or revue."

The very first song he wrote, and one that made it all the way to opening night, was the antique Viennese waltz "One More Kiss," with its underpinnings of Strauss and Lehar as well as a good measure of Romberg and Friml. Sondheim saw this song as something of a self-test to see if he could successfully pull off the old style.

Sondheim later said there was no attempt to conceive of an overall score for *Follies*; "it's just two different kinds of songs." There were the book songs, to spell out the disillusionment of the four main characters, and the Follies numbers, which re-created the virtuosity of the Weismann Follies, as the troupe is called in Goldman's book.

Several of the show numbers are interspersed throughout the evening—three alone in what was known as the Montage: "Rain on the Roof," a husband-and-wife-team vaudeville duet; "Ah, Paris!," a tribute to the City of Lights (at the expense of every other world capital) with Cole Porter–ish panache; and the DeSylva-Brown-Henderson-like "Broadway Baby," one of the show's two anthems of survival. The other, delivered as a star turn, and one of the many late arrivals to a score that was only

125

two-thirds written when the show left for Boston tryouts, is "I'm Still Here."

Irving Berlin inspired the opening, "Beautiful Girls" (heavy shades of "A Pretty Girl Is Like a Melody," which debuted at Broadway's New Amsterdam Theatre in Act II, Episode 5 of the *Ziegfeld Follies of 1919*, and which was grandly reenacted in MGM's 1936 *The Great Ziegfeld*). Porter's influence appears again in "The Story of Lucy and Jessie," with some debt to *Lady in the Dark*'s "The Saga of Jenny," by Kurt Weill and Ira Gershwin; and "Losing My Mind," whose inspiration has been attributed, by Sondheim expert Rick Pender, among others, to George Gershwin's "The Man I Love." A Dorothy Fields–type playful lyric was also detected. Hal Prince referred to it as the character's Helen Morgan song. (Morgan was the torch singer in *Show Boat*.) Others have considered it Arlen-esque. Also in the mix, two of Sondheim's most melodic songs, Ben's "Too Many Mornings" and Sally's "In Buddy's Eyes."

Once Prince was involved, there was a solid nine-month developmental phase. Sondheim and Goldman "gradually realized that every time, in each rewrite, we would read each version and it was too plotted." Out went a chunk of story line, "and just have the party, and then it was still too plotted."

The two "finally woke up to the fact that we should have no plot at all. It should just be these emotional relationships at a party." The reason for the party is because Dimitri Weismann's Theatre is scheduled to be torn down and replaced by a parking lot. What better time and place to meet and reminisce?

Sondheim said that removing the plot gave him the confidence to go ahead with the freeform structures of both *Company* and *Follies*.

The original *Follies* cast, from left; Gene Nelson (Buddy), Alexis Smith (Phyllis), Dorothy Collins (Sally), John McMartin (Ben), and Yvonne DeCarlo (Carlotta). Smith was initially set to sing the heartbreaker "Losing My Mind," but then it was determined Collins had the stronger voice.

THE BUMPY ROAD TO GET "HERE"

"I'm Still Here" nearly wasn't.

But like the many twists of fate detailed in the song—a bluesy, unsympathetic confessional number that traces the social upheavals and personal setbacks of the twentieth century—things have a way of turning out.

The solo was created for the character Carlotta Campion, best described as a resilient veteran of

Yvonne DeCarlo's television fame thanks to *The Munsters* lent her box office appeal and credence to share star billing on *Follies*, despite her relatively small role. Still, her star status was reinforced with her signature number, "I'm Still Here."

Hollywood and the road, and played by Yvonne DeCarlo, a former 1950s screen siren who never met a desert costume she didn't improve before she segued into the '60s sitcom *The Munsters*—which, admittedly, made her a box office draw for *Follies*.

DeCarlo auditioned for the role of Phyllis but lacked the country club hauteur. As the always-game Carlotta, however, she was made to order, something her song, "Can That Boy Foxtrot!" was not. (Like *The Munsters*, it was a one-note joke, with the punchline delivered in the title.)

Replacing it with "I'm Still Here" came late in the Boston run, when pressures on the show were at fever pitch and DeCarlo had trouble keeping the lyrics straight. Sondheim claimed he had found his inspiration in James Goldman's suggestion that Carlotta was a survivor who had been through a lot, followed by his own quizzing of DeCarlo about her life and career. Likely taking a gentlemanly approach, Sondheim later said he based the number on Joan Crawford; dancing in her scanties certainly seems in character for the former Lucille LeSueur.

The song has since proved more indomitable than the show.

DeCarlo recorded it for Capitol Records' feeble attempt at producing a cast album—there were technical deficiencies on top of the mistaken decision not to preserve the score as a two-record set—but, like the lyrics suggest, sometimes you just have to go with what you've got.

Nancy Walker recorded a pitch-perfect rendition of the song at a 1973 *Sondheim: A Musical Tribute* (actually, the first of its kind in what would be decades' worth of celebrations in his honor), and her version still sets the standard. Millicent Martin sang it in the 1977 *Side by Side by Sondheim* in the UK, and several others followed, including Cleo Laine, Elaine Paige, Shirley Bassey, even Sammy Davis Jr. Ann Miller, in a sequined blue dress, performed it in a much-admired 1998 *Follies* production at the Paper Mill Playhouse in Millburn, New Jersey. Shirley MacLaine delivered it with bowdlerized lyrics tweaked by Sondheim himself for the 1990 Mike Nichols's movie *Postcards from the Edge*. Elaine Stritch vowed not to sing it until she was eighty but jumped the gun four years early.

To compensate for the folly of Capitol Records, an all-star *Follies in Concert* was presented, filmed, and recorded at Avery Fisher Hall at New York's Lincoln Center on September 6 and 7, 1985, accompanied by the New York Philharmonic. Sondheim acknowledged that the leads—Barbara Cook as Sally, George Hearn as Ben, Mandy Patinkin as Buddy, and Lee Remick as Phyllis—were all too young for their roles, but that was not an issue in concert.

The role of Carlotta, and with it, "I'm Still Here," went to Carol Burnett, which seemed an odd choice. A treasure, to be sure, Burnett lacked the character's inherently tawdry sense. The reason for the casting might finally have been explained in May 2022.

In a poignant profile of Burnett, *Washington Post* theatre critic Peter Marks, on the occasion of her receiving the Stephen Sondheim Award from the Signature Theatre in Arlington, Virginia, made public a letter Sondheim had written to the awards committee in which he personally recommended Burnett for the honor—making her the final recipient of the award to be handpicked by its namesake.* (Sondheim had written the letter in 2019, but the ceremony was put on hold because of the pandemic.)

The story also told how the two had met, in 1960. She was in a TV studio doing a musical number in her charwoman character for a Dick Van Dyke special. "And this young man came up to me and introduced himself and said, 'I'm Stephen Sondheim, and I really liked what you were doing.' I had no idea who he was," Burnett told Marks.

In the ensuing years, Burnett had done a flashy "Side by Side" production number on her *The Carol Burnett Show* with Bernadette Peters and Tony Roberts, and, following the 1985 Lincoln Center *Follies in Concert*, Sondheim personally chose her for Broadway's 1999 revue of his songs, *Putting It Together*. In 2005, for his seventy-fifth birthday at the Hollywood Bowl, she delivered *Company's* challenging "Getting Married Today."

Sondheim's letter: "We all know, Carol Burnett is a multitude of talents. To begin with, she can sing, and I mean sing! Her singing, in fact, is the most underrated gift she has. Then she can act, and not only that, sing and act at the same time, which is not as easy as it sounds. Especially if you also happen to be one of the funniest women alive. And then, of course, there's her graciousness, which is one of the reasons that people love her as much as they do."

The very definition of "I'm Still Here."

The 1985 *Follies in Concert* at Lincoln Center reunited Sondheim with Lee Remick, who performed the role of Phyllis. The event also starred Barbara Cook (Sally), George Hearn (Ben), and Mandy Patinkin (Buddy), and featured Carol Burnett (Carlotta), Betty Comden (Emily), Adolph Green (Theodore), Liliane Montevecchi (Solange LaFitte), and Elaine Stritch (Hattie Walker).

---

* Established in 2009, the Stephen Sondheim Award is presented to an individual who has made career contributions to the American Musical Theatre that have included interpretations, support, or collaborations of or with the works of Sondheim. Recipients have included Angela Lansbury (2010), Bernadette Peters (2011), Patti LuPone (2012), Harold Prince (2013), Jonathan Tunick (2014), James Lapine (2015), John Weidman (2016), Sir Cameron Mackintosh (2017), John Kander (2018), and Audra McDonald (2019).

Four years after *Follies*, its choreographer and codirector Michael Bennett assembled a group of dancers and created *A Chorus Line*, a concept musical in the tradition of *Company* and *Follies* but a monument all its own. Six years after that, he presented another monument: *Dreamgirls*.

"Michael Bennett suggested that the ghosts of people who were not characters in the show should go through the show, atmospherically, with the combination of the lighting that Hal was talking about that allowed us to play scenes simultaneously," Sondheim said. This also canceled the need for an extra set. "And while we're doing that, behind you there are shadowy figures who are pieces of scenery. The showgirls' ghosts were pieces of scenery. The characters' ghosts were their younger selves. So there are two levels of old figures in it."

Because of the ambitiousness of *Follies*, Prince wanted Michael Bennett to choreograph, which Bennett agreed to do, with the provision that he would also codirect, an arrangement that invariably leads to ambiguities in responsibilities and clashes of ego. These happened. Bennett found the script incomprehensible from the start, according to his associate, Bob Avian. And if *Company* had D. A. Pennebaker's documentary on its cast recording as a permanent reminder of what went on, *Follies* had the journal and memories of Ted Chapin, who later became president of the Rodgers & Hammerstein Organization. As a twenty-year-old college student, Chapin served as a gofer on *Follies* during its pre-opening. Thirty-two years later, in 2003, he published *Everything Was Possible: The Birth of the Musical Follies*. In it, Chapin diplomatically makes clear that Bennett disliked Goldman's book and the librettist's intransigence beyond adding a line here and there. Bennett wanted Neil Simon to come in and add laughs to the book, a notion derided by Sondheim for years afterward.

The two levels of figures Sondheim mentioned, at least the women, have their magic moment with "Who's That Woman?," also known as "the mirror number." It was not what Sondheim had originally imagined; he wanted six women dancing with a gap in the lineup to represent a chorus member who had died. (Asked by British interviewer Melvyn Bragg why he didn't direct, Sondheim replied, "Because I have no visual sense.") Avian said leaving space for the missing dancer just ended up looking like a mistake.

As choreographed by Bennett, the older women, led by Mary McCarty, gather their tap shoes and go through the steps of one of their old routines, which, as one of the women recalls, left her winded at nineteen. Bennett then had the women perform their dance while their younger selves, their so-called ghosts, appeared "in mirror-laden costumes, performed a perfect mirror image of the number upstage, past and present merging in a perfect circle at the number's climax," wrote Bennett biographer Ken Mandelbaum. As throughout the show, the ghosts' costumes are done in black and white, in contrast to the bold colors worn by the reunion attendees.

Donna McKechnie told Ted Chapin that Bennett "designed dance numbers in such a way that he could determine the exact bar of music at which the audience would start to clap, and that repetition was one of the keys."

"Who's That Woman?" assured applause at every performance. The number dazzled and served as the connective tissue necessary for the audience to link the characters' pasts with their present. At one point, before the intermission was removed, the song closed Act I.

"The mirror number in *Follies* and the opening of *Company* are the two best numbers I ever saw in my life," said Sondheim.

—

"They impart a strangely poetic quality to the show, like Fates in ancient tragedy, plumed and glittering looming over the mix-ups of mortal men," *Life* magazine's theatre critic, Tom Prideaux, said of Florence Klotz's "marvelous" costumes and Boris Aronson's "shadowy stairways and parapets." This was especially true with the half-hour "Loveland" sequence that closed the show with

what Sondheim considered a dream ending: Buddy's nervous breakdown.

In the show, pasts and presents collide, at least six Follies-style songs emerge, and opulence abounds. And theatregoers were catapulted into a brave new world that clearly was too new, or too different, for them to deal with and digest.

"Compacted of memory, dreams and desire, the illusions and disillusions of love, the shifting structure of the self, *Follies* fuses all into one of the great haunting themes of the Western mind: Time," *Time* critic Ted E. Kalem said in what was essentially an all-out rave, with a few minor reservations that mostly had to do with how the audience might respond. During the "Loveland" episode, "Each of the four principals does a song or dance number denoting his or her folly: Buddy's is self-hatred; Sally's, being in love with love; Phyllis's, a blurred identity; Ben's self-proving quests, no satisfying goals."

Time followed up three weeks later with a ten-page cover story devoted to lauding *Follies*, but to cap off the opening notice, Kalem wrote, "Rarely have such searching, unsentimental questions and answers been put to a Broadway audience with such elegance and expertise."

TOP: The showstopping "Who's That Woman?" number was conceived by Sondheim as something else entirely before Michael Bennett went to work and put his own stamp on it. Alexis Smith is shown here in red.

ABOVE: The "Loveland" finale to *Follies*, which gave the audience a total escape from reality.

LIGHTS! CAMERA! INACTION!

Bette Davis heard Yvonne DeCarlo's rendition of "I'm Still Here" on the *Follies* cast album and exclaimed, "That could have been written for me."

This reputedly happened in 1973 in Australia, where the movie legend was touring with her New York–based publicist, John Springer, for a series of tributes, although when informed, in 2013, of Davis's reaction, Sondheim said, "I would say that's apocryphal."

But fun to imagine. According to Springer, he apprised another client of his, Hal Prince, about Davis's reaction and how her raspy-voiced interpretation might play in a *Follies* movie.

With Prince amenable to the idea, Springer said he approached Shirley MacLaine and Frank Sinatra, as well as the one-time romantic leads of *Singin' in the Rain*, Gene Kelly and Debbie Reynolds, to see if they might be interested in the Buddy and Sally roles. He then went to Henry Fonda, who'd never done a musical, and asked him to play Benjamin Stone.

Affirmative responses from all.

Essentially casting from his client roster, Springer put in a call to Elizabeth Taylor, to gauge her interest in Phyllis Stone. She didn't say no.

Hearing of Springer's offer, Taylor's husband, Richard Burton, who was also a client, insisted that if Elizabeth played Phyllis, then *he* should be Benjamin, to which Fonda, in the publicist's words, gallantly replied, "Let him play it."

The endgame was to cast a name in every part. Gloria Swanson, whose glamorous posing in front of the wreckage of the Roxy Theatre had originally inspired the mood of the stage production was set to sing "One More Kiss"; Leslie Caron, "Ah, Paris!" Springer was even determined to find a role for Shelley Winters.

Joan Crawford, Springer's stellar but demanding client, then claimed dibs on "Broadway Baby," which, performed by former stage and radio singer Ethel Shutta at age seventy-four, stopped the stage production of *Follies* at every performance at the Winter Garden.

"I won't work with the bitch again," Springer quoted Davis as saying about Crawford, "but we wouldn't be in the same scenes." (The two had not gotten along when filming the 1962 movie *Whatever Happened to Baby Jane?*)

No matter. The hearty effort proved one colossal . . . folly.

Hal Prince flew to Culver City to meet with MGM, allegedly came to creative blows with studio head Daniel Melnick, and summarily withdrew the project—although Ted Chapin in *Everything Was Possible* suggests the problem was that James Goldman was not included in the talks. When asked about the project, Prince confirmed that he and Sondheim did pitch a *Follies* movie to Melnick with a plan to include MGM veterans and to use their old movies in flashbacks.

"My idea was to make it about movies and about the last night of MGM, because you could see that was actually happening," he said about the fabled studio whose fortunes were crumbling at that point. Prince repeated what Springer had said about Davis and Crawford and the songs they wanted to sing.

"We had that all lined up," said Prince, "and I said, 'If all the other people, the Lana Turners and the Dorothy Lamours, come, we'll pay them a stipend and give all the money to charity.'"

That lit the spark, Sondheim and Prince believed, for MGM to compile old musical clips from its vaults and produce the 1974 anthology *That's Entertainment!* instead of *Follies*.

Both *New York Times* critics, Clive Barnes and Walter Kerr, were negative, leaving the show's box office future in doubt. Then came the Tony nominations, eleven in total, and then the Tonys themselves. There were seven wins,* but not for Best Musical. That went to *Two Gentlemen of Verona*. Collecting his Tony, *Verona* playwright John Guare told the crowd he was an investor in *Follies*.

The Broadway production closed July 1, 1972, losing its entire capitalization. Later that same month it ran for one week at the Municipal Opera Association of St. Louis, Missouri, before it opened on July 22 at the brand-new Shubert Theatre in Century City, California, where it prematurely closed on October 1. A national tour was canceled.

As high as the show aims, its presentation frustrates. Ben's lament "The Road You Didn't Take," mirroring sentiments also found in Robert Frost's "The Road Not Taken," seemingly applies to opportunities missed not only by Benjamin Stone but by *Follies* itself.

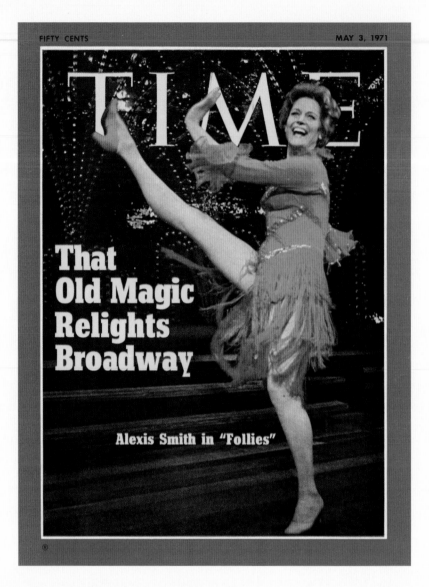

Critics were divided over their reaction to *Follies*; *Time* magazine was not.

Then–Harvard student Frank Rich, reviewing a Boston preview of *Follies* for the *Crimson*, observed, "The world of the dead Follies and the present intermingle constantly in Sondheim's work," but that "a large part of the chilling fascination of *Follies* is that its creators are in essence presenting their own funeral." ("That part of Rich's piece stymied everyone," said Chapin. "Fortunately, it turned out not to be.")

"Eighty percent of *Follies* is the best show ever," Michael Bennett said in hindsight, while producer Cameron Mackintosh, who presented its West End premiere in 1987, pronounced it "one of the most brilliantly flawed shows ever written."

---

* Sondheim for score; Prince and Bennett for direction; Alexis Smith for leading actress; Bennett for choreography; Aronson for scenic design; Klotz for costumes; and Tharon Musser for lighting. Dorothy Collins, Gene Nelson, and James Goldman were also nominated for their respective roles.

A STABLES-IZING INFLUENCE

Cameron Mackintosh has a producing record that would turn Ziegfeld green.

Among his London and New York presentations are *Cats*, *Les Misérables*, *The Phantom of the Opera* (directed by Hal Prince), *Miss Saigon*, and *Hamilton*.

But it was Sondheim who gave him his first success, in 1976, after Mackintosh picked up the rights to a small revue that jazz singer Cleo Laine and her husband, musician John Dankworth, offered as a benefit for their theatre, The Stables, in Buckinghamshire, England.

The show, *Side by Side by Sondheim*, was narrated by broadcaster and director Ned Sherrin with various selections from the Sondheim songbook—all but unknown in the UK—performed by Millicent Martin, Julia McKenzie, and David Kernan.

"That's four performers and two pianos and it's not *Les Miz*, so for a young producer it was possible," Sondheim said years later.

Mackintosh remembered that at the time, the investment was indeed small, and "the least I'll get is good notices." He added, "It was the first time I ever experienced an overnight hit."

"It was the one where we got to be on the map a bit," Sondheim admitted, calling the reaction "very lucky."

Side by Side by Sondheim, the title taken from the number in *Company*, opened at the Mermaid Theatre in Blackfriars on May 4, 1976, and almost immediately generated word of mouth, to say nothing of establishing a Sondheim cult that essentially never ceased to exist.

"I think it was absolutely the rolling stone that started his deserved reputation," said Mackintosh.

The revue later moved to larger theatres in the West End before Hal Prince transferred it to Broadway, where it opened in 1977 and holds the distinction of having its entire cast nominated for Tonys.

The 1977 revue *Side by Side by Sondheim* starred, from left: Julia McKenzie, David Kernan, and Millicent Martin; Ned Sherrin directed and narrated. The modest show, produced by a then-neophyte Cameron Mackintosh, helped establish the Sondheim reputation on both sides of the Atlantic.

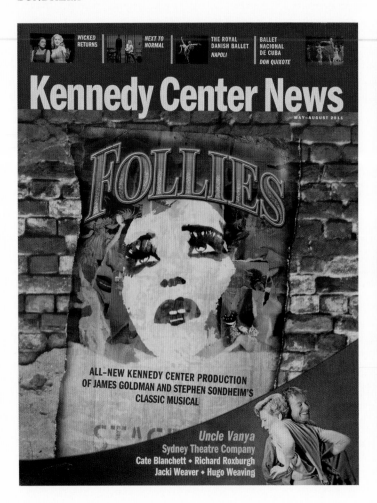

Cameron Mackintosh's $3 million 1987 version of *Follies* at the Shaftesbury Theatre included four replacement songs written by Sondheim, including one delivered by Diana Rigg, as Phyllis, called "Ah, But Underneath." Julia McKenzie was Sally; Daniel Massey, Ben; and David Healy, Buddy. Dolores Gray struck gold with "I'm Still Here." Mike Ockrent directed. Bob Avian choreographed. *Phantom of the Opera* set designer Maria Bjornson handled the look, which evoked a warehouse under construction more than the exulted Roxy. James Goldman reworked the book, though he told the *Washington Post*, "All of us who were involved in the show when it was originally done were very proud of it." In fact, "we thought the show was carved in marble." Nevertheless, "the more I looked at it, the more I didn't like it anymore."

Goldman said he was ending a "terrible marriage" when he and Sondheim wrote the original and "in the midst of a divorce when it went into production, and everything was awful." Once he was remarried, Goldman said, he "didn't feel that way anymore, and I didn't want my characters to feel that way. It isn't what I wanted the evening to say about growing older, about regret, about the passage of youth, and the fading of beauty and times gone by."

The West End restaging ran for 644 performances.

Follies has been revisited, revamped, and revived so many times that every production practically smacks of a world premiere. Engagements have included its 1987 West End debut, along with a 1998 Paper Mill Playhouse in New Jersey version, and a 2011 Kennedy Center mounting that made it to Broadway.

Following the 2017 National Theatre production of *Follies*, which starred Imelda Staunton as Sally and was directed by Dominic Cooke, a feature-film adaptation was announced.

Yet the challenge continued. New York City Center's Encores! mounted *Follies* as a concert in 2007, with Donna Murphy as Phyllis, Victoria Clark as Sally, Victor Garber as Ben, Michael McGrath as Buddy, and Christine Baranski as Carlotta. Casey Nicholaw directed and choreographed, and the production followed the "Loveland" sequence done in London, with its stab at an upbeat ending while retaining Goldman's original book.

The Kennedy Center spent five years and $7.3 million mounting a 2011 revival with Bernadette Peters as Sally, Jan Maxwell as Phyllis, Danny Burstein as Buddy, Ron Raines as Ben, Elaine Paige as Carlotta, and Linda Lavin as Hattie ("Broadway Baby"), which moved to Broadway, where its limited run was extended. The total cast numbered forty.

Since then, there have been versions of various sizes and lengths at Los Angeles's Ahmanson Theatre, in 2012, with Victoria Clark as Sally; London's Royal Albert Hall, in 2015, with Christine Baranski as Phyllis, Betty Buckley as Carlotta, and Lorna Luft as Hattie; and a 2016 Australian concert version.

With Imelda Staunton as Sally, Dominic Cooke directed a winningly received 2017 revival at London's National Theatre, with every character provided a ghost.

Two years later, it was announced Cooke was directing a film version, although no further details were given. Only a few years before, there had been talk of Rob Marshall (*Chicago*, *Into the Woods*) directing Meryl Streep for the screen.

"James Goldman's skillful book nods as much to the golden age of movie musicals as to Broadway," Cooke said in a statement when the project was announced. "It feels like natural material to turn into a movie."

III.

Sondheim's most recognizable song, "Send in the Clowns," arrived neither by accident nor arduous labor, beyond the fact that "it certainly had to be tailored" to the voice of Glynis Johns, for whom the song was written, as she said with understandable possessiveness.

Johns, playing a circa-1900 leading lady of the Swedish stage—one whose status never rose beyond touring—delivers the wistful dream ballad in Act II of the fifth and most elegant collaboration between Sondheim and Prince, *A Little Night Music*. The number comes at the moment when the Johns character, Desirée Armfeldt, arrives at the conclusion that too much time has elapsed in the romance between her and the former lover she was hoping to bring back into her life, fifty-ish lawyer Fredrik Egerman. For his part, Fredrik is still tantalized by his eighteen-year-old virgin bride (his second wife), Anne.

"I have a voice, but not a singing voice," Johns said nearly thirty years after her Tony-winning performance as Desirée. "I must say, Steve was gracious to say I was musical. I could keep on note."

"There was a spot in the second act which required a song," Sondheim said. But when it came to casting a leading lady, "we had not expected to get anybody who could sing because we needed somebody who had great glamour and style and a sense of stage comedy. And we thought to get a lady like that, of what we call of a certain age, and at the same time somebody who could sing, was probably unlikely."

In anticipation, he wrote very few songs for Desirée. She had a number with her daughter, mother, and chorus in Act I, "The Glamorous Life," highlighting the downtrodden joys of acting on tour, and a duet with Fredrik, "You Must Meet My Wife," in which she mostly "supplied the punchlines" about her young rival's naïveté, but "none for her in the second act, and in this spot in the second act, which is sort of the climactic scene between her and her lover, I had intended to write a song for the man, who was cast as a singer. And then we found that we had cast Glynis Johns, and she could sing."

Her voice was always distinctive. Born in Pretoria, South Africa, to Welsh parents who were performing there, Johns made her British stage debut in 1935, at age twelve, as a child ballerina. Three years later, she started appearing in British films, most

"When I'm writing a song," Sondheim said, "I try to be the character. A good actor will not let you know the end of the play while he's playing any scene. He will leave the rest of his journey—that awful word used these days—unknown, so he has someplace to go."

Len Cariou, as Fredrik, and Glynis Johns, as Desirée, in the original 1973 Broadway production of A *Little Night Music*. Because of Cariou's commanding voice, the Act II ballad was intended to be his. Instead, it became Johns's—and Sondheim's—big number, "Send in the Clowns."

memorably as a seductive mermaid who not unexpectedly disrupts a household in the 1948 comedy *Miranda*. Her role as a pubkeeper in director Fred Zinnemann's 1960 epic about Australia, *The Sundowners*, earned her an Oscar nomination for supporting actress, although she was perhaps best known as the mother in Disney's *Mary Poppins*. She sang "Sister Suffragette."

"She had a nice little silvery voice," said Sondheim, describing its sound as breathy to the extent that long phrases might prove a challenge. In a more technical vein, her lines "came directly out of the scene instead of being discursive," said Sondheim.

"That's really what 'less is more' is about—it's about being less discursive both musically and lyrically."

—

Rehearsals for *A Little Night Music* began on Sunday, December 10, 1972, before the company headed to Boston for tryouts on January 15, 1973. By then, Sondheim had written fourteen of the show's sixteen numbers. Only half the songs had been written when rehearsals began.

"That's par for the course for Steve. He's such a procrastinator, it takes some of the joy out of doing the show," said Prince. "The very first song Steve wrote, he said, 'I brought in a *liebesliede* [German for love songs] group, standing around a piano.' I said, 'Why?' He said, 'It looks nice.' I proceeded to worry about it. Then the idea of their singing the overture occurred to me."

"I had no solo until two days before the gypsy run-through," Johns recalled, crediting Prince for urging book writer Hugh Wheeler to rewrite the second-act confrontation scene, although Johns said the new dialogue still had not completely clarified Desirée's eventual acceptance that Fredrik, played by Len Cariou, loves his young wife.

Cariou, she said, always liked a big lunch, so while he was off for a meal, she, Wheeler, and Prince sat on the stage floor, and Prince had Johns tell the playwright what Desirée was feeling at this pivotal moment. Prince took note, then waited for Cariou to return from lunch.

"Then Hal said, 'Now I'd like the two of you to play the scene and ad-lib it,'" said Johns. "Hal was at the root of Steve's writing this song," because during the ad-libbing, Prince phoned Sondheim and told him to get over to the theatre. "So, Steve arrived around four in the afternoon and watched it."

At the moment Prince had phoned, Sondheim was, in fact, working on Cariou's song for the couple's confrontation, which he was basing on Wheeler's original monologue for Fredrik. Prince told Sondheim he now wanted a song for Desirée, and this moment was the best place for it; Sondheim countered by saying, "It's Fredrik's scene—he's the antagonist. He listens." That was when Prince made Sondheim watch how the scene was now being directed, with the focus on Desirée.

Afterwards, Prince and Sondheim went out for a drink and discussed what the new song might be. "It was never to be a soaring ballad. It's a song of regret," said Sondheim. "It is the song of a lady who is too upset and too angry to speak, meaning to sing, for a very long time."

That is why the song is delivered in "short, breathed phrases," said Sondheim. Desirée "is furious. She doesn't want to make a scene in front of Fredrik, because she recognizes that his obsession with his eighteen-year-old wife is unbreakable. So she gives up."

Without going so far as to suggest that the song wrote itself, Sondheim did admit that once he thought to present the lyrics in Desirée's big number as a series of questions, the writing process became clear, and the perpetual procrastinator knocked out the song "essentially overnight . . . I thought, I've got to write a song with short phrases. What better short phrases than questions, [which] ordinarily would not come

"I felt that she was entirely wrong for the part," Hal Prince said of Hermione Gingold (right) who played the world-weary mother of Desirée (Glynis Johns, seen here sitting with Sheila K. Adams). "I thought of her as a comic." He also fretted over Gingold's vanity; would she play a woman of seventy-four? "But Mr. Prince," she told him at the audition, "I *am* seventy-four." Sondheim later found out she was seventy-five.

ITCHING TO BE SWITCHING ROLES

Len Cariou, a native of Manitoba, Canada, was performing the title role in *Oedipus* at Minneapolis's Guthrie Theatre when the script to *A Little Night Music*, sans any Sondheim lyrics, arrived in the summer of 1972.

"It read really beautifully," said Cariou, "like [a Jean] Anouilh play." Sondheim had the same opinion. He even told Prince he didn't see why it had

Laurence Guittard played the other man in Desirée's life, the conceited—and married—Carl-Magnus, whose actions inspire his long-suffering wife, Charlotte (Patricia Elliott), to muse "Every Day a Little Death."

to be musicalized. Prince told him to keep an open mind and go home and write.

The role of Desirèe's vainglorious nobleman lover, Carl-Magnus, had been earmarked for Cariou—a role he did not want but knew would lead at some point to his having to sing for Sondheim when he auditioned.

Prince then offered him the role of Fredrik, and by December 1972—rehearsals had been postponed until he could make himself available—Cariou started commuting between Minneapolis and New York, performing as Oedipus on weekends and rehearsing Fredrik during the week.

When Sondheim introduced "Send in the Clowns" for Desirée—in the spot originally intended for a song for Fredrik—Cariou said Sondheim looked at him and said, "Sorry."

"I was a little pissed off. But what could you say?" said Cariou. "I got to sing the reprise."

Cariou stayed with *A Little Night Music* for a year. Five years later, he was Sweeney Todd.

to me." Johns recalled Sondheim coming back the next morning at ten. He sat down and played the number.

The whole time he was working on the score, said Johns, Sondheim wrote at night and turned his entire day upside down, and the schedule turned him into a physical wreck. "He didn't eat, sleep, or drink, and there he was coming through with these marvelous duets." She referred to Sondheim during his creative process as "this strange creature. But as soon as everything was written, his whole face cleared up."

When Sondheim introduced "Send in the Clowns" at rehearsal, with its Brahms-like opening notes, "I knew from the first note this was a real tearjerker," Johns said, "and I didn't know how I was going to get through it."

Sondheim advised, "Well, sing it hundreds and hundreds of times until you stop crying."

A Little Night Music

—

The genesis of *A Little Night Music* started just after the opening of *West Side Story*, in 1957. Prince, who routinely discussed show ideas with Sondheim even before they worked together on *West Side Story*, said, "We wanted to do something based on the kind of material that's called a 'masque,'" which went back to Elizabethan times, and denoted a courtly presentation with music, dancing, singing, and playacting; think of *A Midsummer Night's Dream.*

"Something that deals with encounters in a country house, love and lovers, and mismatched partners," said Prince. "Such masques frequently have people of all ages from a child to an old lady who's seen it all, and there are lots of foolish crises. Love and foolishness tie in with age."

After all those years, Prince still wanted to do a masque, but, after his investors had lost money on *Follies*, the principal goal "was about having a hit."

From the time he began producing (before becoming a producer *and* director), with *The Pajama Game* and *Damn Yankees*, Prince worked with the same core group of 175 investors. To distinguish himself from the Merricks, Haywards, and others, he found ways to take risks while still expanding artistic boundaries. More often than not, his investors were satisfied. Then, in 1965, came a bonanza from the unlikely source of a Russian shtetl: *Fiddler on the Roof.* Produced by Prince, the show paid its investors back 352 percent.

"There are scores where you go into the theater humming the tune, because you know exactly what's going to come next," Sondheim said. "I find that kind of music uninteresting and no fun. On the other hand, you don't have to be supremely dissonant. You just have to have some freshness or surprise going on someplace." Here, Boris Aronson's sketch of the Armfeldt Family manse as seen on the cover of the show's original program.

"It's very important in the commercial theatre to return the investment," Prince said in a 2012 interview, in which he also stated, "After a bunch of successes at the box office, it gave us the right to have failures that did something we divined was important for the musical theatre form."

Prince would write his investors and say, "'I'm not certain you'll ever see this money again, but you've been doing just fine,' and then we'd do *Follies*, or *Pacific Overtures* . . . you do a show that you *had* to do for artistic reasons that, in fact, ultimately, in [the] case of both those shows, are somewhat historical."

And yet, because of *Follies*, completing the financing of *A Little Night Music* was problematic, with Prince contemplating holding backers' auditions for the first time since he started out. Ultimately, *A Little Night Music* proved both artistically and financially successful.

To that point, Prince said, "I still believe you have to take your audience somewhere, and don't underestimate how damn smart they are and how they want to be stimulated."

As for Sondheim, he flat-out stated that he wrote for "myself, primarily. But I write for myself as a member of the audience. I want the audience to like—well, not like, but to understand and be intrigued by something I write.

"But, like most writers, I write something that I would like to stand in the back of the theatre and watch."

—

"Hal Prince and I wanted to do a romantic musical, and we tried many years earlier to get the rights to a play called *Ring Round the Moon*," a parody by Jean Anouilh of upper-class vanity involving twin brothers, said Sondheim, "and we couldn't get the rights. So, ten years later, when we had the chance again, we tried again, and again couldn't get the rights, so we decided we would try to find the nearest things to that."

Sondheim suggested screening the 1955 Ingmar Bergman comedy of adultery, *Smiles of a Summer Night*. "We wanted to get the musical to take place over a weekend, in some kind of elegant surround, and deal with romance," said Sondheim. Much of the latter part of the Bergman movie takes place at the country estate of Desirée's judgmental and world-weary mother, a former courtesan who believes the summer night smiles three times: on the young, on the fools, and on the old. When Desirée asks why she doesn't pen her memoirs, Madame Armfeldt replies, "My dear daughter, I was given this estate for promising *not* to write my memoirs."

"The Bergman picture, though it's darker—it's more about death—nevertheless provided us with a springboard," said Sondheim.

Anouilh had dithered on the *Ring Round the Moon* rights, and then made the fatal mistake of standing up Hal Prince, who had flown all the way to Paris to meet with him. End of relationship—although, as *A Little Night Music* was about to open for tryouts in Boston, Prince again heard from the French playwright's agent, who was now ready to offer the rights. The producer gladly told him what to do with them.

By contrast, Prince said, dealing with Bergman's representative in America, the Beverly Hills–based old-school agent Paul Kohner, was "extraordinary." The master Swedish filmmaker simply asked for the same deal Prince had offered Christopher Isherwood when adapting the author's *Goodbye to Berlin* into *Cabaret*.

That was accomplished in one phone call, said Prince, "and we went to work."

Among those attending the screening of *Smiles of a Summer Night*, at Prince's invitation, was the novelist and playwright Hugh Wheeler. Wheeler, British-born but a longtime American resident, had written the 1961 play *Big Fish, Little Fish*. He was signed to *A Little Night Music* in early 1972, and six weeks and several drafts later, he had changed Desirée's teenage son Fredrik into a teenaged daughter named Fredrika, along with other alterations.

"The songs that I'd written originally were too dark for Hal," Sondheim said. Prince wanted what he described as more *schlag*, which is Viennese for "whipped cream." "Then, I said, but it's going to be so lightweight. And he said, 'No, no. There can still be knives underneath.'"

There were some. "Every Day a Little Death," was delivered by the Countess Charlotte Malcolm (Patricia Elliott), the wife of Desirée's lover, with an assist from Fredrik's young wife Anne (Victoria Mallory), and it spells out all the evils that men do emotionally. It originally was prefaced by "My Husband the Pig," which was eventually dropped. (The full "'My Husband the Pig" / "Every Day a Little Death" was performed by Julie Andrews in the 1993 *Sondheim: Putting It Together*.)

A musical duel, set in waltz time, between Fredrik and the Count, "In Praise of Women," takes place before an actual duel with firearms. Said duel leads to young wife Anne running off with Henrik (Mark Lambert), Fredrik's sexually frustrated seminary student son; thereby showing Fredrik to be the fool he is, and that he inevitably belongs with Desirée.

Before the show's consequent happy ending, the libidinous maid Petra (D. Jamin-Bartlett) gets in her two cents' worth in a song called, "The Miller's Son," about how sex can be fun, not just remunerative. At the other end of the spectrum was "Later," Henrik's dirge-like song of sexual frustration—even his cello sounds lonely—which is interpolated with Fredrik's "Now." In that song Fredrik contemplates seducing his wife Anne; meanwhile, in "Soon," Anne promises that she is ready to consummate the marriage, at least in theory.

Sondheim hinted that he might have included more knives than Prince would've liked. "I didn't want it to become just frivolous and sentimental, so there's a good deal of irony and, to put it immodestly, I always like it better than I think I'm going to ... because I'm so reluctant to do anything this kind of light in the first place, and I'm always surprised at how well—I'm sure I'm invoking the wrath of God—but I'm always surprised by how well it holds up.

"It's a much stronger piece for something that seems to be very whipped cream than I remembered."

—

The other song Sondheim needed to deliver before opening was the Act I closing number. "A Weekend in the Country" is an elaborate ensemble piece that brings all the characters to the Armfeldt estate to play out their romantic farce in a birch forest that set designer Boris Aronson mounted on sliding plastic panels. To create the set, Aronson used images based on memories of his St. Petersburg childhood combined with the surrealist painter René Magritte's *Blank Signature*. The song begins with Petra handing Anne an invitation that the young wife immediately rejects because she has become aware of Fredrik's involvement with Desirée. Charlotte persuades Anne to attend in spite of herself, then Carl-Magnus invites himself along, and things build from there.

"I remember standing in the lobby at the end of the first act of *Night Music* and somebody saying, 'Oh, that "Weekend in the Country" is so hummable,'" said Sondheim. "Well, of course it's hummable. She just heard eleven choruses of it and came out for a cigarette."

The BBC celebrated Sondheim's ninetieth birthday in 2020 by rebroadcasting its first-ever Sondheim Prom—short for promenade concert—from 2010. The concert was conducted by David Charles Abell in London's Albert Hall, and it featured Bryn Terfel, Maria Friedman, Simon Russell Beale, Julian Ovenden, Daniel Evans, Caroline O'Connor, Jenna Russell, and (shown here with the birthday boy) Dame Judi Dench, who had starred as Desirée in the 1995 National Theatre production of *A Little Night Music*.

There were the usual glitches. In Boston, a banquet table that was meant to glide gracefully from stage left to center came rushing on so fast that the arranged dinner settings went flying. Another time, the table left the stage so abruptly it shoved standing actors into their chairs. Adjustments were made.

On February 20, five days before opening night, with the company back in New York and previewing at the Shubert, Glynis Johns was hospitalized with what was later called a viral infection. Johns, in fact, had been suffering from what seemed pre-opening jitters in extremis. Her understudy, Barbara Lang, went on for her.

"Glynis was almost fired," said Bill Evans, who was then the press associate on *A Little Night Music* and later became the director of media relations for the Shubert Organization. "They even brought Glynis's father to see if that could help her."

What jolted her was the news that Tammy Grimes was brought in to look at the show, with the thought of having her assume the role, although Prince thought Grimes was too young to play Desirée. (As it happened, that plan likely would not have played out. "When Tammy had come to see the show, she went backstage afterwards and started criticizing the red dress," among other demands, said Evans. At that point, he added, the powers-that-be "hesitated.") Showbiz columnist Earl Wilson wrote that Johns experienced "a miraculous recovery."

Johns made it back for opening night, proclaiming that only she would sing her songs. Which she did. *A Little Night Music* gave Sondheim his first good review in the

Times; make that a rave. "The real triumph belongs to Stephen Sondheim, who wrote the music and lyrics," wrote a smitten Clive Barnes, who called the score "a celebration of 3/4 time" and the show itself "heady, civilized, sophisticated, and enchanting."

Most of the other notices followed suit. *A Little Night Music* was that wonderful combination: a prestige hit with commercial chops. Jean Simmons headed up the national company and then the 1975 London production, with Hermione Gingold reprising her Broadway role as Desirée's former courtesan of a mother, Madame Armfeldt. Margaret Hamilton—yes, the Wicked Witch from *The Wizard of Oz*— took the role for the national tour.

Over the next few decades, revivals abounded.

"Shows should look differently," said Sondheim. "It's really the director and designer's vision. One of the things I enjoy is when there is a so-called reinterpretation of the work visually."

Commenting on director Sean Mathias's 1995 London National Theatre production, with Judi Dench as Desirée and Sian Phillips as a very youthful-looking Madame Armfeldt, Sondheim said, "This *Night Music* looks entirely different from what Hal Prince's production did in 1973—entirely different, which is one of the things I like about it. If it looked like Hal's production, then it's just not as much fun."

Taina Elg played Desirée in Sydney, in November 1973, and Trevor Nunn directed a hugely scaled-down 2008 production that moved to the West End before landing on Broadway in 2009 with Catherine Zeta-Jones and Angela Lansbury as the two Armfeldts. They were followed in the roles by Bernadette Peters and Elaine Stritch. New York City Opera staged the work in 1990, 1991, and 2003, as have other

Trevor Nunn directed a 2009 Broadway revival of *A Little Night Music*, for which Catherine Zeta-Jones (center) won a Tony as Desirée and Angela Lansbury was nominated for her portrayal of Madame Armfeldt. Here, Zeta-Jones and Lansbury share their opening-night curtain call with Alexander Hanson, who played Fredrik.

One of Desirée's gowns, by Florence Klotz. A graduate of the Parsons School of Design, Klotz, known as "Flossie," assisted the eminent costumer Irene Sharaff on *The King and I* before establishing a formidable name for herself and winning six Tonys, three of which were for *Follies*, *A Little Night Music*, and *Pacific Overtures*.

opera companies, including those in Houston and Los Angeles, although Sondheim still insisted the work was not an opera—but an operetta.

"About forty percent to fifty percent of *Night Music* is dialogue," he said. "The operetta style of some songs is what gives it that flavor—the ensemble pieces, the trios, et cetera. Those are different in flavor and style than most Broadway shows." In addition, *Night Music* lacks recitative; that is, singing dialogue.

There was a movie made with Elizabeth Taylor in 1978, which is best overlooked, though it did spawn a glorious revision of "The Glamorous Life," now told through the eyes of young Fredrika, who is anticipating the arrival of her long-absent actress mother. Audra McDonald frequently performed the song in concert to a deservedly rapturous reception.

The original Broadway production played the Shubert until September 15, 1972, then moved to the larger Majestic Theatre, where it closed on August 3, 1974, after 644 performances. It received eleven Tony nominations and won six, including awards for Patricia Elliott as Featured Actress (Charlotte), Wheeler's book, and Florence Klotz's costume design.

A remarkably composed Glynis Johns accepted her award for Leading Actress in a Musical, by saying, "I'm surprised, but I would like to thank Hal Prince for giving me the strength and the confidence to go on in the show, and [producer] Ruth Mitchell, and Hugh Wheeler, and Steve Sondheim, for writing such wonderful music, particularly 'Send in the Clowns,' which I adore singing."

After fidgeting in his seat, Sondheim heard prolonged applause amid shouts of "bravo" when his name was announced for best original score. He kissed presenter Celeste Holm, said he was sharing his Tony with musical director Harold Hastings and orchestrator Jonathan Tunick for "the most extraordinary orchestrations in theatre history," delivered what he called "a low bow to Ingmar Bergman," and praised Hal Prince who "made it all possible" and "directed with unmatched brilliance and freshness."

Rex Harrison presented the Best Musical Tony to Hal Prince, who summoned longtime associate Ruth Mitchell to the stage with him and, somewhat elliptically, thanked those people who were there that night, "and they know who they are, for keeping the faith."

Perhaps he was referring to his investors, who ended up receiving a 125 percent return on their investment.

WHEN RUEFUL BECOMES TUNEFUL

Like her clarion-clear renditions of Joni Mitchell's "Both Sides Now" and Pete Seeger's "Turn, Turn, Turn," Judy Collins brought a haunting quality to "Send in the Clowns" and sparked the recording frenzy that turned the ballad into Sondheim's biggest hit.

The spark was first lit when a friend sent Collins the cast album and alerted her to the song. Collins read the album credits, knew Hal Prince, and phoned him. He suggested she contact Jonathan Tunick.

"His orchestration, which includes the English horn phrase at the top, was one of the great secrets," said Collins. The recording "started to go crazy in England. It was immediately on the charts and was a big hit over there."

Judy Collins's rendition of "Send in the Clowns" spent twenty-seven weeks on the *Billboard* Pop Singles chart, starting in 1975. Explaining the song's title, Library of Congress musicologist Mark Horowitz said, "If you're in the circus and there's an accident—say the trapeze artist falls down—they would 'send in the clowns' to distract the audience [from] a bad situation."

As to what drew her to the number in the first place, Collins said it was either "my DNA or by listening to my father sing all the best songs of Rodgers and Hart, of Rodgers and Hammerstein, which I grew up on."

Sondheim credited Bobby Short, the so-called Saloon Singer whose saloon happened to be the Café Carlyle in the Hotel Carlyle on Manhattan's Upper East Side, with discovering the song, having first heard it when *A Little Night Music* was trying out in Boston. "And then my memory is that Judy Collins picked it up, but she recorded it in England. Sinatra heard it and recorded it." Between Judy Collins and Sinatra, "they made it a hit."

And despite Sondheim's often shrugging off the song's immense success—the Collins version won Song of the Year at the 1976 Grammys—"Frank Sinatra said it was one of the ten favorite songs he ever sang," said Bill Evans.

"Steve was very proud of that."

When asked if original cast recordings were the definitive recordings, Sondheim replied, "Of course they are, in the way that the first time for anything is the best. In that sense, my favorite rendition of 'Send in the Clowns' is Glynis Johns's."

The original cast recording session took place Sunday, March 18, 1973, in the same Columbia Records Thirtieth Street Studio C where the *Company* recording was done, as well as those for *My Fair Lady* and *West Side Story*. Goddard Lieberson had been retired for three years—which explains why his imprimatur is not on *Company*—but he stepped back into the ring after seeing *A Little Night Music* at the Shubert Theatre.

"It seems like a traditional show, but it isn't," said Lieberson, who conducted the day's session as if it were an opera. Ten violins were added to the seventeen-piece orchestra that played nightly on Broadway, along with another horn.

Assisting Lieberson was Thomas Z. Shepard, who had produced the *Company* album and would go on to do those for other Sondheim shows, including the London production of *Night Music*, and Broadway's *Pacific Overtures*, *Sweeney Todd*, *Merrily We Roll Along*, and *Sunday in the Park with George*, as well as *Follies in Concert*.

Sondheim said that an extra fifteen minutes were allotted to Johns so she could record "Send in the Clowns," "to take into account that she would be hysterical. I mean, Glynis Johns has never sung in her life before on a stage. We were terrified, because she was a nervous lady to begin with."

There turned out to be no cause for alarm. "We got into the recording studio, she did things in one take. No problem at all. In fact, she was disappointed there wasn't more than one take on 'Send in the Clowns.' First take—out, print."

Sondheim said, "The first person who brings your song out of the womb is the one to whom you give your heart. So, generally," he said, in regard to first cast recordings, "it's not so much they're definitive, but they're the ones you love, at least as a composer."

In 2022, the Turner Classic Movies Film Festival in Hollywood included a screening of *The Last of Sheila*, with a screenplay by Stephen Sondheim and Anthony Perkins. "A game of murder among wealthy vacationers turns into the real thing," was its program description.

A PUZZLEMENT

The Last of Sheila has its virtues, and they are James Coburn, James Mason, Dyan Cannon, the South of France, and a screenplay by, in the order in which they are listed, Stephen Sondheim and Anthony Perkins.

Sondheim credited the endeavor to Herbert Ross. Having choreographed *Anyone Can Whistle* and *Do I Hear a Waltz?* on Broadway, Ross went on to establish himself as a Hollywood director after he first caused a splash by choreographing the musical numbers for William Wyler's 1968 *Funny Girl*. Once the movie-musical cycle faded out, Ross directed a series of successful film adaptations of plays (*The Owl and the Pussycat*; *Play It Again, Sam*; *The Sunshine Boys*), along with some original dramas (*The Turning Point*). He returned to musicals in 1984, with *Footloose*.

It was Ross who said to Sondheim, while *A Little Night Music* was being written, "'Why don't you write plays?' I said I thought they'd be too hard to write, and I didn't have any ideas except for mysteries," said Sondheim. "He said, 'Okay, what about movies?' I plotted one and didn't want to write it alone, so I asked Tony Perkins, who was a murder-mystery fan and a friend and who I knew to be a very funny writer, to do it with me. I plotted it alone, then we wrote alternate scenes."

A few years earlier, Sondheim and Perkins had been heavily engaged in staging elaborate scavenger hunts that kicked off at Sondheim's residence and then took place all over Manhattan. These would

take a month for the two of them to plot, and they would invite about twenty members of their show business circle to play: Ross and his wife, the dancer Nora Kaye; Lee Remick; Roddy McDowall; Mary Rodgers, Phyllis Newman; Adolph Green. The group later expanded to include Mike Nichols, Leonard Bernstein, and André Previn, who called the games "both fun and lethal." Clues would be planted in various hideaways, such as the furthest lane of a bowling alley, or the apartment of Tony Perkins's mother, Janet, who would offer participants coffee and cake—which featured the next clue written in the icing.

"You'd pull up to Sondheim's house and there were all of these limousines parked outside, in preparation for the game to begin," remembered Grover Dale, who was living with Perkins at the time. "The first time I saw all the limos, I thought, 'Oh, someone must be getting married.'"

"One of the guests was Peter Shaffer," said Sondheim, referring to the playwright of *Amadeus* and *Equus*. "Peter is a friend, and he said he and his twin brother Tony used to write murder-mystery novels under a pseudonym before they became playwrights. He asked if I would set [one] up next time I went to England so Tony could play it."

S T E P H E N   S O N D H E I M
June 13, 1973

To the Company, Crew and Orchestra of "A Little Night
Music":

You're all invited to a screening of "The Last of
Sheila" Tuesday night, June 19, at 11:00 P.M., at
Warner Brothers, 666 Fifth Avenue, 6th Floor Screening
Room. This is the murder mystery that Tony Perkins
and I wrote, about which Variety said, "Witless",
The Hollywood Reporter said, "Magnificent", Rex Reed
said, "A disaster", and Liz Smith said, "Brilliant".
Regardless of what the Friday papers say, I'd like
you all to come.

You can each bring one guest. You don't need a ticket
for the screening but, due to the paranoid quality of
life in New York, you <u>will</u> need tickets to get into
the Warner Brothers building. You can get them from
George Martin. Those who don't like the movie or
reveal the plot will have their solos taken away.

Steve

Sondheim posted this open invitation backstage at the Shubert Theatre, welcoming colleagues to a special screening of the movie he had written with Anthony Perkins, *The Last of Sheila*. Rex Reed and Liz Smith were both columnists for New York's *Daily News*. George Martin was *A Little Night Music*'s production stage manager.

Sondheim did just that. "Peter Shaffer was sent to the bathroom to pick up the clue, which was under the sink. He picked it up, looked in the mirror, and behind him was Tony Perkins with a gun in his hand! Bang bang, you're dead!"

Sondheim went on to say, "He was so terrified. I mean, of all people, Tony Perkins just a couple of years after *Psycho*!"

Also worth noting is that Tony Shaffer wrote the 1971 stage mystery *Sleuth*, a great success on the West End, Broadway, on tour, and onscreen in 1972 with Laurence Olivier and Michael Caine. (Caine also starred in a 2007 remake, with Jude Law.) Its original title was *Who's Afraid of Stephen Sondheim?* The character of Andrew Wyke, a mystery writer who lives in a gadget-filled mansion, is based on him.

Sondheim explained, "I saw the script and said to the producer, 'You can't call it that. Nobody knows who I am.' That wasn't false modesty. It's just that, even these days, my name is mostly familiar to people who are interested in musical theater."

On Herbert Ross's suggestion to pen a script, Sondheim enlisted his friend Anthony Perkins (left, on the South of France location for *The Last of Sheila*). "He'd never done any writing at all," Sondheim said, "but I knew he had exactly my kind of mind and take, and he's much more into murder mysteries than I am."

Much of the plot of *The Last of Sheila* is anchored to a movie producer's yacht and the ensuing scavenger hunt to uncover who among his so-called friends killed his gossip columnist wife, Sheila (for whom the yacht is named). James Coburn plays Clinton, the cigar-puffing producer with the reflexes of a cobra. Dyan Cannon, who gained twenty pounds for the role, is the bold-as-brass Hollywood agent Christine, a dead ringer for the real-life ten-percenter Sue Mengers. James Mason, who ends up acting as the movie's version of Agatha Christie's Hercule Poirot, plays Philip, a once-prestigious film director now reduced to doing dog commercials.

"There are two parts to it: the melodrama part, where people wander around in a darkened house, and there are a murderer, [a] murder, and [a] victim," Sondheim said. "Then everybody, even the victim, gets to play the second part, which is to prove who the murderer is."

Originally, Sondheim and Perkins set the action during a snowbound weekend on Long Island. Ross suggested the action be moved to the Côte d'Azur and focused on showbiz.

Providing the movie its true veracity is Cannon's Mengers, who was then at the top of her game. "The first time she asked me to a party," Cannon said about Mengers's lack of a filter, "she said, 'Will you wash your face before you come? I want people to see what you look like.'" Among Mengers's clients were four people attached to

The *Sheila* cast, from left: James Mason, Raquel Welch, James Coburn, Joan Hackett, Ian McShane, Dyan Cannon, and Richard Benjamin. Cannon did an in-your-face impersonation of Hollywood agent Sue Mengers; Herbert Ross diplomatically described the character as "human, gamy, but not common."

Sheila—Anthony Perkins, director Ross, Dyan Cannon, and another star, Richard Benjamin—to say nothing of Barbra Streisand, Clint Eastwood, Ryan O'Neal, Ali MacGraw, Candice Bergen, Gene Hackman, George C. Scott, Tuesday Weld, Mike Nichols, Peter Bogdanovich, Bob Fosse, and Gore Vidal.

In an odd twist of fate, the closing credits of *Sheila* roll as Bette Midler's "Friends" plays on the soundtrack.

Forty years later, Bette Midler starred on Broadway in John Logan's bitingly entertaining one-character play, *I'll Eat You Last: A Chat with Sue Mengers*—as Mengers.

—

Like so many things created by Sondheim, *The Last of Sheila* developed its own cult following, despite its loquacity.

In 2012, New Line Cinema announced plans for a *Last of Sheila* remake, with Joel Silver set to produce, although the film never came to fruition.

Rian Johnson, writer-director of the 2019 whodunit *Knives Out*, tipped his hat to *The Last of Sheila* while doing publicity for his film, and he suggested moviegoers see it as a prelude to his picture. The earlier film was "so funky and so '70s and so cool," he told *Entertainment Tonight*. "It's like a murder mystery party and, of course, it goes horribly wrong, and someone dies." For the 2022 *Knives Out* sequel, titled *Glass Onion* and again starring Daniel Craig, Sondheim briefly appeared as himself.

Sondheim found a certain satisfaction in putting together the pieces of the *Sheila* puzzle. "It's fitting a certain amount of information into a pattern. You make a pattern out of a series of discrete bits of information and try to make it graceful, so you won't feel the effort behind it. In that sense, lyric writing is a puzzle. As a matter of fact, it is more like a jigsaw puzzle than a crossword. It is about words, but they have to fit so they bleed and join the way jigsaw pieces do into an overall pattern in which the cracks are virtually invisible."

As for the denouement, Sondheim said, "the final twenty minutes were an explanation of what you thought you had seen and what you hadn't. When I was plotting it, I thought I've got to make it 'quote' cinematic—people have to be breaking down something or stabbing or shooting each other, even though it may be seen through a rearview mirror."

The production was not without its problems. Actors' egos clashed, security issues presented themselves, and, as Richard Benjamin recollected, Herbert Ross arrived on the location "on the first day and said, 'We've got a little problem.' The boat that they were going to use burned up."

"I was into primal therapy," Dyan Cannon coolly remembered about it all. "I just screamed my way out of it."

—

Sondheim continued writing mysteries. He and Perkins fashioned two, *The Chorus Girl Murder Case* and *Crime and Variations*. The former was commissioned by Michael Bennett, who had a production deal with Universal following the studio's purchase of the rights to *A Chorus Line*. Bob Avian described the plot as being about "girls getting murdered in the middle of huge production numbers," and Sondheim and Perkins's treatment as "so complicated we could hardly figure it out." Meanwhile, *Crimes and Variations* was apparently a six-episode anthology meant for a cable channel. Neither was produced.

In 1996, *Getting Away with Murder*, a two-act straight play Sondheim wrote with George Furth, opened and very quickly closed on Broadway, after getting on its feet the year before at San Diego's Old Globe Theatre under the title *The Doctor Is Out*. "It concerns a group of people in therapy and their psychiatrist," said Sondheim. The doc is dead, and his patients attempt to find out who did it.

Reviewing the show for the *New York Times*, Vincent Canby praised the cast—John Rubinstein, Terrence Mann, Christine Ebersole, Jodi Long, Josh Mostel—but said Sondheim and Furth backed themselves into corners and ended up with something less satisfying than "Christie's *Witness for the Prosecution* and Anthony Shaffer's *Sleuth*, or even *The Last of Sheila*, the densely clued, bitchily funny film written by Stephen Sondheim and Anthony Perkins."

WINTER GARDEN THEATRE
PREVIEWS BEGIN WED. EVG. DEC. 31st • OPENS SUN. EVG. JAN. 11th

"Steve relies very, very heavily on his book writers for tone and for language," said *Pacific Overtures* librettist John Weidman. "He requires raw material from his collaborator before he can sit down and go to work."

EAST GREETS WEST

"Whether or not the show bombs, and regardless of whether you love it or loathe it, it's certainly the most bizarre and unusual musical ever to be seen in a commercial setting," Sondheim said in an attempt to drum up pre-opening interest in the Broadway engagement of *Pacific Overtures*.

The concept was daring in itself. The timeframe covered 125 years of Japanese history, starting with Commodore Matthew Perry's visit to Japan in 1853 under the guise of delivering a friendly letter of greeting from U.S. President Millard Fillmore to His Imperial Majesty, the Emperor of Japan. In fact, the mission was to open Japan's isolated feudal society to Westernization—and not just by Americans, but by trade invaders from Britain, Holland, France, and Russia. This social and political account was to be told dramatically from the Japanese perspective, musically with Japanese modality, narratively by a Japanese character credited as "reciter," and theatrically in Japanese Kabuki* and Bunraku** fashion by an all-Asian-American, all-male cast.

And all in time for the American Bicentennial.

—

"I have an idea for a play about the opening of Japan; can we talk about it?" John Weidman wrote to Hal Prince, whom he knew through his father, Jerome, the author and librettist of *Fiorello!* and *I Can Get It*

for You Wholesale. At the time that John Weidman contacted Prince, he had also written to Major League Baseball commissioner Bowie Kuhn in the hope of scoring an internship, but he struck out. Weidman also applied to Yale Law School and was accepted. He graduated (Class of '74), but in the end decided against a career in law.

"At Harvard [as an undergraduate], I majored in East Asian history. I thought I knew something no one else did. I had no ambition to write a play. I had no training. I just thought I can do this while I'm at Yale."

In the summer of 1973, Weidman secured a fifteen-minute meeting with Prince and hit the jackpot: Prince offered him $500—"a fortune in those

---

* Traditional song and dance theatre in which highly stylized song, mime, and dance are expressed through exaggerated emotional gestures and body movements.

** Theatre in which puppeteers outfitted in black and visible to the audience manipulate large figures to chanted narration and musical-instrument accompaniment.

Boris Aronson's Tony-winning sets for *Pacific Overtures* were inspired by nineteenth-century Japanese prints and marked his fourth and final collaboration with Sondheim and Prince. Sondheim, in turn, said the sets inspired him when it came to fashioning the score.

days," said Weidman—to develop what the twenty-two-year-old had pitched as a realistic historic drama. The project moved apace. "I had finished several drafts of the play, and we had a reading of it."

"Potent theatrical storytelling," was Prince's appraisal of Weidman's text. Then, Prince struck upon an idea of where the story should go next.

"I was coming into New York from New Haven for casting sessions when Hal called me up and said, 'You know what? . . . I think it needs to be a musical.'"

—

"The play was confined to a series of scenes around a negotiating table in which the Japanese were hoodwinked by the mendacity of the American group," Prince told chronicler Foster Hirsch. "I felt the play wouldn't reach enough people. It needed to get beyond specifics. It needed size, and I realized then that music was how to give it size."

Weidman said Prince played "ringmaster" and "bullied" Sondheim "into engaging with the material."

"Steve really thought I was crazy," Prince said.

"At first I thought it could never work," said Sondheim, echoing sentiments he had expressed about many a previous work of his. "I liked the play, but I didn't see how music would fit."

Florence Klotz's Tony-winning costumes for *Pacific Overtures* underscored the plot's focus on Westernization, and theatricalized the cultural invasion of Japan by foreign powers.

"He twisted Steve Sondheim's arm a bit," Weidman said, "and he twisted it some more, and pretty soon we were all sitting in a room together and talking about how to make it into a musical." He added, "The content of the play is quite different from the content of the musical, so we really went back and started over."

"Often, what appeals to Hal will not appeal to me, and vice versa," said Sondheim. "Usually what happens is that Hal drags me into his vision. You commit yourself to something and then after a while, if it has any interest at all, you fall in love with it."

The two-and-a-half-hour *Pacific Overtures* premiered at the Winter Garden Theatre in January 1976. It was a unique stage spectacle built upon a series of often-intimate sequences that, upon first encounter, might have seemed disconnected.

Told through the lives of two men, Manjiro, a fisherman, and Kayama, a samurai, the story begins as a fable, depicting an ancient culture that is proudly untouched by modernity. Manjiro has been living in Boston after being taken there years before by American sailors, and now he has come home to warn the shogun of the United States' plans to launch an expedition to Japan. Kayama is ordered by the shogun's advisors to block the arrival of the American ships and to force them to retreat. Together, Kayama and Manjiro devise a scheme to construct a treaty house—a place for the dignitaries to meet—that will effectively prevent the Americans from technically setting foot on Japanese soil, which is forbidden by royal decree. The plan succeeds but not before Kayama's wife, Tamate, kills herself when she sees American ships in the harbor and assumes Kayama's plan has failed. Act I ends with American ships leaving Japanese waters.

Act II traces the rocky but rapid rise of modernity, starting with the arrival of the Western powers, who land in force, armed with fleets of ships and with cannons that are likened to fire-breathing dragons. Their commanders demand access to ports and the freedom to trade, and swift commercial inroads are made. The samurai

Kayama goes full bureaucrat as he robotically assimilates to Western culture, while the fisherman Manjiro, who is aware of the pitfalls of a society he once embraced, goes full samurai and kills Kayama and the shogun's advisors. The emperor, shown as a child (in puppet form) in the first number of Act I, is now an adult and assumes his rightful role as leader of Japan—one who declares his country to be a staunch ally of Western culture.

"What we've done," Sondheim said, "is to posit in our heads a mythical Japanese playwright who has come to New York and who sees a couple of Broadway shows. He then goes back home and writes a musical about Commodore Perry's visit to Japan."

Sondheim considered that such a premise would "give us the tone and style of the show. And that's how we're preventing it from becoming *The King and I*."

—

What awakened Sondheim to Japanese culture, he said, was accompanying Hal Prince to Japan for two weeks.

"We began to realize as we got deeper into the material that there was something about Kabuki that was so powerful and so clearly connected to the subject matter," said Prince, who expressed disappointment when their guides scheduled only half-hour visits to Kabuki and Noh* plays, "but, in fact, we stayed much longer." One performance witnessed by Prince and Sondheim "lasted over six hours, and we were enthralled." And inspired. "I began to see a trajectory that took you from Kabuki to Ginza in the 1970s, which is as Western as you can get."

"Not that it was in any way an epiphany," said Sondheim, "but just to be there, and see the ladies with obis** in the department stores . . . buying Chanel . . . and see the contrast to what was and what is now."

His takeaway: "They're the ultimate culture in 'Less is more.' They are *the* minimalist culture—look at the Japanese screen," which Sondheim did, at New York's Metropolitan Museum of Art. "I remember stepping out of the elevator, and there was a three-panel screen." To his amazement, "the first panel was absolutely blank; the second panel was absolutely blank except for the end of a bird's tail; and the third panel had the rest of the bird and a tree." That's when it struck Sondheim: "I thought: Ohhhhh, it's all about less is more."

Sondheim's intention became "to echo musically the whole cultural idea of less is more. Meaning, we're just going to take this one chord and, by making tiny little variations on it, we're going to gradually build it up and sustain it so that the audience never gets bored."

What he accomplished is a panoply of theatrical styles.

As an opening number, "The Advantages of Floating in the Middle of the Sea," with its touches of Kabuki and Noh tinged with Broadway values, is showy and sprawling, yet serious. The haiku-like "There Is No Other Way," which portends a ritual

ABOVE: Mako (center), whose full name was Makoto Iwamatsu, received an Oscar nomination as Best Supporting Actor in Robert Wise's 1966 WWII drama *The Sand Pebbles* and was nominated for a Tony for his role as the Kabuki Reciter in *Pacific Overtures*. In addition to narrating, he also portrayed both the Shogun and the Emperor as the story unfolded.

OPPOSITE: Actor Soon-Tek Oh, who played Tamate, wife of Kayama in the all male, Kabuki-style production, is greeted backstage at the Winter Garden Theatre by Elizabeth Taylor after an April 1976 performance. Later that same year, in Vienna, the star filmed the movie version of *A Little Night Music* for director Hal Prince.

---

* Dating back to the fourteenth century and still prominent today, Noh theatre combines music and poetry in its drama and is further distinguished by its elaborate costumes and elegant, yet intense style.

** Traditional sashes worn around the waist.

suicide, blends Eastern and Western sounds using a harp, wood flute, and percussion. "Chrysanthemum Tea," like *A Little Night Music*'s "A Weekend in the Country," advances the action, but this time with lyrics delivered by a shogun's mother as she slowly poisons her son. Gilbert and Sullivan, John Philip Sousa, and touches of the can-can and a Cossack dance are the main influences in "Please Hello," a showstopping patter song that opens Act II and gives each Western power a grand entrance. The placid "Pretty Lady" is sung by three foreign sailors positioning themselves to take unfair advantage of an innocent Japanese woman. The distinctly grave "A Bowler Hat" encapsulates Kayama's Westernization step-by-step.

"I was trying to start with kind of faux Japanese-scale music and, as the country gets Westernized, to gradually make the music more Western," said Sondheim. "The last number is really a Westernization of the opening number."

That is "Next," of which it could be said that it is to Tokyo what *Company*'s "Another Hundred People" is to New York City.

Sondheim took particular pride in "Someone in a Tree" and how it fit several pieces of a puzzle together and tells its story *Rashomon*-style; that is, from various perspectives. As Weidman said, the number takes place "in the Treaty House when the Americans have finally come ashore to deliver their letter. Nothing happened; they brought the letter, they dropped it off, and they left."

It was Prince who wanted a musical number at that exact moment, "so the idea for what became 'Someone in a Tree' was something that got talked about." Weidman wrote bits and pieces of dialogue, "and maybe even a clean version of a scene with the samurai under the floorboards and the kid in a tree."

"Someone in a Tree" also tells of the way history is interpreted and misinterpreted. First, there is an old man telling his version of what he believes is going on, and then his ten-year-old self appears and gives his side of the story. While the elder man embellishes the report with his biases, the younger glides over certain facts with his innocence. Then enters a third witness, a samurai who has been lurking underneath the treaty house, interpreting the events only from what he can hear but cannot see.

No two storytellers tell the same story.

But each recognizes that he is an important participant in history.

"WE'RE NOT WRITING A HISTORY BOOK"

Sondheim said he "kept a very limited harmonic language" within the score to *Pacific Overtures*, "with very little harmonic motion in the songs."

In fact, the show "had static songs, harmonically. They don't go anywhere."

In the case of "Someone in a Tree," the two chords on which the song was built and its "endless rhythmic vamp" were elements that "bored the audience to death in some cases."

He chalked this up to the relentlessness found in Japanese music.

"The score of *Pacific Overtures* holds together," he said, "because it has the same harmonic texture and the same lack of variety within the songs, as opposed to a score like *Follies*, which is *built* on variety."

Pacific Overtures, which Prince categorized as "documentary vaudeville," plays "fast and loose with Japanese history, something that made me uncomfortable," said John Weidman. "But Hal said to me once, 'We're not writing a history book here, we're writing a musical comedy, okay?'"

Weidman added that when the show was eventually produced in Japan, "I expected them to say, 'Now, wait a minute, the shogun did die, but nobody killed him,' but they seemed to be okay with that."

Visually, the original Broadway production was a stunner; Boris Aronson won another Tony for his scenic design, as did Florence Klotz for her epic and elaborate costumes. Aronson neatly splashed the stage with Japanese prints and dazzling collages, pulling off his visual trick with newly developed Xerox color copier technology that allowed the audience to be enveloped in atmosphere.

Theirs were the only two Tonys *Pacific Overtures* received, out of ten nominations. At the ceremony, Sondheim received the longest and loudest round of applause from the audience when his Original Score nomination was announced, but this was the year of *A Chorus Line*, which swept the Tonys. Michael Bennett's musical had become a phenomenon; it also crushed *Chicago*, which did stumbling business in its original run until it finally found a mass audience thanks to a stylized 1996 City Center Encores! concert version that quickly transferred to Broadway and has been running ever since.

Reviews for *Pacific Overtures* were all over the map. "Very serious" and "almost inordinately ambitious," Barnes wrote in the *Times*, citing Sondheim's lyrics as "devilish, witty, and delightfully clever," and calling the composer "the most remarkable man in the Broadway musical today." But Barnes found the score sometimes at odds with "the conceptual format" of Weidman's book, which threw the dramatics of the show off-balance. This did not help sell tickets. *Women's Wear Daily* critic Howard Kissel, who was a lifelong admirer of Sondheim,* called *Pacific Overtures* "the most original, the most profound, the most theatrically ambitious of the Prince-Sondheim collaborations [and] a triumph of sophistication, taste, and craft." That old *Follies* champion, T. E. Kalem, in *Time*, found it "as arid and airless as the moon." John Simon branded it "tripe and pretentiousness combined."

Revisiting the critics in 2004, when *Pacific Overtures* was restaged at Studio 54 by the Japanese director Amon Miyamoto, with B. D. Wong as the Reciter, *Variety* contacted Simon, who was contrite about his initial reaction. "It is better than, perhaps, I first thought," Simon said. "Some things can be immediately appreciated, and others have to be digested more slowly, which is true of more lasting works. Very few of those can be grasped right away."

Kissel said in 2004: "It remains one of the most extraordinary pieces I've ever seen. The other is *Sweeney Todd*."

Pacific Overtures ran only 193 performances and lost its entire investment—"no surprise to most of our investors," said Prince, "but I believe they were proud to have been part of it."

"One of the things that interested me about *Pacific Overtures* was to see if you could do a musical of ideas," said Sondheim.

"I think you can. I think we did, and I'm very proud of the show."

---

* Kissel wrote for New York's *Daily News* in 2010 when, on a list for a liver transplant, he refused an organ donation to attend the revival of *Anyone Can Whistle*, the first New York revival in forty-six years. Kissel got a different liver at a later date.

OPPOSITE ABOVE:
After the York Theatre Company presented a well-received 1984 revival directed by Fran Soeder, the Shubert Organization moved the production to the Promenade Theatre on the Upper West Side of Manhattan; with Sondheim, from left, Kevin Gray (who played Kamaya), Ernest Abuba (the Reciter), and Tony Marino (Lord Abe).

OPPOSITE BELOW:
"Mr. Doyle's genius," critic Terry Teachout wrote of John Doyle's 2017 Classic Stage Company revival of *Pacific Overtures*, with George Takei (center) as the Reciter, "lies in his ability to pare down a script to its essence . . . The simplicity of the presentation means that Mr. Sondheim's gorgeous score, an amalgam of Ravel-like harmonies, pentatonic melodic shapes, and glittering percussion, stands out in the highest possible relief."

RICHARD BARR   CHARLES WOODWARD
ROBERT FRYER   MARY LEA JOHNSON   MARTIN RICHARDS
PRESENT

ANGELA LANSBURY   LEN CARIOU

IN

Sweeney Todd
THE DEMON BARBER OF FLEET STREET

A MUSICAL THRILLER

MUSIC AND LYRICS BY
STEPHEN SONDHEIM

BOOK BY
HUGH WHEELER

BASED ON A VERSION OF "SWEENEY TODD" BY CHRISTOPHER BOND

DIRECTED BY
HAROLD PRINCE

PRODUCTION DESIGNED BY
EUGENE LEE

COSTUMES DESIGNED BY
FRANNE LEE

LIGHTING DESIGNED BY
KEN BILLINGTON

ORCHESTRATIONS BY
JONATHAN TUNICK

MUSICAL DIRECTOR
PAUL GEMIGNANI

DANCE AND MOVEMENT BY **LARRY FULLER**

ASSOCIATE PRODUCERS
DEAN & JUDY MANOS

ASSISTANT TO MR. PRINCE
RUTH MITCHELL

Original Broadway Cast Recording on **RCA** Records and Tapes

URIS THEATRE
50th STREET WEST OF BROADWAY

"*Sweeney Todd,*" Sondheim said, "is built out of about three or four themes. Not all the songs, but most of them. It's not an opera—it's not completely through-composed, but a lot of it is."

BLOODY HELL

In terms of fictional nineteenth-century monsters, Sweeney Todd,
who would become the subject of Stephen Sondheim's 1979 masterwork,
was twenty years younger than Mary Shelley's creature in *Frankenstein*, forty
years older than Robert Louis Stevenson's Edward Hyde,* and fifty years older
than Bram Stoker's bloodsucking Dracula. Todd made his debut in 1846, in the
first installment of an eighteen-week serialization in populist London
publisher Edward Lloyd's *People's Periodical and Family Library*.

Lloyd also published the popular *Varney the Vampire* series, which appeared a year before Sweeney's introduction. Publisher Lloyd kept his authors anonymous, but later research revealed that both Varney and Sweeney were products of the imagination of James Malcolm Rymer, who, protecting his own social standing, was not particularly keen to be associated with Lloyd's "penny dreadfuls"—cheap, best-selling pulp periodicals for those who couldn't afford books.

Sweeney's tale was lurid. He was a homicidal barber on Fleet Street. "I'll cut your throat from ear to ear, if you repeat one word of what passes in this shop," he warns Tobias, a young apprentice whom he's in the process of hiring.

"Yes, sir, I won't say nothing . . . as I may be made into veal pies at Lovett's," the boy responds—referring to a shop run by a Mrs. Lovett, known for her meat pies, despite the sinister quality of their filling.

A year after his introduction on the page, Sweeney appeared on the stage, in *The String of Pearls*, by the actor-playwright–stage manager George Dibdin Pitt. The drama's subtitle was, "The Fiend of Fleet Street." Other stage versions followed, as did two British movies both titled *Sweeney Todd*, in 1926 and 1928, followed by a sound version in 1936 starring an appropriately named Tod Slaughter. In 1956, the same year he starred as Eliza Doolittle's father in Broadway's *My Fair Lady*, British music hall star Stanley Holloway recorded the seven-minute "Sweeney Todd, the Barber," credited to R. P.

---

* Alter ego of Dr. Henry Jekyll.

Weston, a writer of novelty songs and comic monologues who was active from 1906 to 1934. In 1959, Malcolm Arnold composed the score—much of it menacing sounding—for the Royal Ballet's *Sweeney Todd*.*

"It's not so dark," Sondheim said of his own interpretation of the Sweeney story, which, as adapted by Hugh Wheeler, was based on Liverpool actor-playwright Christopher Bond's 1973 *Sweeney Todd, The Demon Barber of Fleet Street*. That version was playing at the Theatre Royal Stratford East** when Sondheim was in London for Angela Lansbury's West End debut in *Gypsy*.

"I went to see it, thought it was terrific, and bought all the published versions—which were all terrible." Sondheim called Bond's version "much richer than the others."

Bond had fleshed out the barber, whose real name is Benjamin Barker, and given him a psychological raison d'être—make that razor d'être—for killing as a means of taking revenge on the crooked Judge Turpin, who framed him and sentenced him to a fifteen-year prison sentence in Australia. With Barker gone, Turpin rapes Barker's beautiful wife, Lucy, and adopts their daughter, Johanna, as his ward. Lucy swallows poison. Returning to London post prison sentence, Barker, now calling himself Sweeney Todd, enters into

THE BRITISH BEE HIVE.

TOP: The character of Sweeney Todd was first introduced in an 1846 serialized story called "The String of Pearls: A Domestic Romance." The pearls in question were snatched from a customer who made the mistake of sitting in Todd's barber chair on London's Fleet Street. Todd's parlor was located next to St. Dunstan's Church and connected to the pie shop of a certain Mrs. Lovett via underground passageway.

BOTTOM: Hal Prince told the *Sweeney Todd* ensemble, "You are prisoners in a factory and collectively driven to cannibalism. You never see the sun because of the soot that covers the roof of the factory." To convey that very message to the audience, a curtain displaying political caricaturist George Cruikshank's "British Bee Hive" hung onstage while the crowd took its seats. The illustration spelled out British society's pecking order.

---

* Both Holloway's "Sweeney Todd, the Barber" and "Malcolm Arnold: Sweeney Todd Suite Op. 68a" can be found on YouTube.

** *A Taste of Honey*, which coincidentally marked Angela Lansbury's Broadway debut when it moved to New York in 1960, and *Oh, What a Lovely War!* premiered with the Stratford's Theatre Workshop company.

an arrangement with his former landlady, Mrs. Lovett, who also happens to love him. (She kept the hairdressing parlor above her pie shop vacant the entire time he was imprisoned. She also safely stashed away his shaving knives.)

With the two now in cahoots, Sweeney goes on a murderous rampage the instant Judge Turpin escapes his clutches in the barber chair. Taking his anger out on others, the barber slits the throats of the victims who sit in his chair, and then he dispatches their corpses into the netherworld of the cellar below, to be ground up and used as filling for Mrs. Lovett's pies.

Her business success is short-lived, however, when Mrs. Lovett herself ends up in the oven at the hands of Sweeney, who disposes of her for having kept secret that the insane beggar woman on the street is, in fact, Barker's wife. After this horrible moment, the apprentice, Toby, slits Barker's throat out of an act of love for Mrs. Lovett.

"It's really kind of funny," Sondheim said. "I mean, nobody takes it seriously . . . it's melodrama. I don't think melodramas are dark."

True, he conceded, "There's a lot of blood," but he also argued, "The attitude is not a real attitude. They're all cartoon figures. I mean, it's an operetta. These are not real people, and they're not supposed to be. They're supposed to be big, larger than life."

Hal Prince, said Sondheim, "always thought it was about the Industrial Revolution,"* what the director viewed as "the collective slavery of sweatshops, assembly lines, the blocking out of nature, sunshine lost to the filthy fog spewing from the smokestacks of factories."

Said Sondheim, "I thought it was about scaring people."

—

Because of his work on *Pacific Overtures*, Sondheim did not begin writing songs for the British period piece until 1977. From the start, he and Prince differed on their visions for the show: Prince saw it as big, and Sondheim saw it as small. A new development also presented itself in terms of working relationship; for the first time since 1970, Prince would be directing the show without also serving as the producer.

Rights to Bond's play had already been secured by the American producers Richard Barr and Charles Woodward, whose previous New York stage credits included Mart Crowley's *The Boys in the Band*, Samuel Beckett's *Krapp's Last Tape*, and Edward Albee's *The Zoo Story* and *Who's Afraid of Virginia Woolf?* Because of the time and expense—the capitalization for *Sweeney* was $1 million—Woodward and Barr were joined by producers Robert Fryer and the husband-and-wife team of Martin Richards and Mary Lea Johnson. Johnson was a daughter of John Seward Johnson, whose father, Robert Wood Johnson, founded the Johnson & Johnson pharmaceutical company. Richards was a former singer and casting director who produced his first show with Fryer, in 1975: Bob Fosse's *Chicago*.** Among Fryer's other productions were *Wonderful Town*, *Auntie Mame*, *Sweet Charity*, *Noises Off*, and the movies *The Boston Strangler* and *Travels with My Aunt*.

---

* The attitude certainly played into people's fears of leaving the safety of an agrarian culture in the country for the degrading atmosphere of the crime- and filth-ridden city.

** Richards won the Oscar in 2003 when the film adaptation of *Chicago* was named Best Picture; he considered the honor "bittersweet" because Mary Lea Johnson and Robert Fryer were no longer living.

Sweeney also marked the first time Sondheim took an idea to Prince, instead of the usual other way around. For Prince, it was not love at first sight. "I don't get it," he told Sondheim. "It's a hoot and a howl, people's theatre, but why do it? It seems campy to me."

He said Sondheim persisted, again in a reversal of their usual roles. What tipped the scales was when Prince began to see Sweeney's act of revenge as an attack on the class system as symbolized by Judge Turpin's omnipotence.

"If Sweeney is victimized by the class system," said Prince, "so is everyone else in the show." That accounted for the decision to change the show's setting from the 1700s to the late nineteenth century, when "the conveyor belt pulled us further and further from harmony, from humanity, from nature," although Prince, along with Sondheim, Hugh Wheeler, and set designer Eugene Lee,* chose to keep the Industrial Revolution metaphor in mind. As far as the audience was concerned, it was only part of the subtext. Prince said that not a word of script needed to be changed.

"Bond's version was that absolutely unreal, old melodrama where you boo the villain," said Hugh Wheeler. "We wanted to make it as nearly as we could into a tragedy." Wheeler fashioned the book as a two-act play, incorporating not only elements of melodrama and Grand Guignol,** but eighteenth-century ballad opera, British music hall, and Brechtian epic theatre—with loosely connected adjunct scenes that addressed the main action.

Once the libretto was completed, said Wheeler, "I encouraged Steve to cannibalize it and make it nearly all music."

—

Sondheim had envisioned the show as a chamber opera staged in a dark, coffin-like setting that would keep audiences on the edges of their seats from beginning to end. "Smoke, some streetlamps, fog rising from the floor, and somebody would pop up beside you and scare you half to death," he said. His music would complement this

Hollywood composer Bernard Herrmann's score to the 1945 movie *Hangover Square*—which Sondheim had seen and adored at age fifteen—inspired Sondheim's own score for *Sweeney Todd*. In the film, the homicidal composer's concerto, with its moody, jagged dissonances, literally sets a concert hall ablaze.

---

* Boris Aronson (1898–1980) had retired.

** Paris's Pigalle District Le Théâtre du Grand-Guignol (1897–1962) specialized in offering naturalistic horror shows.

BUILDING A CATHEDRAL

"We analyzed a Bach fugue," Sondheim recalled of his student days with Milton Babbitt, when the instructor said, "You see, he takes these four notes, and he builds a cathedral out of them."

Sondheim let out an elated sigh.

"I had always appreciated Bach intellectually, but until we started analyzing what Bach was doing, it didn't get to my heart."

The lesson Sondheim learned was, "The four notes determine the entire structure of the piece. They determine the little counterphase . . . You don't have to write so many themes. You just take them and develop them and work with them."

Noting that this "implies many different kinds of harmonies, because you can harmonize any tune a thousand different ways," he said that the question then becomes, "What is the implicit harmony of the tune? And what is the implicit rhythmic stress of the tune? Do you want to maybe stretch that out for another purpose? Do you want to use it as accompaniment figures, or as counterfigures?

"The whole point," he said, "is [to] make the most out of the least . . . to me, the principle of all good art anyway, although Tolstoy might disagree."

sense of unease, and he long knew the source he wanted to emulate.

"When I was fifteen years old, I saw a movie called *Hangover Square*, another epiphany in my life," said Sondheim. "It was a moody, romantic, gothic thriller starring Laird Cregar, about a composer in London in 1900 who was ahead of his time. And whenever he heard a high note, he went crazy and ran around murdering people."

The trailer for the movie, which also starred Linda Darnell and George Sanders, promised "The true story of a murderer whose soul is in turn possessed by love of music, love of women, and the lust to kill!"

"It had an absolutely brilliant score by Bernard Herrmann,* centered around a one-movement piano concerto," said Sondheim, who wanted "to pay homage to the Hollywood composer with this show" because "I had realized that in order to scare people, which is what *Sweeney Todd* is about—the only way you can do it, considering that the horrors out on the street are so much greater than anything you can do on the stage, is to keep music going all the time."

Finding this to be "the principle of suspense sequences in movies," Sondheim said, "*Sweeney Todd* not only has a lot of singing, it has a lot of underscoring." Every main character has an individual motif, and Sondheim estimated that *Sweeney* contained only 20 percent dialogue. Depending on the production, there are anywhere between twenty-five to thirty songs.

The intensity of the music combined with the claustrophobia of the venue were meant "to keep the audience in a state of tension," Sondheim emphasized, "to make them forget they're in a theatre, and to prevent them from separating themselves from the action."

To that end, "I based a lot of the score on a specific chord that Herrmann uses in almost all his film work and spun it out from that."

Sondheim relied heavily on counterpoint, inversion, and angular harmonies. Another strong influence, plainly heard in "The Ballad of Sweeney Todd," which opens the show and is played throughout, was "Dies Irae," a thirteenth-century Latin poem used as a Requiem Mass, and which warns that the world will be reduced to ashes.

Sondheim said the work "is one of my favorite tunes and is full of menace."

---

* Herrmann scored several Alfred Hitchcock films, including *Vertigo*, *North by Northwest*, and *Psycho*.

—

Kiss the tight little coffin goodbye. *Sweeney*'s scenic designer Eugene Lee discovered an abandoned iron foundry in Rhode Island, where he had been the resident designer at Trinity Repertory Company in Providence since 1967.* Lee would convert the foundry's rambling rusty hulk into an oppressive Victorian Era factory for the *Sweeney* backdrop.

"Hal was not looking for a foundry," said Sondheim. "It's just that Eugene thought it would make the stylish setting that Prince was looking for." Prince said the producing team paid $25,000 for the structure so it could be dismantled and adjusted to the stage; the *Daily News* reported it cost $100,000 and took three weeks to move and resurrect.

Rather than the contained spook-house atmosphere that Sondheim desired, *Sweeney Todd* was destined for the vast Uris Theatre,** the biggest house on Broadway, only seventy seats shy of a two-thousand-person capacity. Because of the magnitude of the set and the production, there would be no out-of-town tryouts. *Sweeney* would get on its feet during a month of previews in front of a gossipy, hard-to-please New York theatre crowd. Prince claimed to be unfazed by the challenge; in London, he had directed Andrew Lloyd Webber and Tim Rice's *Evita**** for producer Robert Stigwood using the same tryout method, and it worked.

Setting the tone for the Industrial Age, Prince inserted a piercing factory whistle blast at the opening, which was heard immediately after the Uris houselights were dimmed. Two laborers dressed for the period then yanked down a silk banner displaying sociopolitical illustrator George Cruikshank's "British Bee Hive," "originally sketched in 1840," according to the British Museum, and depicting "a vast range of Britain's professions within a strictly divided pyramid-based social hierarchy." At the top—"by lineal descent," the illustration spells out—sat Queen Victoria.

Meanwhile, the *Sweeney Todd* audience had already been greeted by a macabre pre-show organ accompaniment while witnessing two gravediggers at work on the lip of the stage.

"I suggested it and auditioned several levels of sound until it was almost unbearable," Prince said of the steam whistle, which would also be heard again every time Sweeney slit a throat.

"Audiences found it unbearable, but we loved to torture them."

---

* Starting in 1975, Lee also was—and has remained, into his eighties—production designer of television's *Saturday Night Live*. In 2003, he would go gargantuan again with the sets to Broadway's *Wicked*.

** Opened in 1972 and renamed the Gershwin in 1983, it is still the largest-capacity theatre on Broadway.

*** The musical, about Argentina's Eva Perón, began as a rock opera concept album released in 1976.

SUREFIRE RECIPE

THE STRANGER AT MRS. LOVETT'S PIE SHOP.

Variations of the character's name included its spelling as Lovatt, as seen in this nineteenth-century illustration for "A String of Pearls." But by any other name, the filling of her meat pies was always the same.

As the tale was spun over the years, Sweeney's accomplice in his nefarious deeds, Mrs. Lovett, went by various Christian names: Amelia, Margery, Maggie, Sarah, Shirley, Wilhelmina, Claudetta, and, most commonly, and as applied in the musical, Nellie.

Her husband's cause of death—he was sometimes identified as Albert—was either from dropsy (an archaic term for edema) or plain old mysterious circumstances. In one version, she and Sweeney met because he was familiar with her pie shop and had run out of places to dump his victims, having all but filled the crypts beneath St. Dunstan's Church.

In the original serial adaptation, Sweeney wasn't out for vengeance; he killed to steal valuables from his victims, and as barbers in those days also doubled as medical practitioners, he was assured no shortage of customers.

Packing human remains into meat pies was a practical solution for them both.

The police eventually caught onto their scheme, but not until word of their handiwork had leaked out to the public. Mrs. Lovett was nearly torn to bits by an outraged mob before police escorted her to Newgate Prison. Sweeney was arrested without incident.

She confessed behind bars, and Sweeney was hanged.

Mrs. Lovett poisoned herself before she met the same fate.

—

Prince and Sondheim did not see eye to eye on the casting of Mrs. Lovett. Prince wanted Patricia Routledge, who would not become familiar to American audiences until she played the hilariously pretentious suburban housewife Hyacinth Bucket on the 1990s BBC sitcom *Keeping Up Appearances.*

Sondheim nixed the choice. "Not sexy enough," he said. "I think Angie would be just perfect."

Angie was Angela Lansbury, but Prince had already put in a call to Routledge in the UK. In fact, he connected Len Cariou—who was already cast in his mind to play Sweeney—with Rutledge on the phone from Vienna, where Prince was directing the film version of *A Little Night Music* with Cariou reprising his Broadway role as Fredrik.

"It's scary having anything to do with it," Routledge told Cariou about *Sweeney.* "When we were kids, it was always something to be afraid of. Even my parents would say to me, 'You'd better be careful, or we'll get Sweeney Todd after you.'"

Sondheim kept pressing for Lansbury. Theatre critic and Lansbury biographer Martin Gottfried suggested that Prince was aware that the *Mame* and *Gypsy* star, and

multiple Tony winner, was the wiser choice, but she was also a more obvious choice, and Sondheim and Prince were now well established for avoiding the obvious. Then again, there was the commercial failure of *Pacific Overtures* to consider; would it not be advantageous to go with a bigger name this time, especially with material of such a downbeat nature?

Not that Sondheim was having an easy go at convincing Lansbury to take the part. "Listen, Steve," she told him, "your show is not called *Nellie Lovett*. It's called *Sweeney Todd*. And I'm not the second banana."

Sondheim countered with, "You carry all the comic weight," but that was not yet evident in the script.

"The score was so huge and sonorous in places," remembered Lansbury, "we had to lighten it." She admitted to going broad with the character, but "what she was doing was despicable and terrible," so the leading lady sensed there was some comic leeway. The question was, how much?

"Hal is a great audience" and "will sit there and laugh," yet Lansbury also recalled his being so hands-off that she thought, "Gee, we're doing this by ourselves. Is this going to be all right?"

"When an actor says, 'I created the character,' I used to think, 'No, you didn't; the authors did,'" said Sondheim. "But I came to understand what it means from their

"The wide-openness of my portrayal had to do with my sink-or-swim attitude toward it," Angela Lansbury said of her *Sweeney Todd* character. "I just figured hell, I've done everything else on Broadway, I might as well go with Mrs. Lovett."

Angela Lansbury as Nellie Lovett and Len Cariou as Sweeney Todd, né Benjamin Barker. Cariou had also starred in *A Little Night Music*. "I've been in two of the best musicals ever written," he told journalist Michael Portantiere in 2016. "Both have Hugh Wheeler in common as book writer, and he doesn't get enough credit."

point of view. Angie would question a line or an emotion or an attitude and say, 'This seems inconsistent.' And if I agreed with her, I changed it. I mean, that's what you do with actors, right?"

Lansbury additionally expressed her doubts about audiences accepting a piece so dark. She, too, had grown up on tales of Sweeney Todd and still felt unsettled by them, and she worried that Americans who were not familiar with his legend would be completely turned off. As Lansbury bluntly asked one journalist when the two spoke privately in her apartment while *Sweeney Todd* was still in previews, "Do you think anyone is going to come and see this?"

Known throughout most of her career for her professionalism as well as her pragmatism, Lansbury later said, "Once the audience had been told by the critics that it was okay, then they went for it."

———

At *Sweeney*'s first public preview, Len Cariou accidentally sprayed stage blood all over conductor Paul Gemignani's music sheets. The blood remained throughout the run, "because it looked so cool," said Gemignani. There were also several walkouts during

A FINE BALANCE BETWEEN MUSICAL AND OPERA

The Houston Grand Opera was the first opera company to perform *Sweeney Todd*, in 1984, in a production directed by Hal Prince and starring Timothy Nolen and Joyce Castle.

The work was revived by the same company in 2015, in a coproduction with the San Francisco Opera and starring Nathan Gunn and Susan Bullock.

In 2011, Théâtre du Châtelet presented *Sweeney* with fifty musicians in the pit. Sondheim told the cast that this production was "his dream *Sweeney*," according to American baritone Rod Gilfry, who sang the title role in Paris.

"*Sweeney*," said Gilfry, "is on the border of musical theater and opera. The roles of Beadle [Judge Turbin's lackey] and Dr. Pirelli [Sweeney's barber rival] have to be classically trained tenors. Pirelli has a high D and high C. Most musical theater singers don't have the chops for that."

Added Gilfry, "*Sweeney* is best done by opera companies."

Stephen Sondheim disagreed, publicly stating that he always considered *Sweeney* to be an

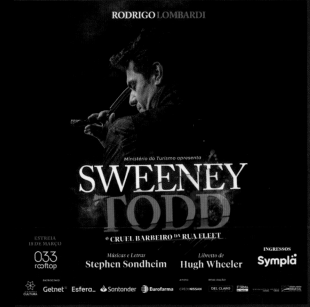

operetta, despite notable productions by the New York City Opera, the Lyric Opera of Chicago, and the Royal Opera House in Covent Garden.

"If it's useful to critics and journalists to have a label as a way of guiding a reader, okay, fine. I find it unimportant."

Conversely, "I do think it's completely arbitrary and very easy to argue that certain operas are musicals. Is *Carmen* an opera or a musical? It's a song-opera. *Carmen* is like *Porgy [and Bess]*. It's almost all sung, but it's essentially songs."

Opera fans are enamored with the performer's voice, not the song, Sondheim told music critic Mark Stryker, along with a reminder that he was raised on musicals and was no opera fan.

"When I go to an opera, I go for the story and the music. If the singer is wonderful, that's gravy. People who love opera are willing to put up with the longueurs. In fact, they enjoy them because they allow the singer to shine. That's the thrill."

Asked if there was one opera that he liked, Sondheim chose Alban Berg's *Wozzeck*—which, like *Sweeney*, features an outsized outcast as its lead.

Berg's 1925 avant-garde work, with its suggestions of military sadism, "says just enough when it's supposed to say it," said Sondheim.

"*Wozzeck* is not a song-opera. It's just one long piece of music."

ACROSS SPREAD:
Productions of *Sweeney Todd* endure around the globe, as evidenced by those in Penzance, UK (2018, opposite top); City of Parañaque, Philippines (2019, opposite bottom); São Paulo, Brazil (2022, above); and Des Moines, Iowa (2023, top).

intermission. Producer Martin Richards claimed a woman hit him with her pocketbook for presenting such a disgusting spectacle on the stage.

"It was three hours long," Cariou said of the first performance. "We had all sorts of problems getting the pie shop on and off the stage." The actors vamped; the intermission ran forty-five minutes so stage technicians could adjust. "For the audience," said Cariou, "that performance was unfair."

Initial word of mouth was not good, but that is often the case at a first preview, especially when there are big names attached. Cariou said that those who remained in the audience on that first night rose to their feet at the end of Act II, and Sondheim met the actor at his dressing room door after the performance.

"They got it," Sondheim said, and the two embraced.

The word at various Broadway hangouts during early previews was decidedly mixed, but it kept improving as the show was tightened. There was even a growing chorus of admirers.

"I think the most unbelievable job of music writing, and I say this with deep reverence and envy," Jule Styne said, "is *Sweeney Todd*."

Not that all the professional reactions were so complimentary. "Disgusting, enough to make you want to throw up in your galoshes! I guess Steve finally got to write a musical that suits his temperament perfectly," Mary Rodgers, paraphrasing Leonard Bernstein's reaction to the show, reported. She chalked up Bernstein's reaction to his own inability to match the unlabored musical flow Sondheim had achieved with *Sweeney*.

The draw of Lansbury, stellar reviews, and eight Tony awards (out of nine nominations), including awards for both lead actors, Sondheim's score, Prince's direction,

"Sweeney and Mrs. Lovett must possess exceptional stage presence, sophisticated knowledge and expertise in music and singing, remarkable acting chops, and physical stamina," director and educator Kent Thompson wrote in his 2019 book *Directing Professionally*. Here, Cariou and Lansbury shown midperformance.

Maternal and murderous: Mrs. Lovett comforts her assistant Toby (Ken Jennings) as she realizes the simple boy has learned too much. He has promised to protect her from the demons that lurk around them ("Not While I'm Around"), only to discover firsthand just who those demons are.

and Best Musical,* propelled the show to 557 performances. In spite of the show's success, *Sweeney* offered investors only a 59 percent return on their initial outlay. Dorothy Loudon, who won a Tony for her role as Miss Hannigan in 1977's *Annie*, and George Hearn, who would later win a Tony as the flamboyant Alban in the 1983 *La Cage aux Folles*, replaced Lansbury and Cariou, and they added four months to the show's run. Hal Prince's final takeaway on the production was that cannibalism is a hard sell.

The 1980 London production, with Denis Quilley and Sheila Hancock, got thrashed by the critics, whose reviews basically let the American creators know they had gotten too big for their britches. The show closed after only 157 performances.

It was a dark period all around. Sondheim had suffered a heart attack three weeks after *Sweeney Todd* opened on Broadway, leaving him "seriously depressed" after his hospitalization.

"I got home, was starting to recuperate, then one morning thought, 'I don't want to live.' I guess it was a delayed reaction to the heart attack. The next day I woke up perfectly fine."

He also stopped smoking and reassessed his diet and physical exercise regime.

Sondheim was forty-nine.

---

* In his acceptance speech, Charles Woodward, speaking for all the producers, thanked the 260 investors in the show, noting "most of them have never invested in the theatre before." He also acknowledged the 150 "from all over the country" who had responded to the producers' *New York Times* ad asking for money.

Sweeney Todd movie director Tim Burton (standing) "likes the musical, and he's not a particular fan of stage musicals," said Sondheim, seen here chatting with Helena Bonham Carter, who played Mrs. Lovett in the film. "But something about this spoke to him, and I absolutely trusted that."

Angela Lansbury and George Hearn filmed *Sweeney Todd* for PBS in 1982, directed by Terry Hughes. Tim Burton directed the 2007 movie version starring Johnny Depp and Helena Bonham Carter. The $50 million production, based on a script by playwright and screenwriter John Logan (*Gladiator*), grossed more than $150 million.

"I'd never heard of Sondheim," said Burton, who stumbled upon the show. "The first time on stage I saw them singing 'Johanna,' and with the throat, you know, the blood, I thought, 'This is a unique juxtaposition of music and image, like a great movie score.'"

Burton originally approached Sondheim about the film rights in the late 1980s. "I said fine," said Sondheim. "Then he went off and did other things." Among them: *Beetlejuice, Batman, Edward Scissorhands, The Nightmare Before Christmas*. But Burton circled back, with Depp on board. He also imagined it, like Sondheim had originally, as an old horror movie.

The film's palette was black-and-white, except for the blood. "We had done tests and experiments with the neck slashing, with the blood popping out," said the film's producer, Richard D. Zanuck. "I remember saying to Tim, 'My god, do we dare do this?'"

Depp modeled his Sweeney on horror leads of the past: Lon Chaney, Boris Karloff, Bela Lugosi, Peter Lorre, and Elsa Lanchester—adapting the Bride of Frankenstein's signature hair streak, which culture writer Sylviane Gold likened to the hair streak sported by intellectual writer Susan Sontag.

According to Bonham Carter, who was domestically partnered with Burton at the time of filming, Sondheim was hesitant about her casting because she was not a singer, while, because of his star power, no one questioned Depp's voice—except Depp. "I may sound like a strangled cat," he warned Burton.

"The fact that he came from a musical background, a rock band, even though he was not a lead singer," Sondheim said, "I knew he was musical."

While driving to the location for the 2007 *Pirates of the Caribbean: At World's End*, Johnny Depp prepared to play Sweeney Todd onscreen by spending "two hours to work and two hours back listening constantly, learning the melodies in the car." With him here, Helena Bonham Carter.

In adapting the Sondheim score for his movie, Burton chucked "The Ballad of Sweeney Todd" into the meat grinder, considering it a stage device that wouldn't translate to the screen, although some thought was given to having horror star Christopher Lee deliver it as a newly written character called the Gentleman Ghost. "It would have been worse if I had done the scenes," said the actor, "but I never got to film them. It's a shame, as the lyrics were wonderful."

With Sondheim's approval, as his contract stipulated, slashes to the property were made. These included Johanna's "Green Finch and Linnet Bird" and the customers' number outside the pie shop, "God, That's Good!" Sondheim also suggested some occasional note changes. He was kept up to date in New York via MP3 files that were sent to him during the fifty days of filming that took place at Pinewood Studios outside London. Jonathan Tunick beefed up the orchestrations from the twenty-seven musicians* that Paul Gemignani had conducted at the Uris to seventy-eight for the big-screen sound Burton desired.

"As the bodies pile up—and land with a sickening squishiness when they slide down the chute from Sweeney's parlor to the basement—the more sensitive may avert their eyes and turn from the movie," *Time* critic Richard Corliss wrote in his glowing review. "But this is gore with an agenda. Having seen where Sweeney came from, and the artistry Burton and Depp bring to his tale, we must keep watching."

Or, as Tim Burton called it, "*The Sound of Music*—with blood!"

---

* Sondheim thanked them, along with Paul Gemignani and Jonathan Tunick, in his Tony acceptance speech.

TAKING *SWEENEY* DOWN TO SIZE

Sweeney Todd had its own Industrial Revolution in 2005, when Scottish director John Doyle mounted a minimalist production on Broadway, with Michael Cerveris and Patti LuPone wielding their knives—and, like members of the rest of the pared-down cast, playing their own musical instruments.

In LuPone's case, that instrument was a tuba.

"It opened the door for other shows," Doyle said, and "allowed for the fact that musicals could be something other than spectacle."

Michael Cerveris and Patti LuPone as Todd and Mrs. Lovett, directed by John Doyle at the Eugene O'Neill Theatre in 2005. "His work demands everything. You have to be intelligent, passionate, emotional, disciplined, and reckless," Cerveris said of Sondheim. "But it also rewards you by making you look good."

This modified mindset continued not only with Doyle's productions of practically every Sondheim title at New York's Classic Stage Company in the East Village, where Doyle served as the artistic director from 2016 until 2022, but also on Broadway, where the glitz was temporarily given a rest and a new generation of shows were welcomed, including *Once*, *The Band's Visit*, *Hadestown*, and *A Strange Loop*—Best Musical Tony winners all.

Doyle was awarded Tonys, too, for his direction of *Sweeney* and his 2006 revival of *Company*, as Best Revival.

"If somebody had said to me, 'That's it: After this, you're not going to direct anymore,' I wouldn't have been devastated. Instead, my life has completely changed," said Doyle, in 2008, as the accolades for *Sweeney Todd* were still pouring in, and he was preparing to make his directorial debut at New York's Metropolitan Opera with *Peter Grimes*, as well as revising Sondheim's *Merrily We Roll Along* for a UK production at the Watermill Theatre in Berkshire.

"Sometimes, when I think maybe it will all end, I think, at least I've got to meet my heroes and sit on Stephen Sondheim's sofa."

In addition to Angela Lansbury, Dorothy Loudon, Sheila Hancock, and Patti LuPone rolling the pie dough, Mrs. Lovett has also been played onstage by the likes of June Havoc, Julia McKenzie, Joanna Lumley, Christine Baranski, Felicity Palmer, Elaine Paige, Judy Kaye, Imelda Staunton, Emma Thompson, and, in Manila and Singapore,

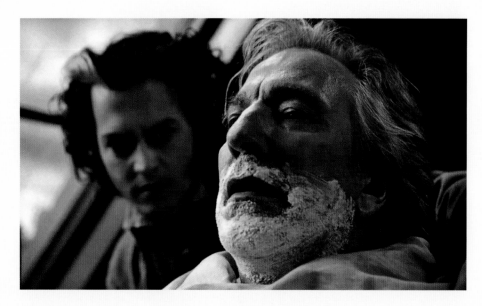

Alan Rickman played evil Judge Turpin, shown here with a lurking Sweeney (Depp) studying his throat as if he were Dracula. "One of the miracles of the film is you kind of forget that it's a musical," Rickman said, "because the speaking and the singing melt into each other."

Lea Salonga. Productions continue to take place all over the world.

In early 2023, Josh Groban and Annaleigh Ashford led a $14-million full-scale Broadway revival of the work, with a cast of twenty-six and, like the 1979 original, an orchestra of twenty-seven. *Hamilton* Tony winner Thomas Kail directed. (Perhaps the ultimate dream cast of the musical still remains to be seen; in 2017, on the BBC's *The Graham Norton Show*, with the principals he mentioned sitting on-camera beside him, Patrick Stewart proposed a *Sweeney Todd* starring Hugh Jackman as Sweeney, Stewart as Judge Turpin—and Ian McKellen as Mrs. Lovett.)

The same month the Groban-Ashford version was to open, the Disney+ streaming service planned to debut a ten-episode animated version of *Sweeney Todd*. The Sondheim score was to be discarded while serving as "the basis of new songs by a rotating stable of songwriters, including *Dear Evan Hansen*'s Benj Pasek and Justin Paul, *Waitress*'s Sara Bareilles, and *Come From Away*'s David Hein and Irene Sankoff," stated a press release.

"I have been inspired by the work of Stephen Sondheim throughout my career as a storyteller," said lead animator Dana Terrace. "I am so honored to be able to carry on his legacy through this new animated series, which will not shy away from the darkest truths of human suffering and depravity, but instead shape them into bite-sized twenty-three-minute 'snacks' you can stream on any device."

Tempus fugit.

—

"I think, if you go through the history of art," Sondheim reflected later in life, "I'll bet you find that the peak of the bell curve is in the forties. I think that's when people are at the combination of their most vigorous and let's call it 'mature.'"

The period also marked "when Hal had just gotten confident as a director, in his late thirties and early forties, so that when we started to work together as writer and director, we were both at our most confident and our most arrogant—meaning, we could try different things, and the shows were successful enough, contrary to popular opinion, so that we could afford to take risks, because people had enough faith in him so he could raise the money."

Furthermore, Sondheim said, "we both were sure of ourselves. And all the writers I chose to write with in those days were in the same boat."

Meaning: "The stuff we wrote was confident."

Sondheim "said it was going to be like a Jule Styne or Irving Berlin musical," orchestrator Jonathan Tunick recalled about 1981's *Merrily We Roll Along*. "And then what was presented to me was a show full of anger and ill will, pessimism and hurt."

TIME TRAVELERS

In keeping with the narrative structure of *Merrily We Roll Along*—which is told in chronological order but backward—this book's account of Sondheim's musical begins in the future, with what will be the 2040 premiere of the movie adaptation of the 1981 Stephen Sondheim–George Furth–Hal Prince musical version of the 1934 George S. Kaufman–Moss Hart melodrama *Merrily We Roll Along*. Easy enough to follow?

Richard Linklater's movie adaptation of *Merrily We Roll Along* has been shooting since 2019. Like the extended production schedule that he took on for his celebrated film, *Boyhood*, the filming of *Merrily We Roll Along* will take place intermittently over the course of many years. Because *Merrily* covers *twenty* years in the relationship of three friends, its long-term production schedule poses more than a few risks. As history has shown, risk is inherent in any project involving Sondheim, otherwise it wouldn't be worth its salt.

The three friends in *Merrily* are Franklin Shepard, a Broadway composer who discards his pals and becomes a Hollywood producer; Charley Kringas, Frank's neurotic but enlightened lyricist partner; and Mary Flynn, a cynical writer unrequitedly in love with Frank and seldom in control of her drinking. (The original characters in the Kaufman and Hart play were Richard, a pretentious playwright of popular shows; Jonathan, a nonconformist painter with high principles; and Julia, a tart-tongued novelist based on Dorothy Parker.)

The theme of the 1934 play and the 1981 musical and, presumably, the 2040 movie is that ambition trumps friendship. The score, arguably, is Sondheim's most robust and varied, as the 1981 original cast album produced by Thomas Z. Shepard* will attest, as will the numerous cabaret and recorded performances of *Merrily*'s "Not a Day Goes By"** and "Old Friends." To carry that message, Linklater cast his movie using actors with musical experience: Paul Mescal (*Carmen*) as Frank, Beanie Feldstein (*Funny Girl*) as Mary, and Ben Platt (*Dear Evan Hansen*) as Charley—who gets to deliver a tour-de-force mental breakdown set to music, called "Franklin Shepard, Inc."

Eighteen years ahead of the movie, in 2022, Daniel Radcliffe played Charley to Lindsay Mendez's

---

* For whom Franklin Shepard was named, in part.

** Which bears a kinship to *Follies'* "Losing My Mind"; Barbara Cook blended them into a medley.

From left: Daniel Radcliffe, Jonathan Groff, and Lindsay Mendez as old friends Charley, Frank, and Mary in director Maria Friedman's December 2022 New York Theatre Workshop revamp of *Merrily We Roll Along*. The engagement, which sold out and also pleased critics, prompted a planned move to Broadway for fall 2023.

Mary and Jonathan Groff's Franklin in a heartily anticipated revival of *Merrily*, directed by Maria Friedman. In 2012, she had staged a well-received London production that was filmed and shown in movie theatres the following year. The 2022 Friedman-Radcliffe version took place at the New York Theatre Workshop on East Fourth Street, where *Rent*, *Slave Play*, and *Hadestown* had previously been born.

"Sondheim's genius was that he left space for every actor to bring their own life into play," said Friedman. "He was open to new interpretations and would roar with laughter when you came up with something he had not thought of."

She also said, "He wrote about people's complexities and relished them. There was never any judgment about people being fractured. He was a kind, loyal man, but God, he could be very . . . direct."

—

The New York Theatre Workshop production was preceded, in 2019, by a deconstructed, intermission-less *Merrily* that was presented by the Fiasco Theater, a troupe

From left: Kenneth MacKenna, Walter Abel, and Mary Philips, who respectively played the characters Richard Niles, Jonathan Crale, and Julia Glenn in George S. Kaufman and Moss Hart's 1934 play *Merrily We Roll Along*. This trio was converted into Franklin Shepard, Charley Kringas, and Mary Flynn for the 1981 musical.

in New York founded in 2009 by three graduates of the Brown/Trinity Rep MFA program: Jessie Austrian, Noah Brody, and Ben Steinfeld.

"We wanted to get in there and have a conversation with Steve," said Brody, who directed the production, which attracted curiosity seekers, Sondheim fans, and mixed reviews.

What immediately surprised the trio "was that he was incredibly open to our ideas," even "some of what we thought were our boldest." More than that, "he would go much further than any of us. He would say, 'Well, if you are going to do that, then why not do this?'" said Steinfeld. "He was a true collaborator."

Seven years prior, in 2012, there were three major productions of *Merrily* in three separate outposts: a New York City Center Encores! concert that featured Colin Donnell as Frank, Celia Keenan-Bolger as Mary, and Lin-Manuel Miranda as Charley; a Cincinnati Playhouse in the Park production directed by John Doyle with Malcolm Gets, Becky Ann Baker, and Daniel Jenkins; and Maria Friedman's London adaptation with Mark Umbers, Jenna Russell, and Damian Humbley.

Friedman's version transferred to the West End for three months, but problems with the book, including an explanation for why Frank repudiates Mary and Charley, remained difficult to resolve.

The bonhomie among cast and crew that greeted the 1981 development of *Merrily*—and the emotional wreckage that followed its critical reception* and immediate demise—can be witnessed in *Best Worst Thing That Ever Could Have Happened*, a feature-length 2016 documentary by original cast member Lonny Price, who was twenty-two at the time he opened on Broadway in the role of Charley Kringas.

His clear-focused film succeeds in showing viewers what it's like to be a young actor singing and dancing in New York. Price captures the blood, sweat, and fears of the cast and creators, showing them as their younger selves (thanks to uncovered ABC News footage) and in fresh interviews thirty-five years after *Merrily*'s opening and closing.

"It was beyond devastating," said Price of the show's sudden death. "Being in that show was everything I had ever wanted."

A Q&A followed the documentary's premiere at the New York Film Festival, where an emotional Sondheim said that he felt he had let the kids down. Hal Prince voiced the same sentiment. Lonny Price related a story from the show's final performance, its sixteenth, and how Prince came to his dressing room.

"He said, 'I'm sorry I didn't give you a hit.' And, when he left, I started to cry because I felt so bad for him. Because to me it was all kind of a gift and glorious. I think Hal is now finally aware, from the film, what a gift he gave us."

---

* As George S. Kaufman would have said, "We got mixed reviews. They were good and rotten."

After *Merrily*, Price graduated to a successful directing career, not only of shows but of events, such as Sondheim's eightieth birthday celebration. Another supporting player from the original cast, Jason Alexander, who was described at twenty-one by Sondheim "as if he had been born middle-aged," went on to play George Costanza on TV's *Seinfeld.** Ann Morrison, who originated the role of Mary, parlayed her performance into other musical roles and established herself on the cabaret circuit, although the path was not easy. Jim Walton, who was catapulted into the role of Frank, continued to find work on Broadway supplemented by his work as the superintendent in his Hell's Kitchen apartment building; he also fathered a child with *Merrily* swing dancer Janie Gleason.

Best Worst Thing That Ever Could Have Happened offered a postscript, suggesting, perhaps, that life can merrily roll along: Many members of the original cast had children who became actors and went on to perform the show all over the world in revised versions that have been embraced by new and more accepting audiences.

—

"As for why I stopped working with Hal," said Sondheim, after he and Prince parted professional ways following the 1981 Broadway collapse of *Merrily*, "he stopped working with me is what happened. He wanted to go off and do other things. He's always worked with other people, and one forgets that directors work with many more people than writers do because it takes much longer to write a show than it does to direct one. And he worked with many other people before our last collaboration."

Prince maintained that if *Merrily* had been a hit, he and Sondheim would have kept working together. "But it flopped, and we both moved on. Of course, I still miss the creative sessions." Sondheim shared the same feeling. The two remained friends.**

Furth continued to tinker with the libretto. He dropped the opening and closing high school graduation scenes and made several other fixes. After he attended a Los Angeles production of William Finn's *March of the Falsettos*, which James Lapine had first directed at Playwrights Horizons in New York, Furth contacted Lapine in the hope that he might bring a fresh approach to *Merrily*. Sondheim was hesitant to revisit the show after its brutal reception on Broadway, but an opportunity arose in La Jolla in 1985. A revised version was tried out and considered an improvement over the original. Still, that production never came to New York.

"I think it's a terrific show, and I thought it was a terrific show even back then when everybody was leaping on it with both feet," Sondheim said around 1998. "I think the major problem with the 1981 production was the production and the casting, and we were all responsible for it—that wasn't just Hal. It was a notion, the idea of casting young and, therefore, inexperienced people, that didn't work out."

Rather than take middle-aged actors and make them look and behave young for those scenes that required it—at one point Franklin Shepard is supposed to be forty-three***—Prince did the reverse: He hired kids and tried to make them look middle-

---

* In 1989, the same year Alexander won a Tony for Leading Actor in a Musical, for *Jerome Robbins' Broadway*.

** Hal Prince died in 2019, at age ninety-one.

*** Jim Walton was twenty-six.

"I THOUGHT, 'MY GOD'"

Darrell Brown has written, arranged, and produced Grammy-winning pop and country songs for and with LeAnn Rimes, Keith Urban, John Mayer, Josh Turner, Neil Young, and others, and it is estimated that his work has sold some seventy-seven million units.

But in 1982, when the Nashville and Los Angeles resident was barely nineteen, he applied for the first ASCAP pop songwriters' workshop, which was being led by Rupert Holmes and set to take place in New York over a twelve-week period.

"I had been playing piano for vocal coaches at the time," said Brown, who won a slot in the workshop. "One night during these twelve weeks, I met these people from the Norwegian Orchestra, including the concert master. They said, 'Come to lunch tomorrow. We're meeting Stephen Sondheim and Hal Prince.' I thought, 'My God.'"

The lunch was to take place on Monday, except, for some reason unknown to Brown, the Norwegian Orchestra left town.

"Naïve as I was," Brown remembered, "that Monday morning I called Hal Prince's office and left a message asking Stephen Sondheim to call me."

Soon enough, the phone rang. "Is Darrell Brown there? This is Steve Sondheim."

"I explained about the Norwegian Orchestra," Brown recalled, "and he said, 'I don't know anybody at the Norwegian Orchestra.' I said, 'No, really,' and he said, 'I have no lunch plans with anybody,' and he started getting really angry."

At that point, Brown uttered "I'm so sorry" into the telephone so many times that he lost count. "And, finally, he said, 'Why did they want you to meet me?'"

"I'm a young songwriter," Brown answered, and Sondheim's voice dropped. "'Oh,' he said. Then, silence."

Somehow, Brown got up the nerve to say, "'Mr. Sondheim, can I meet you?' And, to my amazement, he said, 'What are you doing now?'

"So, I combed my hair, brushed my teeth, put on deodorant," and Brown raced from where he was staying in Midtown to Sondheim's Turtle Bay townhouse.

"I walk in, and he introduces me to Betty Comden and Adolph Green. They were judging the Young Playwrights Awards. So, I sat down at the table, and we ended up having dinner. They were all so kind."

Afterward, Sondheim started to keep track of Brown's songwriting progress, heard his music, and a friendship developed.

"Every week we had dinner. He was working on *Sunday in the Park with George* at the time, and, one day, he said to me, 'Sit down and play me a song.' I nervously touched his piano. He listened to my song, which I thought was complete, only when I played it for him, I could tell it wasn't. He didn't scold me. He didn't point out where the corners came apart. He asked me where I thought they came apart, and what was my own reaction. He was the first person to tell me how to experience what I was feeling. He was the first, and it was *him*."

One particular incident lingers in Brown's memory. Sondheim played him the score to *Merrily We Roll Along*, which had been shot down by Broadway critics (and audiences) the year before.

Darrell Brown turned a faux pas into a friendship with Sondheim.

"He said, 'I don't understand. They asked me to give this to them, I gave this to them, and then they threw it back at me.' And as he was saying this, he suddenly looked twenty-five to thirty years younger, like a physical transformation had taken place. He was in his fifties at the time, but the young man in him came out. It was remarkable. He looked young all over again. I didn't know what to say. All I could think to do was put my arm around his shoulder."

Brown's professional songwriting started to take off four years later, and the friendship with Sondheim gradually went from weekly dinners to monthly, tri-monthly, yearly, and then occasional phone conversations.

"He ended up in a very nice personal relationship with someone, and his time became precious. I understand. But his affinity for helping people on their way up—what can I say? He knew everything started in chaos. He knew you had to go into the ether and cross the dream line, and then bring back the chaos. You get to edit it, change things, and move things around. He knew the process and the beautiful turmoil required for that birthing to take place.

"Only as I got older was I able to understand the multiverse dimensions of the gifts he put before me.

"He knew who he was, and the influence he had, the weight he carried, and he also knew that vulnerability is not a weakness, but a superpower."

aged at the start of the show, then allowed them to become their younger selves as the plot progressed backward in time.

Prince agreed he could never come to grips with how the production should look. Usually, he relied on the scenery, but a metaphor like the one he found for *Sweeney Todd* never materialized for *Merrily*. (Eugene Lee again did the scenic design.) "We decided on a gymnasium for the basic set," said Prince. "Bad idea."

"It's one of the few times in his life when he's made such a mistake," said Sondheim. "The idea was fine: He wanted to do the show as if it were put on by kids, as if they had designed the costumes and the sets, and unfortunately, when he got to looking at it during the tech rehearsals, he realized he had made a mistake, and so had to do the best he could to retract and try to make the show work by putting on those sweatshirts and things like that." The sweatshirts worn by the actors spelled out who their characters were, either their names ("Frank," "Mary," "Charley") or where they stood: "Best Friend," "Ex-Wife," and so on.

"But the set was always oppressive," said Sondheim, "and there was nothing one could do about it."

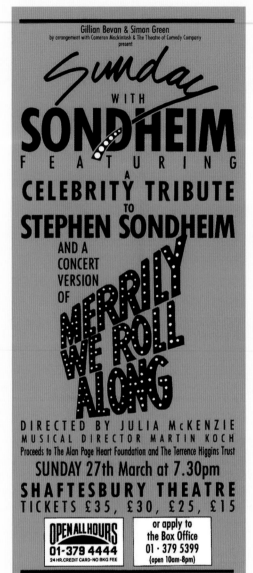

Gillian Bevan & Simon Green
by arrangement with Cameron Mackintosh & The Theatre of Comedy Company
present

Sunday

WITH

SONDHEIM

FEATURING

A

CELEBRITY TRIBUTE

TO

STEPHEN SONDHEIM

AND A CONCERT VERSION OF

MERRILY WE ROLL ALONG

DIRECTED BY JULIA McKENZIE
MUSICAL DIRECTOR MARTIN KOCH
Proceeds to The Alan Page Heart Foundation and The Terrence Higgins Trust

SUNDAY 27th March at 7.30pm
SHAFTESBURY THEATRE
TICKETS £35, £30, £25, £15

OPEN ALL HOURS
01·379 4444
24 HR. CREDIT CARD·NO BKG FEE

or apply to
the Box Office
01·379 5399
(open 10am-8pm)

LEFT, OPPOSITE, AND FOLLOWING SPREAD: Hopping the *Merrily* bandwagon: Despite its swift departure from Broadway, the vehicle has gotten a lot of mileage through the years, thanks to its stirring score and near-constant efforts to snap its book into shape. Here, various posters herald the show's arrival in London's West End (1988, left), Philadelphia's Temple University (2015, opposite), Northwestern University in Evanston, Illinois (2022, following spread left), and Southwest London (2022, following spread right).

Previews proved difficult. Theatregoers found themselves lost in the incomprehensible book, with its twenty-six different characters; walkouts became a nightly routine. "The hatred the audience had for the show was so intense that it put up a curtain between them and the performers," remembered Robert Hofler, who went on to be an editor at *Life* and *Variety*. "The rejection was that intense."

The gossip columnist Liz Smith, normally a booster of Broadway shows, ran a lead item that tracked 140 walkouts during one preview alone. Daisy Prince, daughter of Hal, was a member of the cast and gave her father nightly reports about how many members of the audience they were losing. By Act II, the Alvin Theatre was half-empty.

"I went to bed night after night in flop sweat," said Hal.

"George and I talked about flaws in the piece," said Sondheim.

The problem, the writers concurred, was "that nobody's interested in a selfish, venal compromiser."

"Like *Pacific Overtures* and *Sweeney Todd*," said Sondheim, "the *Merrily* score is very much inter-related. Blocks of music are utilized in different contexts and time periods to suggest the emotional colors underlying the relationships."

This resulted in a consolidation of musical themes. "Usually," he said, "you start with the song in the first act and then you might have fragments or a full reprise in the second act. I thought, 'Well, suppose we start with the fragments.'"

"Our Time" goes into "Rich and Happy." "Like It Was" goes into "Old Friends" and "Good Thing Going." "The Hills of Tomorrow" / "Merrily We Roll Along" goes like "One Foot, Other Foot," in Rodgers and Hammerstein's *Allegro*; the theme comes and goes throughout.

The score also contained that rare thing in a Sondheim musical: a traditional overture, and this one fired on all cylinders.

"Opening Doors" inspired Sondheim, at age fifty, to remember what it was like to be and sound twenty-five. He also called it his most personal song. It conjures up the period when he and his friends were trying to break through professionally; in this case, Mary (as in Rodgers, which explains why the character in *Merrily* is called Mary), and Hal Prince, who always insisted that the trio met at the 1949 opening night of *South Pacific*, where Hal and Mary were each other's dates and Sondheim was with the Hammersteins. (Sondheim disputed that memory but let Prince adhere to the story.)

"Opening Doors," Sondheim explained in *Finishing the Hat*, "describes what the struggle was like for me and my generation of Broadway songwriters."

While he felt frustrated at the time, "in retrospect it strikes me as the most exhilarating period of my life."

Benjamin "Britten shows up a lot in the stuff I write," Sondheim said. "*Sunday in the Park with George* is a Britten score, I think. I'm very fond of English music."

REGENERATION

I.

The major theme in 1984's *Sunday in the Park with George** can be found in Act II, in the song "Move On." According to *Stephen Sondheim and the Reinvention of the American Musical* author Robert L. McLaughlin, the song "suggests that the past is transformed into the future in the now, the present moment."

That might sound like a lot to digest, but "if it works," Sondheim wrote in the second volume of his memoirs, *Look, I Made a Hat*, "'Move On' feels like a satisfying and touching resolution . . . it's tribute to my First Principle: Less Is More."

After six collaborative efforts with Hal Prince, Sondheim did move on; although, at first, because of the negative reception that greeted *Merrily We Roll Along*, he threatened to take up writing mysteries instead of musicals. He also took into consideration the age factor: "I really don't know any composer from the theatre, I think, who's written really good stuff after the age of fifty, which is a very young age," he said. Sondheim was fifty-two.

As it turned out, he did not forsake the theatre. What he did was downsize. He went from Broadway to Off-Broadway. Actually, smaller than Off-Broadway: He went to a nonprofit workshop.

Producer Lewis Allen, whose plays included works by Sam Shepard, Horton Foote, and Herb Gardner, as well as the musical *Annie*, proposed that Sondheim adapt Nathanael West's *A Cool Million*, which satirically set the Horatio Alger myth on its ear. In addition, he proposed writer-director James Lapine as Sondheim's collaborator. But Sondheim found the West novel, despite its 1930s Depression-era setting, too similar to *Candide*, which he had worked on with Hal Prince and Leonard Bernstein.**

---

* Although the title says George, in the show the character is referred to as Georges, at least in the first act.

** Lapine later moved ahead with *A Cool Million*, loosely adapting it under the new title *Luck, Pluck and Virtue*. It opened at the La Jolla Playhouse in 1993 and starred Neil Patrick Harris, who also played the lead in the 1995 production at New York's Atlantic Theater Company. The music was composed by Allen Shawn. Reviews were lukewarm.

"I compare him to Stravinsky and *Le sacre du printemps* because no one has ever heard anything like that before," Adam Guettel said of Sondheim and his music. "When it is said he is much imitated, it is his musical phrasing that is imitated, much more than the content." Standing at right, Sondheim's new collaborator, librettist and director James Lapine. Working together, in 1984 they created the highly innovative *Sunday in the Park with George.*

Sondheim passed, but he invited Lapine over to his home and handed him a joint.

The conversation got around to "theme and variations, because that's a kind of show I had always wanted to do," said Sondheim, who showed Lapine "a French magazine I had that was devoted to variations on the *Mona Lisa*. And we started talking about paintings."

Lapine mentioned that when he was at Yale he had done a stage piece based on the 1884 *A Sunday Afternoon on the Island of La Grande Jatte* by the French pointillist painter Georges Seurat. "And he said, 'Did you ever notice there are over fifty people in it, and nobody's looking at anybody else?' We started to speculate why. Suddenly I said, 'It's like a stage set, you know. It's like a French farce, isn't it? You know, maybe those people aren't supposed to be seen with each other,'" Sondheim recalled.

The two discussed how a story might be developed out of this, "and then James said the crucial thing: 'Of course, the main character's missing.' I said, 'Who?' He said, 'The painter.'

"As soon as he said that we knew we had a show. It would be more than a stunt. It would be a play about a man and his landscape and how he controls it.

"And how hard it is to make art."

—

"My life changed when I started working with Lapine because, for the first time, I was working with a whole other generation. James represented a whole new way of looking at the theatre, a new way of playwrighting that was nowhere near as conservative as what I'd come from."

The change suited Sondheim. "I found myself writing with more formal looseness than I had before, allowing songs to become fragmentary, like musicalized snatches of dialogue," he said. "I worried less about punctuating the piece with applause and concentrated more on the flow of the story itself."

"I didn't really know Steve's shows," said Lapine, who was twenty years younger than Sondheim, hailed from Mansfield, Ohio, and had a background in photography and graphic design before he went on to experimental theatre. The only Sondheim show he had ever seen when the two met had been *Sweeney Todd*.

"I came from a whole other world." Lapine had directed three shows, but only one musical: William Finn's 1981 *March of the Falsettos*. As for the possibility of working with Sondheim, "It took a little while for me to figure out who he was and what he did."

Using a postcard of the Seurat painting, Lapine traced and dissected the characters and how they connected with one another or did not. Sondheim then tossed out questions about the way these people lived and thought, so he could get to know them.

"I'd always loved that painting," said Lapine, who remembered that "I just sat down without a plan and began to write about the painter and the people in the canvas, inventing relationships as I went. I showed the first six or seven pages to Steve." Discussions were held, "and the ideas started to jell. At one point I wanted to follow the entire life of the painting—from its creation down to the present time. But that book was so thick, we ended up taking out the middle and jumping right to the present."

Lapine said that even when he was well underway with the book, he kept wondering when Sondheim was going to get around to writing the first song. Only later did Lapine learn, "It takes him a long time to write a song because, as he says, he doesn't want to write the wrong song."

"I guess it comes from my training under Oscar," Sondheim told Lapine. "Always think character and story, and then you think about the song."

For Sondheim's part, he operated within his usual framework: He said that the play Lapine was writing really did not need any songs.

—

"Once you say the artist is the main character, then you know at least one of your themes is going to be about creativity. The other interesting thing was that pointillism does exactly what we were trying to do," said Sondheim, and that was "take this image and that image—meaning emotional images, character, et cetera—and make them so they all finally come together and make a whole that tells a story."

Lapine had a commission from Playwrights Horizons, located in what was then a gamey section on far West Forty-Second Street, to deliver a project, and he asked the company's artistic director, André Bishop,* if there might be interest in a new musical that involved Stephen Sondheim. Bishop did not have to be asked twice.

"Even then," Bishop is quoted as saying in Lapine's 2021 book *Putting It Together*, a history of the making of *Sunday in the Park with George*, "Sondheim was a god to people like me."

A reading of the first act—which still had no songs—was held on November 1, 1982, with Sondheim playing only the opening chords. Sondheim then wrote the first song, the title number, while Lapine was visiting the actual site in Paris where Seurat had gathered the group featured in his painting. Seurat was twenty-six when he unveiled his most famous work in 1886. In all, the work contains forty-eight characters, including Seurat's mother and his mistress; Lapine named her Dot, in a tip of the hat to Seurat's pointillist style.

Songs were being written. "Steve would start by writing couplets of a song," said Lapine. "He'd say, 'Well, should it be this?' or 'Should it be this?,' and he'd read maybe four different couplets that encapsulated what the song was about or what the character was saying. And I just intuitively would say, 'Oh, I think it's the second one because I hear them talking like this.'"

Sondheim and Lapine visited the Art Institute of Chicago, where the Seurat painting still hangs. In addition to studying the work, they were shown X-ray images that had been taken of the seven-by-ten-foot canvas to show the multiple layers beneath the visible surface, exposing the different versions and revisions Seurat had made. As for the artist himself, he had a common-law wife and together they had two children who perished in infancy. Seurat died at the age of thirty-one, never having achieved critical or commercial success.

Back at Playwrights Horizons, a workshop was planned for June 1983, with subscribers to the nonprofit theatre company invited to attend. According to André Bishop, as chronicled by Lapine, while money was being raised for the event, Dorothy Hammerstein stepped forward with her checkbook "because she and Steve were quite close."

Meanwhile, Dorothy Rodgers, the widow of Richard, was then the head of the New York State Council on the Arts, which funded groups like Playwrights Horizons, and she balked at the idea that a nonprofit was proceeding with a commercial venture,** or at least one written by a Broadway composer (whom she did not particularly like). Rodgers threatened to withhold council funding.

Bishop wrote her a sharply worded rebuke, basically telling her she would be crazy to think a half-written musical about a pointillist painter was commercial material.

"Point taken" was her brief reply, said Bishop.

"And she stopped making trouble."

—

OPPOSITE: "Like very few others, she sings and acts at the same time," Sondheim said of Bernadette Peters (seen here with him in 1990), who has been described as his muse. "Most performers act and then sing, act, and then sing," he said. "Bernadette is flawless as far as I'm concerned."

* Since serving as artistic director of Playwrights Horizons from 1981 to 1991, Bishop has been artistic director of Lincoln Center Theater and has produced more than eighty plays and musicals on Broadway.

** The environment has since changed, with lines blurred between what differentiates nonprofit from commercial.

"Once you have actors cast and you hear them, the writing gets easier and easier because the reality of it's clear," Lapine said. "By the time we got to workshop, we probably had maybe two-thirds of the first act."

Bernadette Peters hailed from Ozone Park in Queens, New York. She had been acting since age three* and had various movie and television credits to her name along with appearances in *Dames at Sea*, a revival of *On the Town*, *George M!*, and *Mack and Mabel*—and had first met Sondheim in the 1970s by saying hello to him in the theatre-district restaurant Joe Allen. Lapine's only familiarity was from having seen her in the 1981 movie *Pennies from Heaven*, but he sent her an invitation to join the workshop. Lapine also included a scene he had written about Seurat's 1886–1887 painting *Les Poseuses*. The work shows nude models posing in front of *A Sunday Afternoon on the Island of La Grande Jatte*. With that, Peters said no thank you.

She later spoke to Sondheim and agreed to take the part. She also suggested to Lapine that Mandy Patinkin would be perfect as Georges. In 2022, Lapine told *CBS Sunday Morning* that back then he knew Patinkin only from the TV commercial for the Broadway run of *Evita*; Lapine had never actually seen the show itself. Patinkin hailed from Chicago's South Side and was a Juilliard-trained actor who won a Tony in 1980 as Leading Actor in a Musical for his performance as Che

Mandy Patinkin, as Georges Seurat in *Sunday in the Park with George*. His character demonstrates the artistic process, no matter the medium.

---

* Peters was also in the second national company of *Gypsy* as a Hollywood Blonde and an understudy for Dainty June.

Guevara in said *Evita*. At the time Lapine contacted him, Patinkin was fresh from playing the role of Barbra Streisand's love interest in *Yentl*.

Sunday in the Park with George now had its stars, with Peters insisting that Patinkin have top billing because his was the character stated in the title. Also cast in the workshop were three actors who did not go the distance with the show—that is, to Broadway—because not only were their parts reduced, but television roles beckoned: they were Christine Baranski, Kelsey Grammer, and Charles Kimbrough. Kimbrough had also been in the original Broadway production of *Company*.

Lapine directed while he simultaneously worked on rewrites in his head. Sondheim was at home composing. "He doesn't like coming to rehearsals, and I don't like having people at my rehearsals—so it was perfect," said Lapine. Occasionally the writer-director would invite Sondheim over to see new material. In addition, Sondheim helped the cast with their vocals and they would "sing through the song and have a little tutorial."

In terms of writing, "it's pleasanter to work in the country, where it's quiet and where you can wander out among the trees. But I don't get as much work done," Sondheim said. "In the city there's more

According to Sondheim and Lapine, one of the characters in the painting *A Sunday Afternoon on the Island of La Grande Jatte* is actually a representation of Seurat's paramour and muse. They named her Dot, and she's the woman shown holding a monkey on a leash. Here, Mandy Patinkin as Georges poses Bernadette Peters's Dot. The mustachioed man looking on is a character named Jules, played by Charles Kimbrough.

pressure. You don't want to leave the room because there's all that chaos going on. So it's more like a monk's cell, in the sense that you're isolating yourself from the world. I think that leads to more work."

But not necessarily speed. Sondheim explained to Lapine that his procrastination dated back to college, where he was so good at his classes that he did not bother to study for exams until the night before.

"In the same way," he said of his adult habits, "I wait, I wait, I wait; and then, Oh, my God, you need this song on Tuesday, and it's Monday night—"

Patinkin vented about the process more than a few times, Lapine writes in his book, but every crisis was eventually resolved—usually when the actor was presented with a new song. Finally, one number showed up and helped define not only the character of Georges and his struggle to create, but also the show itself, "Finishing the Hat." It also completed Act I.

"It's a song that the Seurat character sings," said Sondheim. "He is having trouble balancing his life with his mistress, who's in bed in the other room, waiting for him to stop painting and come to bed. And he can't stop, and she resents it."

"Steve Sondheim comes over to play this song they want me to put in that night," Patinkin said in 2020. "And Sondheim sits down and before he's even halfway through it, his shirt . . . is just sopping wet."

By the time Sondheim finishes—this is the song's first public hearing—"he is a complete wreck," said the actor. "Terrified to look at anybody in the eye. Certain that it's a disaster. That he's just delivered nothing."

As such, Patinkin said, "The definition of the word 'genius' is a guy like Steve Sondheim."

—

Even though the show's second act had yet to be written, two benefit previews, at $250 a ticket ($700 today), took place while the production played its brief workshop run. VIPs were sprinkled among the Playwrights subscribers: Lee Remick, photographer Richard Avedon, Dorothy Hammerstein, Dorothy Rodgers, playwright Terrence McNally, Arthur Laurents, and Leonard Bernstein, who walked up to Lapine, planted a big kiss on his lips—and used his tongue, or at least tried to, said Lapine—and declared, "If I give you another $250, can I see the second act?"

With only three more performances to go before wrapping up their Playwrights stint, Sondheim and Lapine decided that Act I was a set piece unto itself and should remain as such. They then began tackling Act II, which took that action forward to modern day, a reception at the Art Institute of Chicago, and dealt with Georges's artist great-grandson, George (Patinkin), and his grandmother, Marie (Peters).

"It's always surprising to me, where shows end up," Lapine said. "You start out wanting it to be A, and you end up with C or D. I was particularly surprised with *Sunday* because Steve never finished the score until the last minute. I remember the actors would come out and deliver monologues where songs were supposed to be. Then Steve would bring in a song and we were so desperate we'd put it onstage with piano accompaniment only. The final numbers were orchestrated on the day the critics came. People thought we were scrambling to rewrite the show. We weren't. We were writing it."

And that was on Broadway, at the Booth Theatre, where, armed with a budget of $2.1 million ($5.7 million today), *Sunday in the Park with George* began a month of previews on April 4, 1984. The move had been facilitated by Bernard Jacobs, president of the Shubert Organization, whose purpose in advancing the show was twofold: to fill one of his theatres* in what was still seamy Times Square, and to mount a prestige attraction—and Sondheim equaled prestige. Jacobs also involved producer Emanuel Azenberg, whose roster of hits included most of the Neil Simon canon, although, as Lapine portrays him in *Putting It Together*, Azenberg was unenthused about the show, which he admitted he did not totally comprehend.

Azenberg was not alone. General reaction from preview audiences was not cordial. It wasn't even quiet. At one point, Jacobs held open the exit door of the theatre so the walkouts wouldn't bang it shut. But the Shubert executive remained unwavering in his support, as did his partner, Shubert CEO Gerald Schoenfeld, who began a one-man word-of-mouth campaign. "Every person interested in the arts has got to see this show," Schoenfeld took to saying at dinner parties, especially if a journalist should be within earshot.

Meanwhile, the stage crew started calling the show "Sunday in the Dark and Bored." Sondheim took the reactions in stride, as did Bernadette Peters, herself a

---

* Lapine's selection of the too-intimate eight-hundred-seat Booth ended up being a tactical error in terms of economics.

GRASPING HIS ORIGINALITY

"I met Sondheim while singing in the bath," Melissa Errico recalled.

"I had been cast as Dot in the 2002 Kennedy Center revival of *Sunday in the Park with George*, and I thought that Dot ought to be introduced naked in a bathtub getting ready for her soon-to-be-canceled date night with Georges, finishing his damned hat."

As an art-history major in college, Errico "thought it would underline her vulnerability and would suit the Impressionist setting of the show, as painting in the period was filled with nudes in baths—Degas and so on."

Whether he "took pity on my naïveté or liked my moxie, he agreed to the idea and even to make small alterations in the lyrics to make it work better."

While she had long been aware of Sondheim, "it was only when I began to sing Dot that I grasped the stature and originality of what he was doing."

She was reminded when she sang "Children and Art" from *Sunday* at Sondheim's ninetieth birthday celebration "at the height of the pandemic, when I was locked inside with my own children, struggling as we all were to continue making some kind of art.

"The song sums up Steve's philosophy—children and art are all we leave behind us—and it somehow reassured me, and maybe others, that we would get through and past that crisis."

Melissa Errico played Dot to Raúl Esparza's Georges in the 2002 Kennedy Center production. Errico took the bold step of suggesting to Sondheim that she make her entrance naked in the tub. He not only approved but offered new lyrics.

veteran of a one-night Broadway flop called *La Strada*. Lapine felt otherwise. The *Washington Post* reported that "he retreated to a tiny downtown loft he rented at the time ('I called it the Anne Frank house'), got stoned, and tried to put the whole project out of his mind."

Matters improved with the Act II additions of the songs "Move On" and "Children and Art." (The fast-paced "Putting It Together," about the difficulties of being an artist, was an earlier and well-received arrival.) The penultimate number, "Lesson #8," in which George shows empathy and an understanding of people *and* art, is *Sunday*'s variation on *Company*'s "Being Alive." Like Act I, Act II concluded with the rousing "Sunday," in which the Seurat painting becomes a majestic *tableau vivant*.

Then there was the six-hundred-pound elephant in the room, which both baffled and bedazzled audiences, depending on how far they were willing to go along with the conceit: the Chromolume, a large metal sculpture created by George that beamed kinetic lights in various shapes and color patterns over the audience.* (*Chromoluminarism* was a term coined by art historians for Seurat's pointillist theory of dividing primary colors into dots for the human eye to blend into a third color.)

Some audience members were still disgruntled, but much of the booing was abated, and an audience was building. The show officially opened May 2, 1984. The majority of the reviews were unsupportive, with the exception of Frank Rich's in the *Times*, which read positive but not enthusiastic. Rich followed up with several appreciative pieces about the show. In all, *Sunday* ran 604 performances.

"Some people came back to see it three and four times," said Azenberg. "When it was over, they'd be sitting there, weeping—like, quiet hysteria—and we would have to wait ten minutes before we could clear the house. It was never going to be a musical that appeals to the bulk of the nation, but it was the perfect Steve Sondheim fan club musical—providing insight into the mysterious Steve and the depth of his passion."

Jake Gyllenhaal and Annaleigh Ashford took on the starring roles in a limited Broadway engagement at the Hudson Theatre in 2017.

---

* A particularly polished Chromolume made its appearance in the 2017 Hudson Theatre Broadway revival of *Sunday* starring Jake Gyllenhaal and Annaleigh Ashford, directed with equal polish by Sarna Lapine, a niece of James's.

YOU I LOVE AND YOU I LOVE
AND YOU AND YOU I LOVE
AND YOU I LOVE AND YOU I LOVE
AND YOU AND YOU I LOVE, I LOVE!

LARS

German set designer and director Lars Linnhoff started doing interpretative sketches of Sondheim productions during the Covid lockdown. "I wanted to draw all the original casts," the artist said, "but that's a lot. So I did what came to mind." Here, a Valentine featuring his favorite Broadway composer.

"HIS SHOWS PULL ME INTO ANOTHER WORLD"

Weaned on a diet of *Starlight Express* from the time he was seven ("I must have seen it ninety times"), German stage director, set designer, and illustrator Lars Linnhoff spent much of his youth videotaping anything he could find on musical theatre off his childhood television set.

"I was thirteen," he said, "and had never heard of Stephen Sondheim." That changed in 2000 thanks to a German TV broadcast of the 1961 *West Side Story*, which was immediately followed by a documentary on Sondheim.

"I was particularly fascinated by this opening scene from *Sunday in the Park with George*," said Linnhoff, remembering how the bare stage on the TV screen began to come alive with cutouts, scenery, and characters.

As soon as he was able, Linnhoff took his first trip to New York, where he saw *Rent*, *A Chorus Line* ("That was something amazing"), and *Spring Awakening*. Having time for one more, "I had to choose between *Legally Blonde*, *The Little Mermaid*, or *Sunday in the Park with George*"—the 2008 Roundabout Theatre import of London's Menier Chocolate Factory production, directed by Sam Buntrock and starring Daniel Evans and Jenna Russell.

He chose *Sunday* "because I wanted to see this scene change I had seen on television."

And yet, he was puzzled when, right before the performance, he read a brief article in a tourist handout about the show's color-and-light-dispensing machine, called a Chromolume.

"I thought, Wait a minute. This is not the show I came to see."

Curtain up, and Linnhoff "didn't understand a word in the show at all," a combination of his still-shaky English and *George*'s elliptical dialogue and lyrics and its nonlinear structure.

Back home, Linnhoff watched a DVD of director Terry Hughes's 1982 *Sweeney Todd* starring Angela Lansbury and George Hearn—and that did it.

Linnhoff was now sold on Sondheim, especially after he pieced together clips from YouTube of John Doyle's minimalist 2005 *Sweeney*, with Patti LuPone and Michael Cerveris.

"It showed me that musical theatre doesn't have to be big, that you don't need a lot of scenery to do the storytelling."

It also convinced him to become a musical director—an ambition realized. His productions, so far, have included *Thrill Me: The Leopold & Loeb Story*; *A Man of No Importance*; *Little Shop of Horrors*; and an evening of eleven new, ten-minute musicals by German composers.

As for experiencing works by Sondheim, Linnhoff is frequently on a plane to catch the latest productions in London.

"His shows pull me into another world," said Linnhoff, calling them "something I want to understand but can never fully explain. I am left with questions, always."

He added, "This is something I enjoy. I grow with his shows."

—

Sunday in the Park with George received the lion's share of Tony nominations that season, ten, but only won two,* for Tony Straiges's Scenic Design and Richard Nelson's Lighting (thank you, Chromolume). The night belonged to the musical *La Cage aux Folles*, with a book by Harvey Fierstein, direction by Arthur Laurents, and a score by Jerry Herman.

Herman, whose star rose with *Hello, Dolly!* and *Mame* in the 1960s, the same decade in which Sondheim's star stalled, said in accepting his Tony, "This award forever shatters a myth about the musical theatre. There's been a rumor around for a couple of years that the simple, hummable show tune was no longer welcome on Broadway. Well, it's alive and well at the Palace!"

The remark was a direct slap in the face of a fellow composer, and everyone knew whose face that was. Sondheim leaned over and said to Lapine, "Welcome to my world." Jack Kroll, the drama and film critic for *Newsweek*, turned his head and said to a fellow journalist sitting next to him, "That wasn't very gentlemanly, was it?"

In his 2022 memoir *I Was Better Last Night*, Harvey Fierstein recounts residual fallout from Herman's comments. When Fierstein personally approached Sondheim, in 2005, with an idea to adapt writer-director Joseph L. Mankiewicz's Oscar-winning 1949 *A Letter to Three Wives* into a musical, Sondheim cut him off with a curt no, which Fierstein attributed to *La Cage*'s long-ago win over *Sunday*—followed by two more *La Cage* Tony victories, in 2004 and 2010, for Best Revival in the same years *Pacific Overtures* and *A Little Night Music* had been revived.

In two more telling anecdotes, Fierstein relates that at home in Connecticut, Sondheim was shocked one day when he opened his utility bill. "Six hundred dollars?" he exclaimed. "Who the hell do they think I am—Jerry Herman?" Likewise, Sondheim's annual birthday honors turned Herman a shade of green. "Sondheim this and Sondheim that," Fierstein quotes Herman as saying. "He's seventy, let's have a concert! He's seventy-five, this calls for a gala! Now, they can take all seventy-six trombones and . . . " The implication was clear where all that brass could go.

A year after the 1984 Tonys, it was announced that *Sunday* had won the Pulitzer Prize for Drama, one of only ten musicals to be so honored since the founding of the awards in 1917.**

At the time of the announcement, Sondheim and Lapine were in the midst of revising the *Merrily We Roll Along* revival, which Lapine would direct in La Jolla. "We were having a production meeting," Sondheim recalled, "and the phone rang, and my informant, whoever it was, said, 'Guess what? You've just won the Pulitzer Prize.'"

Sondheim wrote down the news on a piece of paper, folded it, then walked over to Lapine, who was talking to a set designer. Sondheim slipped Lapine the note.

"I wish I could say there was some great dramatic reaction," said Sondheim. "There wasn't.

"He just opened it and he said, 'Oh, that's nice.'"

---

* Ten years later, for the first London production, *Sunday* would win Best Musical at the Olivier Awards. In 2007, a West End revival was named Outstanding Musical Production.

** The others are *Of Thee I Sing*, *South Pacific*, *Fiorello!*, *How to Succeed in Business Without Really Trying*, *A Chorus Line*, *Rent*, *Next to Normal*, *Hamilton*, and *A Strange Loop*.

MIRACLE ON FIFTY-FIFTH STREET

The Lebanese-American family of the New York–based actor, playwright, and poet George Abud, whose Broadway acting credits include *The Band's Visit*, has been playing the oud*—a pear-shaped, four-stringed, fretless predecessor of the lute—for four generations.

"It mirrors the range, height, and capacity of the human voice," the thirty-one-year-old said in 2022. It was with oud in hand that Abud experienced an exceptional encounter with "Mr. Sondheim."

The meeting happened at a "Lobby Project" called "A Sondheim Remix" organized by Jeanine Tesori, the composer of *Kimberly Akimbo*, *Fun Home*, and *Caroline, or Change*, and herself frequently referenced as an inheritor of the Sondheim mantle. Presentation of the project took place in the atrium of New York's City Center prior to a June 25, 2014, Encores! Off-Center performance of Jonathan Larson's *tick, tick . . . BOOM!*, starring Lin-Manuel Miranda.

"This is just a note to tell you how much I loved your version of 'Children and Art,'" Sondheim wrote to George Abud (here, with his oud) after his performance at City Center. "I was moved to tears by the connection between it and your father. Thank you for being part of the celebration."

Participation in the so-called Lobby Contest included the following prompt: "Choose ANY song or piece of music from Stephen Sondheim's *Sunday in the Park with George*," said the rules, along with the encouragement to "Create your own take on this piece."

Five winners were to be chosen.

Abud's first thought: "The only way to get into the woods is to go through it." Sitting at home with his oud, he started playing the underscore to "Children and Art," "manipulating it into an Arabic rhythm, then whistling over it and seeing if I could put it in a rhythmic way."

Once Abud got the structure on point, he "found my life parallels this song almost to a T." Besides also being named George, Abud never knew his

---

* In Arabic, *oud* means "wood."

grandfather, also named George, as is the case in Act II of *Sunday*. Abud's grandmother, like Marie in the show, also frequently lamented that her husband, *this* George's grandfather, was not around to see and hear his grandson play the oud.

While he refashioned the lyrics, Abud was both intimidated and driven by the notion that "this is Sondheim. I can't do approximate rhymes."

After submitting his entry, Abud ended up one of the chosen five, and "later heard from Jeanine Tesori's assistant, 'You'll play it for Stephen Sondheim.'"

Abud gasped.

The night arrived. "Jeanine comes up to me and says, 'George, will you open?'"

Sondheim was already in the atrium, "and I'm thinking, 'How do I approach him?' That's when an associate of Jeanine's came up and offered to hold my oud."

As Abud walked around the crowd of 250 people, he wondered what he might say to Sondheim.

"I was too terrified to go up to him, and then Jeanine comes over and says, 'We're about to start.' So, I look around, and the lady holding my oud is standing next to Stephen Sondheim. I *have* to go over there.

"Sondheim has his drink in his hand, and he says, 'Ooh, is that an oud?' 'Yes, Mr. Sondheim.' 'Will you be playing tonight?' 'Yes, I will, Mr. Sondheim.' And he engaged me in this five-minute talk. He asked, 'Have you ever heard a crwth?' [pronounced "kroo-wth"] 'No, Mr. Sondheim.' 'Well,' he said, 'it's a Celtic oud.' This was right up his alley."

It was now time to perform. "He patted me on the back and said, 'Have a good time up there.' I floated to the stage."

As Abud performed, "I could see that he watched me so thoughtfully. I was on Cloud Nine, and then I looked over again, and Sondheim has collapsed, his head is in his hands, crying. He's so red, and he's not shy about it. I'm thinking, 'Am I doing something wrong?'"

When Abud concluded, "Sondheim wiped away his tears, leapt to his feet, and burst into applause."

It wasn't until Abud got home at one a.m. that he learned the subtext of the evening. Jeanine Tesori had sent around an email: That very night, she wrote, Sondheim arrived at the stage door "and pulled me aside. 'Jeanine,' he said, 'Mary Rodgers died today, and my heart is broken. I had to show up for these young people, but I just can't stay to see the show.'"

What happened next was something Tesori called "a tiny miracle on Fifty-Fifth Street."

"George Abud sang his rendition of 'Children and Art,' gently accompanying himself on the oud. Tears streamed down Steve's face. He ended up staying after all, his heart clearly broken, but also full," her email said.

"Stephen Sondheim wasn't a father, but he parented a lot of us, and he made a lot of work. So, yes. Children. And Art."

II.

During the fourth week of the month-long workshop production of *Sunday in the Park with George* at Playwrights Horizons in 1983, Stephen Sondheim and James Lapine stepped across the street for dinner. Suddenly, amid their typical small talk, Sondheim blurted out, "I want to write my next show with you."

"What?" said Lapine, caught off guard by the statement.

Sondheim repeated himself.

The only response Lapine could imagine was "We haven't even finished writing this one."

"I always wanted to do a fairy tale," said Sondheim, "so I suggested that to James, and that we invent our own fairy tale sort of quest."

"A lot of it," Sondheim said of *Into the Woods*, "has to do with parent to child, teacher to student, the passing on of knowledge, the precepts, a kind of emotional circularity that occurs from generation to generation."

The two worked on that "for a bit, and it didn't seem to be panning out."

Lapine had another thought, "of taking fairy tales, which he pointed out are very short pieces, and therefore not worthy of expansion, but by combining a number of them perhaps we could get a full-length piece. And it grew that way."

This would become *Into the Woods*.

—

By "quest" Sondheim meant that their musical should be "like *The Wizard of Oz*, where you start here and you've got to get to there, and you have a number of adventures along the way . . . but always with a goal at the end."

Among the possibilities for their agenda, said Lapine, were *1001 Arabian Nights* and, with a tip of the hat to his collaborator's love of computer games, *Dungeons & Dragons*.

Sondheim noticeably backpedaled on being a *Dungeons & Dragons* fan but did point out that it was a quest game.

"You're going for a treasure or something like that," he said.

As a child, Sondheim was a great admirer of the L. Frank Baum *Oz* books. Beyond those, "I was not exposed to fairy tales very much, except through Walt Disney pictures." Lapine, he said, had a better understanding of fairy tales than he. "But I read all the *Oz* books, and was enchanted by the *Oz* books, and love the movie *The Wizard of Oz*."

Sondheim also fondly recalled "reading *The Hobbit*, too, when I was a kid—and so, the idea of a series of adventures with strange creatures and unexpected twists and turns of fate and funny things and melodramatic things and sorcery and all that sort of thing appealed to me, and I thought, knowing James's imagination, it would be fun to utilize that."

Lapine claimed no Disney influence or memories whatsoever, although he had vivid recollections from childhood of the *Grimms' Fairy Tales* illustrations, even more than he had of the stories themselves.

As for their approach to adapting the various fairy tales—Cinderella, for example—Sondheim and Lapine eschewed the familiar Charles Perrault* version, in which she loses a glass slipper and has a fairy godmother and which Walt Disney used in his 1950 screen adaptation. Instead, their Cinderella relies on the "darker and bloodier" (Lapine's words) tale by the Brothers Grimm,** whose version encompassed a gold slipper and assistance from mystical, eye-pecking birds. Grimms' Cinderella also visits the palace of the Prince three times, while Perrault's heroine only pops in once. By her showing up multiple times, Sondheim and Lapine realized, there were more chances for more adventures.

"The Cinderella tale is a very hard one to figure out," said Sondheim. "You have a girl who, on the one hand, lives in a house where she's mistreated, ill-used, and poor. And then she goes to another house and meets the most handsome man in the kingdom, and the richest, and he wants to marry her—and she can't make up her mind which [life] she wants. And you think, 'What's that story about?'"

Jack and the Beanstalk's unwitting benefactor, the Giant, greeted theatregoers when *Into the Woods* originally played on Broadway, starting in 1987. A facsimile was sought when the 2022 revival played at the St. James Theatre.

---

* French author and member of the Académie Française who lived from 1628 to 1703.

** Jacob (1785–1863) and Wilhelm (1786–1859), German archivists of folklore.

Sondheim and Lapine with their *Into the Woods* Witch, Bernadette Peters.

Sondheim made the further distinction that *Into the Woods* leans not so much on fairy tales, but on folk tales—except for Jack and the Beanstalk, "which is totally an English invention," he noted.

The next step was to weave the adventures of the protagonists together by a common thread and avoid being *too* imaginative with the audience's preconceived notions about the characters.

"It seems like so much fun to say to yourself, 'Hey, let's make Cinderella really nasty and make her stepsisters really wonderful girls,'" said Sondheim. "Or, 'Hey, let's make Little Red Riding Hood a nymphet.' You can do that for a sketch, but to try to sustain an audience's interest over an evening by totally or even partially subverting characters they've known or loved all their lives is not only perverse—it doesn't work."

For a deeper understanding of their characters, Sondheim and especially Lapine, who was already well versed in the theories of Freud and Jung, studied analyses of the effects fairy tales have on children that were conducted by the child psychologist Bruno Bettelheim,* the Jungian theorist Marie-Louise von Franz, and folklorists Iona and Peter Opie.

"I wanted to do something that was very plotted," said Lapine, "and the great challenge with all these characters was to keep all the balls in the air at the same time."

---

* Sondheim told Ned Sherrin in a British TV interview in 1990 that he thought Bettelheim's 1976 *The Uses of Enchantment: The Meaning and Importance of Fairy Tales* was given too much credit for inspiring *Into the Woods*, blaming this on the fact that it was the only book on the subject out there.

Some of the balls got bounced. After a few drafts, out went the Three Little Pigs. Likewise, Rumpelstiltskin.

"It just got too complex," said Sondheim.

One idea remained in place: that three of the characters should represent the three stages of adolescence.

They would be Red Riding Hood, Jack, and Cinderella.

—

Sondheim's original plan was to create rap music for the Witch, blues for the Wolf, folk songs for Jack, and operetta for Cinderella. In the end, he broke away from those constraints.

Initially, "I chose these things because I thought the colors were right for the characters," he said, "but then, rather than make it schematic, I just used it where I thought it was useful."

He also played with the idea of "a lot of ditty-like tunes" that would emulate nursery rhymes: eight-, sixteen-, and thirty-two-bar tunes offering "a lot of rhythmic propulsion to try to keep a bounce going."

Joanna Gleason, as the Baker's Wife, shared some thoughts about her character with Sondheim, and what she told him ended up incorporated into a song. The Baker was played by Chip Zien.

Ultimately, "what I decided to do with this one was, instead of picking character themes, to take sort of idea themes. For example, it all takes place in the woods, except for the Prologues to the two acts, and so I have a 'journeying' theme . . . essentially, a rhythmic theme, not a melodic theme, and it's just kind of skipping through the woods."

The rhythm remains throughout, until Jack—"of Jack and the Beanstalk fame," said Sondheim—arrives with his mother, and then "it becomes a waltz rhythm." Mother and son have a cow, "and Jack doesn't want to sell it because the cow is a friend." So the rhythm shifts slightly, and the mother sings of the cow's every liability.

Crosscut to Little Red Riding Hood—a youngster with as fresh a mouth as anyone would ever fear, let alone the Baker and his Wife, who desperately want a child—and her rhythm takes on a different meter as she sings of going off to grandmother's house.

As for the Witch, "suddenly the feeling of the music changes" again. Her underscoring "is a little slower and in a different key . . . and becomes more sinister."

The plot, Sondheim said, "concerns five magic beans," and there are five notes that represent each of the five beans. The "bean theme" recurs throughout the show, "just in various guises."

Explaining, Sondheim said, "It's sort of fun to follow that theme throughout the show. It's used upside down. It's used backwards in many ways. But the five beans, every time they have a relevance to the plot, that theme crops up."

WHEN A WRONG MAKES A SONG

Joanna Gleason won the 1988 Tony as Leading Actress in a musical for *Into the Woods* and figures that she spent two years of her life devoted to the show—from the time of its 1986 workshop at San Diego's Old Globe Theatre through its Broadway opening at the Martin Beck Theatre* on November 5, 1987. She then stayed with the musical for several months into its run.

Gleason originated the role of the Baker's Wife and noted that she and the Baker were strictly a creation of James Lapine's imagination and not something he borrowed from Grimm. Chip Zien played the Baker.

Gleason also said that if you carefully examine *Into the Woods*, "it's really the Baker and his Wife's story."

Act I is about how they want a child, and Act II is about how they are trying to survive.

Recalling her experience with *Into the Woods* for a 2000 Paley Center for Media discussion on Stephen Sondheim, Gleason said that one night at home her phone rang and it was Sondheim calling.

"Terrifying," she admitted, "and he said, 'I'm writing you a number for Act II. Any thoughts?'"

She recalled telling him that the Baker's Wife had a thing for the Prince—in fact, the Prince seduces her—"and," Gleason told Sondheim, "she must think, 'This is ridiculous. What am I doing here? I'm in the wrong story.' And he said, 'Okay, see you tomorrow.'"

"Three o'clock the next day," said Gleason, Sondheim showed up with the song for her and the Prince, "Any Moment."

The song begins, and as soon as she is kissed, the Baker's Wife turns to the audience and sings: "This is ridiculous. What am I doing here? I'm in the wrong story."

---

* The theatre was renamed for celebrity caricaturist Al Hirschfeld in 2003.

"So, we have one rhythmic theme, which is the journey," said Sondheim. "And one melodic theme, which is the beans. And I have one harmonic theme, which is the Witch's chord when she casts a spell."

The spell she casts has caused her neighbors, the Baker and His Wife, to be incapable of having a child, because years before, the Baker's father stole vegetables from the Witch's garden.

That musical construction, Sondheim said, "is enormously important. At one point, when she sends the Baker out on his task"—in order to lift the curse, he must find a cow as white as milk, a cape as red as blood, hair as yellow as corn, and a slipper as pure as gold—"the chord in a different position suddenly starts to take on a harmonic color."

Sondheim considered "these three themes, the melodic one, the rhythmic one, the harmonic one . . . the glue that holds the whole show together."

He called Act I the "I Wish" portion of the show. And yet, he emphasized, in order to get what they want, "the characters have to transgress a bit." For example, Jack is a thief (stealing the Giant's eggs and harp) and a murderer (he slays the Giant, which ticks off the Giant's Wife, but that's for Act II). Then there's Cinderella, who "goes to the ball and pretends to be somebody else. That's called lying."

Put together, Sondheim said, "all their transgressions add up to a huge transgression in the second act." Enter Mrs. Giant. "What have they brought on themselves? And, having discovered what they brought on themselves—which is nothing more or less than the end of the world—they have to band together and become some sort of community and have some kind of inter-responsibility and not just be each for himself." Because, he said, they have "to save the world, to put it back together again."

The anthem presented at this juncture, "No One Is Alone," is not pat and sentimental, as some accusers would have it.*

---

* One critic wrote that it turned the show into "a didactically communitarian fable."

211

"It means we are all responsible for each other, that every action we take, from the smallest one, from the tiniest thing you tell your wife or husband, has consequences and can spread, and you must therefore always be responsible for your actions. In that sense, it's 'No man is an island.'"

Or, as Sondheim put it on another occasion, "You can't just go stealing gold and selling cows for more than they're worth, because it affects everybody else."

—

"We had 'Boom, Crunch.' And that was changed to 'The Last Midnight,'" said Bernadette Peters, who played the Witch on Broadway, after Sondheim mentioned over lunch at his Connecticut home that the role was available.

"I remember being handed the song and James telling me, 'I'd really like to put this into the show tomorrow.' I said, 'Tomorrow?' I didn't know when the critics were coming, but we had to get the song up and running. I remember people in the wings, watching and listening when I sang it the first time."

The show had Act II issues, just like *Sunday in the Park*. How to tie all those loose ends together? Some tightening was done. Lapine was also dealing with a problem he had not had before: an abundance

Princes in wolves' clothing: Christopher Sieber and Gregg Edelman were behind the fur in the 2002 Broadway revival.

of producers, "whereas *Sunday* we just did it on our own." Production costs in the intervening years had skyrocketed, although they were nothing compared to what they would become. (Likewise, ticket prices.) Ergo, more producers were needed.

"*Into the Woods* wasn't, in many ways, all that pleasant either because we had so many people chattering to us about, 'It's too dark, it's too this, it's too that,'" said Lapine. "What was nice about *Sunday* is everybody left us alone . . . no one in any way was breathing down our necks with notes."

The reviews—some charming, some Grimm—at least sparked curiosity when it came to seeing the show; word of mouth built as time went on, which also proved

helpful for the show's success. In the Tony race, despite *Into the Woods'* ten nominations, the show was facing *The Phantom of the Opera*. The show with the falling chandelier trounced the one with the growing beanstalk. Still, in addition to Gleason, Lapine also won for his book and Sondheim for his score.

Mandy Patinkin and Lee Remick presented Sondheim with his Tony, and, beyond expressing enormous surprise, the winner looked happier than he ever had before at an awards ceremony. He thanked the producers "for the courage to put on *Into the Woods*," the ensemble cast, Lapine (whom he thanked "not only for this show, but for *Sunday in the Park with George*"), Paul Gemignani, Jonathan Tunick, "and also Paul Ford, world's most tireless rehearsal pianist and a memory bank of every show that has ever been written for any musical on any continent."

In the ensuing years, tours, revivals, reunions, concerts, a New York Shakespeare Festival rendition in Central Park, and an Encores! transfer to Broadway in 2022 have kept the *Into the Woods* flame burning, as have both modest and elaborate versions that are performed wherever English is spoken—to say nothing of Catalan, Norwegian, Hebrew, and Danish. Terry Gilliam and choreographer Leah Hausman together directed a summer 2022 production at Theatre Royal Bath, England, that highlighted the show's visual possibilities—in contrast to the version that was simultaneously running on Broadway, with its scaled-down scenery and few props (save for a marvelous cow) and emphasis on performances, directed by Lear deBessonet.

Since 1996, there has also been an approved, officially licensed, fifty-minute "Junior Adaptation" made for school and juvenile companies.

The vocal keys might be different, and Act II is missing, but the lifeforce is there.

"BLIMEY, THAT'S AWESOME"

Jacqui Dankworth, from Northampton, England, saw the original Broadway company of *Into the Woods* "in New York with my mum, and I thought, 'Someday, I'm going to do that.'"

Dankworth had her eye on the role of the Baker's Wife, but realized Cinderella was more suited to her age. Only a few years before, Dankworth was introduced to Sondheim's work when "Mum played the *Sweeney Todd* CD, and I thought, 'I must see it.' I had to be seventeen or eighteen."

She got her wish. "I got the last ticket to the last performance when Sheila Hancock and Denis Quilley played in it in the West End."

Dankworth, a graduate of Guildhall School of Music & Drama, has acted with the Royal Shakespeare Company, and she finally got her chance with *Into the Woods* in 1990. The production, directed by Richard Jones, marked the show's West End premiere. She played Cinderella.

"Stephen Sondheim and James Lapine came in during dress rehearsals," Dankworth recalled, "and Sondheim sort of redirected the scene."

It was the moment when Cinderella was twisting the hair of the ugly stepsisters before they gallivanted off to the Prince's ball. Sondheim observed how Dankworth handled the hair.

"He told me, 'If you do it like *this*, you will get the laugh.' And I remember Richard saying, 'Jacqui, why are you doing it like that?'" She fumbled for what to say. "I was stuck between a rock and a hard place."

Jacqui Dankworth saw *Into the Woods* on Broadway and knew that someday she would be in the show. Her wish came true.

Cleo Laine (front, right) played the Witch in the 1988–1990 national tour of *Into the Woods*. Behind her, from left: Tracy Katz, Robert Duncan McNeill, Kathleen Rowe McAllen, and Ray Gill.

Dankworth also played Beth, the mother of Frank's son, in a 1992 production of *Merrily We Roll Along* at the Haymarket Theatre, in Leicester.

When it came to the song "Not a Day Goes By," she remembered, "Sondheim wanted it really angry, not sentimental—fiery and cynical. It's about the end of a relationship. When I listen to the cast recording now, I think, 'Blimey, that's awesome.'"

She said when it came to his giving notes, Sondheim was "strict and intense. It was about the work and nothing personal. I found it inspiring. He was trying to draw out the best of you, not humiliate you. He was incredible."

Accomplished in her own right as an actor and a music performer, Dankworth knows that of which she speaks.

Her mum is the incredible jazz singer Cleo Laine; her dad, the incredible musician John Dankworth.

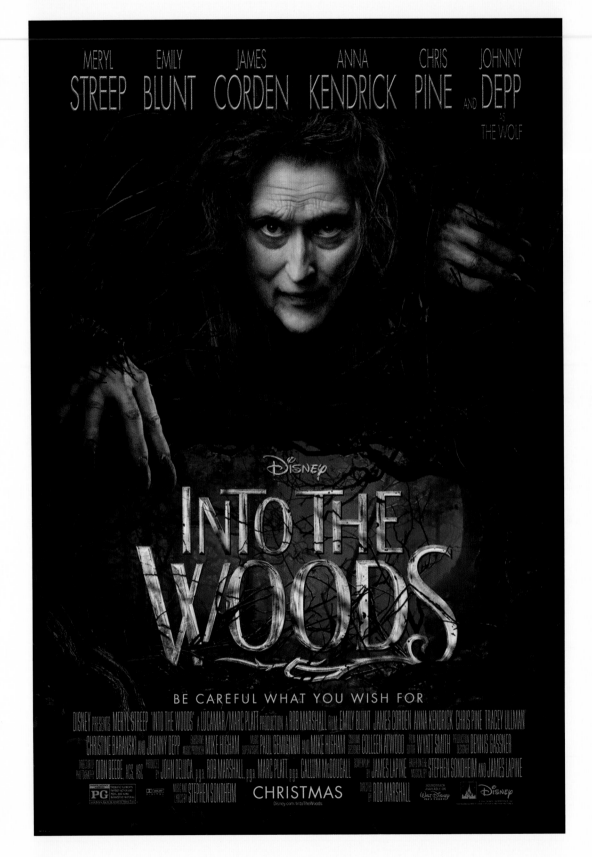

—

Rumblings of a movie version of *Into the Woods* started reverberating in the 1990s, with various names bandied about for various roles: Robin Williams as the Baker; Goldie Hawn, his Wife; Cher, the Witch; Steve Martin, the Wolf; Danny DeVito, the Giant.

In 2014, Disney came through with James Corden, Emily Blunt, Meryl Streep, Johnny Depp, and Frances de la Tour in those roles—actually, de la Tour appeared as Mrs. Giant. Anna Kendrick was Cinderella. Rob Marshall, who did the movie version of *Chicago*, directed from Lapine's screenplay.

The film's $50 million budget was considered skimpy; at the time, Disney had recently spent nearly $200 on *Maleficent*, but *Into the Woods* was considered a greater financial risk.* Shooting took place in rural England starting in late September 2013. If one listens carefully, "The Sun Won't Set," from *A Little Night Music*, can be heard as the waltz melody being played during the Prince's ball in the film.

Marshall thought to cast Streep because of her ease with ABBA in the screen version of *Mamma Mia!*, but the multi-Oscar winner, who was then sixty-five, demurred at taking on Sondheim and Lapine's evil sorceress.

"When I turned forty," Streep said, "I got three witch offers in one year, and no other offers. Three offers to play a witch, but no love-interest things, no woman-scientist-adventurists, no 'I'm out saving the world,' no nothing. Just witches. I thought, 'God, there's got to be another way.'"

Eventually, she changed her mind and took on the part.

Act II of the show was condensed for the screen, although death and destruction still make appearances. More importantly, the Witch still sang "Children Will Listen."

She does so at the end of the film, while the Baker tells his baby the story of recent events.

OPPOSITE: Plans had been afoot to turn *Into the Woods* into a movie for two decades, at least. Initially, Meryl Streep turned down the role of the Witch. She said she'd been getting too many similar offers.

---

* It more than made back its costs, grossing nearly $215 million its first year.

"How could one inconsequential angry little man cause such universal grief and anguish? More important, why would he?" Sondheim posited in regard to his and John Weidman's chilling 1990 effort. "That's what *Assassins* is about."

DEATH AND LOVE

I.

"We're not going to apologize for dealing with such a volatile subject," Stephen Sondheim said, referring to himself and his *Pacific Overtures* collaborator John Weidman, on their second joint effort, *Assassins*.

The musical serves as a kaleidoscopic portrait— its creators shied away from calling it a revue—rife with dramatic license about nine Presidential assassins, four of whom were successful in carrying out their plots: John Wilkes Booth (who targeted Abraham Lincoln), Charles Guiteau (James A. Garfield), Leon Czolgosz (William McKinley), and Lee Harvey Oswald (John F. Kennedy). Other assassins who executed failed attempts were featured: Giuseppe Zangara (Franklin D. Roosevelt), Samuel Byck (Richard M. Nixon), Sara Jane Moore and Lynette "Squeaky" Fromme (Gerald Ford), and John Hinckley (Ronald Reagan).

"Nowadays," Sondheim said in 1990, as the first production of *Assassins*, directed by Jerry Zaks, was preparing to premiere at Playwrights Horizons, "virtually everything goes."

The idea for the show, Sondheim's fourteenth, had been sparked by Charles Gilbert Jr. Sondheim had run across his 1979 fringe-musical script, titled *Assassins*, while serving on the board of a theatre group dedicated to finding new works for Off-Broadway. Gilbert's libretto featured a fictitious Vietnam vet turned presidential assassin.

Gilbert, who later headed the musical theatre program at the University of the Arts in Philadelphia, was fresh out of graduate school when he was browsing the stacks of the Carnegie Library of Pittsburgh. He ran across a book of biographical sketches—including verse, journal entries, and courtroom transcripts—about real-life assassins. "There was something about that, having their own words, that was both spooky and entertaining to me," Gilbert said.

"For example," Sondheim remembered, "there was a poem that Charles Guiteau wrote on the day of his execution which began, 'I am going to the Lordy.' In fact, I quote two lines from it in one of my songs. That poem, and the letters and diaries, was what was most interesting about" Gilbert's script.

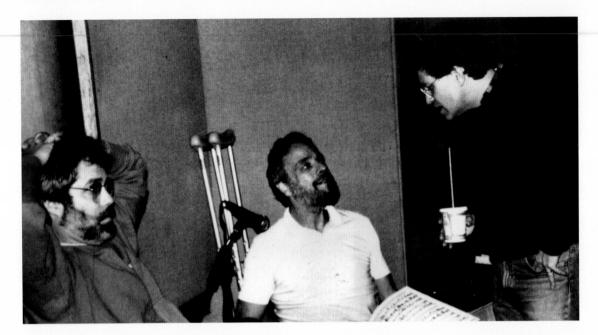

Gilbert had also written in "a sort of Sidney [*sic*] Greenstreet* figure . . . as sort of the spirit of evil, who would appear sporadically and read quotations from various politicians' letters." However, Sondheim said, "the narrative seemed to weigh the piece down, so [the theatre board] never did it. But I thought, 'I wish I had had that idea.'"

Thanks to a Ford Foundation grant, Gilbert did see his show mounted in Pittsburgh, first in a workshop and then as a full-length production. The action began at a sideshow shooting gallery with a barker shouting, "Step right up! Hit the Prez and win a prize!"

Having evidently kept Gilbert's name, his show title, and his opening scene in mind, Sondheim mentioned them years later to Weidman, who was sold on the title alone.

"I said, 'Let me see if I can track down Charles Gilbert,' and I did, and I wrote him a letter, and I said, 'Could we use your idea? We won't use your show, just the idea of *Assassins*.'"

"I was baffled that he tracked me down," remembered Gilbert. "I wrote back and proposed that we collaborate, but he phoned and said that was very gracious, but he had John Weidman in mind."

An agreement was arranged, and Sondheim and Weidman proceeded with *Assassins*.

———

"Steve will admit that one of the things he likes to rely on his collaborators for is research," said Weidman, who, as one who long felt at home in a research library, relished the arrangement. "It's work, but it's painless. You sit around, you read. It's not like trying to write."

"Assassins is *Sweeney Todd*," said Sondheim, seen here in the studio with librettist John Weidman (left) and director Jerry Zaks, during the first cast recording in 1991. "It's about righting a wrong, and how, if you do it the wrong way, you're in a lot of trouble."

---

* Sydney Greenstreet was a rotund British character actor in the Golden Era of Hollywood, known for his semisinister roles in *Casablanca* and *The Maltese Falcon*.

Recording session for the original Playwrights Horizons production of *Assassins*; from left: Victor Garber, Jonathan Hadary, and Greg Germann, who played John Wilkes Booth, Charles Guiteau, and John Hinckley Jr.

The two met and discussed the project on a weekly basis for months.

"We first decided that we would do assassinations starting with Julius Caesar. Just the whole idea of assassins from the whole world. And we realized it was too unwieldy," said Sondheim. "So we eventually narrowed it down to just presidential assassins."

"I felt very free to write whatever I wanted," Weidman said, "and I was drawing on a lot of different styles in which I had written in the past because that seemed to be what the material required."

"The idea that people from different eras would have scenes together was exciting," said Sondheim. "I loved the notion that John Wilkes Booth could talk with somebody who lived fifty years after he died." In the finished scenario, it is Booth who convinces Lee Harvey Oswald inside the Dallas Book Depository that he will be making a name for himself if he kills JFK.

"Once the barriers are down," said Sondheim, "you can allow yourself to cross eras and find parallels and contrasts."

While *Assassins* does not glorify its nine lethal characters, it does present them as human beings who, collectively, were shut out of the American Dream—thus asking the audience to question what roles their fellow citizens played in disenfranchising them, which some people find akin to questioning patriotism.

"One of the things we found out as we looked at them is that we were not writing about shooting at the President of the United States," Weidman said. "What's provocative and upsetting and disturbing is the lives they led up to that point and what those lives reveal."

A few of the assassins—in Sondheim's words, "some were less than crazy, and some were more than crazy"—were portrayed humorously, some disturbingly.

The sixteen-member cast included Debra Monk as Sara Jane Moore, Annie Golden as "Squeaky" Fromme, Victor Garber as Booth, Jonathan Hadary as Guiteau, and Terrence Mann as Czolgosz.

Sondheim and Weidman's *Assassins* opened at Playwrights Horizons on December 18, 1990, but the timing—as reflected in the reviews—could not have been more inopportune.

AND THE OSCAR GOES TO . . .

Broadway's chief sophisticate matched up with a popular comic strip and won an Oscar—only in Hollywood.

Thirty-seven days after *Assassins* closed in New York, Sondheim collected the coveted golden statuette for Best Song, although he was not present at the ceremony.

His win was for "Sooner or Later (I Always Get My Man)," one of five songs* he wrote that appeared in Warren Beatty's *Dick Tracy*, a colorful 1930s-style adaptation of the comic strip about the famous fictional crime detective. In the film—and at the Academy Awards show that year—the seductive number was performed by Madonna.

Three of the songs in the movie were written for her character, Tracy's girlfriend, Breathless Mahoney. Beatty played Tracy.

---

* The others were the Tin Pan Alley–like "Back in Business" and "Live Alone and Like It" (sung in the background by Mel Tormé), the Gershwin-esque "More," and "What Can You Lose?," flamboyantly delivered onscreen by Mandy Patinkin as the character 88 Keys, Breathless Mahoney's Piano Man.

マドンナはクラクラするほどセクシーで小悪魔的。
マリリン・モンローとジェシカ・ラビットのまさにブレンド。
—タイム誌—

ディック トレイシー

January 17, 1991, brought the launch of Operation Desert Storm led by American forces against Iraq after it had invaded neighboring Kuwait.

Assassins ran its seventy-three scheduled performances at Playwrights Horizons. Immediate plans to move it to a larger house, let alone Broadway, ran out of steam.

—

Repeating the pattern of other Sondheim shows, *Assassins* found its audience through subsequent productions.

Eighteen months after the Playwrights Horizons engagement, in August 1992, artistic director Eric D. Schaeffer gave the show a fresh airing at the then-two-year-old Signature Theatre in Arlington, Virginia, which would quickly establish itself as the nation's unofficial Sondheim showcase outside of New York.

"We projected images of Kennedy's funeral on the set while the assassins pointed their guns right into the audience," Schaeffer said of the engagement, which sold out its late August–to–early October run. "People questioned me about it. 'What's to

OPPOSITE: Sondheim's musical contributions to Warren Beatty's 1990 *Dick Tracy* included "Sooner or Later (I Always Get My Man)," performed by Madonna (depicted here in the film's Japanese poster). Sondheim won the Academy Award for Best Song.

"I didn't know if I could do his stuff justice, and he wasn't sure either," Madonna said of the Sondheim material.

"Sooner or Later" is a nightclub song that a sexy chanteuse sings at a microphone in front of the band. Madonna delivers it at the Club Ritz dressed in a black-sequined dress made for her by film and stage costume designer Milena Canonero.

Sondheim was in the recording studio and on set while Madonna worked. "Her phrasing and timing are terrific," he said, "very sexy." He also praised the "style and grace" of her dancing.

This was Sondheim's second film with Beatty; he'd also worked on the score for *Reds*, the director's 1981 biography of American journalist John Reed, although, as Beatty said, "I don't very much like music in my films." Dave Grusin ended up finishing the score—Sondheim needed to get back to *Merrily We Roll Along*—and yet the film still contains Sondheim's effective "Goodbye for Now," a song that spells out the anguish of long-distance relationships.

Sondheim's "I Never Do Anything Twice," a double-entendre number also known as "The Madame's Song," was introduced by nightclub impresario Régine in Herbert Ross's 1976 film, *The Seven-Per-Cent Solution*, but the song truly caught fire when Millicent Martin delivered it onstage that same year in *Side by Side by Sondheim*.

Sondheim's other notable screen work—his first—was for director Alain Resnais's 1974 '30s-period French film *Stavisky*, starring Jean-Paul Belmondo as a seductive and influential real-life swindler.

The *Stavisky* soundtrack represents the only full-orchestra film score composed by Sondheim—which makes it all the more valuable, given that, as he said himself, "During my formative years, movies really molded my entire view of the world."

question?' I ask. I feel it's important to go out on the edge and put the audience in [the assassins'] minds."

London got its first look at *Assassins* not long after. Sam Mendes, then twenty-six and serving in his new capacity as artistic director of the Donmar Warehouse, directed a version that also introduced the song "Something Just Broke," to reflect the public's mourning of a fallen president. It has remained in the show ever since.

"The reviews there were the exact opposite of the reviews in New York," said Weidman. "They were good."

The Donmar production ran from October 29, 1992, until January 9, 1993, while, in America, colleges, universities, and regional companies began picking up *Assassins*, resulting in more than four hundred productions nationwide over the next decade.

There was interest generated by producers in New York, Weidman said, "but they didn't feel like a good fit with the sensibility of the show"—that is, until director Joe Mantello proposed a production for the Roundabout Theatre Company. "He had a smart idea for one very small adjustment in one of the scenes early on, and that was it." Mantello suggested introducing the women, "Squeaky" and Sara Jane, earlier.

"*Assassins* is very much a collection of songs," said Sondheim. "Some motifs are used over and over again, particularly 'Hail to the Chief,' and a couple of others." He called the show, "in the old-fashioned sense, a musical comedy—whether people think it's a comedy or not . . . a collection of songs." No attempt was made, he said, to create "a 'score' except insofar as it relates to the characters." What emerges is "eclectic—different kinds of style, reflecting the period and reflecting the characters."

Scheduled to open at Broadway's Music Box Theatre on November 29, 2001, the Roundabout *Assassins* was then canceled and put on lengthy hold in the wake of the September 11 attacks. In the spring of 2004, Roundabout mounted the production at Broadway's Studio 54. Neil Patrick Harris played both the Balladeer—not at all like Sydney Greenstreet but more like folk singer Pete Seeger or Woody Guthrie—and Lee Harvey Oswald. Marc Kudisch played the Proprietor of the carnival with the shooting gallery; Denis O'Hare, Charles Guiteau; Mario Cantone, Samuel Byck; Mary Catherine Garrison, "Squeaky"; and Michael Cerveris, John Wilkes Booth.

OPPOSITE: The 1992 *Assassins* at London's Donmar Warehouse, directed by Sam Mendes; from left: Cantwell (John Hinckley Jr.), Henry Goodman (Charles Guiteau), Gareth Snook (Lee Harvey Oswald), David Firth (John Wilkes Booth), Paul Harrhy (Giuseppe Zangara), and Louise Gold (Sara Jane Moore).

RIGHT: Will Swenson (center) as Charles Guiteau in Classic Stage Company's *Assassins*, accompanied on clarinet, guitar, and flute by Brad Giovanine (left), Rob Morrison, and Katrina Yaukey. According to Weidman, one of his and Sondheim's original thoughts was to write a musical about the Paris Peace Conference of 1919, but then Sondheim remembered Charles Gilbert's *Assassins*.

This time, reviews were out of the ballpark. Cerveris (Featured Actor in a Musical) and Mantello (Direction) won Tonys, as did the show itself for Best Revival of a Musical, and also for Lighting Design and Orchestrations. It was not that the show had changed since 1991, although Mantello had given it a flashy new veneer; the world itself had changed.

That became all the more obvious when director John Doyle staged his hot-ticket, postpandemic* Classic Stage Company version in late 2021. This time the musical instruments were mostly in the pit and not—per Doyle's usual style—on the backs of the actors.

Will Swenson appeared as Guiteau, Judy Kuhn as Sara Jane Moore, and Steven Pasquale as Booth. All three actors stood out, although no one single person could hope to compete with the show's overriding message that domestic terrorists now lurk everywhere.

---

* The run was regrettably cut short by a resurgence of Covid.

II.

"In my mind," said Donna Murphy, whose performance as Fosca in Stephen Sondheim and James Lapine's 1994 one-act musical, *Passion*, won her a Tony as Best Actress in a Musical, "I assumed this role is going to Patti LuPone. How is it not going to Patti LuPone?"

"*Passion* is closer to a chamber opera," Sondheim said, comparing it to Benjamin Britten's *The Rape of Lucretia*, "in which, although there is dialogue, there is a sense of through-composition." Here, Marin Mazzie and Jere Shea, on Broadway in 1994.

Murphy had auditioned for Lapine before, for one of his productions of *Merrily We Roll Along*. "Kind of a cool customer," she called him. "I sang 'Not a Day Goes By,' and he said, 'Well, that's not how I imagined it.'"

Sondheim, on the other hand, "was smiling" during her *Passion* audition and, as she later learned, was thinking to himself, "That's pretty good." But as she also learned, by "pretty good" he was referring not to her performance but to "what I wrote."

At the time she tried out for Sondheim and Lapine, Murphy, a native New Yorker who is one of seven children, was playing the Whore in Michael John LaChiusa's *Hello Again* at Lincoln Center. Prior to that she did a summer-stock production of *Oliver!* starring Davy Jones, formerly of The Monkees, as Fagin.

"While the show itself has been dividing opinion (an expected part of any Sondheim preview process)," reported the New Yorker, "the performance of its female lead, Donna Murphy, has brought uniform acclaim." Murphy won a Tony for her role as the cloying, cunning Fosca.

Murphy's agent described Fosca to her as "a consumptive, nineteenth century neurotic," and Murphy knew this was not something she could pull together in one night. Sondheim and Lapine wanted her to audition the next day.

Murphy sent word that she needed more time so that "I have a sense of what I might be able to do here." The noncommittal response she received in return was, "Well, hopefully, there'll be another casting session."

"I'd grown more trusting of my decisions," Murphy said in retrospect.

The following Monday she received a call. "They can see you Thursday."

Murphy used the time to immerse herself in the song she had been sent, "I Read." The setting is a remote military outpost in 1863 Italy, and the sickly, homely Fosca sings it to her handsome cousin Giorgio. He is an army corporal separated from his beautiful mistress, Clara, who is married. But the relentless, love-starved Fosca is obsessed with him. Weak from melancholy and her illness, yet strong enough to manipulate, Fosca sings "I Read" when she returns Giorgio his copy of Rousseau.

Murphy said she found Fosca's entire character in that one song because it contained "the nature of who that woman was, the types of experiences she had, how she saw herself, how self-aware she was of how she was viewed, the rage, the self-pity, and the deep, deep yearning for connection—so many things."

Sondheim took notice. "I asked her how she locked into the character," he said, "and Donna said it was something very personal."

She knew it so well, it turned out, that Sondheim would eventually publicly state that Murphy's audition for *Passion* was the best audition he had ever witnessed.

"I wanted to open the show that night."

—

After *Sweeney Todd*, *Passion* marked only the second time that Sondheim had initiated a project. In 1983, he saw Italian film director Ettore Scola's *Passione d'Amore*, based on the 1869 serialized novel *Fosca*, by Iginio Ugo Tarchetti.*

"I wanted to make a musical piece out of it without thinking for one reason why," said Sondheim. "I never think why. You get attracted to a story, and you do it, for whatever series of reasons, whether they're psychological or theatrical, or a combination of both. I just wanted to do it."

"I was less convinced when I saw the movie," Lapine said after Sondheim had pitched *Passione d'Amore* to him as the basis for "a great musical." Once Lapine read the novel, however, "I found my way into the story." He also said that Sondheim wrote a great deal of music for the piece—most theatre historians and critics consider *Passion* a chamber opera,** an assessment Sondheim found "fair"—and this caused Lapine to believe the show should be sung through.

---

* Sometimes compared to Edgar Allan Poe for the darkness in his writing, Tarchetti, like his character Giorgio, was in the military.

** A work performed with a small group rather than a full orchestra.

"This can't be sung through," Sondheim told him. "The ear needs a rest so the music can be 'heard.'"

Expanding on that, Sondheim said, "First of all, I don't much like opera because I like the contrast between the spoken word and the song word. To me, the spoken word is another kind of music." He also compared *Passion* to an old Warner Bros. movie that would have starred Bette Davis, Errol Flynn, and Olivia de Havilland—as Fosca, Giorgio, and Clara.

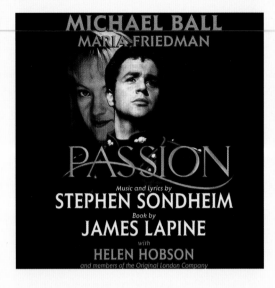

"Sondheim's new musical drama is one of his darkest, but also one of his most exciting; a hard, stormy, unsettling and spellbinding piece of theatre," London *Sunday Times* critic John Peter wrote about the 1996 West End production, directed by Jeremy Sams. As Fosca, "Maria Friedman gives the finest and most harrowing performance of her career. This is unlike anything I have seen in musical theatre."

"*Passion* seemed like a one-act musical," said Sondheim. (It would turn out to be just that, with a running time of one hour, fifty minutes.) "Meantime, James Lapine had read a book called *Muscle*, by Sam Fussell." The full title of the 1991 memoir was *Muscle: Confessions of an Unlikely Bodybuilder*, and in it Fussell traced his own transformation from a "stork-like" Oxford scholar to a steroid-using, protein-powder-devouring devotee of a New York City YMCA. As a bodybuilder, *Muscle*'s hero "goes to California to compete in contests, then collapses and returns to normal," said Sondheim. "I read it, and it seemed like a one-act, too. Click! Together they'd make a full evening." Two one-act musicals. The tie that bound? "Both books are about appearances."

Muscle came first. After a reading of a first draft, Sondheim was reportedly dissatisfied with his music, and the one-act was shelved.* Focus then centered on *Passion*. A reading was held. By that time, Murphy had been cast as Fosca, Marin Mazzie as Clara, and Peter Gallagher as Giorgio, but he was then called away on movie assignments. Jere Shea was cast as Giorgio, and *Passion* moved ahead and into previews at the Plymouth Theatre on Broadway.

The show begins with the naked Giorgio and Clara in bed; their song is "Happiness."

"The first two thirds of the show, the duets between Giorgio and Clara are . . . in major keys," said Sondheim, "and Fosca's keys are mostly minor." As the show progresses, "things start to switch. Not that Clara becomes minor, but Fosca becomes major."

The concept behind *Passion*, he said, "is that nothing comes to a conclusion. Musically, the idea is to make it one long rhapsody, so the audience will never applaud [and is] never encouraged to think that something is over, because I didn't want the mood broken and the audience being made conscious it was in a theatre."

Also to be considered was how homely Fosca should be. There was the effect her looks would have on Giorgio, let alone on the audience.

"Donna is a gorgeous woman," said Sondheim. "During previews, we kept putting a prosthetic nose on her, a receding hairline—and all the time it looked like a beautiful

---

* Lapine revisited *Muscle* in 2001, with a score by William Finn. Reviewing its premiere in Chicago, the *Variety* critic found the concept "intriguing" but the reality "off-kilter."

Sondheim is flanked by *Passion* costume designer Jane Greenwood (right) and set designer Adrianne Lobel at the home of set-design collector Douglas Colby (left), in 2017. The occasion was Sondheim's receipt of the New York State Writers Hall of Fame award from the Empire State Center for the Book. Under observation is a Jo Mielziner design concept for *The Girls Upstairs*, which eventually became *Follies*.

woman made up to look ugly. Finally, we settled for a couple of moles because she knows how to *act* ugly."

"I thought about the fact that she probably wasn't somebody who groomed herself daily, so I didn't bathe for a couple of days. I didn't wash my hair," said Murphy. "I remember my husband—I was eating breakfast the way I thought that she would eat, and he said, 'I really respect that you are preparing for this, but do I have to have breakfast with Fosca?'"

Previews proved rocky. Audiences laughed in places where they should not have. They also were not buying into the idea that Giorgio would ever leave Clara for Fosca.

"I was old enough to be asked my opinion of *Passion*," said Adam Guettel. He and his parents "had just seen a preview and been invited back to Steve's house. He asked me what I thought, and I mistakenly said, 'I've never seen anything like it. I think just the idea of making a show about this is extraordinary.'"

The statement fell short of a compliment, something Guettel had not thought of in the moment. He was immediately apprised otherwise.

Guettel explained, "For any creative person, forget about somebody in his league, who had invested what he had invested, and someone his age at that point, starting to have a quiet dialogue within himself about whether or not he's losing it, or even whether he's past it—you don't trifle with 'Utterly original,' 'I've never seen anything like it,' 'Who would attempt such a thing?' In any creative person's mind, this is going to have either an overt 'but' or a covert 'but' following it. He's of course waiting for that. Even if it's not said, it's there."

Sondheim's response "was sharp and immediate," said Guettel, "and I learned that lesson. But that's true of all of us. If you don't hear, 'I was so moved. It is absolutely gorgeous,' then, no thank you."

229

Reviews were beyond respectful, but *Passion* closed after only 280 performances. "Brilliant but gloomy" was the assessment—especially compared to the critic-proof Broadway adaptation of *Beauty and the Beast*, which Disney had opened that same season.

Passion still holds the distinction of being the shortest-running show to be named Best Musical at the Tonys. Awards also went to Murphy, Sondheim, and Lapine.

PBS filmed the Broadway production in 1995. In 1996, *Passion* opened in London, directed by Jeremy Sams, with Maria Friedman as Fosca, Michael Ball as Giorgio, and an intermission. For a 2002 Sondheim Celebration, the Kennedy Center staged *Passion*, directed by Eric Schaeffer from the Signature Theatre. Judy Kuhn starred as Fosca, a role she reprised in 2013 for John Doyle's Classic Stage Company, which also starred Ryan Silverman as Giorgio and Melissa Errico as Clara.

As for Patti LuPone, who was, in fact, offered Fosca before Donna Murphy auditioned, the star finally played the part in 2003 at the Ravinia Festival in Chicago and again in 2005 in a concert version at the Rose Theater in New York that was telecast on *Live from Lincoln Center*.

In her memoir, LuPone expressed regret over not having accepted the role in the first place, but she was otherwise engaged: to play Norma Desmond in the London premiere of Andrew Lloyd Webber's *Sunset Boulevard*.*

Once in London, she wrote, she went to see Sam Mendes's Donmar Warehouse production of *Assassins*. Sitting there, she asked herself two questions.

The first was, "Would Andrew be pissed off that I saw a Sondheim musical?"

And the second: "Why couldn't I be in a Sondheim musical?"

---

* Despite contractual obligations to LuPone, Lloyd Webber cast Glenn Close to open the Broadway production. LuPone took him to court, where she received an undisclosed settlement.

III.

In the very last days of spring in 2022 in Manhattan,
Ted Sperling presented a concert he had conceived,
stage-directed, music-directed, hosted, and performed on
piano, along with a cast of four and a musical accompaniment
of seven. Called *Isn't It Bliss?: Sondheim on Love*, the recital
was part of the 92nd Street Y's fifty-year-old Lyrics and
Lyricists series. Sperling said he put it together to show
an aspect of Sondheim that most people usually do not
associate with him: his romantic side.

Sperling, a multifaceted and Tony-winning musical director, conductor, orchestrator, and arranger, was a student at Yale when he first met Sondheim, who had been invited to speak to a select group of students at the university. Sperling had not been one of those selected, he said, but he showed up anyway and used the occasion to ask if he could make changes to the Sondheim musical that the student theatre group was putting on. Sondheim replied by saying his musicals had been put together by professionals and, therefore, were not to be tampered with. Through an ensuing correspondence, Sperling said, Sondheim did permit him to make some adjustments. The two remained in contact, and, in 1984, a year after Sperling graduated from Yale, Sondheim and Paul Gemignani invited him to play the synthesizer in the pit of *Sunday in the Park with George*. Sperling's career was launched.

Sperling's 2022 program at the Y included "Love Is in the Air" (cut from *A Funny Thing Happened on the Way to the Forum*), "Take Me to the World" (*Evening Primrose*), "By the Sea" (*Sweeney Todd*), "Good Thing Going" (*Merrily We Roll Along*), and "Too Many Mornings" (*Follies*). He also introduced a song he admitted would be unfamiliar to most of the audience, "The Best Thing That Ever Happened."

The song, which pays homage to Harold Arlen, never made it to Broadway and neither did the show it came from, the third and final of the Sondheim–John Weidman collaborations. Initially titled *Wise Guys* but ultimately called *Road Show*—in between, it also took on the names *Gold!* and *Bounce*, as well as four different directors, including, at one stage (in Chicago, at the Goodman Theatre) Hal Prince—the project dealt with the real-life Addison and Wilson Mizner. The brothers were high-stakes gamblers who ran through money and Alaska, California, New York, and eventually Florida, where they developed Palm Beach and Boca Raton, even if their Mizner Development Corporation went bankrupt in 1926.

Along the way, Addison (1872–1933) was known as "the gay father of South Florida architecture," while Wilson (1876–1933) ended up as "America's most fascinating outlaw," a description reputedly coined by writer Anita Loos.

Wise Guys was first presented in a 1999 sneak peek at the New York Theatre Workshop, with Sam Mendes directing, Nathan Lane as Addison, and Victor Garber as Wilson. It then went through a long, circuitous development phase.

When Hal Prince took over, in 2003, said Sperling, "he said, 'What this show needs is girls!'" So a love interest named Nellie was introduced, and she and Wilson sang "The Best Thing That Ever Happened." In the Chicago production, Richard Kind was Addison; Howard McGillin, Wilson; and Michelle Pawk, Nellie.

Eventually, the show and the song underwent a switch. As time went on, the song became a duet for Addison and his boyfriend, Hollis.

The result, Sperling said, was "the most warm-hearted, full-throttle love song in the Sondheim canon."

———

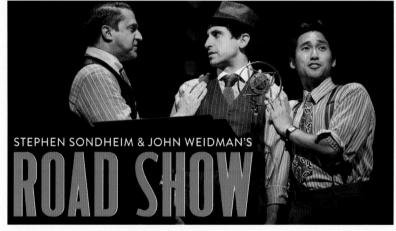

"I think we just worked on it too long," Sondheim said in 2004, after the many incarnations of the show had come and gone. In truth, Sondheim had been interested in the tale of the Mizners as early as 1956, when he did a demo recording for Hal Prince of a song called "I Wouldn't Change a Thing," which Sperling also played at the Y.

"When I first read about them," Sondheim said of the brothers, "I was fascinated by the way Wilson was the jack-of-all-trades and the master of none. I wanted to explore what's behind that kind of restlessness that occurs when somebody can't find his talent and flits from one thing to another, as Wilson did in real life."

Wilson's primary gift was scamming, but he "also was a playwright, a manager of prizefighters and hotels, a gold prospector, a screenwriter, and also a famous wit, socialite, and con artist." In 1926, as manager of the Brown Derby restaurant, Wilson named the Los Angeles watering hole after the headgear sported by two of his role

OPPOSITE TOP: *Road Show* went by several names, and through several concepts and directors, but the subject matter had interested Sondheim since he was in his twenties: the exploits of the Brothers Mizner—Addison was an architect who helped build Florida, and Wilson was a con man who ended up a shill in Hollywood.

OPPOSITE BOTTOM: Raúl Esparza (left) played Wilson, and Brandon Uranowitz (center) was Addison in the 2019 Encores! Off-Center production of *Road Show*, with Jin Ha (right) as Wilson's lover, Hollis Bessemer.

RIGHT: Howard McGillin played Wilson Mizner to Richard Kind's Addison in the summer of 2003 when Hal Prince took over the direction and the show was called *Bounce*.

Limited Engagement Starts June 20th

BOUNCE
A New Musical Comedy

Call: 312.443.3800

Order Online 24/7 at
www.goodman-theatre.org

Music and lyrics by
Stephen **Sondheim**   John **Weidman**   Book by

Directed by
Harold **Prince**

"THE BEST REGIONAL THEATER IN THE U.S." — TIME MAGAZINE, MAY 2003

Goodman

models, New York State governor Al Smith and Western lawman Bat Masterson.

"Addison," Sondheim said of the older brother, "was primarily an architect and remained an architect for the rest of his life. He was somebody who had found himself."

Sondheim gave Weidman the 1953 book *The Legendary Mizners* by *New Yorker* writer Alva Johnston and told him to take a good look at Wilson. "Well," Weidman said after reading it, "just based on this one book, [Wilson] strikes me as a jerk, but his brother is interesting."

While Sondheim continued to be captivated by Wilson, Weidman found himself intrigued "in the way in which the personalities of the two Mizner brothers intersected," and "helped each other and destroyed each other." That, along with "the context of the America in which their story took place," he said, "all felt like it had the right size and scope to be a musical."

And yet, the elements never jelled. "I don't think, in a way, we ever really got on the same page about what we were writing about," Weidman said.

"We started with a very energetic musical comedy," Sondheim said in 2003. "We always had an image of Bob Hope and Bing Crosby. The score reflects Hope-Crosby movies* and the sound of 1950s and 1960s theatre scores." He called it "a chronological musical comedy."

The show bounced around over the years, picking up some directors' touches and losing some others. Mendes's version was "not without its comic aspects but Serious with a capital S," said Sondheim. "Hal tried to blend the two [and] liked the whole idea of the epic quality, but it got lost in the shuffle."

A one-night reading was held at New York's Public Theater in February 2006, to allow the authors to reassess what they had made so far. Richard Kind was again Addison; Marc Kudisch was Wilson; Bernadette Peters, the brothers' mother; John Cullum, their father; and Gavin Creel was Hollis.

More than two years later at the Public, in November 2008, *Road Show* was staged by John Doyle. Sondheim wrote a new song, "Brotherly Love," to establish the siblings' complicated relationship. Michael Cerveris played Wilson and Alexander Gemignani, son of Paul, was Addison. The two had played the roles under Eric Schaeffer's direction when the Kennedy Center staged its 2002 Sondheim Celebration. Theirs are also the voices on the 2009 *Road Show* Original New York Cast Recording.

By Rick Pender's count,** *Road Show*, under its various names, went through more than thirty songs, only six of which made it into every production.

"The challenges of *Road Show*," Doyle said in 2008, "are not only in the tremendous number of places we visit along the way, but also in the fact that the brothers are complex and, according to some, not particularly likeable."

Doyle posited that "the idea that people have to be likeable in order to make a good musical is, I believe, questionable.

"These characters are complex and selfish and yet capable of love and kindness, just like all of us."

---

* From 1940 through 1962, Hope the comic and Crosby the crooner made seven successful *Road* pictures together, starting with *The Road to Singapore*.

** Pender was executive editor and publisher of the website *Everything Sondheim*, managing editor of the *Sondheim Review*, which was published quarterly from 1994 until 2016, and author of the comprehensive *The Stephen Sondheim Encyclopedia*.

SUNDAY IN SPRINGFIELD WITH STEVE

"I still can't believe we got him," *The Simpsons* writer Michael Price said about Sondheim's 2007 appearance on the animated show. After Sondheim (second from right) recorded his sequence, Price told the guest star that they just needed one more thing—for Sondheim to play the entire score from *Sweeney Todd!* "He frowned," Price recalled, "and then played those first low rumble notes of the opening number with a big smile on his face. Unforgettable."

Steve Martin and Martin Short, move over: Enter Stephen Sondheim and Krusty the Clown.

The mismatch took place on *The Simpsons* during the Fox animated series' 2007 season,* when Krusty, voiced by Dan Castellaneta, desperately needs songs for a primetime special.

Enter Stephen Sondheim, voiced by Stephen Sondheim.

Except, when Sondheim hands Krusty the sheet music, the joyless jester goes ballistic—all he can see, he screams, are "complex harmonies, intricate lyrics, pithy observations on human life. *What is this junk?!*"

Krusty tells Sondheim simply to do what he did with *Cats.*

"I didn't write *Cats,*" Sondheim tells him.

Krusty demands Sondheim just give him "a peppy vamp."

Sondheim sits down at the piano and offers to add a counterpoint.

An agitated Krusty repeats his instruction.

Sondheim starts tinkling out a lively vamp, then muses, "Hey, this peppy stuff isn't bad. Maybe I *will* write that jingle for Buzz Cola."

At which point Sondheim rhymes the name of the soft drink with "Ayatollah."

---

* Average weekly viewership that season: 8.6 million.

IV.

It started as a spiky
vamp and then turned
into a religion.

When Sondheim turned eighty, in 2010, his birthday candles illuminated both sides of the Atlantic, particularly in his native Manhattan.

An all-star concert was held in Avery Fisher Hall, and another at City Center. Elaine Stritch devoted her Café Carlyle engagement to him. The Henry Miller Theatre on West Forty-Third Street was renamed the Stephen Sondheim.

The icing on the cake was surely *Sondheim on Sondheim*, a Broadway revue conceived and directed by James Lapine, featuring live performances of the Sondheim oeuvre along with video clips projected supersize and showing the man himself talking about his life and work . . . nearly choking up when discussing Oscar Hammerstein, taking care to explain his writing tools (Blackwing pencils and a shot glass), and even opening up about finding love late in life.*

The cast included Barbara Cook, Norm Lewis, Leslie Kritzer, Erin Mackey, Euan Morton, Matthew Scott, and God. No, really: God. The Almighty appeared in a new song Sondheim had written exclusively for the occasion, a laugh-filled satire about the awe in which he is held.

And whose picture was it that appeared on the giant video screen when "God" was sung?

Stephen Sondheim's.

Purely meant to be tongue-in-cheek, the song was nonetheless taken seriously in some quarters.

"He used irony to poke fun at his living legend," said Sondheim-obsessed podcaster and lyricist Kaley McMahon (whose *Aladdin* satire, *Twisted*, has seven million views on YouTube). "But I felt the song called out to me because the arts are a religion, and he stands for excellence that I can always aspire to, because, after all, he is God."

In 1998, *Newsweek* reported on a forty-five-year-old San Francisco writer who every year hosted like-minded friends to celebrate Sondheim's March 22 birthday, complete with T-shirts and meat pies. The newsmagazine went on to tell how New Jersey's

Among the tributes paid to Sondheim for his eightieth birthday in 2010 was *Sondheim on Sondheim*, a revue conceived and directed by James Lapine. A new number was added to the song canon for the occasion: "God" was part paean, part parody—depending upon one's point of view.

---

* When Sondheim was sixty, he said in interviews, he fell in love for the first time, with Peter Jones, a dramatist. They reportedly remained friends until Sondheim's death. In 2017, Sondheim married Jeff Romley, who survived him.

Paper Mill Playhouse was flooded with ticket orders from Australia, France, China, and twenty-six U.S. states when the theatre announced it was doing *Follies*.

Sondheads, as *Newsweek* called them, were also responsible for positioning themselves strategically outside the Plymouth Theatre and yelling at anyone who dared to walk out on *Passion*.

Sondheim himself was not immune to this heightened sense of attention.

When one fan—make that fanatic—sent him a chocolate cake for his birthday, Sondheim wrote back and asked for the recipe.

Rent composer-lyricist Jonathan Larson (left) and Stephen Sondheim, in the early 1990s. Sondheim had been offering the young musician advice from the time Larson was a college student.

The 2021 movie musical *tick, tick . . . BOOM!*, set in 1990, took its beat from a real-life 1992 stage monologue written and performed by the rock composer, lyricist, and playwright Jonathan Larson about his efforts to find producers for his dystopian musical, *Superbia*.

The film's titular time bomb refers to his being days away from turning thirty; "Older than Stephen Sondheim when he had his first show," Larson laments as the camera pans over the back cover of the original *West Side Story* soundtrack LP.

The plot contains another time-clock device. Larson, succumbing to an undiagnosed aortic aneurysm, would be dead at thirty-five on the very eve of proving the promise Sondheim recognized early on: the first Off-Broadway preview of what will become Larson's Pulitzer- and Broadway Tony-winning spin on *La Bohème*, the runaway hit *Rent*.

In truth, Larson and Sondheim had been corresponding from the time the former, an acting major at New York's Adelphi University, had first sought advice from the veteran.

As portrayed by Andrew Garfield, under Lin-Manuel Miranda's direction, Larson cloaks his seminaked ambition in earnestness, though the veneer couldn't protect Larson's relationship with the dancer Susan (Alexandra Shipp)—a parallel to Georges Seurat and Dot in *Sunday in the Park with George*, a snippet of which Larson is seen watching on TV. (Larson pens his own "Sunday," only his is based on his experience as a waiter in a diner, not a painter in a park.)

In the movie, as in real life, Sondheim attends a tryout for new composers and offers Larson this assessment: "First-rate lyric. And tune." Quick cut to Larson telling his club-venue audience: "Those five words were enough to keep me going for the next two years."

At his lowest ebb after a fruitless backers' audition of *Superbia*, Larson returns home to an answering-machine message from the Great Influencer himself, words the real Sondheim recorded for the film based on his actual sentiment to Larson: "It's first-rate work and has a future, and so do you."

Sondheim asks if it is all right to call Larson later with some comments.

"Meanwhile," he said, "be proud."

Stephen Sondheim, by Jama McMahon, 2021. McMahon and
Sondheim share the same birthday, March 22, albeit six decades
apart. She was also company manager at the Classic Stage Company
in 2017, when Sondheim attended the opening night of their *Pacific
Overtures*. She gave him a souvenir pin he liked.

LATER

"Sometimes," Stephen Sondheim said as he approached his eightieth birthday in 2010, "I think if I hear one more song I have written, I will kill myself."

He laughed.

"As he got older," Sam Mendes recalled, "his emotions were closer to the surface—ironic for someone who was sometimes accused of a lack of warmth in his work." Mendes remembered having supper alone with Sondheim at his home on Forty-Ninth Street, "during which he described the legendary production of *The Tempest* by Giorgio Strehler. When he spoke about the final moments, and of Prospero accepting that his powers were gone, he burst into tears and retired to the bathroom."

"The thing that's startling," said composer Stephen Flaherty (*Ragtime, Once on This Island*, and thirty years Sondheim's junior), "is when you think of how he, for decades and decades, was the preeminent writer for the American musical theatre. He was always in production, always involved with something, and yet he always found the time to mentor, to return every individual letter and email."

The guidance extended beyond correspondence. Flaherty frequently witnessed Sondheim at various venues around New York lending support at early workshops and readings of new works. "You would think he would be so rarified and so removed from the everyday world, and he was the opposite of that."

There was also a playful side to him. When he showed up at the Classic Stage Company for opening night of their *Pacific Overtures* in 2017, the company manager, Jama McMahon, greeted him and his guest, Sondheim's then-collaborator, playwright David Ives (*Venus in Fur*). The two were at work on a musical about Spanish film director Luis Buñuel based on two of his movies, *The Discreet Charm of the Bourgeoisie* (1972) and *The Exterminating Angel* (1962).

"I was wearing a little lapel pin of Sondheim I'd bought years ago, made by this Australian guy [Tyson Armstrong]," McMahon recalled in 2022, "and when I met Sondheim, I thought, 'This is my chance to say something. What do I do?' So I took the little lapel pin off and said, 'I want to show you this,' and handed it to him. 'Oh, my God,' he said. 'This is hilarious. This is the funniest thing I have ever seen.'" And he handed it back to me. 'No, no,' I said. 'You can keep it.' And he was like a little kid. 'I get to keep this?' he said. 'I can keep it?'"

He not only kept it, but before and during the performance of *Pacific Overtures* he kept taking it out of his pocket. When he wasn't inspecting it, he was rubbing it in David Ives's face.

"David," Sondheim said, "is there a pin of *your* face?" And, "David, there's no pin of your face, is there?"

And a bit later, he said, "But I promise when our show opens, someone will do a pin of your face."

Sondheim was both encouraging and inspirational when Lin-Manuel Miranda (here, at the 2021 Times Square Sondheim memorial) revealed his idea to do a musical about Alexander Hamilton. Williams College music professor W. Anthony Sheppard likened *Hamilton*'s prologue to "the opening of *Sweeney Todd*, with each character singing about the title character before the title character speaks."

The Buñuel project was scrapped, or so it seemed. By April 2021, official word came down that it would not happen. On the other hand, in September 2021, Nathan Lane spilled the beans on the *Today* show that he and Bernadette Peters had recently participated in a private reading of a new Stephen Sondheim–David Ives musical, so hope for the show sprang up again—under the title *Square One*. By March 2023, the title became *Here We Are*, and a limited production was scheduled for that September in The Shed at Manhattan's Hudson Yards, under the direction of Joe Mantello.

"I'm not a retiring type," said Sondheim. "I'm not a golf player. I can't imagine sitting in front of the television. Painful as it is, writing is still fun, and I don't have anything else to do."

And yet, there was the inevitable.

"Aging is no fun. My memory isn't sharp. All your energies diminish. You don't want to make any more friends than you've made, and they're all dying anyway." He also found himself increasingly homebound, out of desire, mostly.

"I don't want to even leave the couch to go to the next room. I rode a bike to Broadway for twenty years. You get to know every pothole in New York. Watch me climb the stairs and you'll know I'm an old man climbing the stairs.

"That also happens at the piano."

—

"If I had to live my life over again, I would have children," Sondheim said in 2009. "That's the great mistake I made. It's too late now. The idea of being a homosexual and raising children was one that was just not acceptable until, my goodness, I'd say the 1970s or 1980s. You want to live long enough to see your children grow up, they're not puppies. The joy is not just to have them, but to watch them change and grow. So, yes, that is a great regret."

Sondheim with his partner, actor-singer-producer Jeff Romley, in 2013, when the composer was among those honored as a Library Lion at the New York Public Library, "for outstanding achievements in their respective fields of arts, culture, letters, and scholarship." Sondheim and Romley were married in 2017.

Stephen Joshua Sondheim died at his Connecticut home at the age of ninety-one. The cause of death was cardiovascular disease. He had had Thanksgiving dinner with friends the night before.

He was generous with his estate, which was estimated to be worth $75 million. Having established the Stephen J. Sondheim Revocable Trust, he left monetary gifts to the Smithsonian Institute, the Museum of New York City, the Library of Congress, the New York Public Library for the Performing Arts, the Dramatists Guild Fund, and the Irish Repertory Theatre company. According to reports, in addition to his husband, Jeff Romley, and his previous companion, Peter Jones, he listed James Lapine among the beneficiaries, along with other friends.

On March 22, 2022, on what would have been Sondheim's ninety-second birthday, Playbill.com posted comments from Angela Lansbury, Chita Rivera, Bernadette Peters, Norm Lewis, Betty Buckley, Raúl Esparza, Donna Murphy, Michael Cerveris, Patti LuPone, Melissa Errico, and several others about the impact he had had on them.

Each remembrance was personal in its own way, but one stood out in particular. Addressing how Sondheim "taught artists to trust that the uniqueness of oneself and one's work is something to be revered, encouraged, and celebrated, not only by others, but, most importantly, by one's own self," Audra McDonald said there was no greater gift.

A Stephen Sondheim Foundation was established. On its behalf, Cameron Mackintosh produced a May 3, 2022, event at London's Stephen Sondheim Theatre and called it *Old Friends*. Staged by Matthew Bourne and Maria Friedman, the all-star evening featured Bernadette Peters, Judi Dench, Imelda Staunton, Michael Ball, Helena Bonham Carter, Petula Clark, Damien Lewis, Julia McKenzie, Julian Ovenden, Sian Phillips, and Jenna Russell, among others—and it sold out so quickly that the live performance had to be broadcast in hi-def to another capacity-filled West End theatre in order to meet the ticket demand.

The night concluded with the entire house singing "Old Friends." There were very few dry eyes in the crowd.

"One of the things I couldn't care less about is posterity," said Stephen Sondheim. "If you can't enjoy life while still alive, what is the point?"

As usual, he gave the statement a quick second thought.

"However, while I'm still alive, I'd like my shows to be done as much as possible."

OPPOSITE: "The worst thing you can do is censor yourself as the pencil hits the paper," Stephen Sondheim (1930–2021) told his students at Oxford. "If you start thinking that way, you won't write anything." He further advised, "If you can put everything down, stream-of-consciousness, no matter how clichéd it may seem, you'll do yourself a service."

ACKNOWLEDGMENTS

Diane Reid, with whom I've shared nearly every Sondheim show (not to mention countless others, as well as several Westminster Dog Shows), voluntarily read every syllable as the manuscript took shape, and she made comments. Oh, did she make comments. One phone call alone lasted four hours.

Her advice and our enduring friendship have been invaluable.

Even when this book was only in the rumor stage, Jane Klain, of the Paley Center for Media in New York City, jumped in to help. It was hardly a surprise that she had heard the rumor; Jani is a super sleuth. Among her professional finds have been *Evening Primrose* and, at Sondheim's urging, the believed-to-be-lost *Password* episode with Sondheim and Lee Remick. In appreciation, Sondheim called Jani "a doll." Twice.

For her near-miraculous abilities and generosity, I second that.

Howard Mandelbaum, of Photofest, was his usual big-hearted self, as he has been on every book I have written. Please, kiddo, let's keep this going.

Barbara Carroll and Kevin McAnarney met me at Becco in the Theatre District for monthly pep talks—and many bottles of Montepulciano. That welcome combination contributed to the book you now hold in your hands.

Jolie and Gary Alony pulled a genie out of a bottle. They understand what I mean, and I still cannot thank them enough.

Mary Corliss supplied magic, but Mary is magical.

Ronny Diamond supplied shelter when the electricity gave out at my place. She is also my dog Kingston's beloved godmother. Cinderella could not ask for more.

David Noh, a fellow journalist, provided a key introduction and equally appreciated laughs. Robert Hofler offered critical insights into Sondheim, but then, he *is* a critic. Chris Hill acted like a personal news clipping service, and it's a good thing I have unlimited message units. My dear friend Pippa Scott told swell tales of her *Auntie Mame* and *The Searchers* costars Rosalind Russell and Natalie Wood. (They also starred in *Gypsy*.) Miranda Tollman provided unflagging enthusiasm and support. Frank Dunlop continued to amaze with his tales of the theatre, to say nothing of his wry wit.

Neighbors Bette and Pavel Kraus, Bob Finkelstein and Don Lemoine, Paromita and Robert Harrington, and Mary Elizabeth Simpson left food at my door during crunch time. Jennifer Gonzales left reference books. This is why one lives in New York City.

I intend to thank the following in person but would first like to acknowledge them here: Patricia Birch, Joan Brower, Michael Dirda, Alan Eichler, Jane Friedman, Tamara Glenny, Foster Hirsch, Louise Kerz Hirschfeld, Barry Kleinbort, Diane Krausz and Robert Infarinato, Sara Kelly Johns, Jane Lahr, Dame Cleo Laine, Christine La Monte and Len Williams, David Landay, Ron Mandelbaum, Matthew Messinger, Judy and Terry Mowschenson, Joan Myers, Sheila Nevins, Marsha Palanci, Ron Pullen, Evelyn Renold, Ethel Sheffer, Laura and David Rudge, Anna and Paul Stolper, Charlene Stolper, Victoria Wilson, Glenn Young, and Kathy Zuckerman.

Special gratitude to those who allowed themselves to be interviewed; you will find yourselves identified in the text and source notes. Those willing to speak but requesting anonymity have had their wishes granted.

I would be remiss in not thanking my long-ago editors at the *New York Post*. They hired me to cover entertainment when I was all of twenty-five, thus furnishing a gateway to such giants as Jerome Robbins, Agnes de Mille, Bob Fosse, Michael Bennett, and, yes, Stephen Sondheim, with whom I shared a particularly memorable dinner with Dorothy Loudon. (One day I shall auction off my diary.)

Finally, and I know I am over my word count, but I cannot say enough about my publisher, Black Dog & Leventhal. Just as you did in 2019 with my *The Amusement Park*, you showed extra care, special thoughtfulness, and impeccable taste.

Deepest thanks to publishing director Becky Koh Hicks, director of marketing Betsy Hulsebosch, associate director of publicity Kara Thornton, senior editor Lisa Tenaglia, and, especially, editor Joe Davidson, who lent a keen and knowledgeable eye to the manuscript and a wonderful temperament to our Monday morning phone calls.

Vodka stingers all around.

—S.M.S.

BIBLIOGRAPHY

BOOKS

Abbott, George. *"Mr. Abbott."* New York: Random House, 1963.

Abbott, Karen. *American Rose: The Life and Times of Gypsy Rose Lee.* New York: Random House, 2011.

Avian, Bob, with Tom Santopietro. *Dancing Man: A Broadway Choreographer's Journey.* Jackson, MS: University Press of Mississippi, 2020.

Behlmer, Rudy, ed. *Memo from David O. Selznick.* New York: Viking Press, 1972.

Bernstein, Jamie. *Famous Father Girl: A Memoir of Growing Up Bernstein.* New York: Harper, 2018.

Beymer, Richard. *Impostor: Or, Who Am I When Not Being Who I Think I Am, or Whatever Happened to Richard Beymer?* N.p.: Booboo Press, 2007.

Block, Geoffrey. *Enchanted Evenings: The Broadway Musical from "Show Boat" to Sondheim and Lloyd Webber.* New York: Oxford University Press, 2009.

Bloom, Ken. *American Song: The Complete Musical Theatre Companion.* New York: Schirmer Books, 2001.

———. *Show & Tell: The New Book of Broadway Anecdotes.* New York: Oxford University Press, 2016.

Bosworth, Patricia. *Montgomery Clift: A Biography.* New York: Harcourt Brace Jovanovich, 1978.

Bouzereau, Laurent. *"West Side Story": The Making of the Steven Spielberg Film.* New York: Harry N. Abrams, 2021.

Bryer, Jackson R., and Richard A. Davidson, eds. *The Art of the American Musical: Conversations with the Creators.* New Brunswick, NJ: Rutgers University Press, 2005.

Burke, John. *Rogue's Progress: The Fabulous Adventures of Wilson Mizner.* New York: G. P. Putnam's Sons, 1975.

Burton, Humphrey. *Leonard Bernstein.* New York: Doubleday, 1994.

Cain, James M. *Serenade.* New York: Alfred A. Knopf, 1937.

Chakiris, George, with Lindsay Harrison. *My West Side Story: A Memoir.* Lanham, MD: Lyons Press, 2021.

Chapin, Ted. *Everything Was Possible: The Birth of the Musical "Follies."* New York: Alfred A. Knopf, 2003.

Citron, Stephen. *Sondheim & Lloyd-Webber: The New Musical.* New York: Oxford University Press, 2001.

Clum, John M. *The Works of Arthur Laurents: Politics, Love, and Betrayal.* Amherst, NY: Cambria Press, 2014.

Collier, John. *Fancies and Goodnights.* New York: Doubleday, 1951.

Comden, Betty. *Off Stage.* New York: Simon & Schuster, 1995.

Curtis, James. *Buster Keaton: A Filmmaker's Life.* New York: Alfred A. Knopf, 2022.

Dachs, David. *Anything Goes: The World of Popular Music.* Indianapolis: Bobbs-Merrill, 1964.

de Mille, Agnes. *A Dance of Death: Lizzie Borden.* Boston: Little, Brown, 1952.

———. *Dance to the Piper.* Boston: Little, Brown, 1952.

Dietz, Dan. *The Complete Book of 1970s Broadway Musicals.* Lanham, MD: Rowman & Littlefield, 2015.

Fierstein, Harvey. *I Was Better Last Night: A Memoir.* New York: Alfred A. Knopf, 2022.

Filichia, Peter. *Strippers, Showgirls, and Sharks: A Very Opinionated History of the Broadway Musicals That Did Not Win the Tony Award.* New York: St. Martin's Press, 2013.

Flinn, Caryl. *Brass Diva: The Life and Legends of Ethel Merman.* Berkeley, CA: University of California Press, 2007.

Ford, Paul. *Lord Knows, At Least I Was There: Working with Stephen Sondheim.* With an introduction by Mandy Patinkin. New York: Moreclacke Publishing, 2022.

Fordin, Hugh. *Getting to Know Him: A Biography of Oscar Hammerstein II.* With an introduction by Stephen Sondheim. New York: Random House, 1977.

Francis, Ben. *Careful the Spell You Cast: How Stephen Sondheim Extended the Range of the American Musical.* London: Methuen Drama, 2023.

Frommer, Myrna Katz, and Harvey Frommer. *It Happened on Broadway: An Oral History of the Great White Way.* Madison, WI: University of Wisconsin Press, 2004.

Furth, George, Stephen Sondheim, and Hal Prince. *Company: A Musical Comedy.* New York: Theatre Communications Group, 1996.

———. *Company: A Musical Comedy.* London: Nick Hearn Books, 2019.

Garebian, Keith. *The Making of "Gypsy."* Toronto: ECW Press, 1994.

———. *The Making of "My Fair Lady."* Buffalo, NY: Mosaic Press, 1998.

Gelbart, Larry. *Laughing Matters: On Writing "M*A*S*H," "Tootsie," "Oh, God!," and a Few Other Funny Things.* New York: Random House, 1998.

Goldman, James, and Stephen Sondheim. *Follies.* New York: Theatre Communications Group, 2011.

Goldman, William. *The Season: A Candid Look at Broadway.* New York: Harcourt, Brace & World, 1969.

Gordon, Joanne. *Art Isn't Easy: The Theater of Stephen Sondheim.* New York: Da Capo Press, 1992.

Gordon, Robert, ed. *The Oxford Handbook of Sondheim Studies.* New York: Oxford University Press, 2014.

Gottfried, Martin. *Balancing Act: The Authorized Biography of Angela Lansbury.* Boston: Little, Brown, 1999.

———. *Sondheim.* New York: Harry N. Abrams, 2000.

Grant, Mark N. *The Rise and Fall of the Broadway Musical.* Boston: Northeastern University Press, 2004.

Hall, Ben M. *The Best Remaining Seats: The Story of the Golden Age of the Movie Palace.* New York: Bramhall House, 1961.

Hall, Margaret. *Gemignani: Life and Lessons from Broadway and Beyond.* Guilford, CT: Applause Theatre & Cinema Books, 2022.

Hamill, Pete. *Why Sinatra Matters*. New York: Little, Brown, 2015.

Hammerstein, Oscar II. *Rodgers & Hammerstein's Carousel: The Complete Book and Lyrics of the Broadway Musical*. New York: Applause Theatre & Cinema Books, 2016.

Harris, Mark. *Mike Nichols: A Life*. New York: Penguin Press, 2021.

Hirsch, Foster. *Harold Prince and the American Musical Theatre*. New York: Applause Theatre & Cinema Books, 2005.

Hofler, Robert. *Money, Murder, and Dominick Dunne: A Life in Several Acts*. Madison, WI: University of Wisconsin Press, 2017.

Horowitz, Mark Eden. *Sondheim on Music: Minor Details and Major Decisions*. Lanham, MD: Rowman & Littlefield, 2019.

———. *The Letters of Oscar Hammerstein II*. New York: Oxford University Press, 2022.

Housez, Lara E. *Becoming Stephen Sondheim: "Anyone Can Whistle," "A Pray by Blecht," "Company" and "Sunday in the Park with George."* Rochester, NY: University of Rochester, 2013.

Ilson, Carol. *Harold Prince: From "Pajama Game" to "Phantom of the Opera" and Beyond*. New York: Limelight Books, 1992.

Irvin, Sam. *Kay Thompson: From "Funny Face" to "Eloise."* New York: Simon & Schuster, 2010.

Jacobs, Alexandra. *Still Here: The Madcap, Nervy, Singular Life of Elaine Stritch*. New York: Farrar, Straus and Giroux, 2019.

Jowitt, Deborah. *Jerome Robbins: His Life, His Theatre, His Dance*. New York: Simon & Schuster, 2004.

Kaiser, Charles. *The Gay Metropolis: The Landmark History of Gay Life in America*. New York: Grove Atlantic, 2007.

Kapilow, Rob. *Listening for America: Inside the Great American Songbook from Gershwin to Sondheim*. New York: Liveright Publishing, 2019.

Kellow, Brian. *Ethel Merman: A Life*. New York: Viking Penguin, 2007.

Kelly, Kevin. *One Singular Sensation: The Michael Bennett Story*. New York: Doubleday, 1990.

Kinne, Wisner Payne. *George Pierce Baker and the American Theatre*. Cambridge, MA: Harvard University Press, 1955.

Kissel, Howard. *David Merrick: The Abominable Showman: The Unauthorized Biography*. New York: Applause Books, 2000.

Knapp, Raymond. *The American Musical and the Formation of National Identity*. Princeton: Princeton University Press, 2006.

Kreuger, Miles. *"Show Boat": The Story of a Classic American Musical*. New York: Oxford University Press, 1977.

Lapine, James. *Putting It Together: How Stephen Sondheim and I Created "Sunday in the Park with George."* New York: Farrar, Straus and Giroux, 2021.

Laurents, Arthur. *Mainly on Directing: "Gypsy," "West Side Story," and Other Musicals*. New York: Alfred A. Knopf, 2009.

———. *Original Story: A Memoir of Broadway and Hollywood*. New York: Applause Theatre Books, 2000.

Laurents, Arthur, Stephen Sondheim, and Jule Styne. *Gypsy*. New York: Theatre Communications Group, 2009.

Lawrence, Carol. *Carol Lawrence: The Backstage Story*. New York: McGraw Hill, 1990.

Lawrence, Greg. *Dance with Demons: The Life of Jerome Robbins*. New York: G. P. Putnam's Sons, 2001.

Leamer, Laurence. *Capote's Women: A True Story of Love, Betrayal, and a Swan Song for an Era*. New York: G. P. Putnam's Sons, 2021.

Lee, Gypsy Rose. *Gypsy: A Memoir*. New York: Dell Publishing, 1959.

Lerman, Leo. *The Grand Surprise: The Journals of Leo Lerman*. Edited by Stephen Pascal. New York: Alfred A. Knopf, 2007.

Logan, John. *I'll Eat You Last: A Chat with Sue Mengers*. London: Oberon Books, 2013.

Long, Robert Emmet. *Broadway, the Golden Years: Jerome Robbins and the Great Choreographer-Directors, 1940 to the Present*. New York: Continuum Books, 2001.

LuPone, Patti, with Digby Diehl. *Patti LuPone: A Memoir*. New York: Three Rivers Press, 2010.

Mack, Robert L. *The Wonderful and Surprising History of Sweeney Todd: The Life and Times of an Urban Legend*. London: Bloomsbury Academic, 2007.

Mandelbaum, Ken. *"A Chorus Line" and the Musicals of Michael Bennett*. New York: St. Martin's Press, 1989.

———. *Not Since "Carrie": Forty Years of Musical Flops*. New York: St. Martin's Press, 1991.

Maslon, Laurence, ed. *Kaufman & Co.: Broadway Comedies*. New York: The Library of America, 2004.

Max, D. T. *Finale: Late Conversations with Stephen Sondheim*. New York: Harper, 2022.

McLaughlin, Robert L. *Stephen Sondheim and the Reinvention of the American Musical*. Jackson, MS: University Press of Mississippi, 2016.

McMillin, Scott. *The Musical as Drama: A Study of the Principles and Conventions Behind the Musical Shows from Kern to Sondheim*. Princeton: Princeton University Press, 2006.

Merman, Ethel, with George Eells. *Merman: An Autobiography*. New York: Simon & Schuster, 1978.

Mirisch, Walter. *I Thought We Were Making Movies, Not History*. Madison, WI: University of Wisconsin Press, 2008.

Molnár, Ferenc. *Liliom: A Legend in Seven Scenes and a Prologue*. Translated by Benjamin F. Glazer. University of North Carolina at Chapel Hill: Project Gutenberg eBook, 2015.

Mordden, Ethan. *Beautiful Mornin': The Broadway Musical in the 1940s*. New York: Oxford University Press, 1999.

———. *Coming Up Roses: The Broadway Musical in the 1950s*. New York: Oxford University Press, 1998.

———. *On Sondheim: An Opinionated Guide*. New York: Oxford University Press, 2016.

———. *One More Kiss: The Broadway Musical in the 1970s*. New York: Palgrave Macmillan, 2003.

———. *Open a New Window: The Broadway Musical in the 1960s*. New York: St. Martin's Press, 2001.

O'Leary, James. "Breakout from the Asylum of Conformity: Sondheim, Laurents, and the Dramaturgy of *Anyone Can Whistle*." In *Sondheim in Our Time and His*. Edited by W. Anthony Sheppard. New York: Oxford University Press, 2022.

Oppenheimer, George. *The View from the Sixties: Memories of a Spent Life*. New York: David McKay, 1966.

Parker, Dorothy. *Not Much Fun: The Lost Poems of Dorothy Parker*. Edited by Stuart Y. Silverstein. New York: Scribner, 2009.

Pender, Rick. *The Stephen Sondheim Encyclopedia*. Lanham, MD: Rowman & Littlefield, 2021.

Poland, Albert. *Stages: A Theatre Memoir*. Wappingers Falls, NY: Albert Poland, 2019.

Preminger, Erik Lee. *Gypsy & Me: At Home and On the Road with Gypsy Rose Lee*. Boston: Little, Brown, 1984.

Prince, Hal. *Contradictions: Notes of Twenty-Six Years in the Theatre*. New York: Dodd, Mead, 1974.

Prince, Harold. *Sense of Occasion*. Milwaukee: Applause Theatre & Cinema Books, 2017.

Purdum, Todd S. *Something Wonderful: Rodgers and Hammerstein's Broadway Revolution*. New York: Henry Holt, 2018.

Quinn, Carolyn. *Mama Rose's Turn: The True Story of America's Most Notorious Stage Mother*. Jackson, MS: University Press of Mississippi, 2013.

Rich, Frank, with Lisa Aronson. *The Theatre Art of Boris Aronson*. New York: Alfred A. Knopf, 1987.

Riedel, Michael. *Razzle Dazzle: The Battle for Broadway*. New York: Simon & Schuster, 2015.

Rodgers, Mary, and Jesse Green. *Shy: The Alarmingly Outspoken Memoirs of Mary Rodgers*. New York: Farrar, Straus and Giroux, 2022.

Rodgers, Richard. *Musical Stages: An Autobiography*. New York: Random House, 1975.

Russell, Rosalind, and Chris Chase. *Life Is a Banquet*. New York: Random House, 1977.

Salsini, Paul. *Sondheim & Me: Recalling a Genius*. Baltimore MD: Bancroft Press, 2022.

Secrest, Meryle. *Somewhere for Me: A Biography of Richard Rodgers*. New York: Alfred A. Knopf, 2001.

———. *Stephen Sondheim: A Life*. New York, Alfred A. Knopf, 1998.

Shapiro, Eddie. *Nothing Like a Dame: Conversations with the Great Women of Musical Theater*. New York: Oxford University Press, 2015.

Sheppard, W. Anthony, ed. *Sondheim in Our Time and His*. New York: Oxford University Press, 2022.

Shevelove, Burt, Larry Gelbart, and Stephen Sondheim. *A Funny Thing Happened on the Way to the Forum*. New York: Applause Theatre Book Publishers, 1991.

Short, Bobby, with Robert Mackintosh. *The Life and Times of a Saloon Singer*. New York: Clarkson N. Potter, 1995.

Shulman, Irving. *West Side Story: A Novelization*. New York: Gallery Books, 2021.

Silverman, Stephen M. *The Amusement Park: 900 Years of Thrills and Spills, and the Dreamers and Schemers Who Built Them*. New York: Black Dog & Leventhal, 2019.

———. *Dancing on the Ceiling: Stanley Donen and His Movies*. New York: Alfred A. Knopf, 1996.

———. *David Lean*. New York: Harry N. Abrams, 1989.

———. *The Fox That Got Away: The Last Days of the Zanuck Dynasty at Twentieth Century-Fox*. Secaucus, NJ: Lyle Stuart, 1988.

———. *Public Spectacles*. New York: E.P. Dutton, 1981.

Simeone, Nigel, ed. *The Leonard Bernstein Letters*. New Haven: Yale University Press, 2013.

Simon, John. *On Theater: Criticism 1974–2003*. New York: Applause Theater & Cinema Books, 2005.

Smith, Helen R. *New Light on Sweeney Todd, Thomas Peckett Prest, James Malcolm Rymer, and Elizabeth Caroline Grey*. London: Jarndyce, 2002.

Sondheim, Stephen. *Finishing the Hat: Collected Lyrics (1954–1981) with Attendant Comments, Principles, Heresies, Grudges, Whines, and Anecdotes*. New York: Alfred A. Knopf, 2010.

———. *Look, I Made a Hat: Collected Lyrics (1981–2011) with Attendant Comments, Amplifications, Dogmas, Harangues, Digressions, Anecdotes, and Miscellany*. New York: Alfred A. Knopf, 2011.

———. "Theatre Lyrics." In *Playwrights, Lyricists, Composers on Theater*. Edited by Otis Guernsey. New York: Dodd, Mead, 1974.

Stevens, George Jr., ed. *Conversations with the Great Moviemakers of Hollywood's Golden Age at the American Film Institute*. New York: Alfred A. Knopf, 2006.

Stevens, Mark, and Annalyn Swan. *Francis Bacon: Revelations*. New York: Alfred A. Knopf, 2021.

Suskin, Steven. *Opening Night on Broadway: A Critical Quotebook of the Golden Era of the Musical Theatre, from "Oklahoma!" (1943) to "Fiddler on the Roof" (1964)*. New York: Schirmer Books, 1990.

———. *Showtunes 1905–1991: The Songs and Careers of Broadway's Major Composers*. New York: Limelight Editions, 1992.

Swayne, Steve. *How Sondheim Found His Sound*. Ann Arbor: University of Michigan Press, 2007.

Taylor, Theodore. *Jule: The Story of Composer Jule Styne*. New York: Random House, 1979.

Thompson, Kent. *Directing Professionally: A Practical Guide to Developing a Successful Career in Today's Theatre*. London: Methuen Drama, 2019.

Thurber, James. *The Years with Ross*. Boston: Little, Brown, 1959.

Turner, Alice K. *The History of Hell*. New York: Harcourt Brace, 1993.

Vaill, Amanda, ed. *Jerome Robbins, By Himself: Selections from His Letters, Journals, Drawings, Photographs, and an Unfinished Memoir*. New York: Alfred A. Knopf, 2019.

———. *Somewhere: The Life of Jerome Robbins*. New York: Broadway Books, 2006.

Viertel, Jack. *The Secret Life of the American Musical: How Broadway Shows Are Built*. New York: Farrar, Straus and Giroux, 2016.

White, E. B. *Here Is New York*. New York: Harper & Brothers, 1949.

Willson, Meredith. *But He Doesn't Know the Territory: The Making of Meredith Willson's "The Music Man."* Minneapolis: University of Minnesota Press, 2009.

Winecoff, Charles. *Anthony Perkins: Split Image*. New York: Advocate Books, 2006.

Wolfe, Tom. *The "Me" Decade and the Third Great Awakening*. New York: Farrar, Straus and Giroux, 1976.

Zadan, Craig. *Sondheim & Co*. New York: Da Capo Press, 1994.

Zinnemann, Fred. *Fred Zinnemann: A Life in the Movies*. New York: Charles Scribner's Sons, 1992.

PERIODICALS, PROGRAMS, AND NEWS SERVICES

Abramovitch, Seth. "Perverted Wolves, Cheating Wives and a Fired 10-Year-Old: The Dark Path to Disney's 'Into the Woods.'" *Hollywood Reporter*, December 10, 2014. https://www.hollywoodreporter.com/news/general-news/perverted-wolves-cheating-wives-a-755359/.

———. "Tony Kushner on Tackling 'West Side Story' with Spielberg: 'We Knew We Were Going into a Complicated Situation.'" *Hollywood Reporter*, December 3, 2021. https://www.hollywoodreporter.com/movies/movie-features/tony-kushner-interview-west-side-story-steven-spielberg-1235054430/.

Allis, Tim. "What Stephen Sondheim Thinks of the 'Merrily We Roll Along' Doc." *Playbill*, November 16, 2016. https://playbill.com/article/what-stephen-sondheim-thinks-of-the-merrily-we-roll-along-doc.

Anonymous. "Charles Gilbert: Full Circle." *Sondheim Review*, Summer 1994.

———. "From Oedipus to 'Me as King Lear.'" *Sondheim Review*, Summer 1998.

———. "Herbert Sondheim, 71, Dead." *New York Times*, August 2, 1966.

———. "Season Program Ratings." *Hollywood Reporter*, May 25, 2007. https://web.archive.org/web/20100129154626/http://www.hollywoodreporter.com/hr/content_display/television/features/e3ifbfdd1bcb53266ad8d9a71cad261604f.

———. "Show Business: Sweet and Sour Sue." *Time*, March 26, 1973. https://content.time.com/time/subscriber/article/0,33009,907002,00.html.

———. "Show Business: The Once and Future Follies." *Time*, May 3, 1971. http://content.time.com/time/subscriber/article/0,33009,876987-7,00.html.

———. *Something for Everyone: Sondheim Tonight!* New York: The Museum of Television & Radio program brochure, 2000.

———. "Sondheim: 'It Was a Hard One to Write.'" *Sondheim Review*, Summer 1994.

———. "Stephen Sondheim Takes Issue with Plan for Revamped 'Porgy and Bess,'" *ArtsBeat* (blog). *New York Times*, August 10, 2011. https://artsbeat.blogs.nytimes.com/2011/08/10/stephen-sondheim-takes-issue-with-plan-for-revamped-porgy-and-bess/.

Arkatov, Janice. "A New Role in an Old Favorite: Glynis Johns returns to 'A Little Night Music.'" *Los Angeles Times*, April 17, 1991. https://www.latimes.com/archives/la-xpm-1991-04-17-ca-126-story.html.

Atkinson, Brooks. "Anatomy of Worldly Success in 'Merrily We Roll Along,' by George S. Kaufman and Moss Hart." *New York Times*, October 1, 1934.

Babbitt, Milton. "Who Cares If You Listen?" *High Fidelity*, February 1958. https://artsillumination.files.wordpress.com/2015/02/who-cares-if-you-listen.pdf.

Baltake, Joe. "There's Nothing Wrong with '62 'Gypsy.'" *Los Angeles Times*, December 27, 1993. https://www.latimes.com/archives/la-xpm-1993-12-27-ca-5840-story.html.

Bandler, Michael J. "What Collaboration Is All About." *Sondheim Review*, Fall 2009.

Barnes, Clive. "Stage: 'Funny Thing' Happens Again." *New York Times*, March 3, 1972.

———. "Theater: 'Company' Offers a Guide to New York's Marital Jungle." *New York Times*, April 27, 1970. https://archive.nytimes.com/www.nytimes.com/books/98/07/19/specials/sondheim-company.html.

———. "The Theatre: 'A Little Night Music.'" *New York Times*, February 26, 1972. https://archive.nytimes.com/www.nytimes.com/books/98/07/19/specials/sondheim-night.html.

Barnett, Gregory. "'Sweeney Todd,' Houston Grand Opera." *Opera News*, July 2015. https://www.operanews.com/Opera_News_Magazine/2015/7/Reviews/HOUSTON__Sweeney_Todd.html.

Barnett, Laura. "Stephen Sondheim, Composer—Portrait of the Artist." *Guardian*, November 27, 2012. https://www.theguardian.com/culture/2012/nov/27/stephen-sondheim-portrait-artist.

Benedict, David. "Sondheim Reshaped American Theatre, Placing It at the Very Heart of American Culture." *Guardian*, November 28, 2021. https://www.theguardian.com/commentisfree/2021/nov/28/rip-stephen-sondheim-revolutionary-in-world-of-musical-theatre.

Berger, Joseph. "New York Military Academy's Sudden Closing, After 126 Years." *New York Times*, September 20, 2015.

Berkvist, Robert. "Arthur Laurents, Playwright and Director on Broadway, Dies at 93." *New York Times*, May 5, 2011.

———. "Stephen Sondheim Takes a Stab at Grand Guignol." *New York Times*, February 25, 1979. https://archive.nytimes.com/www.nytimes.com/books/98/07/19/specials/sondheim-guignol.html.

Bixby, Suzanne. "Jumping In." *Sondheim Review*, Summer 2010,

———. "Sixty Years of Sparks: Hal Prince Says He and Sondheim Energize Each Other." *Sondheim Review*, Spring 2010.

———. "Two-Way Street." *Sondheim Review*, Fall 2010.

Blau, Eleanor. "Jule Styne, Bountiful Creator of Song Favorites, Dies at 88." *New York Times*, September 21, 1994.

Blumenthal, Ralph. "The Legacy of a Stage-Struck Teacher: Dusty Treasures Reveal a Golden Era for Broadway, TV and Ethel Burns (Who?)." *New York Times*, October 22, 1998.

Bosworth, Patricia. "From the Archives: Elaine Stritch, Barbara Barrie, Larry Kert, and the Cast of 'Company' on Modern Marriage," *Playbill*, September 16, 2018. https://www.playbill.com/article/from-the-archives-elaine-stritch-barbara-barrie-larry-kert-and-the-cast-of-company-on-modern-marriage.

Brantley, Ben. "Stephen Sondheim, the Man Who Felt Too Much." *New York Times*, March 15, 2020.

Breglio, John. "Letters: A Song for Stephen Sondheim, by Julie Andrews and Others." *New York Times*, November 30, 2021.

Brill, Amy. "Saturday Night Special." *Talk*, February 2000.

Brockes, Emma. "Big Beasts of Broadway . . . Stephen Sondheim and James Lapine on the Art of Writing Musicals." *Guardian*, July 10, 2016. https://www.theguardian.com/stage/2016/jul/10/stephen-sondheim-james-lapine-interview-writing-musicals-into-the-woods.

———. "Stephen Sondheim: A Life in Music." *Guardian*, December 20, 2010. https://www.theguardian.com/culture/2010/dec/20/stephen-sondheim-life-music-profile.

Brown, Liz. "She Had Rhythm, She Had Music." *Newsday*, January 6, 2008.

Brown, Royal S. "'A Little Night Music' in the Studio." *High Fidelity*, July 1973.

Burke, Tom. "Steve Has Stopped Collaborating." *New York Times*, May 10, 1970.

Calta, Louis. "Rodgers and Sondheim Preparing a Musical." *New York Times*, December 6, 1964.

Canby, Vincent. "A Most Sinister Gathering of Not-So-Usual Suspects." *New York Times*, March 18, 1996.

———. "Theater Review: A Morality Tale About Everybody's Fall Guy." *New York Times*, April 5, 1995.

Carnelia, Craig. "In Conversation with Stephen Sondheim." *Sondheim Review*, Fall 2008.

Christiansen, Richard. "Flaws and All, 'Follies' Still Vintage Sondheim." *Chicago Tribune*, February 7, 1999. https://www.chicagotribune.com/news/ct-xpm-1999-02-07-9902060057-story.html.

Coe, Richard. "Tryouts: Here to Broadway or Bust." *Washington Post*, September 30, 1979. https://www.washingtonpost.com/archive/lifestyle/1979/09/30/tryouts-here-to-broadway-or-bust/6ad5acd9-3f33-48a8-93e9-3f1c9d5fda51/.

Cohen, Patricia. "'Sweeney Todd' (2005 Revival)." *New York Times*, April 13, 2020. https://www.nytimes.com/interactive/2020/04/13/t-magazine/sweeney-todd-revival.html.

Corliss, Richard. "'Sweeney Todd': Horror and Humanity." *Time*, December 21, 2007. http://content.time.com/time/arts/article/0,8599,1697909,00.html.

Crews, Chip. "Broadway's Bernadette Peters: Viva the Diva, Her Fans Say." *Los Angeles Times*, January 12, 1999. https://www.latimes.com/archives/la-xpm-1999-jan-12-ca-62620-story.html.

Dawson, Jeff. "Tim Burton Explains Why Musicals Still Cut It." (London) *Sunday Times*, January 6, 2008. https://www.thetimes.co.uk/article/tim-burton-explains-why-musicals-still-cut-it-zjh88x9m0d0.

DeGregory, Priscilla. "Stephen Sondheim Left Behind an Estate Worth an Estimated $75 Million." *New York Post*, January 23, 2022. https://nypost.com/2022/01/23/stephen-sondheim-left-behind-an-estate-worth-an-estimated-75-million/.

Dowd, Maureen. "Bravado Softened by Vulnerability." *New York Times*, December 12, 2021, section ST, p. 1.

Downes, Olin. "Hubbard Hutchinson." *New York Times*, December 30, 1934.

Dyer, Richard. "A First Time for Everything: With World Premiere, the BSO Finally Steps into the World of Composer Milton Babbitt." *Boston Globe*, January 13, 2005. http://archive.boston.com/news/globe/living/articles/2005/01/13/a_first_time_for_everything/.

Dziemianowicz, Joe. "'Sondheim': It's Uneven Stephen." (New York) *Daily News*, April 23, 2010.

Emmrich, Stuart. "For the Cult of Sondheim, 'Merrily We Roll Along,' and On, and On, and . . ." *Los Angeles Times*, March 4, 2019. https://www.latimes.com/entertainment/arts/la-et-cm-merrily-we-roll-along-20190304-story.html.

Errico, Melissa. "Get Out of My Light, Honey. I'm Auditioning Here." *New York Times*, September 1, 2019.

Feldman, Adam. "Stephen Sondheim: The Infomercial." *Time Out New York*, April 29–May 5, 2010.

Fierberg, Ruthie. "Mandy Patinkin Shares the Story Behind Hearing *Sunday in the Park with George*'s 'Finishing the Hat' for the 1st Time." *Playbill*, July 2, 2020. https://playbill.com/article/mandy-patinkin-shares-the-story-behind-hearing-sunday-in-the-park-with-georges-finishing-the-hat-for-the-1st-time.

Fleming, John. "Salvaging Sondheim." *Tampa Bay Times*, June 24, 2001, updated September 10, 2005. https://www.tampabay.com/archive/2001/06/24/salvaging-sondheim/.

Foundas, Scott. "Film Review: 'Into the Woods.'" *Variety*, December 17, 2014. https://variety.com/2014/film/reviews/film-review-into-the-woods-1201381097/.

Fowler, Glenn. "Armina Marshall Is Dead at 96; Co-Founder of the Theatre Guild." *New York Times*, July 22, 1991.

Fox, David J. "Rewrite by Sondheim." *Los Angeles Times*, September 9, 1990. https://www.latimes.com/archives/la-xpm-1990-09-09-ca-389-story.html.

Franks, Alan. "Stephen Sondheim: 'My Ideal Collaborator Is Me.'" *Times* (of London), April 25, 2009. https://www.thetimes.co.uk/article/stephen-sondheim-my-ideal-collaborator-is-me-j0ghgwbz072.

Friedman, Samuel G. "The Words and Music of Stephen Sondheim." *New York Times Magazine*, April 1, 1984.

Funke, Lewis. "The Year of the Adamses." *New York Times*, April 20, 1969.

Furth, George, Hal Prince, and Stephen Sondheim. *Company: Original Cast in Concert* program. New York: Bradford Graphics, April 11 and 12, 1993.

Galuppo, Mia. "Richard Linklater Musical to Be Filmed Over 20-Year Span." *Hollywood Reporter*, August 29, 2019. https://www.hollywoodreporter.com/news/general-news/richard-linklater-film-merrily-we-roll-along-be-shot-20-years-1235414/.

Gardner, Elysa. "'Sondheim on Sondheim': A Love Song to a Musical Master." *USA Today*, April 23, 2010.

Gardner, Lyn. "The Amazing Mr. Musicals." *Guardian*, January 24, 2008. https://www.theguardian.com/stage/2008/jan/24/theatre.musicals.

Gilbert, Sophie. "Stephen Sondheim's Knotty Vision of Musical Theater." *Atlantic*, December 3, 2021. https://www.theatlantic.com/culture/archive/2021/11/stephen-sondheim-death-musical-theater/620860/.

Gioia, Ted. "Is Old Music Killing New Music?" *Atlantic*, January 23, 2022.

Gold, Sylviane. "Demon Barber, Meat Pies and All, Sing on the Screen." *New York Times*, November 4, 2007. https://www.nytimes.com/2007/11/04/movies/moviesspecial/04gold.html.

Gordon, John Steele. "My Uncle, Oscar Hammerstein." *Commentary*, April 2011. https://www.commentary.org/articles/john-steele-gordon/my-uncle-oscar-hammerstein/.

Green, Jesse. "Side by Side: Stephen Sondheim and Angela Lansbury on a Lifetime in Theatre." *New York*, December 21–28, 2009.

———. "THEATRE: A Funny Thing Happened on the Way to the Punch Line." *New York Times*, June 27, 2004.

———. "When You're a Shark, You're a Shark All the Way." *New York*, March 15, 2009.

Grover, Stephen. "Bringing a New Show to the Broadway Stage Is High Drama in Itself." *Wall Street Journal*, February 27, 1973, p. 1.

Guare, John. "Savoring a Moment: A Conversation with Stephen Sondheim." *Lincoln Center Theatre Review*, Summer 2004.

Gussow, Mel. "Books of the Times: Peeks at the Complexities of a Very Private Genius." *New York Times*, July 21, 1998.

———. "Prince Recalls the Evolution of 'Follies.'" *New York Times*, April 9, 1971.

———. "Prince Revels in 'A Little Night Music.'" *New York Times*, March 27, 1973.

———. "Stage: 'Frogs' in a Pool." *New York Times*, May 23, 1974. https://archive.nytimes.com/www.nytimes.com/books/98/07/19/specials/sondheim-pool.html.

———. "Theater: 'Company' Anew." *New York Times*, July 29, 1970.

Hagerty, James R., and Anne Steele. "Moon, June Left Marooned: Pop Songs Embrace Imperfect Rhymes." *Wall Street Journal*, February 19–20, 2022.

Hale, Mike. "Adoring, and Parodying, Sondheim." *New York Times*, February 26, 2019.

Hammerstein, Oscar II. "From the Drama Mailbag." *New York Times*, September 5, 1943.

———. "In Re 'Oklahoma!'" *New York Times*, May 23, 1943.

Harriman, Margaret Case. "Words and Music." *New Yorker*, November 15, 1940. https://www.newyorker.com/magazine/1940/11/23/words-and-music-3.

Hawkins, Robert F. "Observations on the Italian Picture Scene." *New York Times*, April 5, 1953.

Henry, William A. III. "Master of the Musical: Stephen Sondheim Applies a Relentless." *Time*, December 7, 1987. https://web.archive.org/web/20070930120011/http://www.time.com/time/magazine/article/0,9171,966141,00.html.

Hernandez, Ernio. "Cut: Christopher Lee and Ghosts are Nixed from 'Sweeney Todd' Film." *Playbill*, May 22. 2007. https://www.playbill.com/article/cut-christopher-lee-and-ghosts-are-nixed-from-sweeney-todd-film-com-140979.

Hershberg, Marc. "'West Side Story' Sequel in the Works As Ethnic Groups Reclaim Their Stories.'" *Forbes*, December 19, 2021. https://www.forbes.com/sites/marchershberg/2021/12/19/west-side-story-sequel-in-the-works-as-ethnic-groups-reclaim-their-stories/.

Hevesi, Dennis. "Ruth Ford, Film and Stage Actress, Dies at 98." *New York Times*, August 14, 2009. https://www.nytimes.com/2009/08/14/theater/14ford-1.html.

Hirschhorn, Clive. "Will Sondheim Succeed in Being Genuinely Japanese?" *New York Times*, January 4, 1976.

Hoffman, Barbara. "Actors Recall Living in Fear of Working with Jerome Robbins—Yet Dying to Work with Him." *New York Post*, July 26, 2018. https://nypost.com/2018/07/26/actors-recall-living-in-fear-of-jerome-robbins-yet-dying-to-work-with-him/.

———. "How the West Was Won." *New York Post*, March 8, 2009.

Hoffman, Theodore. "Review: 47 Workshop." *Kenyon Review*, Spring 1955.

Hofler, Robert. "Critical Response." *Variety*, December 12, 2004.

Horowitz, Mark Eden. "'Really Weird': The Story of 'Anyone Can Whistle' with Lots of Details." *Sondheim Review*, Winter 2010.

Howard, Horatia. "50 Years of 'West Side Story.'" *Telegraph*, July 7, 2008.

Huffman, Kristin. "Rich and Rewarding." *Sondheim Review*, Summer 2009.

Isenberg, Barbara. "Meet Mr. Plucky: To James Lapine, Directing His New Play 'Luck, Pluck & Virtue' Means Booting Horatio Alger Smack Dab into the '90s." *Los Angeles Times*, August 1, 1993. https://www.latimes.com/archives/la-xpm-1993-08-01-ca-19137-story.html.

———. "Sondheim, Songless: The Master Minus the Music? Well, He's Been Playing with Puzzlers for Years and Now Takes a Turn at Mystery Playwriting with 'The Doctor Is Out.'" *Los Angeles Times*, September 10, 1995. https://www.latimes.com/archives/la-xpm-1995-09-10-ca-44084-story.html.

Isherwood, Charles. "'Saturday' Boasts Sound of Sondheim Tuning Up." *Variety*, February 20, 2000. https://variety.com/2000/film/reviews/saturday-night-saturday-boasts-sound-of-sondheim-tuning-up-1200460534/.

Jefferson, Margo. "Listen to 'Company,' Tune Out the Book." *New York Times*, October 15, 1995.

Jones, Chris. "Appreciation: Stephen Sondheim, as Great an American Composer and Lyricist as Ever Lived." *Chicago Tribune*, November 26, 2021. https://www.chicagotribune.com/nation-world/ct-aud-nw—20211126-dbise7agvfbyteq7s6tebtowvi-story.html.

———. "Muscle." *Variety*, June 14, 2001. https://variety.com/2001/legit/reviews/muscle-3-1200468803/.

Jones, Chris, Sid Smith, and Michael Phillips. "The Team Behind 'Bounce.'" *Chicago Tribune*, June 22, 2003.

Kakutani, Michiko. "Sondheim's Passionate 'Passion.'" *New York Times*, March 20, 1994.

———. "Theater; Beyond Happily Ever After." *New York Times*, August 30, 1987.

Kalem, Ted E. "Seascape with Frieze of Girls." *Time*, April 12, 1971.

Kanfer, Stefan. "The Once and Future Follies." *Time*, May 3, 1971.

Keating, John. "New Musical 'Hot Spot' on the Spot." *New York Times*, April 14, 1963.

Kellaway, Kate. "Maria Friedman: 'Sondheim Was a Kind Man, but God, He Could Be Very Direct.'" *Guardian*, February 13, 2022. https://www.theguardian.com/stage/2022/feb/13/maria-friedman-sondheim-was-a-kind-man-but-he-could-be-very-direct-legacy-menier-chocolate-factory-interview.

Kelly, Kevin. "Sondheim Struggles to Write Words AND Music." *Boston Globe*, March 8, 1970.

King, Susan. "Dyan Cannon and Richard Benjamin Fondly Look Back at 'The Last of Sheila.'" *Los Angeles Times*, January 24, 2020. https://www.latimes.com/entertainment-arts/movies/story/2020-01-24/dyan-cannon-and-richard-benjamin-fondly-look-back-at-the-last-of-sheila.

Kit, Borys. "New Line to Remake Murder Mystery 'The Last of Sheila' (Exclusive)." *Hollywood Reporter*, June 18, 2012. https://www.hollywoodreporter.com/business/business-news/new-line-remake-last-sheila-murder-mystery-338801/.

Koehler, Robert. "Legend in His Own Time." *Variety*, October 15, 1999.

Kornbluth, Jesse. "Storytelling with Sondheim." *Harvard Magazine*, January–February 2011. https://www.harvardmagazine.com/2011/01/storytelling-with-sondheim#.

Lane, Nathan, Marianne Elliott, and Beanie Feldstein. "Nathan Lane, Marianne Elliott and Beanie Feldstein Remember Stephen Sondheim." *Variety*. December 2, 2021. https://variety.com/2021/theater/people-news/nathan-lane-beanie-feldstein-stephen-sondheim-1235123585/.

Lawson, Mark. "'Anyone Can Whistle' Review—Sondheim Flop Gets a Blazing Revival." *Guardian*, April 6, 2022. https://www.theguardian.com/stage/2022/apr/06/anyone-can-whistle-review-southwark-playhouse-london-sondheim.

Lebrecht, Norman. "The Unsung Sondheim." *Evening Standard* (London), April 10, 2012. https://www.standard.co.uk/culture/theatre/the-unsung-sondheim-7428423.html.

Leifeste, Luke. "Meet Eugene Lee, the Crazy Stylish 78-Year-Old Man Who Literally Built 'SNL.'" *GQ*, July 26, 2017. https://www.gq.com/story/meet-eugene-lee-the-man-who-built-snl.

Levin, Anne. "Restoration of Highland Farm to Preserve Hammerstein Legacy." *Town Topics*, May 8, 2019. https://www.towntopics.com/wordpress/2019/05/08/restoration-of-highland-farm-to-preserve-hammerstein-legacy/.

Leyden, Liz. "In Good Company." *Williams Magazine*, Spring 2020. https://magazine.williams.edu/2020/spring/feature/in-good-company/.

Lipton, James. "Stephen Sondheim, The Art of the Musical." *Paris Review*, no. 142, Spring 1997. https://www.theparisreview.org/interviews/1283/the-art-of-the-musical-stephen-sondheim.

Lyons, Margaret. "From 'South Park' to 'Knives Out,' Pop Culture Is Steeped with Sondheim." *New York Times*, March 12, 2020.

Malkin, Marc, and Chris Willman. "Stephen Sondheim to Be Saluted at Grammys by Rachel Zegler, Cynthia Erivo, Ben Platt, Leslie Odom Jr. (EXCLUSIVE)." *Variety*, March 23, 2022. https://variety.com/2022/music/news/stephen-sondheim-grammys-ben-platt-cynthia-erivo-leslie-odom-rachel-zegler-1235213093/.

Marchese, Joe. "'Assassins' Enduring Popularity." *Sondheim Review*, Winter 2015.

Marks, Peter. "For Carol Burnett, the Sondheim Award Is Personal." *Washington Post*, May 19, 2022. https://www.washingtonpost.com/theater-dance/2022/05/19/carol-burnett-sondheim/.

Martinez, Al. "Harry at Your Head." *Los Angeles Times*, May 21, 1994. https://www.latimes.com/archives/la-xpm-1994-05-21-me-60284-story.html.

Max, D. T. "Stephen Sondheim's Lesson for Every Artist." *New Yorker*, February 14, 2022. https://www.newyorker.com/culture/the-new-yorker-interview/stephen-sondheim-final-interviews.

McLellan, Dennis. "Musical Theatre Icon Stephen Sondheim Dead at 91." *Los Angeles Times*, November 26, 2021. https://www.latimes.com/obituaries/story/2021-11-26/stephen-sondheim-dead-at-91.

Mendes, Sam. "Sam Mendes on Stephen Sondheim: 'He Was Passionate, Utterly Open, and Sharp as a Knife.'" *Guardian*, November 29, 2021. https://www.theguardian.com/stage/2021/nov/29/sam-mendes-stephen-sondheim-passionate-sharp-knife-musicals.

Millstein, Gilbert. "A Funny Man Happened." *New York Times*, June 3, 1962.

Milzoff, Rebecca. "The Rehearsal Pianist." *New York*, November 30, 2013. https://nymag.com/news/frank-rich/composer-john-kander-2013-12/.

Miranda, Lin-Manuel. "Stephen Sondheim, Theater's Greatest Lyricist." *T Magazine*, October 16, 2017. https://www.nytimes.com/2017/10/16/t-magazine/lin-manuel-miranda-stephen-sondheim.html.

Murray, Christopher. "'Saturday Night' Is a Cheery Time Capsule: Sondheim at Age 23." *Observer*, November 18, 2014. https://observer.com/2014/11/saturday-night-is-a-cheery-time-capsule-sondheim-at-age-23/.

Narvaez, Alfonso S. "H. M. Margolis, 80, Industrialist." *New York Times*, November 3, 1989.

Newsweek staff. "Sondheim's Still Here." *Newsweek*, June 12, 1992. https://www.newsweek.com/sondheims-still-here-199396.

Obama, Barack. "Remarks on Presenting the Presidential Medal of Freedom." Hosted by President Barack Obama; guest, Stephen Sondheim. U.S. Government Publishing Office, November 24, 2015. https://www.govinfo.gov/content/pkg/DCPD-201500840/pdf/DCPD-201500840.pdf.

Olson, John. "'Assassins': A Chronology." *Sondheim Review*, Spring 2011.

Page, Tim. "Stephen Sondheim, Central Figure in American Musical Theater, Dies at 91." *Washington Post*, November 26, 2021. https://www.washingtonpost.com/local/obituaries/stephen-sondheim-central-figure-in-american-musical-theater-dies-at-91/2021/11/26/939fea1c-4f06-11ec-b0b0-766bbbe79347_story.html.

Paris, Francesca. "How Williams College Sparked Stephen Sondheim's Career." *Berkshire Eagle*, November 27, 2021. https://www.berkshireeagle.com/news/northern_berkshires/how-williams-college-sparked-stephen-sondheims-career/article_4a770d16-4fa6-11ec-b0ac-0f26adab6f27.html.

Paulson, Michael. "Tony-Winning 'Company' Revival Will End Broadway Run July 31." *New York Times*, July 21, 2022. https://www.nytimes.com/2022/06/21/theater/company-broadway-closing.html.

Pender, Rick. "Sondheim and Rich Go to College." *Sondheim Review*, Spring 2009.

Peyser, Marc. "Send in the Fanatics." *Newsweek*, May 25, 1998.

Phillips, Michael. "Stephen Sondheim Devoured Cinema. Here's How His Movie Love Fed His Own Work, on Stage and Screen." *Chicago Tribune*, November 29, 2021. https://www.chicagotribune.com/entertainment/movies/michael-phillips/sc-ent-sondheim-movies-phillips-1128-20211129-y22pcegy2fbhxfwrzpidffcdsq-story.html.

Piepenburg, Erik. "'60s Sondheim TV Show Is Now on (Legal) DVD," *New York Times*, October 25, 2010.

———. "Five Questions for Donna Murphy." *ArtsBeat* (blog), *New York Times*, April 7, 2010. https://artsbeat.blogs.nytimes.com/2010/04/07/five-questions-for-donna-murphy/.

Pollack-Pelzner, Daniel. "Why 'West Side Story' Abandoned Its Queer Narrative." *Atlantic*, March 1, 2020. https://www.theatlantic.com/culture/archive/2020/03/ivo-van-hoves-west-side-story-steeped-stereotypes/607210/.

Portantiere, Michael. "The Greatest Gift." *Sondheim Review*, Spring 2012.

———. "Old Friends: Mary Rodgers Shared Thoughts About 70 Years of Knowing Sondheim." *Sondheim Review*, Fall 2014. Talkin' Broadway. https://www.talkinbroadway.com/page/rialto/past/2014/072214.html.

Poundstone, William. "A Funny Thing Happened on the Way to Broadway." *Advocate*, August 1, 1989.

Prince, Hal. "In the Words of Hal Prince." *Cue*, April 10, 1971.

Quindlen, Anna. "George Oppenheimer, Drama Critic and Writer for Stage and Screen." *New York Times*, August 16, 1977.

Reed, Rex. "Sweeney Soars." (New York) *Daily News*, March 3, 1979.

Rich, Frank. "Conversations with Sondheim." *New York Times Magazine*, March 12, 2000.

———. "Stage: 'Sunday in the Park with George.'" *New York Times*, May 3, 1984.

———. "Vulture: A Return to 'Company.'" *New York*, August 16, 2021. https://www.vulture.com/2021/08/company-cast-album-stephen-sondheim-jonathan-tunick.html.

Richards, David. "The Lowdown on Sondheim's Partner." *Washington Post*, April 20, 1997. https://www.washingtonpost.com/archive/lifestyle/style/1997/04/20/the-lowdown-on-sondheims-partner/689f219b-c989-475a-8cb0-a451c108b3e5/.

Ring, Trudy. "Sondheim's 'A Little Night Music' Gets a Queer Twist." *Advocate*, February 4, 2022. https://www.advocate.com/theater/2022/2/04/sondheims-little-night-music-gets-queer-twist.

Robert, Terri. "Glynis Johns: Still Tearful in 'Clowns.'" *Sondheim Review*, Summer 1998.

Robson, Leo. "Mandy Patinkin on Stephen Sondheim: 'I Got to Be in the Room with Shakespeare. Who Gets That?'" *New Statesman* (UK edition), November 29, 2021. https://www.newstatesman.com/culture/music/2021/11/mandy-patinkin-on-stephen-sondheim-i-got-to-be-in-the-room-with-shakespeare-who-gets-that.

Rollyson, Carl. "More Than a Girl with a Gimmick." *Wall Street Journal*, January 7, 2011. https://www.wsj.com/articles/SB10001424052748704034804576025691968347626.

Rosen, Barbara. "The Mackintosh 'Follies.'" *Washington Post*, July 8, 1987. https://www.washingtonpost.com/archive/lifestyle/1987/07/08/the-mackintosh-follies/b9c37c98-1637-49e0-8649-6e75929e90c3/.

Rosen, Jody. "The American Revolutionary." *T Magazine*, July 8, 2015. https://www.nytimes.com/interactive/2015/07/08/t-magazine/hamilton-lin-manuel-miranda-roots-sondheim.html.

Rosenberg, Donald. "Sondheim Talks Hammerstein, Songwriting and 'Sondheim on Sondheim,' Coming to PlayhouseSquare." (Cleveland) *Plain Dealer*, May 13, 2002. https://www.cleveland.com/musicdance/2012/05/sondheim_story.html.

Rosenblum, Joshua. "Musical Dramatist: In His Sixty-Year Career, Stephen Sondheim Has Transformed the Broadway Musical and the American Theatre." *Opera News*, February 2022.

Ross, Lillian. "Enchanted Evenings," *New Yorker*, March 31, 2008. https://www.newyorker.com/magazine/2008/04/07/enchanted-evening/amp.

Rothstein, Mervyn. "Richard Barr, 71, Stage Producer and Theater League Head, Dies." *New York Times*, January 10, 1989.

Rubin, Rebecca. "'West Wing' Reunion: Marlee Maitlin and Bradley Whitford Discuss Sondheim, Sorkin, and 'Wonderfully Sexual Middle-Aged' Representation." *Variety*, 2022. https://variety.com/2022/film/news/bradley-whitford-tick-tick-boom-marlee-matlin-coda-1235169944/.

Salisbury, Mark. "A Pie-in-the-Sky Dream Come True." *Los Angeles Times*. December 28, 2007. https://www.latimes.com/archives/la-xpm-2007-dec-28-et-helena28-story.html.

Salsini, Paul. "Among the Night People." *Sondheim Review*, Summer 1994.

———. "'As Always, Steve': Corresponding with Sondheim, Note by Note." *Milwaukee Journal Sentinel*, December 8, 2021. https://www.jsonline.com/story/entertainment/arts/2021/12/07/corresponding-stephen-sondheim-note-note/8851136002/.

Savage, Mark. "Barbra Streisand: 'I've Always Had the Right to Sing What I Want.'" BBC News, August 4, 2021. https://www.bbc.com/news/entertainment-arts-58056164.

Schiff, Stephen. "Deconstructing Sondheim." *New Yorker*, February 28, 1993. https://www.newyorker.com/magazine/1993/03/08/deconstructing-sondheim.

Shirley, Don. "Revisiting 'Company' of Days Past: Original Cast, Creators of 1970 Musical Gather for Reunion Benefit." *Los Angeles Times*, January 25, 1993. https://www.latimes.com/archives/la-xpm-1993-01-25-ca-1587-story.html.

———. "Robert Fryer; Producer, Former Ahmanson Director." *Los Angeles Times*, May 31, 2000. https://www.latimes.com/archives/la-xpm-2000-may-31-me-35862-story.html.

Silverman, Stephen M. "Elaine Stritch, Broadway Legend and TV Star, Dies." *People*, July 17, 2014. https://people.com/celebrity/elaine-stritch-dies/.

———. "Stephen Sondheim Hated Lady Gaga's 'Sound of Music' Performance at the Oscars." *People*, March 17, 2015. https://people.com/celebrity/stephen-sondheim-hated-lady-gagas-sound-of-music-performance-at-the-oscars/.

Simon, John. "A Little Knife Music." *New York*, March 19, 1979.

Simon, Paul. "Isn't It Rich?" *New York Times Book Review*, October 31, 2010.

So, Jimmy. "'Sondheim on Sondheim': American Musical Theatre in Six Songs." *Daily Beast*, July 11, 2017. https://www.thedailybeast.com/sondheim-on-sondheim-american-musical-theater-in-six-songs.

BIBLIOGRAPHY

Solomon, Alisa. "On Jewishness, as the Fiddle Played." *New York Times*, October 20, 2013.

Sondheim, Stephen. "The Musical Theatre: A Talk with Stephen Sondheim." *Dramatists Guild Quarterly*, Autumn 1978.

———. "Stephen Sondheim in a Q&A Session: Part I." *Dramatists Guild Quarterly*, no. 1, 1991.

———. "Stephen Sondheim Recalls 'Allegro,'" pamphlet to *Allegro* CD, 2007, from comments Sondheim made at City Center Encores!, New York, March 1994.

Sondheim, Stephen, and Anthony Shaffer. "Theater; Of Mystery, Murder, and Other Delights." *New York Times*, March 10, 1996. https://archive.nytimes.com/www.nytimes.com/books/98/07/19/specials/sondheim-shaffer.html.

Springer, John. "'Follies'; A Movie That Wasn't." *New York Times*, April 8, 2001.

Stryker, Mark. "'I'm Not an Opera Fan': A 2009 *Free Press* Interview with Theater Composer Stephen Sondheim." *Detroit Free Press*, November 26, 2021. https://www.freep.com/story/entertainment/music/2021/11/26/stephen-sondheim-pondered-opera-musicals-2009-free-press-interview/8770543002/.

Syme, Rachael. "Mandy Patinkin Is Still Singing." *New Yorker*, October 11, 2020. https://www.newyorker.com/culture/the-new-yorker-interview/mandy-patinkin-is-still-singing.

Tallmer, Jerry. "Comedy Tonight." *Village Voice*, May 17, 1962.

Teachout, Terry. "Learning to Love Stephen Sondheim." *Wall Street Journal*, November 28, 2018. https://www.wsj.com/articles/learning-to-love-stephen-sondheim-1543427965.

———. "'Pacific Overtures' Review: Shortening Sondheim." *Wall Street Journal*, May 4, 2017. https://www.wsj.com/articles/pacific-overtures-review-shortening-sondheim-1493944200.

———. "Sondheim at 90." *Commentary*, March 2020. https://www.commentary.org/articles/terry-teachout/broadway-musical-talent-sondheim/.

———. "What Jerome Robbins Knew That Leonard Bernstein Didn't." *Commentary*, November 2019. https://www.commentary.org/articles/terry-teachout/what-jerome-robbins-knew-that-leonard-bernstein-didnt/.

Teeman, Tim. "Stephen Sondheim: Nearly Everything on Broadway Is Commercial." *Times* (of London) *Saturday Review*, March 3, 2012.

Turner, Kyle. "Love Is 'Company': Director Marianne Elliott on Her Revival of Sondheim's Classic Musical," *Interview*, April 27, 2020. https://www.interviewmagazine.com/art/company-marianne-elliott-broadway.

Vallance, Tom. "George Furth: Actor and Playwright Who Collaborated with Stephen Sondheim on the Musical 'Company.'" *Independent*, August 27, 2008. https://www.independent.co.uk/news/obituaries/george-furth-actor-and-playwright-who-collaborated-with-stephen-sondheim-on-the-musical-company-909609.html.

Variety staff. "Color-Blind 'Company.'" *Variety*, December 10, 1995. https://variety.com/1995/legit/news/color-blind-company-99130362/.

Vlessing, Etan. "Dominic Cooke Sets Movie Adaptation of Stephen Sondheim's 'Follies.'" *Hollywood Reporter*, November 14, 2019. https://www.hollywoodreporter.com/movies/movie-news/dominic-cooke-sets-movie-adaptation-stephen-sondheims-follies-1254884/.

Weinstock, Matt. "Loveland." *Paris Review*. November 29, 2013. https://www.theparisreview.org/blog/2013/11/29/loveland/.

Wiegand, Chris. "How We Made 'West Side Story.'" *Guardian*. September 18, 2017. https://www.theguardian.com/stage/2017/sep/18/how-we-made-west-side-story-stephen-sondheim-chita-rivera-musicals.

———. "'I'm a Great Audience—I Cry Very Easily': Stephen Sondheim in His Own Words." *Guardian*. November 27, 2021. https://www.theguardian.com/stage/2021/nov/27/im-a-great-audience-i-cry-very-easily-stephen-sondheim-in-his-own-words.

Winer, Linda. "The Gift of Sondheim Keeps on Giving." *Newsday*, April 23, 2010.

———. "A Lyric Landmark." *Newsday*, March 12, 2000.

Wong, Wayman. "Her 'Passion' Is Acting." *Sondheim Review*, Summer 1994.

Wood, Mark Dundas. "Anyone Can Whistle—Or Can They?" *Backstage*, May 14, 2002.

Zolotow, Sam. "Perkins to Star in Stage Musical." *New York Times*, March 14, 1969.

FEATURE FILMS, DOCUMENTARIES, VIDEOS, RECORDINGS, BROADCASTS, AND PODCASTS

"*Anyone Can Whistle* 2022 Revival, in Rehearsal." WhatsOnStage channel, March 25, 2022. YouTube. https://www.youtube.com/watch?v=hp4iosX646k.

Beatty, Warren, and Trevor Griffiths. *Reds*. Written by Warren Beatty and Trevor Griffiths; directed and produced by Warren Beatty; music and lyrics for "Goodbye for Now" by Stephen Sondheim; music by Dave Grusin; starring Warren Beatty, Diane Keaton, Edward Herrmann, Jerzy Kosinski, Jack Nicholson, Paul Sorvino, and Maureen Stapleton. December 4, 1981. Finland, U.K., New York City, Washington, DC, and Los Angeles: Barclays Mercantile, Industrial Finance, and JRS Productions. Distributed by Paramount Pictures.

Berman, John, Deborah Apton, and Victoria Thompson. "Stephen Sondheim: My 'West Side Story' Lyrics Are 'Embarrassing.'" ABC News, December 8, 2020. https://abcnews.go.com/Entertainment/stephen-sondheim-west-side-story-lyrics-embarrassing/story?id=12345243.

Brown, Bob. "Stephen Sondheim: The Man Behind the Music." Interview by Bob Brown; hosted by Hugh Downs; guest, Stephen Sondheim. *20/20*, ABC News, 1994. YouTube. https://www.youtube.com/watch?v=zGDoe-2A-Hk.

Brown, Jeffrey. "Stephen Sondheim on the Times and Rhymes of His Life." Interview by Jeffrey Brown; created by Robert MacNeil and Jim Lehrer; guest, Stephen Sondheim. *MacNeil-Lehrer NewsHour*, December 8, 2010. Washington, DC: PBS NewsHour Productions. https://www.pbs.org/newshour/show/composer-stephen-sondheims-life-times-and-rhymes.

Cash, Jim, and Jack Epps Jr. *Dick Tracy*. Written by Jim Cash and Jack Epps Jr., based on characters created by Chester Gould; directed and produced by Warren Beatty; music and lyrics for "Sooner or Later (I Always Get My Man)," "More," "Live Alone and Like It," "Back in Business," and "What Can You Lose?" by Stephen Sondheim; starring Warren Beatty, Al Pacino, Madonna, Glenne Headly, and Dustin Hoffman. Disney World premiere June 14, 1990. Burbank, CA: Touchstone Pictures, Silver Screen Partners IV, and Mulholland Productions. Distributed by Buena Vista Pictures.

Colbert, Stephen. *The Colbert Report*. Hosted by Stephen Colbert; created by Jon Stewart and Ben Karlin; written by Stephen Colbert, Paul Dinello, Eric Drysdale, Glenn Eichler, Barry Julien, Opus Moreschi, Tom Purcell, Meredith Scardino, Scott Sherman, and Max Werner; guest, Stephen Sondheim. Comedy Central, December 14, 2010. https://www.cc.com/video/ouqrnm/the-colbert-report-stephen-sondheim.

———. *The Late Show with Stephen Colbert*. Hosted by Stephen Colbert; written by Caroline Lazar; guest, Stephen Sondheim. CBS, September 15, 2021. YouTube. https://youtu.be/GKSYeMgamIA.

———. *The Late Show with Stephen Colbert*. Hosted by Stephen Colbert; written by Nicole Conlan, Felipe Torres Medina, Asher Perlman, and Kate Sidley, produced by Spartina Productions; guest, Bradley Whitford. CBS, May 27, 2021. YouTube. https://youtu.be/CiA9GG7Mbhw.

Cramer, Ned. *The American Musical Theatre*. Produced by Ned Cramer, associate produced by Ethel Burns; directed by Neal Finn; conducted by Irwin Kostal; hosted by Earl Wrightson; guest, Stephen Sondheim. WCBS-TV, Paley Center for Media, October 15, 1961. YouTube. https://youtu.be/0udP4_1tarY.

"Documentary: Avant-Garde Composer Milton Babbitt." NPR, January 31, 2011. https://www.npr.org/sections/deceptivecadence/2011/04/10/133372983/npr-exclusive-new-documentary-on-the-late-composer-milton-babbitt.

Douglas, Andrew. *Great Performances: Keeping Company with Stephen Sondheim*. Directed by Andrew Douglas; produced by David Sabel; series produced by Bill O'Donnell; executive produced by David Horn; starring Stephen Sondheim, Marianne Elliott, Katrina Lenk, Patti LuPone, Adrian Lester, Raúl Esparza, and other members of the 1970, 1995, 2006, 2018, and 2021 casts. PBS, May 27, 2022. https://www.pbs.org/wnet/gperf/keeping-company-with-sondheim-about/13669/.

Douglas, Mike. *The Mike Douglas Show*. Hosted by Mike Douglas; guest, Stephen Sondheim. June 14, 1977. Philadelphia: Westinghouse Broadcasting Company.

Fine, Sylvia. *Musical Comedy Tonight*. Written and hosted by Sylvia Fine; directed by Stan Harris; produced by Eric Lieber; starring Carol Burnett, Richard Chamberlain, John Davidson, Agnes de Mille, Sandy Duncan, Rock Hudson, Ethel Merman, Bernadette Peters, and Bobby Van. PBS, October 1, 1979. YouTube. https://www.youtube.com/watch?v=_7Z30RWK5l4.

Fishko, Sarah. "The Real-Life Drama Behind 'West Side Story.'" *Fishko Files*, NPR, January 7, 2009. https://www.npr.org/2011/02/24/97274711/the-real-life-drama-behind-west-side-storynakes.

Gennaro, Liza. Oral History Sound Recording. Interviewed by Liza Gennaro; guests, George and Ethel Martin. Goshen, NY: New York Public Library for the Performing Arts, January 17 and February 25, 2003.

Gill, Brendan. "The Creative Process" series. Hosted by Brendan Gill; guests, Stephen Sondheim and Harold S. Prince. New York Public Library for the Performing Arts. Recorded June 2, 1975. Streamed for one showing only by the New York Public Library on March 21, 2022.

Goldman, James. *Evening Primrose*. Written by James Goldman, based on "Evening Primrose" by John Collier; music and lyrics by Stephen Sondheim; directed by Paul Bogart; produced by Willard Levitas; executive produced by John Houseman for Gramercy Productions, Inc.; starring Anthony Perkins, Charmian Carr, Dorothy Stickney, and Larry Gates. *ABC Stage 67*, ABC, November 16, 1966.

Gross, Terry. "'Fresh Air' Remembers Broadway Legend Stephen Sondheim (Part 1)." *Fresh Air*. Hosted by Terry Gross; guest, Stephen Sondheim, from a 2010 interview. NPR, December 1, 2021. https://www.npr.org/transcripts/1060439722.

———. "How Rodgers and Hammerstein Revolutionized Broadway," *Fresh Air*. Hosted by Terry Gross; guest, Todd Purdum. NPR, April 9, 2018. https://www.npr.org/2018/05/28/614469172/how-rodgers-and-hammerstein-revolutionized-broadway.

———. "Stephen Sondheim: Examining His Lyrics and Life." *Fresh Air*. Hosted by Terry Gross; guest, Stephen Sondheim. NPR, February 16, 2012. https://www.npr.org/2012/02/16/146938826/stephen-sondheim-examining-his-lyrics-and-life.

"Harold Prince on Stephen Sondheim." masterworksbwayVEVO channel, February 2, 2016. YouTube. https://www.youtube.com/watch?v=ZaO8Rjc9WSU.

Hilferty, Robert. *Portrait of a Serial Composer*. Directed by Robert Hilferty and Laura Karpman; starring Milton Babbitt. 2010. YouTube. https://www.youtube.com/watch?v=JuTRWHAd_IM.

Homan, Katy. *Cameron Mackintosh: The Musical Man*. Directed and produced by Katy Homan; presented by Alan Yentob; starring Cameron Mackintosh; guest starring Stephen Sondheim. BBC, September 11, 2017. YouTube. https://youtu.be/a6WIWKjilU4.

Kantor, Michael. *Broadway Musicals: A Jewish Legacy*. Written and directed by Michael Kantor; executive produced by Barbara Brilliant; coproduced by Sylvia Cahill and Jan Gura; narrated by Joel Grey. PBS, January 1, 2013. Ghostlight Films.

Kushner, Tony. *West Side Story*. Written by Tony Kushner, based on the stage musical book by Arthur Laurents based on a conception of Jerome Robbins; music by Leonard Bernstein; lyrics by Stephen Sondheim; directed by Steven Spielberg; produced by Steven Spielberg, Kristie Macosko Krieger, and Kevin McCollum; starring Ansel Elgort, Ariana DeBose, David Alvarez, Mike Faist, Rita Moreno, and Rachel Zegler. New York premiere, November 29, 2021. New York and New Jersey: Amblin Entertainment and TSG Entertainment, distributed by 20th Century Studios.

Lane, Jeffrey. *The 1988 Tony Awards*. Written and coproduced by Jeffrey Lane; directed by Walter C. Miller; produced by David J. Goldberg; executive produced by Don Mischer; hosted by Angela Lansbury. CBS, June 5, 1988. YouTube. https://youtu.be/S1TYwKVVH-M.

Lansbury, Angela. "Angela Lansbury—on *Anyone Can Whistle*." masterworksbwayVEVO channel, 2012. YouTube. https://www.youtube.com/watch?v=YtBwhsHCu_s&t=6s.

Lapine, James. *Into the Woods*. Written by James Lapine, based on the stage musical; music and lyrics by Stephen Sondheim; directed by Rob Marshall; produced by Rob Marshall, John DeLuca, Marc Platt, and Callum McDougall; starring Meryl Streep, Emily Blunt, James Corden, Anna Kendrick, Chris Pine, Tracey Ullman, Christine Baranski, and Johnny Depp. New York premiere, December 8, 2014. London, Surrey, and Kent: Walt Disney Pictures, Lucamar Productions, and Marc Platt Productions. Distributed by Walt Disney Studios.

———. *Passion*. Written and directed by James Lapine, based on the stage musical; music and lyrics by Stephen Sondheim, based on the film *Passione d'amore* by Ettore Scola, based on the novel *Fosca* by Iginio Ugo Tarchetti; starring Donna Murphy, Jere Shea, and Marin Mazzie. *American Playhouse*. PBS, September 29, 1996. Michael Brandman Productions.

———. *Six by Sondheim*. Directed and executive produced by James Lapine; "Send in the Clowns" directed by Autumn de Wilde; "I'm Still Here" directed by Todd Haynes; produced by Liz Stanton; executive produced by Frank Rich and Sheila Nevins (for Home Box Office); edited by Miky Wolf; starring Stephen Sondheim, Jarvis Cocker, Audra McDonald, Darren Criss, Jeremy Jordan, Laura Osnes, Jackie Hoffman, America Ferrera, and Will Swenson. HBO, December 9, 2013.

Laurents, Arthur. *Gypsy*. Written by Arthur Laurents, based on his book for the stage musical based on the memoirs of Gypsy Rose Lee; music by Jule Style; lyrics by Stephen Sondheim; directed by Emile Ardolino; produced by Emile Ardolino, Cindy Gilmore, and Bob Weber; starring Bette Midler, Cynthia Gibb, Peter Riegert, Jennifer Rae Beck, and Edward Asner. CBS, December 12, 1993. Storyline Entertainment, All Girl Productions, and RHI Entertainment.

Lee, Gypsy Rose. *Gypsy Rose Lee and Her Friends*. Hosted by Gypsy Rose Lee; guest, Ethel Merman. 1965. YouTube. https://youtu.be/yqCgnX0s0M8.g

Lehman, Ernest. *West Side Story*. Written by Ernest Lehman, based on the stage musical book by Arthur Laurents based on a conception of Jerome Robbins; music by Leonard Bernstein; lyrics by Stephen Sondheim; directed by Robert Wise and Jerome Robbins; produced by Saul Chaplin, Walter Mirisch, and Robert Wise; starring Natalie Wood, Richard Beymer, Russ Tamblyn, Rita Moreno, and George Chakiris. New York premiere, October 18, 1961. New York and Hollywood: Seven Arts Productions, released through United Artists.

Levien, Sonya, and William Ludwig. *Oklahoma!*. Written by Sonya Levien and William Ludwig, based on the stage production directed by Rouben Mamoulian, with music by Richard Rodgers, book and lyrics by Oscar Hammerstein II, based on *Green Grow the Lilacs* by Lynn Riggs, choreography by Agnes de Mille; directed by Fred Zinnemann; produced by Arthur Hornblow Jr.; starring Gordon MacRae, Gloria Grahame, Gene Nelson, Charlotte Greenwood, Eddie Albert, James Whitmore, Rod Steiger, and Shirley Jones. New York premiere, October 11, 1955. Magna Theatre Corporation. Initial general release by RKO Radio Pictures.

Levin, Bernard. *The Levin Interviews*. Hosted by Bernard Levin; guest, Stephen Sondheim. BBC, April 26, 1980.

Lipton, James. "Stephen Sondheim Interviewed by James Lipton in 1994 at the Actor's Studio." *Inside the Actor's Studio*. Created, hosted, and executive produced by James Lipton; guest, Stephen Sondheim. Greenleaf Productions, 1994. YouTube. https://www.youtube.com/watch?v=fDpE7Ki4jMs.

Lunden, Jeff. "'Showboat.'" *All Things Considered*. NPR, April 17, 2000. https://www.npr.org/2000/04/17/1073053/npr-100-i-showboat-i.

Matlin, Marlee, and Bradley Whitford. "Actors on Actors—Full Conversation." *Variety*. Presented by Amazon Studios, 2022. YouTube. https://youtu.be/Bswrux2wfXQ.

McHenry, Jackson. "How 'Documentary Now' Made the Sondheim-Alike Musical 'Co-op' for Its 'Company' Episode." *Vulture*, February 27, 2019. https://www.vulture.com/2019/02/documentary-now-making-of-co-op-musical.html.

McPartland, Marian. *Marian McPartland's Piano Jazz*. Hosted by Marian McPartland; guest, Stephen Sondheim. NPR, 1994. https://www.npr.org/2011/12/30/144485557/stephen-sondheim-on-piano-jazz.

Meyer, Nicholas. *The Seven-Per-Cent Solution*. Written by Nicholas Meyer, based on his novel; directed by Herbert Ross; Produced by Stanley O'Toole, Herbert Ross, Arlene Sellers, and Alex Winitsky; "The Madame's Song (I Never Do Anything Twice)," by Stephen Sondheim, starring Nicol Williamson, Robert Duvall, Alan Arkin, Laurence Olivier, Vanessa Redgrave, and Joel Grey. October 25, 1976. Universal Pictures.

Meyers, Seth. "Patti LuPone Shares Memories of Working with Stephen Sondheim." *Late Night with Seth Meyers* channel. NBC, December 14, 2021. YouTube. https://www.youtube.com/watch?v=r0dLINWDXPE.

Mulaney, John. "Seth Meyers & Richard Kind on Sondheim & 'Co-Op.'" Eli Bolin channel, September 25, 2018. YouTube. https://www.youtube.com/watch?v=9uNoHYimK2A.

Mulaney, John, and Seth Meyers. *Original Cast Album: Co-Op*. Lyrics by John Mulaney and Seth Meyers; music by Eli Bolin; directed by Alex Buono; produced by John Mulaney, David Cress, John Sullivan, Matt Pacult, Tamsin Rawady, and Alice Mathias; executive produced by Lorne Michaels, Andrew Singer, Rhys Thomas, Alex Buono, Fred Armisen, Bill Hader, and Seth Meyers; starring Helen Mirren, Alex Brightman, Renée Elise Goldsberry, Taran Killam, Richard Kind, John Mulaney, Paula Pell, and James Urbaniak. *Documentary Now!* IFC, February 27, 2019.

Myers, Pete. *PM*. Hosted by Peter Myers; guest, Stephen Sondheim. July 21, 1973. BBC Radio. Audible.

Newman, Edwin. "*Into the Woods*: A Conversation with Stephen Sondheim and James Lapine." Hosted by Edwin Newman; guests, Stephen Sondheim and James Lapine. PBS, 1991. Broadway History channel. YouTube. https://youtu.be/9Bjr0LbDKks.

Oppenheimer, George, and Stephen Sondheim. "Burglar Episode." *Topper*, season 1, episode 9. Written by George Oppenheimer and Stephen Sondheim; directed by Philip Rapp; produced by John W. Loveton; starring Anne Jeffreys, Robert Sterling, Leo G. Carroll, and Lee Patrick. CBS, December 4, 1953. YouTube. https://www.youtube.com/watch?v=27UPeAROS6M.

———. "Hiring the Maid." *Topper*, season 1, episode 3. Written by George Oppenheimer and Stephen Sondheim; directed by Philip Rapp; produced by John W. Loveton; starring Anne Jeffreys, Robert Sterling, Leo G. Carroll, and Lee Patrick. CBS, October 23, 1953. YouTube. https://www.youtube.com/watch?v=g0WzaUfpI2U.

———. "Preparations for Europe." *Topper*, season 1, episode 36. Written by George Oppenheimer and Stephen Sondheim; directed by James V. Kern; produced by John W. Loveton; starring Anne Jeffreys, Robert Sterling, Leo G. Carroll, and Lee Patrick. CBS, June 11, 1954. YouTube. https://www.youtube.com/watch?v=Q2DNdq5V8SM.

Orr, Matthew, and Merv Rothstein. "Remembering Stephen Sondheim." Produced by Matthew Orr and Merv Rothstein. NYT News, November 29, 2021. YouTube. https://www.youtube.com/watch?v=S-T4-g_x4NA&t=491s.

Parks, Hildy. *The 1971 Tony Awards*. Written by Hildy Parks; directed by Clark Jones; produced by Alexander H. Cohen; hosted by Lauren Bacall, Angela Lansbury, Anthony Quayle, and Anthony Quinn. CBS, March 28, 1971. YouTube. https://www.youtube.com/watch?v=nCB_r7iSoEY.

———. *The 1973 Tony Awards*. Written by Hildy Parks; directed by Clark Jones; produced by Alexander H. Cohen; hosted by Rex Harrison, Celeste Holm, Eddie Albert, Rossano Brazzi, Yul Brynner, Diahann Carroll, Sandy Duncan, Nanette Fabray, Helen Gallagher, Ken Howard, Paula Kelly, Alan King, Cleo Laine, Michelle Lee, Donna McKechnie, Jerry Orbach, Christopher Plummer, Walter Slezak, Alexis Smith, Tommy Steele, Peter Ustinov, and Gwen Verdon. CBS, March 25, 1973. YouTube. https://www.youtube.com/watch?v=s89lQaC_yog.

Pennebaker, D. A. *Original Cast Album: Company*. Directed by D. A. Pennebaker; music and lyrics by Stephen Sondheim; produced by Chris Dalrymple, Delia Doherty, Chester Feldman, and Peter Hansen; executive produced by Daniel Melnick; associate produced by Judy Crichton; starring Dean Jones, Elaine Stritch, Barbara Barrie, Stephen Sondheim, Thomas Z. Shepard, Harold Hastings, George Furth, and Harold Prince. New York Film Festival premiere, September 1970. PBS.

Rodgers, Richard, and Oscar Hammerstein II. *Oklahoma!* Written by Richard Rodgers (music) and Oscar Hammerstein II (book and lyrics), from their stage production based on *Green Grow the Lilacs* by Lynn Riggs; directed by Trevor Nunn; produced by Chris Hunt, Andy Picheta, and Richard Price; starring Hugh Jackman, Josefina Gabrielle, Maureen Lipman, and Shuler Hensley. September 26, 1999. Kew, Victoria, Australia: Umbrella Entertainment.

Sangare, Omar. "In Conversation with Stephen Sondheim." Hosted by Omar Sangare; guest, Stephen Sondheim. Omar Sangare, November 30, 2012. YouTube. https://www.youtube.com/watch?v=k7A0rHcYiMY.

Semprún, Jorge. *Stavisky*. Written by Jorge Semprún; directed by Alain Resnais; music by Stephen Sondheim; executive produced by Alesandre Mnouchkine and Georges Dancigers; starring Jean-Paul Belmondo, Anny Duperey, and Charles Boyer. Cannes Film Festival premiere May 15, 1974. Paris and Rome: Cérito Films, Ariane Films, and Euro-International Films, released by Cinemation Industries.

Sherrin, Ned. "Sondheim on Newsnight 1990." *Newsnight*. Hosted by Ned Sherrin; guest, Stephen Sondheim. BBC, 1990. YouTube. https://youtu.be/k8ayRl1VL9E.

Simon, Scott. *Weekend Edition Saturday*. Written and hosted by Scott Simon. NPR, November 27, 2021. https://www.npr.org/2021/11/27/1059485840/opinion-in-sondheims-essential-lyrics-a-soundtrack-for-life.

Sondheim, Stephen. *Stephen Sondheim in His Own Words*. Hosted by Pete Myers, André Previn, Bernard Levin, Roy Plomley, Jeremy Isaacs, and Mark Lawson; guest, Stephen Sondheim. BBC Audio, 2021.

———. "Stephen Sondheim on Glynis Johns." masterworksbwayVEVO, March 4, 1013. YouTube. https://www.youtube.com/watch?v=oSgyBoyoXnc.

———. "Stephen Sondheim on *Into the Woods*." masterworksbwayVEVO, August 1, 2012. YouTube. https://www.youtube.com/watch?v=seZyx0bNHBA.

Sondheim, Stephen, and Adam Guettel. *The Art of Songwriting with Stephen Sondheim and Adam Guettel*. Hosted by Adam Guettel; directed by Jeremy Levine and Landon Van Soest; produced by the Dramatists Guild Foundation, the Legacy Project; series conceived by Jonathan Reynolds; music by David Shire; guest, Stephen Sondheim. September 2009. YouTube. https://www.youtube.com/watch?v=TofC3KD-h8M.

BIBLIOGRAPHY

Sondheim, Stephen, and Hugh Wheeler. *A Little Night Music*. Music and lyrics written by Stephen Sondheim; book by Hugh Wheeler, suggested by a film by Ingmar Bergman; directed by Kirk Browning (City Opera production directed by Scott Ellis); produced by John Goberman; starring Sally Ann Howes, George Lee Andrews, Regina Resnik, Kevin Anderson, Beverly Lambert, Michael Maguire, Maureen Moore, Danielle Ferland, and the New York City Opera. *Live from Lincoln Center*, PBS, November 7, 1990. YouTube. https://youtu.be/8nfd98fE9T8.

Sondheim, Stephen, and James Lapine. *Sunday in the Park with George*. Music and lyrics written by Stephen Sondheim; book written by James Lapine; directed by Terry Hughes; written by James Lapine (book) and Stephen Sondheim (music and lyrics), based on their stage musical; produced by Iris Merlis; executive produced by Emanuel Azenberg, Michael Brandman, Bernard B. Jacobs, and Gerald Schoenfeld (The Shubert Organization); starring Mandy Patinkin and Bernadette Peters. *American Playhouse*. PBS, June 16, 1986.

Spigelgass, Leonard. *Gypsy*. Written by Leonard Spigelgass; based on the book of the stage musical by Arthur Laurents based on the memoirs of Gypsy Rose Lee; music by Jule Styne; lyrics by Stephen Sondheim; directed and produced by Mervyn LeRoy; starring Rosalind Russell, Natalie Wood, and Karl Malden. November 1, 1962. Burbank, CA: Warner Bros.

"Stephen Sondheim—The Story So Far . . . Finale." masterworksbwayVEVO channel, June 17, 2022. YouTube. https://www.youtube.com/watch?v=wi1Jf8AeAQQ.

Stevens, George Jr. *The Kennedy Center Honors: A Celebration of the Performing Arts*. Written and produced by George Stevens Jr.; produced by Don Mischer; directed by Louis J. Horvitz. CBS, December 29, 1993. YouTube. https://www.youtube.com/watch?v=ZaB1XWZwbF4.

"The Story So Far . . . *Sweeney Todd*." masterworksbwayVEVO channel, February 25, 2022. YouTube. https://www.youtube.com/watch?v=jvJ0xXGnTXo.

Wheeler, Hugh. *A Little Night Music*. Written by Hugh Wheeler, based on his book for the stage musical based on Ingmar Bergman's *Smiles of a Summer Night*; music and lyrics by Stephen Sondheim; directed by Harold Prince; produced by Elliott Kastner; starring Elizabeth Taylor, Diana Rigg, Len Cariou, Lesley-Anne Down, Hermione Gingold, and Laurence Guittard. September 30, 1977. Vienna: New World Pictures.

WEBSITES AND SOCIAL MEDIA PLATFORMS

American Theatre Editors. "Disney+ Announces Plans for 'Sweeney Todd' Animated Series." American Theatre, April 1, 2022. https://www.americantheatre.org/2022/04/01/disney-announces-plans-for-sweeney-todd-animated-series/.

Anonymous. "The 1970s." The Town Hall. http://thetownhall.org/the-1970s.

———. "About." Rodgers and Hammerstein: The Official Website, 2021. https://rodgersandhammerstein.com/about/.

———. "The British Bee Hive." British Library. https://www.bl.uk/collection-items/the-british-bee-hive.

———. "Cover Versions of 'Tonight' written by Leonard Bernstein, Stephen Sondheim." SecondHandSongs. https://secondhandsongs.com/work/54466/versions.

———. "Documentary: Avant-Garde Composer Milton Babbitt." NPR, January 31, 2022. https://www.npr.org/sections/deceptivecadence/2011/04/10/133372983/npr-exclusive-new-documentary-on-the-late-composer-milton-babbitt.

———. "George Oppenheimer." IMDB.com. https://www.imdb.com/name/nm0649183/.

———. "Hangover Square—Trailer." IMDB.com. https://www.imdb.com/video/vi1459077913/?ref_=tt_vi_i_1.

———. "Maestro of Broadway." Academy of Achievement, July 5, 2005. https://achievement.org/achiever/stephen-sondheim/#interview.

———. "Master Showman." Academy of Achievement, June 22, 2007. https://achievement.org/achiever/harold-prince/#interview.

———. "Milton Babbitt." The Pulitzer Prizes. https://www.pulitzer.org/winners/milton-babbitt.

———. "'On Sondheim': The Musical-Theater Legend at 80." NPR, April 21, 2010. https://www.npr.org/2010/04/21/124907187/on-sondheim-the-musical-theater-legend-at-80.

———. "Remembering George School Alum Stephen Sondheim, '46." George School, November 29, 2021. https://www.georgeschool.org/remembering-george-school-alum-stephen-sondheim-46/.

———. "Remembering Stephen Sondheim." Boston Symphony Orchestra. https://www.bso.org/events/boston-pops-sondheim-tribute.

———. "Topper." IMDB.com. https://www.imdb.com/title/tt0045447/fullcredits/?ref_=tt_cl_sm.https://www.imdb.com/title/tt0045447/fullcredits/?ref_=tt_cl_sm.

———. "Topper." Sondheim.com, 2004. http://www.sondheim.com/works/topper/.

———. "*West Side Story*: Birth of a Classic, Birth of a Musical." Library of Congress. https://www.loc.gov/exhibits/westsidestory/westsidestory-exhibit.html.

———. "*West Side Story*: Birth of a Classic, The Legacy of *West Side Story*." Library of Congress. https://www.loc.gov/exhibits/westsidestory/westsidestory-legacy.html.

Blevins, Joe. "Stephen Sondheim Was Not Impressed with the Film Version of *West Side Story*." The A.V. Club, April 7, 2016. https://www.avclub.com/stephen-sondheim-was-not-impressed-with-the-film-versio-1798245982.

Boone, John. "'Knives Out' Director Rian Johnson Reveals 3 Movies to Watch Ahead of His Whodunit." *Entertainment Tonight*, November 25, 2019. https://www.etonline.com/knives-out-director-rian-johnson-reveals-3-movies-to-watch-ahead-of-his-whodunit-134682.

Breen, Kerry. "Broadway Legend Stephen Sondheim Took Time to Mentor Young Creatives. Here's What It Meant to Them." *Today*, December 30, 2021. https://www.today.com/popculture/broadway-legend-stephen-sondheim-took-time-mentor-young-creatives-here-t243972.

Bulkeley, Kelly, PhD. "The Horrors of the Dream Ballet in 'Oklahoma!'" *Psychology Today*, February 21, 2018. https://www.psychologytoday.com/us/blog/dreaming-in-the-digital-age/201802/the-horrors-the-dream-ballet-in-oklahoma.

Dee, Jake. "Natalie Wood's 10 Best Movies, According to Rotten Tomatoes." ScreenRant, August 25, 2020. https://screenrant.com/natalie-wood-best-movies-rotten-tomatoes/.

Del Toro, Guillermo (@RealGDT). "There are some of the dance number shots that are extremely (if not impossible) to decipher and almost all of them require brain-surgery levels of precision. I was elated from the purity of his audiovisual painting strokes-." Twitter, February 26, 2002, 12:53 p.m. https://twitter.com/RealGDT/status/1497631034719887361.

Evans, Greg. "Daniel Radcliffe to Star in Off Broadway Revival of Sondheim's 'Merrily We Roll Along.'" *Deadline*, March 7, 2022. https://deadline.com/2022/03/daniel-radcliffe-off-broadway-stephen-sondheim-merrily-we-roll-along-1234972678/.

———. "Stephen Sondheim Writing New Musical 'Square One,' Reveals Plans to Stephen Colbert." *Deadline*, September 12, 2021. https://deadline.com/2021/09/stephen-sondheim-stephen-colbert-new-musical-square-one-1234838060/.

———. "'You'll Need to Be Sitting Down for This One': Emails Between Stephen Sondheim and Marianne Elliott Chronicle the Birth of a 21st Century 'Company.'" *Deadline*, June 8, 2022. https://deadline.com/2022/06/stephen-sondheim-marianne-elliott-new-emails-company-evolution-1235037493/.

Filichia, Peter. "You Don't Know Jack!" TheaterMania, November 13, 2006. https://www.theatermania.com/new-york-city-theater/news/you-dont-know-jack_9439.html.

Floyd, Jerry. "Sondheim&Signature: Side by Side with Eric D. Schaeffer." Stephen Sondheim Stage, 1998. http://www.sondheim.com/interview/sig.html.

Gans, Andrew. "Angela Lansbury, Audra McDonald, Bernadette Peters, Norm Lewis, Patti LuPone, More Remember Stephen Sondheim." *Playbill*, March 22, 2022. https://www.playbill.com/article/angela-lansbury-audra-mcdonald-bernadette-peters-norm-lewis-patti-lupone-more-remember-stephen-sondheim.

Gilbert, Charles. "A Tale of Two Assassins." Chas. Gilbert (personal website), 2001. http://www.chasgilbert.com/articles/assassins.html. (URL inactive; information based on 2001 printout.)

Gribber, Mark. "Sweeney Todd—Man or Myth?" Crime Library, 2007. https://web.archive.org/web/20080405180719/http://www.crimelibrary.com/serial_killers/weird/todd/index_1.html.

Hammerstein, Oscar II. "*Oklahoma!* Musical Script." The Musical Lyrics. https://www.themusicallyrics.com/b/348-broadway-musical-scripts/3611-oklahoma-musical-script.html.

Hannemann, Wolfram. "Introduction to 'West Side Story.'" in70mm.com, April 11, 2009. https://in70mm.com/festival/bradford/year/2009/intro/wolfram/west_side_story/index.htm

Janiga, Bruce (comp.). "Side by Side with Sondheim." Stephen Sondheim Stage, 1998. http://www.sondheim.com/interview/cyber.html.

Jones, Kenneth. "Stephen Sondheim Talks to Playbill.com." *Playbill*, December 7, 2010. https://www.playbill.com/article/stephen-sondheim-talks-to-playbillcom-com-174172.

Khoury, Peter. "Stephen Sondheim and the Australian Connection to His Work." *On Stage*, June 1, 2022. https://theatreheritage.org.au/on-stage-magazine/itemlist/tag/Stephen%20Sondheim.

Kimmel, Bruce. "Reds." Sondheim.com. http://www.sondheim.com/works/reds/.

Lenker, Maureen Lee. "Remembering That Time Stephen Sondheim Won a Grammy for Song of the Year." *Entertainment Weekly*, April 2, 2022. https://ew.com/awards/grammys/stephen-sondheim-send-in-the-clowns-grammy-song-of-the-year-judy-collins/.

Lockhart, Keith. "Tribute to Stephen Sondheim." Boston Symphony Orchestra, 2022. https://www.bso.org/pops/Sondheim-Tribute.

McCartney, Paul (@PaulMcCartney). "We have lost a great talent but his music will live long and prosper." Twitter, November 27, 2021. https://twitter.com/PaulMcCartney/status/1464542203469045769.

McNally, Terrence. "Landmark Symposium: *West Side Story*." Moderated by Terrence McNally; panelists, Leonard Bernstein, Arthur Laurents, Jerome Robbins, and Stephen Sondheim. Dramatists Guild, 1985; posted February 9, 2022. https://www.dramatistsguild.com/thedramatist/landmark-symposium-west-side-story.

McPhee, Ryan. "The Daily Distraction: A Funny Thing Happened to Whoopi Goldberg on the Way to Broadway." *Playbill*, May 8, 2020. https://playbill.com/article/the-daily-distraction-a-funny-thing-happened-to-whoopi-goldberg-on-the-way-to-broadway.

Oppenheimer, George. "George Oppenheimer Papers, 1943–1977." New York Public Library Archives & Manuscripts. https://archives.nypl.org/the/21265.

Peck, Justin (justin_peck). "It hit me like a gut-punch . . . It became a north-star guiding me back to New York, where I moved at age 15 to study dance and theatre." Instagram, November 15, 2021. https://www.instagram.com/p/CWTfgNLrdPn/.

Pollack-Pelzner, Daniel. "The Hidden History of 'Oklahoma!'" Oregon Artswatch, November 19, 2018. https://www.orartswatch.org/the-hidden-history-of-oklahoma/.

BIBLIOGRAPHY

Price, Michael (@mikepriceinla). "When he finished playing and singing he asked 'is that it? We done?' I said 'just one more thing. Please play me the entire score to Sweeney Todd.' He frowned . . . and then played those first low rumble notes of the opening number with a big smile on his face. Unforgettable." Twitter, November 27, 2021. https://twitter.com/mikepriceinla/status/1464489697481134085.

Rice, Patricia. "'Sweeney Todd' Was Always Meant to Be an Opera." St. Louis Public Radio, May 21, 2012. https://news.stlpublicradio.org/arts/2012-05-21/sweeney-todd-was-always-meant-to-be-an-opera.

Rymer, James Malcolm. *The String of Pearls; or, the Barber of Fleet Street, a Domestic Romance*. Edited by Alex Crary and Matthew McAnelly. The James Malcolm Rymer Collection, University of Wisconsin, Green Bay. http://salisburysquare.com/TSOP/content/TSOP.1850.UNC.chap.001.xml. Originally published in 1850.

Shook, Gregory. "Five New Graduates Awarded Hubbard Hutchinson Fellowships." Williams College, press release, July 8, 2020. https://communications.williams.edu/news-releases/7_8_2020_hutchinson/.

Singer, Barry. "What to Know About Sondheim's 'Saturday Night'—According to Stephen Sondheim." *Playbill*, March 7, 2019. https://playbill.com/article/what-to-know-about-sondheims-saturday-nightaccording-to-stephen-sondheim.

Solomon, Alisa. "Six Things You May Not Have Known About 'Fiddler on the Roof.'" *Smithsonian Magazine*, September 19, 2014. https://www.smithsonianmag.com/arts-culture/six-things-you-may-not-have-known-about-fiddler-roof-180952771/.

Teeman, Tim. "Up Close and Very Personal with the Real Stephen Sondheim." *Daily Beast*, November 27, 2021. https://www.thedailybeast.com/broadway-giant-stephen-sondheim-dead-at-91.

Thompson, Anne. "'Beauty and the Beast': How Bill Condon Built Hollywood's Most Expensive Musical." *IndieWire*, March 14, 2017. https://www.indiewire.com/2017/03/420-disney-beauty-and-the-beast-bill-condon-emma-watson-musical-1201791591/.

Wolf, Matt. "Stephen Sondheim Turns 80." Stage Whispers. https://www.stagewhispers.com.au/articles/193/stephen-sondheim-turns-80.

Zubrow, Keith. "'West Side Story' Lyrics Still Embarrass Sondheim." *60 Minutes Overtime*, CBS News, February 16, 2020. https://www.cbsnews.com/news/stephen-sondheim-on-a-21st-century-west-side-story-60-minutes-2020-02-16/.

SOURCE NOTES

TUNING UP

page 1: *"I'm interested in the theatre . . . is paramount to me"*: Terry Gross (host), "Stephen Sondheim: Examining His Lyrics and Life," *Fresh Air*, NPR. February 16, 2012, https://www.npr.org/2012/02/16/146938826/stephen-sondheim-examining-his-lyrics-and-life.

page 1: *"I don't think . . . making them human"*: Emma Brockes, "Big Beasts of Broadway . . . Stephen Sondheim and James Lapine on the Art of Writing Musicals," *Guardian*, July 10, 2016, https://www.theguardian.com/stage/2016/jul/10/stephen-sondheim-james-lapine-interview-writing-musicals-into-the-woods.

page 1: *"Writers write what they want to see on a stage"*: Bob Brown (interviewer), Hugh Downs (host), Stephen Sondheim (guest), "Stephen Sondheim: The Man Behind the Music," *20/20*, ABC News, 1994, YouTube, March 21, 2020, video, https://www.youtube.com/watch?v=zGDoe-2A-Hk.

page 1: *The show . . . "deadened world"*: Michiko Kakutani, "Sondheim's Passionate 'Passion,'" *New York Times*, March 20, 1994, section 2, pp. 1, 30.

page 2: *"If I consciously sat down . . . I wouldn't know how to do it"*: *Newsweek* staff, "Sondheim's Still Here," *Newsweek*, June 21, 1992, https://www.newsweek.com/sondheims-still-here-199396.

page 2: *"Write what you believe . . . never used his kind of imagery again"*: Dramatists Guild Foundation, *The Art of Songwriting with Stephen Sondheim and Adam Guettel*, Adam Guettel (host), Jeremy Levine and Landon Van Soest (directors); the Dramatists Guild Foundation, the Legacy Project (producers), David Shire (music), September 2009, New York, YouTube, April 28, 2020, video, https://www.youtube.com/watch?v=TofC3KD-h8M.

page 2: *"Order out of chaos . . . people make art"*: Terry Gross (host) and Stephen Sondheim (guest), "'Fresh Air' Remembers Broadway Legend Stephen Sondheim (Part 1)," *Fresh Air*, NPR, December 1, 2021, https://www.npr.org/transcripts/1060439722.

page 2: *"Modern literature . . . ambitious and complex"*: Adam Kirsch, "Why Stephen Sondheim Is America's Greatest Living Writer," *Wall Street Journal*, March 12, 2021, https://www.wsj.com/articles/why-stephen-sondheim-is-americas-greatest-living-writer-11615565018.

page 2: *"A poem . . . exists in time"*: Jeffrey Brown (interviewer), Robert MacNeil and Jim Lehrer (producers), "Stephen Sondheim on the Times and Rhymes of His Life," *MacNeil-Lehrer NewsHour*, PBS, December 8, 2010.

page 2: *"Opera is designed . . . as swiftly as possible"*: Jackson R. Bryer and Richard A. Davison, eds., *The Art of the American Musical: Conversations with the Creators* (New Brunswick, NJ: Rutgers University Place, 2005), p. 202.

page 2: *upon first exposure, Critics often did not know what to make of his work.*: Stephen Sondheim, conversation with author, August 6, 1981.

page 2: *"I try not to read my reviews . . . that you've been speared"*: Laura Barnett, "Stephen Sondheim, Composer—Portrait of the Artist," *Guardian*, November 27, 2012, https://www.theguardian.com/culture/2012/nov/27/stephen-sondheim-portrait-artist.

page 3: *with vodka, later wine*: Laura Barnett, "Stephen Sondheim, Composer—Portrait of the Artist," *Guardian*, November 27, 2012, https://www.theguardian.com/culture/2012/nov/27/stephen-sondheim-portrait-artist.

page 3: *"I've never thought for one minute . . . waste of time"*: Emma Brockes, "Stephen Sondheim: A Life in Music," *Guardian*, December 20, 2010, https://www.theguardian.com/culture/2010/dec/20/stephen-sondheim-life-music-profile.

page 3: *chart-toppers*: "Cover Versions of 'Tonight' written by Leonard Bernstein, Stephen Sondheim," SecondHandSongs, https://secondhandsongs.com/work/54466/versions.

page 3: *"two and a half million copies"*: Mark Savage, "Barbra Streisand: 'I've Always Had the Right to Sing What I Want,'" BBC News, August 4, 2021, https://www.bbc.com/news/entertainment-arts-58056164.

page 3: *licensing agency*: masterworksbwayVEVO, "Stephen Sondheim—on *Into the Woods*," YouTube, August 1, 2012, video, https://www.youtube.com/watch?v=seZyx0bNHBA.

page 5: *music by Eli Bolin*: Eli Bolin, "John Mulaney, Seth Meyers & Richard Kind on Sondheim & 'Co-Op,'" YouTube, September 25, 2018, video, https://www.youtube.com/watch?v=9uNoHYimK2A.

page 5: *aping . . . and* Working: Jackson McHenry, "How 'Documentary Now' Made the Sondheim-Alike Musical 'Co-op' for Its 'Company' Episode," *Vulture*, February 27, 2019, https://www.vulture.com/2019/02/documentary-now-making-of-co-op-musical.html.

page 5: *"The lyrics are crowded"*: Mike Hale, "Adoring, and Parodying, Sondheim," *New York Times*, February 26, 2019, section C, p. 1.

page 5: The Morning Show: David Benedict, "Sondheim Reshaped American Theatre, Placing It at the Very Heart of American Culture," *Guardian*, November 28, 2021, https://www.theguardian.com/commentisfree/2021/nov/28/rip-stephen-sondheim-revolutionary-in-world-of-musical-theatre.

page 5: *"I'm more than delighted, I'm thrilled"*: Etan Vlessing, "Dominic Cooke Sets Movie Adaptation of Stephen Sondheim's 'Follies,'" *Hollywood Reporter*, November 14, 2019, https://www.hollywoodreporter.com/movies/movie-news/dominic-cooke-sets-movie-adaptation-stephen-sondheims-follies-1254884/.

page 5: *"so he would be the best"*: Eli Bolin, "John Mulaney, Seth Meyers & Richard Kind on Sondheim & 'Co-Op,'" YouTube, September 25, 2018, video, https://www.youtube.com/watch?v=9uNoHYimK2A.

page 7: *writing partner*: Mia Galuppo, "Richard Linklater Musical to Be Filmed over 20-Year Span," *Hollywood Reporter*, August 29, 2019, https://www.hollywoodreporter.com/news/general-news/richard-linklater-film-merrily-we-roll-along-be-shot-20-years-1235414/.

page 8: *"We have lost . . . prosper"*: Paul McCartney (@PaulMcCartney), "We have lost a great talent but his music will live long and prosper," Twitter, November 27, 2021, 2:30 a.m., https://twitter.com/PaulMcCartney/status/1464542203469045769.

page 8: *"You have two kinds . . . all spectacles"*: Frank Rich, "Conversations with Sondheim," *New York Times Magazine*, March 12, 2000, section 6, p. 38.

page 9: *"the only awards . . . with cash"*: Stephen Sondheim, *Look, I Made a Hat: Collected Lyrics (1981–2011) with Attendant Comments, Amplifications, Dogmas, Harangues, Digressions, Anecdotes, and Miscellany* (New York: Alfred A. Knopf, 2011), p. 50.

page 9: *Hamburg Steinway*: Sondheim and Guettel, in *The Art of Songwriting*.

page 9: *"As a composer . . . 'Send in the Clowns.'"*: President Barack Obama (host), Stephen Sondheim (guest), "Remarks on Presenting the Presidential Medal of Freedom," U.S. Government Publishing Office, November 24, 2015, https://www.govinfo.gov/content/pkg/DCPD-201500840/pdf/DCPD-201500840.pdf.

SPIRITUAL PRESENCE

I.

page 11: *his Prohibition-era characters*: James Thurber, *The Years with Ross* (Boston: Little, Brown, 1959), Kindle edition.

page 11: *"constantly screw up his life"*: *Something for Everyone: Sondheim Tonight!* (New York: The Museum of Television & Radio program brochure, 2000), p. 7.

page 11: *a likely eleven*: "*Topper*: Full Cast & Crew," IMDB.com, https://www.imdb.com/title/tt0045447/fullcredits/?ref_=tt_cl_sm.

page 11: *to as many as twenty-nine*: George Oppenheimer, *The View from the Sixties: Memories of a Spent Life* (New York: David McKay, 1966), pp. 256–257.

page 11: *Howard Lindsay*: Craig Zadan, *Sondheim & Co.* (New York: Da Capo Press, 1994), p. 8.

page 13: *"one of the writers for Topper"*: William Poundstone, "A Funny Thing Happened on the Way to Broadway," *Advocate*, August 1, 1989, p. 62.

page 13: *theatre-owning family*: Meryle Secrest, *Stephen Sondheim: A Life* (New York: Alfred A. Knopf, 1998), p. 96.

page 13: *Capehart phonograph player*: "Maestro of Broadway," Academy of Achievement, July 5, 2005, https://achievement.org/achiever/stephen-sondheim/#interview.

page 13: *"but I could read it"*: Marian McPartland (host), Stephen Sondheim (guest), *Marian McPartland's Piano Jazz*, NPR, 1994, https://www.npr.org/2011/12/30/144485557/stephen-sondheim-on-piano-jazz.

page 13: *"trotted back to my bedroom"*: McPartland, *Marian McPartland's Piano Jazz*.

page 13: *Sondheim on Sondheim*: Performance attended by author, April 23, 2010.

page 13: *over his father's and follow along*: D. T. Max, "Stephen Sondheim's Lesson for Every Artist," *New Yorker*, February 14, 2022, https://www.newyorker.com/culture/the-new-yorker-interview/stephen-sondheim-final-interviews.

page 14: *"a nice lady"*: *Six by Sondheim*, James Lapine (director), Liz Stanton (producer), James Lapine and Frank Rich (executive producers), Miky Wolf (editor), HBO, 2013.

page 14: *"didn't see my own father"*: "Maestro of Broadway."

page 15: *"my tendency to hysteria"*: William A. Henry III, "Master of the Musical: Stephen Sondheim Applies a Relentless," *Time*, December 7, 1987, https://web.archive.org/web/20070930120011/http://www.time.com/time/magazine/article/0,9171,966141,00.html.

page 15: *"American Noël Coward"*: "Show Business: The Once and Future Follies," *Time*, May 3, 1971, http://content.time.com/time/subscriber/article/0,33009,876987-7,00.html.

page 15: *"hobnobbing with Leonard Bernstein"*: "Maestro of Broadway."

page 15: *"creature of public opinion"*: Brockes, "Sondheim: A Life in Music."

page 15: *"chaos of home"*: Joseph Berger, "New York Military Academy's Sudden Closing, After 126 Years," *New York Times*, September 20, 2015, section A, p. 14.

page 16: *"a year of organ there"*: McPartland, *Marian McPartland's Piano Jazz*.

page 15: *"always with unconscious elegance"*: John Steele Gordon, "My Uncle, Oscar Hammerstein," *Commentary*, April 2011, https://www.commentary.org/articles/john-steele-gordon/my-uncle-oscar-hammerstein/.

page 15: *"homespun quality of his work"*: Stephen Sondheim, introduction to *Getting to Know Him: A Biography of Oscar Hammerstein II* by Hugh Fordin (New York: Random House, 1977), p. xi.

page 15: *"I thought that was thrilling"*: Henry, "Master of the Musical."

page 16: *"melodies ever written"*: Sondheim, in *Six by Sondheim*.

page 16: *"emotional truth and reality"*: Jeff Lunden, "'Showboat,'" *All Things Considered*, NPR, April 17, 2000, https://www.npr.org/2000/04/17/1073053/npr-100-i-showboat-i.

page 16: *"as well as writing songs"*: Jones, "Stephen Sondheim Talks to Playbill.com," *Playbill*, December 7, 2010, https://www.playbill.com/article/stephen-sondheim-talks-to-playbillcom-com-174172.

page 17: *"No two productions are alike"*: Jones, "Sondheim Talks."

page 17: *seeking out new vistas*: Stephen Sondheim, *Finishing the Hat: Collected Lyrics (1954–1981) with Attendant Comments, Principles, Heresies, Grudges, Whines, and Anecdotes* (New York: Alfred A. Knopf, 2010), p. xx.

page 18: *freshening up the Sondheim residence*: Fordin, *Getting to Know Him*, p. 171.

page 18: *"She sort of foisted me"*: Sondheim, in *Six by Sondheim*.

page 18: *in the family manse*: Anne Levin, "Restoration of Highland Farm to Preserve Hammerstein Legacy," *Town Topics*, May 8, 2019, https://www.towntopics.com/wordpress/2019/05/08/restoration-of-highland-farm-to-preserve-hammerstein-legacy/.

page 18: *"more a Hammerstein than a Sondheim"*: Henry, "Master of the Musical."

page 18: *"Steve was not warm"*: Todd S. Purdum, *Something Wonderful: Rodgers and Hammerstein's Broadway Revolution* (New York: Henry Holt, 2018), Kindle edition.

page 18: *"wounds have been inflicted"*: Secrest, *Sondheim: A Life*, p. 37.

page 18: *Sondheim's early efforts*: Paul Salsini, "'As Always, Steve': Corresponding with Sondheim, Note by Note," *Milwaukee Journal Sentinel*, December 8, 2021, https://www.jsonline.com/story/entertainment/arts/2021/12/07/corresponding-stephen-sondheim-note-note/8851136002/.

page 18: *"George School's own Rachmaninoff"*: "Remembering George School Alum Stephen Sondheim '46," George School, November 29, 2021, https://www.georgeschool.org/remembering-george-school-alum-stephen-sondheim-46/.

page 19: *of Cherokee descent*: Daniel Pollack-Pelzner, "The Hidden History of 'Oklahoma!,'" Oregon Artswatch, November 19, 2018, https://www.orartswatch.org/the-hidden-history-of-oklahoma/.

page 19: *keen on the property*: Oscar Hammerstein II, "In Re 'Oklahoma!,'" *New York Times*, May 23, 1943, p. 1.

page 19: *"ever need know"*: Richard Rodgers, *Musical Stages: An Autobiography* (New York: Random House, 1975), p. 209.

page 19: *"you're making a mistake"*: Rodgers, *Musical Stages*, p. 217.

page 19: *set them to music*: Fordin, *Getting to Know Him*, p. 186.

page 20: *"in almost ten years"*: Rodgers, *Musical Stages*, p. 207.

page 20: *"anybody else reading that play would not have seen"*: Lin-Manuel Miranda, "Stephen Sondheim, Theater's Greatest Lyricist," *T Magazine*, October 16, 2017, https://www.nytimes.com/2017/10/16/t-magazine/lin-manuel-miranda-stephen-sondheim.html.

page 20: *"What could be more ridiculous?"*: Agnes de Mille, interview with author, New York City, November 21, 1979.

page 20: *"they have their own magic"*: James Lipton (host) and Stephen Sondheim (guest), "Stephen Sondheim Interviewed by James Lipton in 1994 at the Actor's Studio," *Inside the Actor's Studio*, Greenleaf Productions, YouTube, November 27, 2021, video, https://www.youtube.com/watch?v=fDpE7Ki4jMs.

page 20: *"everything they were going over to fight for"*: Stephen M. Silverman, *Public Spectacles* (New York: E. P. Dutton, 1981), pp. 64–71.

page 21: *"the battlefield for his emotions"*: Leo Robson, "Mandy Patinkin on Stephen Sondheim: 'I Got to Be in the Room with Shakespeare. Who Gets That?,'" *New Statesman* (UK edition), November 29, 2021, https://www.newstatesman.com/culture/music/2021/11/mandy-patinkin-on-stephen-sondheim-i-got-to-be-in-the-room-with-shakespeare-who-gets-that.

page 21: *"really radically new in the theater"*: Terry Gross (host) and Todd Purdum (guest), "How Rodgers and Hammerstein Revolutionized Broadway," *Fresh Air*, NPR, May 28, 2018, https://www.npr.org/2018/05/28/614469172/how-rodgers-and-hammerstein-revolutionized-broadway.

page 22: *his willingness to experiment*: "Maestro of Broadway."

page 22: *"It might also be boring"*: De Mille, interview with author.

page 22: *twenty-two curtain calls and a standing ovation*: Silverman, *Public Spectacles*, p. 64.

page 22: *"much more than to his work"*: Mark Eden Horowitz, *Sondheim on Music: Minor Details and Major Decisions* (Lanham, MD: Rowman & Littlefield, 2019), p. 210.

page 22: *a servant girl he has just encountered*: Ferenc Molnár, *Liliom: A Legend in Seven Scenes and a Prologue*, trans. Benjamin F. Glazer (1921; University of North Carolina at Chapel Hill: Project Gutenberg, 2015), https://www.gutenberg.org/files/48749/48749-h/48749-h.htm.

page 23: *"I cry very easily"*: Brockes, "Sondheim: A Life in Music."

page 24: *Lucifer, or Darth Vader*: Kelly Bulkeley, Ph.D, "The Horrors of the Dream Ballet in 'Oklahoma!,'" *Psychology Today*, February 21, 2018, https://www.psychologytoday.com/us/blog/dreaming-in-the-digital-age/201802/the-horrors-the-dream-ballet-in-oklahoma.

page 24: *"as the curtain falls"*: Oscar Hammerstein II, "*Oklahoma!* Musical Script," The Musical Lyrics, https://www.themusicallyrics.com/b/348-broadway-musical-scripts/3611-oklahoma-musical-script.html.

II.

page 24: *"I, of course . . . 'bah-duh-duh-duh'"*: Omar Sangare, "In Conversation with Stephen Sondheim," YouTube, November 30, 2021, video, https://www.youtube.com/watch?v=k7A0rHcYiMY.

page 24: *teaching at Williams in 1939*: Rick Pender, "Sondheim and Rich Go to College," *Sondheim Review*, Spring 2009, p. 17.

page 24: *"and everybody hated him . . . he was very dry"*: Stephen Schiff, "Deconstructing Sondheim," *New Yorker*, February 28, 1993, https://www.newyorker.com/magazine/1993/03/08/deconstructing-sondheim.

page 24: *"the skies opening up . . . and some don't"*: Schiff, "Deconstructing Sondheim."

page 25: *"opening night of* A Chorus Line*"*: Jack Viertel, *The Secret Life of the American Musical: How Broadway Shows Are Built* (New York: Farrar, Straus and Giroux, 2016), p. 15.

page 25: *"unlikely to be successful"*: David Dachs, *Anything Goes: The World of Popular Music* (Indianapolis: Bobbs-Merrill, 1964), p. 294.

page 26: *linking the tales into one coherent story*: Steve Swayne, *How Sondheim Found His Sound* (Ann Arbor: University of Michigan Press, 2007), pp. 138–139.

page 26: *"fairly different from the film"*: Pete Myers (host), Stephen Sondheim (guest), *The Lively Odds*, January 2, 1977, BBC, retrieved from *Stephen Sondheim in His Own Words* (BBC Audio, 2021).

page 26: *at Robert Barrow's encouragement*: Bernard Levin (host) and Stephen Sondheim (guest), *The Levin Interviews*, BBC, April 26, 1980.

page 26: *went on to become . . . for the* New York Times: Olin Downes, "Hubbard Hutchinson," *New York Times*, December 30, 1934, p. 108.

page 26: *their pursuit of the creative arts*: "Five New Graduates Awarded Hubbard Hutchinson Fellowships," Williams College, press release, July 8, 2020, https://communications.williams.edu/news-releases/7_8_2020_hutchinson/.

page 26: *setting up a cot in the dining room*: Martin Gottfried, *Sondheim* (New York: Harry N. Abrams, 2000), p. 16.

page 26-27: *"We would spend . . . compositional analysis"*: "'On Sondheim': The Musical-Theater Legend at 80," NPR, April 21, 2010, https://www.npr.org/2010/04/21/124907187/on-sondheim-the-musical-theater-legend-at-80.

page 27: *appreciated, even comprehended*: Robert Hilferty and Laura Karpman (directors), Milton Babbitt (star), *Portrait of a Serial Composer*, 2010, available on Roger Sessions, YouTube, April 11, 2013, video, https://www.youtube.com/watch?v=JuTRWHAd_IM.

page 27: South Pacific *instead*: Richard Dyer, "A First Time for Everything: With World Premiere, the BSO Finally Steps into the World of Composer Milton Babbitt," *Boston Globe*, January 13, 2005, http://archive.boston.com/news/globe/living/articles/2005/01/13/a_first_time_for_everything/.

page 27: *"for his life's work . . . private tutorial"*: "Milton Babbitt," The Pulitzer Prizes, https://www.pulitzer.org/winners/milton-babbitt.

page 27: *"What it amounts . . . make it cohere"*: Max, "Stephen Sondheim's Lesson for Every Artist."

page 27: *"He said . . . 'You haven't, have you?'"*: James Lipton, "Stephen Sondheim, The Art of the Musical," *Paris Review*, no. 142, Spring 1997, https://www.theparisreview.org/interviews/1283/the-art-of-the-musical-stephen-sondheim.

page 27: *"They show up all the time in my stuff"*: "Maestro of Broadway."

page 27: *"No one could have . . . Broadway musical"*: Zadan, *Sondheim & Co.*, pp. 6–7.

page 28: Libeled Lady, A Day at the Races: "George Oppenheimer," IMDB.com, https://www.imdb.com/name/nm0649183/.

page 28: *He took his idea to Yale*: Theodore Hoffman, "Review: 47 Workshop," *Kenyon Review*, Spring 1955, p. 302.

page 29: *thinly disguised versions of writers*: Anna Quindlen, "George Oppenheimer, Drama Critic and Writer for Stage and Screen," *New York Times*, August 16, 1977, p. 36.

page 29: *"Pay no attention . . . dropping a name"*: Dorothy Parker, *Not Much Fun: The Lost Poems of Dorothy Parker*, edited by Stuart Y. Silverstein (New York: Scribner, 2009), p. 46.

page 29: *"to prepare . . . a sonnet"*: Oppenheimer, *The View from the Sixties*, p. 256.

page 29: *"He had . . . by name"*: Oppenheimer, *The View from the Sixties*, p. 257.

page 29: *weekly stipend of $300*: "Topper," Sondheim.com, http://www.sondheim.com/works/topper/.

page 29: *character actress Kathleen Freeman*: George Oppenheimer and Stephen Sondheim (writers), Philip Rapp (director), John W. Loveton (producer), "Hiring the Maid," *Topper*, season 1 episode 3, CBS, October 23, 1953, available on YouTube, video, https://www.youtube.com/watch?v=g0WzaUfpI2U.

page 29: *gets Cosmo indicted*: George Oppenheimer and Stephen Sondheim (writers), Philip Rapp (director), John W. Loveton (producer), "Burglar," *Topper*, season 1 episode 9, December 4, 1953, available on YouTube, video, https://www.youtube.com/watch?v=27UPeAROS6M.

page 29: *"like music . . . everyone votes—for"*: George Oppenheimer and Stephen Sondheim (writers), James V. Kern (director), John W. Loveton (producer), "Preparations for Europe," *Topper*, season 1 episode 36, CBS, June 11, 1954, available on YouTube, video, https://www.youtube.com/watch?v=Q2DNdq5V8SM.

page 29: *"We alternated writing scripts"*: "Maestro of Broadway."

page 29: *"A song, like a play . . . where you began"*: Ned Cramer (producer), Ethel Burns (associate producer), Neal Finn (director), Irwin Kostal (conductor), Earl Wrightson (host), Stephen Sondheim (guest), *The American Musical Theatre*, WCBS-TV, October 15, 1961.

page 29: *worsened by the arrival of his mother*: Zadan, *Sondheim & Co.*, pp. 8–9.

page 29: *revealed himself to be bipolar*: Secrest, *Sondheim: A Life*, p. 97.

page 29: *drama critic for Long Island's* Newsday: "George Oppenheimer Papers, 1943–1977," New York Public Library Archives & Manuscripts, https://archives.nypl.org/the/21265.

page 29: *an industrial spy with epilepsy*: Secrest, *Sondheim: A Life*, p. 103.

page 29: *"The company . . . was able to crack"*: Michael J. Bandler, "What Collaboration Is All About," *Sondheim Review*, Fall 2009, p. 25.

STREET FIGHTERS

page 30: *"There are two lyrics . . . on paper"*: Pete Myers (host), Stephen Sondheim (guest), *PM*, BBC Radio, July 21, 1973.

page 31: *Oppenheimer introduced Sondheim*: Bryer and Davison, *Art of the American Musical*, p. 192.

page 31: *Martin Gabel*: Arthur Laurents, *Original Story: A Memoir of Broadway and Hollywood* (New York: Applause Theatre Books, 2000), p. 334.

page 31: *Henry Margolis*: Robert Emmet Long, *Broadway, the Golden Years: Jerome Robbins and the Great Choreographer-Directors, 1940 to the Present* (New York: Continuum Books, 2001), p. 97.

page 31: *La Côte Basque*: Alfonso S. Narvaez, "H. M. Margolis, 80, Industrialist," *New York Times*, November 3, 1989, section D, p. 18.

page 31: *told Bernstein that* Serenade *was trash*: Humphrey Burton, *Leonard Bernstein* (New York, Doubleday, 1994), pp. 247–248.

page 31: *"but then . . . a film of* Serenade*"*: Bryer and Davison, *Art of the American Musical*, p. 192.

page 32: *"Depends who you ask"*: "Maestro of Broadway."

page 32: *"Robbins . . . gangs in New York"*: Patricia Bosworth, *Montgomery Clift: A Biography* (New York: Harcourt Brace Jovanovich, 1978), p. 136.

page 32: *"Arthur and Lenny were"*: Terrence McNally (moderator), Leonard Bernstein, Arthur Laurents, Jerome Robbins, and Stephen Sondheim (panelists), "Landmark Symposium: *West Side Story*," Dramatists Guild, 1985, posted February 9, 2022, https://www.dramatistsguild.com/thedramatist/landmark-symposium-west-side-story.

page 33: *knockdowns . . . were commonplace*: Jesse Green, "When You're a Shark, You're a Shark All the Way," *New York*, March 15, 2009.

page 33: *he wrote . . . propaganda*: Robert Berkvist, "Arthur Laurents, Playwright and Director on Broadway, Dies at 93," *New York Times*, May 6, 2011, section B, p. 10.

page 33: *definitively new world, American*: Amanda Vaill, *Somewhere: The Life of Jerome Robbins* (New York: Broadway Books, 2006), p. 90.

page 33: *expand* Fancy Free *into a full-blown musical*: Stephen M. Silverman, *Dancing on the Ceiling: Stanley Donen and His Movies* (New York: Alfred A. Knopf, 1996), p. 107.

page 34: *floating crap game?*: Nigel Simeone ed., *The Leonard Bernstein Letters* (New Haven: Yale University Press, 2013), pp. 343-345.

page 34: *larger ballet mid-act*: "*West Side Story*: Birth of a Classic, Birth of a Musical," Library of Congress, https://www.loc.gov/exhibits/westsidestory/westsidestory-exhibit.html.

page 34: *"It's not a dream sequence . . . lyricism and peace"*: Jerome Robbins, interview with author, February 10, 1980.

page 35: *1994 . . . Encores! revival*: Performance attended by author, March 2, 1994.

page 35: *"It changed . . . fix that show"*: Bryer and Davison, *Art of the American Musical*, p. 193.

page 35: *gang violence in Southern California*: Simeone, *Leonard Bernstein Letters*, p. 343.

page 35: *"unprepossessing . . . clothes"*: Arthur Laurents, *Mainly on Directing: Gypsy, West Side Story, and Other Musicals* (New York: Alfred A. Knopf, 2009), p. 334.

page 35: *Dakota apartment building*: Dennis Hevesi, "Ruth Ford, Film and Stage Actress, Dies at 98," *New York Times*, August 14, 2009, https://www.nytimes.com/2009/08/14/theater/14ford-1.html.

page 36: *"liked what he heard"*: Chris Wiegand, "How We Made 'West Side Story,'" *Guardian*, September 18, 2017, https://www.theguardian.com/stage/2017/sep/18/how-we-made-west-side-story-stephen-sondheim-chita-rivera-musicals.

page 36: *"A young lyricist . . . as do we all"*: Horatia Howard, "50 Years of 'West Side Story,'" *Telegraph*, July 7, 2008.

page 36: *"It's a job"*: Bryer and Davison, *Art of the American Musical*, p. 192.

page 37: *directed for New York's Second Stage*: Performance attended by author, February 16, 2000.

page 37: *played the part at Second Stage*: Amy Brill, "Saturday Night Special," *Talk*, February 2000.

page 37: *"revisit old work"*: Barry Singer, "What to Know About Sondheim's *Saturday Night*—According to Stephen Sondheim," *Playbill*, March 7, 2019, https://playbill.com/article/what-to-know-about-sondheims-saturday-nightaccording-to-stephen-sondheim.

page 38: *"There's a lot of plot . . . that's ever existed"*: Wiegand, "How We Made 'West Side Story.'"

page 38: *"Not only was I . . . verging on myth"*: Sondheim, *Finishing the Hat*, p. 25.

page 38: *"liked to work . . . the phone a lot"*: "Maestro of Broadway."

page 38: *Actors Studio in the '50s: subtext*: Sondheim, *Finishing the Hat*, p. 57.

page 38: *"words and intention collide"*: Foster Hirsch, *Harold Prince and the American Musical Theatre* (New York: Applause Theatre & Cinema Books, 2005), p. 75.

page 38: *"did something . . . that doesn't date"*: Wiegand, "How We Made 'West Side Story.'"

page 38: *"I wanted . . . word on Broadway"*: Keith Zubrow, "'West Side Story' Lyrics Still Embarrass Sondheim," *60 Minutes Overtime*, CBS News. February 16, 2020. https://www.cbsnews.com/news/stephen-sondheim-on-a-21st-century-west-side-story-60-minutes-2020-02-16/.

page 38: *Robbins acknowledged*: McNally, "Landmark Symposium."

page 39: *"He was perfect . . . 'Please don't'"*: Wiegand, "How We Made 'West Side Story.'"

page 39: *"Arthur would come . . . as a dance"*: McNally, "Landmark Symposium."

page 39: *"They could only come . . . in those days"*: Grover Dale, interview with author, March 21, 2022.

page 39: *"I went into the rehearsal room . . . in front of somebody else"*: James Lapine, *Putting It Together: How Stephen Sondheim and I Created "Sunday in the Park with George"* (New York: Farrar, Straus and Giroux, 2021), pp. 106–107.

page 40: *add musical notes to "Somewhere"*: Burton, *Leonard Bernstein*, p. 275.

page 40: *"You came out scarred . . . with good work"*: Wiegand, "How We Made 'West Side Story.'"

page 40: *Another grab from* Candide: Laurent Bouzereau, *"West Side Story": The Making of the Steven Spielberg Film* (New York: Harry N. Abrams, 2021), p. 18.

page 40: *replacement for the balcony scene*: Geoffrey Block, *Enchanted Evenings: The Broadway Musical from "Show Boat" to Sondheim and Lloyd Webber* (New York: Oxford University Press, 2009), p. 252.

page 40: *Bernstein had his heart set*: Burton, *Leonard Bernstein*, p. 275.

page 40: *"I thought . . . 'a lot to me'"*: Zubrow, *"West Side Story* Lyrics."

page 40: *"We argued . . . he was absolutely right"*: McNally, "Landmark Symposium."

page 40: *"He'd written . . . ballet called Conch Town"*: Wiegand, "How We Made 'West Side Story.'"

page 40: *"would sketch out . . . 'being poetic!'"*: Wiegand, "How We Made 'West Side Story.'"

page 41: *"I don't think it was planned that way"*: Randy Kennedy, "Tunnel Vision; Three Note Mystery Haunts Riders on No. 2 Line," *New York Times*, January 9, 2002, section B, p. 3.

page 41: *"people . . . 'hear it?'"*: Jim Dwyer, "Under Broadway, the Subway Hums Bernstein," *New York Times*, February 20, 2009, https://www.nytimes.com/2009/02/21/nyregion/21about.html.

page 41: *"Afraid of taking a chance . . . defend every point"*: Gottfried, *Sondheim*, p. 49.

page 41: *"Somebody . . . in my mouth"*: "Maestro of Broadway."

page 42: *George Abbott and Richard Rodgers among them*: Hal Prince, *Contradictions: Notes on Twenty-Six Years in the Theatre* (New York: Dodd, Mead, 1974), p. 30.

page 42: *constructive criticism*: McNally, "Landmark Symposium."

page 42: *"My version . . . raise the money"*: McNally, "Landmark Symposium."

page 42: *"This is the first . . . cast accordingly"*: McNally, "Landmark Symposium."

page 42: *eight-week rehearsal period*: McNally, "Landmark Symposium."

page 42: *"a battleground"*: Sara Fishko, "The Real-Life Drama Behind 'West Side Story,'" *Fishko Files*, NPR, January 7, 2009, https://www.npr.org/2011/02/24/97274711/the-real-life-drama-behind-west-side-storynakes.

page 42: *"violence . . . and fractured bones"*: Carol Lawrence, *Carol Lawrence: The Backstage Story* (New York: McGraw Hill, 1990), pp. 42–43.

page 43: *"When I wrote . . . ever seen in my life"*: Melissa Errico, "Get Out of My Light, Honey. I'm Auditioning Here," *New York Times*, September 1, 2019, section AR, p. 4.

page 43: *"Which was itself generous of him"*: Melissa Errico, email to author, May 6, 2022.

page 43: *"'West Side Story' is a work of art"*: Richard L. Coe, "Tryouts: Here to Broadway or Bust," *Washington Post*, September 30, 1979, https://www.washingtonpost.com/archive/lifestyle/1979/09/30/tryouts-here-to-broadway-or-bust/6ad5acd9-3f33-48a8-93e9-3f1c9d5fda51/.

page 43: *"Chita . . . good time"*: Wiegand, "How We Made 'West Side Story.'"

page 43: *"stared . . . with bravos"*: Lawrence, *Carol Lawrence*, pp. 2–3.

page 44: *"Death is . . . a logical ending to a story"*: "Maestro of Broadway."

page 44: *"I didn't think it would last three months"*: Barbara Hoffman, "How the West Was Won," *New York Post*, March 8, 2009, p. 43.

page 44: *only studio to bid on the property*: Prince, *Contradictions*, p. 43.

page 44: *"Not many laughs . . . But I'm glad he did"*: "Maestro of Broadway."

page 44: *first played her "Maria"*: Gottfried, *Sondheim*, p. 48.

page 44: *"I wasn't sure . . . you can't get onstage"*: Robbins, interview with author.

page 44: *according to producer Walter Mirisch*: Walter Mirisch, *I Thought We Were Making Movies, Not History* (Madison, WI: University of Wisconsin Press, 2008), Kindle edition.

page 45: *Other names on the table . . . and Jill St. John*: Wolfram Hannemann, "Introduction to 'West Side Story,'" in70mm.com, April 11, 2009, https://in70mm.com/festival/bradford/year/2009/intro/wolfram/west_side_story/index.htm.

page 45: *admitted she was not Hispanic*: Mirisch, *Making Movies*.

page 46: *over-orchestrating it with too many musicians*: Mirisch, *Making Movies*.

page 46: *"I think . . . it seemed to have a lot of impact on the world"*: Robbins, interview with author.

page 47: *redeveloped into Lincoln Center*: George Stevens, Jr., ed., *Conversations with the Great Moviemakers of Hollywood's Golden Age at the American Film Institute* (New York: Alfred A. Knopf, 2006), p. 470.

page 47: *"That's one story"*: Robbins, interview with author.

page 47: *"in his usual vaguely dishonest manner"*: Simeone, *Leonard Bernstein Letters*, p. 437.

page 47: *He wanted his name removed from the picture*: Mirisch, *Making Movies*.

page 48: *"I don't think* West Side Story*'s a good movie at all because . . . I'm not scared"*: Joe Blevins, "Stephen Sondheim Was Not Impressed with the Film Version of 'West Side Story,'" The A.V. Club, April 7, 2016, https://www.avclub.com/stephen-sondheim-was-not-impressed-with-the-film-versio-1798245982.

page 48: *Robbins said he would still cast the two*: Silverman, *Public Spectacles*, p. 77.

page 48: *"You can't update* West Side Story*"*: Robbins, interview with author.

page 48: *"There was a plan . . . meant updating the orchestration"*: Bruce Janiga, comp., "Side by Side with Sondheim," Stephen Sondheim Stage, 1998, http://www.sondheim.com/interview/cyber.html.

page 48: *"Other shows have evolved from it"*: Robbins, interview with author.

page 48: *"dance Robbins's choreography . . . dazzling effects"*: Ken Mandelbaum, *"A Chorus Line" and the Musicals of Michael Bennett* (New York: St. Martin's Press, 1989), pp. 23–24.

page 49: *"the libretto . . . and local dialects"*: *"West Side Story*: Birth of a Classic—The Legacy of *West Side Story*," Library of Congress, https://www.loc.gov/exhibits/westsidestory/westsidestory-legacy.html.

page 50: *"He's Stephen Sondheim"*: Seth Abramovitch, "Tony Kushner on Tackling 'West Side Story' with Spielberg: 'We Knew We Were Going into a Complicated Situation,'" *Hollywood Reporter*, December 3, 2021, https://www.hollywoodreporter.com/movies/movie-features/tony-kushner-interview-west-side-story-steven-spielberg-1235054430/.

page 50: *"The whole thing . . . feels fresh"*: Stephen Colbert (host) and Stephen Sondheim (guest), *The Late Show with Stephen Colbert*, September 15, 2021, available on *The Late Show with Stephen Colbert*, "Stephen Sondheim Is Still Writing New Works, As 'Company' Returns to Broadway," YouTube video, https://youtu.be/GKSYeMgamIA.

page 50: *"brain-surgery levels of precision"*: Guillermo del Toro (@RealGDT), "There are some of the dance number shots that are extremely (if not impossible) to decipher and almost all of them require brain-surgery levels of precision. I was elated from the purity of his audiovisual painting strokes." Twitter, February 26, 2022, 12:53 p.m., https://twitter.com/RealGDT/status/1497631034719887361.

page 51: *"What happened to that young woman . . . happened to her"*: Marc Hershberg, "'West Side Story' Sequel in the Works As Ethnic Groups Reclaim Their Stories," *Forbes*, December 19, 2021, https://www.forbes.com/sites/marchershberg/2021/12/19/west-side-story-sequel-in-the-works-as-ethnic-groups-reclaim-their-stories/.

page 51: *"What is . . . culturally appropriated"*: Hershberg, "'West Side Story' Sequel in the Works."

page 51: *he didn't even know any Puerto Ricans* or *poor people*: Zadan, *Sondheim & Co.*, p. 14.

page 51: *"The ethnic warfare . . . Hatfields and the McCoys"*: Daniel Pollack-Pelzner, "Why 'West Side Story' Abandoned Its Queer Narrative," *Atlantic*, March 1, 2020, https://www.theatlantic.com/culture/archive/2020/03/ivo-van-hoves-west-side-story-steeped-stereotypes/607210/.

page 51: *"It is an anti-racist, democratic musical"*: Abramovitch, "Tony Kushner on Tackling 'West Side Story.'"

GOT IT

page 52: *"He places value on . . . the notes"*: Theodore Taylor, *Jule: The Story of Composer Jule Styne* (New York: Random House, 1979), p. 202.

page 53: *"Home was a strange word . . . Or did it?"*: Gypsy Rose Lee, *Gypsy: A Memoir* (New York: Dell Publishing, 1959), p. 141.

page 53: *Gypsy's account of her own life . . . with humor added*: Carolyn Quinn, *Mama Rose's Turn: The True Story of America's Most Notorious Stage Mother* (Jackson, MS: University Press of Mississippi, 2013), p. xi.

page 53: *with the aim of having Jerome Robbins stage it*: Laurents, *Original Story*, p. 376.

page 54: *"I wasn't naked . . . blue spotlight"*: Carl Rollyson, "More Than a Girl with a Gimmick," *Wall Street Journal*, January 7, 2011, https://www.wsj.com/articles/SB10001424052748704034804576025691968347626.

page 54: *Grinding out her book . . . on a rented typewriter*: Keith Garebian, *The Making of "Gypsy"* (Toronto: ECW Press, 1994), p. 29.

page 56: *same killer instincts in Merrick*: Erik Lee Preminger, *Gypsy & Me: At Home and On the Road with Gypsy Rose Lee* (Boston: Little, Brown, 1984), p. 42.

page 56: *to enlist Betty Comden and Adolph Green*: Garebian, *Making of "Gypsy,"* p. 32.

page 56: *a guest who said she had been the lover of Gypsy Rose Lee's mother*: Laurents, *Original Story*, p. 376.

page 57: *"Maybe he would be a good idea for 'Gypsy.'"*: Amanda Vaill, ed., *Jerome Robbins, By Himself: Selections from His Letters, Journals, Drawings, Photographs, and an Unfinished Memoir* (New York: Alfred A. Knopf, 2019), p. 215.

page 57: *"He tries . . . these words as she can"*: Margaret Case Harriman, "Words and Music," *New Yorker*, November 15, 1940, https://www.newyorker.com/magazine/1940/11/23/words-and-music-3.

page 58: *"not bright"*: Laurents, *Original Story*, p. 378.

page 58: *she still would be ideal in a revival of* Gypsy: Silverman, *Public Spectacles*, p. 78.

page 59: *"I was in a room . . . that I've ever seen in my life"*: Rebecca Milzoff, "The Rehearsal Pianist," *New York*, November 30, 2013, https://nymag.com/news/frank-rich/composer-john-kander-2013-12/.

page 59: *initially foresaw as a Rose ballet*: Sondheim, *Finishing the Hat*, pp. 75–77.

page 59: *Jule Styne . . . played the piano, and Sondheim sang*: Taylor, *Jule*, p. 210.

page 59: *"When I wrote 'Small World' . . . '[Sinatra] needs a song'"*: "Maestro of Broadway."

page 59: *telling Loretta what she could go do with herself*: Lapine, in *Six by Sondheim*.

page 59: *she made up for in boldness, brassiness*: Ethel Merman, interview with author, June 1, 1978.

SOURCE NOTES

page 59: *"Gypsy . . . was a full-fledged play"*: Ethel Merman with George Eells, *Merman: An Autobiography* (New York: Simon & Schuster, 1978), p. 202.

page 59: *"You're dead wrong . . . It wouldn't work as a straight play"*: Taylor, *Jule*, p. 201.

page 60: *the two bickered over that distinction for the rest of their lives*: Vaill, *Robbins, By Himself*, p. 344.

page 60: *"Ethel . . . would be a winner"*: Laurents, *Mainly on Directing*, p. 22.

page 60: *"I'll do anything you want me to"*: Laurents, *Original Story*, p. 378.

page 60: *had to coax her into delivering a line*: Caryl Flinn, *Brass Diva: The Life and Legends of Ethel Merman* (Berkeley, CA: University of California Press, 2007), Kindle edition.

page 60: *"Ethel told me her public would be alienated . . . so the passage was cut"*: Stephen Citron, *Sondheim & Lloyd-Webber: The New Musical* (New York: Oxford University Press, 2001), p. 90.

page 60: *"I got sympathy . . . People cried"*: Merman, *Merman: An Autobiography*, p. 205.

page 60: *"It's supposed to . . . not a nice lady"*: Cramer, *American Musical Theatre*.

page 60: *Her faux interest . . . is all meant to trap him*: Michael Kantor (writer and director), Barbara Brilliant (executive producer), Sylvia Cahill and Jan Gura (coproducers), Joel Grey (narrator), *Broadway Musicals: A Jewish Legacy*, PBS, 2013, Ghostlight Films.

page 60: *"And . . . he's caught"*: Cramer, *American Musical Theatre*.

page 60: *"Rose would . . . blindside the audience"*: Sondheim, *Finishing the Hat*, p. 56.

page 60: *Merman's Gypsy contract . . . plus living expenses*: Merman, *Merman: An Autobiography*, p. 202.

page 61: *"'The night before . . . giving you birth'"*: Kakutani, "Sondheim's Passionate 'Passion.'"

page 61: *"She didn't want me on earth . . . I was an inconvenience"*: Sondheim, in *Six by Sondheim*.

page 61: *"because I've told so many people . . . that I laugh at them now"*: Max, "Stephen Sondheim's Lesson for Every Artist."

page 61: *he died in 1966*: "Herbert Sondheim, 71, Dead," *New York Times*, August 2, 1966, p. 28.

page 61: *"My stepmother and I forced him . . . he missed the worry"*: Henry, "Master of the Musical."

page 61: *"the last few years"*: Tim Teeman, "Up Close and Very Personal with the Real Stephen Sondheim," *Daily Beast*, November 27, 2021, https://www.thedailybeast.com/broadway-giant-stephen-sondheim-dead-at-91.

page 61: *"It never happened"*: Source, conversation with author, August 15, 2022.

page 62: *Merrick didn't bite*: Swayne, *How Sondheim Found His Sound*, p. 57.

page 62: *"First, it had been agreed . . . I thought"*: Taylor, *Jule*, p. 200.

page 62: *Merrick said to give him a week*: Taylor, *Jule*, p. 197.

page 62: *"with more guts than I thought possible"*: Taylor, *Jule*, p. 198.

page 62: *"I never had the good fortune . . . They were her life"*: Gypsy Rose Lee (host) and Ethel Merman (guest), *Gypsy Rose Lee and Her Friends*, 1967, available on Alan Eichler, "Ethel Merman, Gypsy Rose Lee Show, 1967 TV," YouTube, video, https://youtu.be/yqCgnX0s0M8.

page 63: *assuming that the listener already knew what he was talking about*: Jule Styne, interview with author, November 29, 1993.

page 63: *"verbal shorthand," or "Stynese"*: Eleanor Blau, "Jule Styne, Bountiful Creator of Song Favorites, Dies at 88," *New York Times*, September 21, 1994, section A, p.

page 63: *"The worst thing about . . . rehearsal"*: Brendan Gill (host), Stephen Sondheim and Harold S. Prince (guests), "The Creative Process" series. New York Public Library for the Performing Arts. Recorded June 2, 1975, streamed online March 21, 2022.

page 63: *"[and] you are . . . two terrible lines"*: Flinn, *Brass Diva*.

page 63: *"I find lyric writing . . . very fulfilling"*: Swayne, *How Sondheim Found His Sound*, p. 255.

page 64: *"That amounts to . . . four dollars and ninety cents"*: Flinn, *Brass Diva*.

page 64: *"Mother . . . smaller royalty checks"*: Preminger, *Gypsy & Me*, p. 187.

page 64: *next door to where Katharine Hepburn had been living*: Katharine Hepburn, interview with author, December 14, 1987.

page 64: *"My father co-signed the loan"*: Max, "Stephen Sondheim's Lesson for Every Artist."

page 64: *Hepburn, barefoot*: Gottfried, *Sondheim*, p. 86.

page 65: *"Jule's shows . . . rather than hit songs"*: Taylor, *Jule*, p. 201.

page 65: *"goes into rehearsal . . . out of your life"*: Fordin, *Getting to Know Him*, p. 330.

page 65-66: *"Gypsy was written . . . Vaudeville"*: Stephen Sondheim to Adam Gopnik, New Yorker Festival, October 10, 2014.

page 66: *"I thought . . . we got along fine"*: Taylor, *Jule*, p. 201.

page 66: *"the most flexible . . . rather than a composer"*: Janiga, "Side by Side with Sondheim."

page 66: *"If he had told me . . . was a bit disappointed"*: Taylor, *Jule*, p. 201.

page 65: *(Arthur Laurents . . . not to be true.)*: Laurents, *Original Story*, p. 389.

page 66: *"The effect . . . horror movie"*: Cramer, *American Musical Theatre*.

page 67: *"Playing poker . . . in my hotel room"*: Peter Filichia, "You Don't Know Jack!," TheaterMania, November 13, 2006, https://www.theatermania.com/new-york-city-theater/news/you-dont-know-jack_9439.html.

page 68: *"I felt she should have gotten the part . . . if they come up"*: Rosalind Russell and Chris Chase, *Life Is a Banquet* (New York: Random House, 1977), p. 202.

page 69: *"The movies destroyed . . . the stage"*: Blau, "Jule Styne."

page 69: *"fidelity to the play . . . the title character"*: Joe Baltake, "There's Nothing Wrong with '62 'Gypsy,'" *Los Angeles Times*, December 27, 1993, https://www.latimes.com/archives/la-xpm-1993-12-27-ca-5840-story.html.

page 70: *"She scared me"*: Styne, interview with author.

page 70: *starring Angela Lansbury*: Performance attended by author, June 21, 1973.

page 70: *"I would be very pleased . . . historical record"*: Patrick Healy, "Streisand in Talks to Play Mama Rose in Film Remake of 'Gypsy,'" *ArtsBeat* (blog), *New York Times*, January 5, 2011, https://artsbeat.blogs.nytimes.com/2011/01/05/streisand-in-talks-to-play-mama-rose-in-film-remake-of-gypsy/.

page 70: *"When I won . . . that was very touching"*: Eddie Shapiro, *Nothing Like a Dame: Conversations with the Great Women of Musical Theater* (New York: Oxford University Press, 2015), p. 85.

page 71: *"Oh, my God, I'm watching my mother"*: Shapiro, *Nothing Like a Dame*, p. 347.

page 71: *Patti LuPone (Rose)*: Patti LuPone with Digby Diehl, *Patti LuPone: A Memoir* (New York: Three Rivers Press, 2010), p. 288.

page 71: *"Gypsy says something . . . wasn't a smash hit"*: Zadan, *Sondheim & Co.*, p. 52.

page 71: *"He had a couple things . . . as a Grand Master of Musical Theater"*: Donald Rosenberg, "Sondheim Talks Hammerstein, Songwriting and 'Sondheim on Sondheim,' Coming to PlayhouseSquare," (Cleveland) *Plain Dealer*, May 13, 2012, https://www.cleveland.com/musicdance/2012/05/sondheim_story.html.

page 71: *"I don't really remember . . . he died before Forum"*: Swayne, *How Sondheim Found His Sound*, p. 127.

page 71: *"He saved my life . . . his presence"*: Fordin, *Getting to Know Him*, p. xiii.

TOGA PARTY

page 72: *"the plays . . . I was still laughing"*: Stephen Sondheim, "The Musical Theatre: A Talk by Stephen Sondheim," *Dramatists Guild Quarterly*, Autumn 1978.

page 73: *"The show's to star . . . a rather tired formula that"*: Cramer, *American Musical Theatre*.

page 74: *Merrick was now producing Forum*: Vaill, *Somewhere*, p. 334.

page 74: *"sent in the form . . . between the eyes"*: Larry Gelbart, *Laughing Matters: On Writing "M*A*S*H," "Tootsie," "Oh, God!," and a Few Other Funny Things* (New York: Random House, 1998), p. 210.

page 74: *"clarity of language . . . true of lyric writing"*: Stephen Sondheim, "Theatre Lyrics," in *Playwrights, Lyricists, Composers on Theater*, edited by Otis Guernsey (New York: Dodd, Mead, 1974), p. 87.

page 74: *time to collect themselves between jokes*: Zadan, *Sondheim & Co.*, p. 68.

page 75: *relentless barrage of gags*: Zadan, *Sondheim & Co.*, p. 68.

page 75: *Harry Gelbart, who was Larry's father*: Al Martinez, "Harry at Your Head," *Los Angeles Times*, May 21, 1994, https://www.latimes.com/archives/la-xpm-1994-05-21-me-60284-story.html.

page 75: *"You want . . . Call Jule Styne"*: Bandler, "What Collaboration Is All About," p. 26.

page 75: *"I suppose you could say it started with Forum"*: Bryer and Davison, *Art of the American Musical*, p. 195.

page 75: *"I recognized . . . Frank Loesser way"*: Sondheim and Guettel, in *The Art of Songwriting*.

page 75: *"more naked" . . . said Sondheim*: Secrest, *Sondheim: A Life*, p. 149.

page 76: *"completely humorless"*: Vaill, *Somewhere*, p. 342.

page 76: *The team had barely cracked Act II*: Harold Prince, *Sense of Occasion* (Milwaukee: Applause Theatre & Cinema Books, 2017), p. 91.

page 76: *"There's a point . . . of the game"*: Bandler, "What Collaboration Is All About."

page 76: *"My wife has been telling me that for years"*: Gilbert Millstein, "A Funny Man Happened," *New York Times*, June 3, 1962, p. 224.

page 77: *"More important . . . he was asserting . . . even theatre"*: Prince, *Sense of Occasion*, pp. 91–92.

page 77: *"The trouble with Zero . . . bon mot"*: Bandler, "What Collaboration Is All About," p. 26.

page 77: *writers' vote of no confidence*: Prince, *Sense of Occasion*, p. 92.

page 77: *"If you don't . . . in the balls"*: Zadan, *Sondheim & Co.*, p. 67.

page 77: *writers threatened to withdraw their play*: Prince, *Sense of Occasion*, p. 92.

page 77: *"I like to think there was no connection between events"*: Gelbart, *Laughing Matters*, p. 211.

page 77: *"The book has . . . the score and the book"*: Bryer and Davison, *Art of the American Musical*, p. 195.

page 77: *"The worst mistake . . . is writing different musicals"*: Max, "Sondheim's Lesson for Every Artist."

page 77: *"Some of the best jokes were cut . . . Stupid"*: Horowitz, *Sondheim on Music*, p. 187.

page 78: *"You can tell from silences . . . You gotta let it play"*: Brockes, "Big Beasts of Broadway."

page 78: *"We thought . . . You'd better call in Jerome Robbins"*: Lipton, "Stephen Sondheim, The Art of the Musical."

page 78: *leftist sympathies and sexual orientation*: Terry Teachout, "What Jerome Robbins Knew That Leonard Bernstein Didn't," *Commentary*, November 2019, https://www.commentary.org/articles/terry-teachout/what-jerome-robbins-knew-that-leonard-bernstein-didnt/.

page 78: *blacklist of . . . directors, and artists*: Deborah Jowitt, *Jerome Robbins: His Life, His Theater, His Dance* (New York: Simon & Schuster, 2004), p. 231.

page 78: *"His fans were so worshipful . . . He took advantage"*: Bandler, "What Collaboration Is All About," p. 26.

page 79: *"had written two opening numbers . . . that was the end of that"*: Max, "Sondheim's Lesson for Every Artist."

page 80: *"He said, 'It's the opening number . . . Let's not do the rest of the show'"*: Lipton, "Stephen Sondheim, The Art of the Musical."

page 80: *what it felt like to work with Robbins and Sondheim*: Debra Levine, email to author, May 11, 2022.

page 80: *"He didn't discuss . . . his work"*: Liza Gennaro (interviewer), George and Ethel Martin (guests), oral history sound recording, Goshen, NY, January 17 and February 25, 2003, New York Public Library for the Performing Arts.

page 80: *Abbott accepted Robbins's takeover*: Prince, *Sense of Occasion*, p. 94.

page 81: *ultimately succeeded in working together on* Fiddler on the Roof: Alisa Solomon, "On Jewishness, as the Fiddle Played," *New York Times*, October 20, 2013, section AR, p. 8.

page 81: *Robbins fed Sondheim . . . reprise for the finale*: Vaill, *Somewhere*, p. 343.

page 81: *"On the other hand . . . uphill fight all the way"*: Citron, *Sondheim & Lloyd-Webber*, p. 101.

page 81: *Clive Barnes's rave review*: Clive Barnes, "Stage: 'Funny Thing' Happens Again," *New York Times*, March 31, 1972, p. 13.

page 83: *"We tried . . . You're welcome"*: Nathan Lane, Marianne Elliott, and Beanie Feldstein, "Nathan Lane, Marianne Elliott and Beanie Feldstein Remember Stephen Sondheim," *Variety*, December 2, 2021, https://variety.com/2021/theater/people-news/nathan-lane-beanie-feldstein-stephen-sondheim-1235123585/.

page 83: *to help Athens out of her woes*: Alice K. Turner, *The History of Hell* (New York: Harcourt Brace, 1993), pp. 26–27.

page 83: *"If you're writing . . . harmonies"*: Horowitz, *Sondheim on Music*, p. 109.

page 83: *"it was like putting on a show in a men's urinal"*: Jesse Green, "THEATRE: A Funny Thing Happened on the Way to the Punch Line," *New York Times*, June 27, 2004, section 2, p. 1.

page 83: *while generally applauding "the theatrical event"*: Mel Gussow, "Stage: 'Frogs' in a Pool," *New York Times*, May 23, 1974, https://archive.nytimes.com/www.nytimes.com/books/98/07/19/specials/sondheim-pool.html.

page 84: *1996 revival*: Performance attended by author, April 18, 1996.

page 84: *"His material . . . was just so brilliantly written"*: Lane et al., "Nathan Lane, Marianne Elliott and Beanie Feldstein Remember Stephen Sondheim."

page 84: *Whoopi Goldberg stepped in*: Performance attended by author, March 6, 1998.

page 84: *"That damn toga . . . You can't look cute in a toga"*: Ryan McPhee, "The Daily Distraction: A Funny Thing Happened to Whoopi Goldberg on the Way to Broadway," *Playbill*, May 8, 2020, https://playbill.com/article/the-daily-distraction-a-funny-thing-happened-to-whoopi-goldberg-on-the-way-to-broadway.

page 84: *"We had somehow managed . . . writing it"*: Bandler, "What Collaboration Is All About," p. 49.

page 85: *"who's very popular . . . as Sondheim"*: Tyler Armstrong. interview with author, April 1, 2022.

NEVER DO ANYTHING TWICE

I.

page 86: *"It was way ahead . . . experimental"*: Zadan, *Sondheim & Co.*, p. 82.

page 86: *"Essentially . . . not particularly interesting"*: Zadan, *Sondheim & Co.*, pp. 86–87.

page 87: *"then you're going to write the same thing you wrote before"*: *New York Times*, "Remembering Stephen Sondheim—NYT News," YouTube, November 29, 2021, video, https://www.youtube.com/watch?v=S-T4-g_x4NA&t=491s.

page 87: *"I just remember thinking . . . really weird"*: Mark Eden Horowitz, "'Really Weird': The Story of 'Anyone Can Whistle' with Lots of Details," *Sondheim Review*, Winter 2010, p. 7.

page 87-88: *"was about so many things . . . what it* was *about"*: Citron, *Sondheim & Lloyd-Webber*, p. 133.

page 88: *treated the audience with condescension bordering on contempt*: Sondheim, *Finishing the Hat*, p. 111.

page 88: *Originally, Laurents conceived of* Anyone Can Whistle *as two different plays*: James O'Leary, "Breakout from the Asylum of Conformity: Sondheim, Laurents, and the Dramaturgy of *Anyone Can Whistle*," in *Sondheim in Our Time and His*, edited by W. Anthony Sheppard (New York: Oxford University Press, 2022), p. 95.

page 88: *"'Well, are we going to' . . . get back in the mood"*: Sondheim, "The Musical Theatre."

page 88: *other money people chimed in with similar sentiments*: Horowitz, "'Really Weird.'"

page 88: *"not a coherent success"*: Bryer and Davison, *Art of the American Musical*, p. 195.

page 89: *deconstructed* West Side Story *for Broadway*: Performance attended by author, February 22, 2022.

page 89: *"Each generation . . . looking at a play"*: Zubrow, "'West Side Story' Lyrics."

page 89: *"I don't really see . . . a conceived score"*: Horowitz, *Sondheim on Music*, pp. 188–189.

page 89: *vocal coach Kay Thompson*: Silverman, *Dancing on the Ceiling*, p. 77.

page 89: *"If you listen . . . at the time"*: Bryer and Davison, *Art of the American Musical*, p. 195.

page 89: *the show's investing angels . . . $16,000 today*: Lara E. Housez, *Becoming Stephen Sondheim: 'Anyone Can Whistle,' 'A Pray by Blecht,' 'Company' and 'Sunday in the Park with George,'* PhD diss. (Rochester, NY: University of Rochester, 2013), p. 35.

page 89: *"It must be good because these guys wrote it"*: Martin Gottfried, *Balancing Act: The Authorized Biography of Angela Lansbury* (Boston: Little, Brown, 1999), pp. 136–137.

page 89: *"It wasn't my style . . . rather quiet person"*: masterworksbwayVEVO, "Angela Lansbury—on *Anyone Can Whistle*," YouTube, August 20, 2012, video, https://www.youtube.com/watch?v=YtBwhsHCu_s&t=6s.

page 89: *"nearly ruined my voice"*: Gottfried, *Balancing Act*, p. 138.

page 89: *Lansbury heard rumblings that she was to be replaced*: Zadan, *Sondheim & Co.*, p. 89.

page 89: *"this wonderful ballet sequence"*: "Angela Lansbury—on *Anyone Can Whistle*."

page 90: *"I remember screaming . . . He was a fence-sitter"*: Zadan, *Sondheim & Co.*, p. 90.

page 90: *"That's tough to swallow for the author"*: Shapiro, *Nothing Like a Dame*, p. 77.

page 91: *"Most extraordinary"*: "Angela Lansbury—on *Anyone Can Whistle*."

page 91: *"Was going out with . . . taken with her"*: Norman Lebrecht, "The Unsung Sondheim," *Evening Standard* (London), April 10, 2012, https://www.standard.co.uk/culture/theatre/the-unsung-sondheim-7428423.html.

page 91: *"Arthur said the song . . . touch with feelings"*: Lebrecht, "The Unsung Sondheim."

page 91: *"She made the right choice"*: Stephen Sondheim at New York City Center, April 10, 2010.

page 91: *"less way out than way off"*: Citron, *Sondheim & Lloyd-Webber*, p. 133.

page 91: *dedicated the score to the record producer*: Robert L. McLaughlin, *Stephen Sondheim and the Reinvention of the American Musical* (Jackson, MS: University Press of Mississippi, 2016), p. 53.

page 91: *"Why did it crash? . . . blind if you do both"*: Lebrecht, "The Unsung Sondheim."

page 91: *"I don't mind . . . been tried before"*: Zadan, *Sondheim & Co.*, p. 95.

page 92: *"They were coming from . . . love story at the center"*: Erik Piepenburg, "Five Questions for Donna Murphy," *ArtsBeat* (blog), *New York Times*, April 7, 2010, https://artsbeat.blogs.nytimes.com/2010/04/07/five-questions-for-donna-murphy/.

page 92: *faithful version to New York's City Center*: Performance attended by author, April 10, 2010.

page 92: *in 2022 at London's Southwark Playhouse*: Performance attended by author, April 21, 2022.

page 92: *"feel quite current . . . to express now"*: "*Anyone Can Whistle* 2022 Revival—In Rehearsals," WhatsOnStage, YouTube, March 25, 2022, video, https://www.youtube.com/watch?v=hp4iosX646k.

page 92: *"Sondheim flop gets a blazing revival"*: Mark Lawson, "'Anyone Can Whistle' Review—Sondheim Flop Gets a Blazing Revival," *Guardian*, April 6, 2022, https://www.theguardian.com/stage/2022/apr/06/anyone-can-whistle-review-southwark-playhouse-london-sondheim.

II.

page 93: *"You can put songs . . . not very good"*: "Remembering Stephen Sondheim."

page 93: *"a sort of forty-year-old secretary . . . totally impractical"*: Stephen M. Silverman, *David Lean* (New York: Harry N. Abrams, 1989), p. 101.

page 93: *soon after the Booth and Hepburn versions*: Sondheim and Guettel, in *The Art of Songwriting*.

page 93: *Rodgers thought the plot was too thin*: Meryle Secrest, *Somewhere for Me: A Biography of Richard Rodgers* (New York: Alfred A. Knopf, 2002), pp. 369–370.

page 94: *Other possibilities . . . Streisand*: Ken Mandelbaum, *Not Since "Carrie": Forty Years of Musical Flops* (New York: St. Martin's Press, 1991), p. 255.

page 95: *"I regret spending a year of my life on Do I Hear a Waltz"*: Horowitz, *Sondheim on Music*, p. 244.

page 95: *referred to the show as a "Why?" musical*: Michael Portantiere, "Old Friends: Mary Rodgers Shared Thoughts About 70 Years of Knowing Sondheim," *Sondheim Review*, Fall 2014, Talkin' Broadway, https://www.talkinbroadway.com/page/rialto/past/2014/072214.html.

page 95: *"It was a terrible, terrible experience"*: Bryer and Davison, *Art of the American Musical*, p. 194.

page 95: *Lerner's lackadaisical work ethic*: Rodgers, *Musical Stages*, p. 317.

page 95: *"You've got to do it . . . in terms of songs"*: Secrest, *Somewhere for Me*, p. 371.

page 95: *"My father . . . should be constructed"*: Myrna Katz Frommer and Harvey Frommer, *It Happened on Broadway: An Oral History of the Great White Way* (Madison, WI: University of Wisconsin Press, 2004), p. 97.

page 95: *"conflicted feelings about his collaborator"*: Fordin, *Getting to Know Him*, p. xii.

page 96: *Rodgers . . . was serving as the show's producer*: Bryer and Davison, *Art of the American Musical*, p. 143.

page 96: *"He felt . . . to rewrite"*: Sondheim and Guettel, in *The Art of Songwriting*.

page 96: *Rodgers . . . fell asleep at a meeting with Franco Zeffirelli*: Laurents, *Original Story*, p. 213.

page 96: *"I watched him grow . . . to a monster"*: Louis Calta, "Rodgers and Sondheim Preparing a Musical," *New York Times*, December 6, 1964, p. 29.

page 96: *wrote of having had an unrequited crush on Sondheim*: Mary Rodgers and Jesse Green, *Shy: The Alarmingly Outspoken Memoirs of Mary Rodgers* (New York: Farrar, Straus and Giroux, 2022), pp. 6–7.

page 96: *because he was both "brilliant" and Oscar's protégé*: Rodgers and Green, *Shy*, p. 122.

page 96: *her love for him did not*: Rodgers and Green, *Shy*, pp. 259–262.

page 96: *"a plane that doesn't take off"*: Sondheim and Guettel, in *The Art of Songwriting*.

page 96: *replying that the words meant all the more*: Letter displayed at Stephen Sondheim exhibit, Lincoln Center Library for the Performing Arts, Winter 2022.

page 96: *a man of infinite talent but limited soul*: Mel Gussow, "Books of the Times: Peeks at the Complexities of a Very Private Genius," *New York Times*, July 21, 1998, section E, p. 7.

page 97: *"I must've . . . five thousand times"*: Sondheim and Guettel, in *The Art of Songwriting*.

page 97: *"In that case, it's the worst thing I've ever read"*: Jimmy So, "Sondheim on Sondheim: American Musical Theatre in Six Songs," *Daily Beast*, July 11, 2017, https://www.thedailybeast.com/sondheim-on-sondheim-american-musical-theater-in-six-songs.

page 97: *"I had every bit . . . and appreciate him for"*: Adam Guettel, conversation with author, May 18, 2022.

page 98: *"Withering . . . next time, fine"*: Guettel, conversation with author.

III.

page 99: *"an old friend of the family . . . 'an hour-long musical'"*: Citron, *Sondheim & Lloyd-Webber*, p. 139.

page 99: *Robinson had dated Foxy Sondheim*: Anthony Perkins, comments at Paley Center for Media, Los Angeles, CA, March 2, 1989.

page 100: *"Everything . . . price tag on it"*: Charles Winecoff, *Anthony Perkins: Split Image* (New York: Advocate Books, 2006), p. 239.

page 102: *"Jim started out . . . I was able to go ahead with it"*: Paul Salsini, "Among the Night People," *Sondheim Review*, Summer 1994, p. 21.

page 102: *"I find it useful . . . also fun"*: Stephen Sondheim, "Stephen Sondheim in a Q&A Session: Part I," *Dramatists Guild Quarterly*, no. 1, 1991.

page 102: *"It has a vaguely amateur . . . I like"*: Erik Piepenburg, "'60s Sondheim TV Show Is Now on (Legal) DVD," *New York Times*, October 25, 2010, section C, p. 2.

page 103: *"Most of the bootleg . . . lent it to people"*: Piepenburg, "'60s Sondheim TV Show."

PRINCELY ACTS

I.

page 104: *"in that stream . . . to what Hammerstein did"*: Bernard Levin (host) and Stephen Sondheim (guest), *The Levin Interviews*, BBC, May 24, 1980, retrieved from *Stephen Sondheim in His Own Words* (BBC Audio, 2021). ·

page 105: *"He said . . . 'musicals is over'"*: Karen Lerner, conversation with author, circa 2003.

page 105: *"sharp . . . fisheye look"*: Sylvia Fine (writer and host), Stan Harris (director), Eric Lieber (producer), Carol Burnett, Richard Chamberlain, John Davidson, Agnes de Mille, Sandy Duncan, Rock Hudson, Ethel Merman, Bernadette Peters, and Bobby Van (stars), *Musical Comedy Tonight*, PBS, October 1, 1979, available on swan555, "*Musical Comedy Tonight*—1979," YouTube, July 29, 2020, video, https://www.youtube.com/watch?v=_7Z30RWK5l4.

page 105: *"But we all know . . . making relationships"*: Sondheim, "The Musical Theatre."

page 105: *"I had thought . . . new Broadway show"*: George Furth, quoted in *Company: Original Cast in Concert* program (New York: Bradford Graphics, April 11 and 12, 1993), p. 3.

page 106: *"We wanted a show . . . not be able to sleep"*: Tom Vallance, "George Furth: Actor and Playwright Who Collaborated with Stephen Sondheim on the Musical 'Company,'" *Independent*, August 27, 2008, https://www.independent.co.uk/news/obituaries/george-furth-actor-and-playwright-who-collaborated-with-stephen-sondheim-on-the-musical-company-909609.html.

page 106: *"We wanted to take . . . wanted to go"*: masterworksbwayVEVO, "Harold Prince on Stephen Sondheim," channel, YouTube, February 2, 2016, video, https://www.youtube.com/watch?v=ZaO8Rjc9WSU.

page 106: *blundering Peace Corps volunteer*: John Keating, "New Musical 'Hot Spot' on the Spot," *New York Times*, April 14, 1963, pp. 97, 99.

page 106: *called in Sondheim to work on two numbers*: Vallance, "George Furth."

page 106: *One of the women . . . extended flirtation*: Alexandra Jacobs, *Still Here: The Madcap, Nervy, Singular Life of Elaine Stritch* (New York Farrar, Straus and Giroux, 2019), p. 90.

page 107: *Furth . . . seek advice from Sondheim*: Sam Zolotow, "Perkins to Star in Stage Musical," *New York Times*, March 14, 1969, p. 48.

page 107: *"had all the chops . . . all I could see"*: Suzanne Bixby, "Sixty Years of Sparks: Hal Prince Says He and Sondheim Energize Each Other," *Sondheim Review*, Spring 2010, p. 21.

page 107: *"Why don't we make . . . what an odd idea"*: Tom Burke, "Steve Has Stopped Collaborating," *New York Times*, May 10, 1970, p. 89.

page 107: *replaced Furth with Larry Blyden*: Furth, quoted in *Company: Original Cast in Concert* program.

page 107: *title* Company *was changed to* Threes: Lewis Funke, "The Year of the Adamses," *New York Times*, April 20, 1969, section D, p. 1.

page 107: *"talked for weeks . . . put them in focus"*: Burke, "Steve Has Stopped Collaborating."

page 107: *"so he could . . . each of his friends"*: Prince, *Sense of Occasion*, p. 145.

page 107: *"George started rewriting . . . I started the songs"*: Burke, "Steve Has Stopped Collaborating."

page 107: Company *was ready for rehearsals by February 1970*: Prince, *Sense of Occasion*, p. 147.

page 107: *"I knew from the beginning . . . fresh with it"*: Burke, "Steve Has Stopped Collaborating."

page 107: *lengthy conversations in his townhouse*: Rodgers and Green, *Shy*, p. 355.

page 107: *gotten him involved in* Do I Hear a Waltz?: Sondheim, *Finishing the Hat*, p. 167.

page 107: *"Well, it's all . . . than the lyrics can"*: Portantiere, "Old Friends."

page 108: *"In* Company . . . *we were . . . island of Manhattan"*: Sondheim, "The Musical Theatre."

page 108: *"Robert bears . . . to live in New York"*: Hal Prince, "In the Words of Hal Prince," *Cue*, April 10, 1971, p. 12.

page 108: *Francis Bacon's experiments*: Mark Stevens and Annalyn Swan, *Francis Bacon: Revelations* (New York: Alfred A. Knopf, 2021), p. 285.

page 108: *"Married life in New York City . . . transparent cages"*: Frank Rich with Lisa Aronson, *The Theatre Art of Boris Aronson* (New York: Alfred A. Knopf, 1987), p. 220.

page 108: *"They only saw a show . . . not to their liking"*: Bob Avian with Tom Santopietro, *Dancing Man: A Broadway Choreographer's Journey* (Jackson, MS: University Press of Mississippi, 2020), p. 59.

page 109: *"These are universal points of view"*: Guettel, conversation with author.

page 109: *"The first choral . . . 'works very well'"*: Horowitz, *Sondheim on Music*, pp. 108–109.

page 109: *"The function of the songs . . . middle of a scene"*: Kevin Kelly, "Sondheim Struggles to Write Words AND Music," *Boston Globe*, March 8, 1970, section A, p. 103.

page 109: *"the only song . . . relationships"*: Sondheim, "The Musical Theatre."

page 109: *It stopped the show*: Stephen Sondheim, quoted in *Company: Original Cast in Concert* program, p. 2.

page 110: *"As a teenager . . . sharing your life"*: Tiffany Babb, phone conversation with author, February 15, 2022.

page 110: *"Tony thought . . . has all the colors"*: Winecoff, *Anthony Perkins*, p. 262.

page 111: *"that I didn't realize . . . to see the show"*: Don Shirley, "Revisiting 'Company' of Days Past: Original Cast, Creators of 1970 Musical Gather for Reunion Benefit," *Los Angeles Times*, January 25, 1993, https://www.latimes.com/archives/la-xpm-1993-01-25-ca-1587-story.html.

page 111: *Jones had contracted hepatitis, which was not true*: Shirley, "Revisiting 'Company.'"

page 112: *"I came offstage . . . 'in two days'"*: Dean Jones, comments at Paley Center for Media in Los Angeles, May 24, 2000.

page 112: *"Dean was . . . sweating the notes out"*: Frank Rich, "A Return to 'Company,'" *Vulture*, August 16, 2021, https://www.vulture.com/2021/08/company-cast-album-stephen-sondheim-jonathan-tunick.html.

page 113: *"I'm a lot like Robert . . . to another human being"*: Patricia Bosworth, "From the Archives: Elaine Stritch, Barbara Barrie, Larry Kert, and the Cast of 'Company' on Modern Marriage," *Playbill*, September 16, 2018, https://www.playbill.com/article/from-the-archives-elaine-stritch-barbara-barrie-larry-kert-and-the-cast-of-company-on-modern-marriage.

page 113: *develop the right finish the number*: Secrest, *Sondheim: A Life*, p. 195.

page 113: *that she not be given the same steps and gestures*: Avian, *Dancing Man*, pp. 54–55.

page 113: *being done in a roadside lap-dance bar*: Avian, *Dancing Man*, pp. 59–60.

page 114: *as famous for the roles she didn't land as the ones she did*: Stephen M. Silverman, "Elaine Stritch, Broadway Legend and TV Star, Dies," *People*, July 17, 2014, https://people.com/celebrity/elaine-stritch-dies/.

page 114: *"The problem is . . . ain't room for both of us"*: Jacobs, *Still Here*, pp. 61–62.

page 114: *likened to Godzilla in a stalled elevator*: Silverman, "Elaine Stritch."

page 114: *from* The Graduate: Jacobs, *Still Here*, p.172.

page 116: *"I told my friend . . . new language on Broadway"*: Steve Ross, conversation with author, May 7, 2022.

page 116: *"Mr. Sondheim's lyrics . . . worthless, and horrid"*: Clive Barnes, "Theater: 'Company' Offers a Guide to New York's Marital Jungle," *New York Times*, April 27, 1970, https://archive.nytimes.com/www.nytimes.com/books/98/07/19/specials/sondheim-company.html.

page 117: *"an original . . . seemed restless"*: Mel Gussow, "Theater: 'Company' Anew," *New York Times*, July 29, 1970, p. 31.

page 117: *"I do* not *understand . . . listening very carefully"*: Burke, "Steve Has Stopped Collaborating."

page 117: *"I never thought . . . It's even nicer to win two"*: Hildy Parks (writer), Clark Jones (director), Alexander H. Cohen (producer), Lauren Bacall, Angela Lansbury, Anthony Quayle, and Anthony Quinn (hosts), *The 1971 Tony Awards*, CBS, March 28, 1971, available on MissPoochSmooch, YouTube, August 9, 2013, video, https://www.youtube.com/watch?v=nCB_r7iSoEY.

page 117: *"West Side Story . . . ranks of the classics"*: Prince, "In the Words of."

page 117: *"Company never played . . . showed a profit"*: Prince, *Sense of Occasion*, p. 156.

page 117: *"My only expectation . . . he would die"*: Henry, "Master of the Musical."

page 118: *"Seeing his works . . . unlucky collaborators"*: John Simon, "Side by Side," *New York*, July 22, 2002, p. 43.

page 118: *"I've only been . . . feeling of it"*: Barbara Isenberg, "Sondheim, Songless: The Master Minus the Music? Well, He's Been Playing with Puzzlers for Years and Now Takes a Turn at Mystery Playwriting with 'The Doctor Is Out,'" *Los Angeles Times*, September 10, 1995, https://www.latimes.com/archives/la-xpm-1995-09-10-ca-44084-story.html.

page 118: *"I think he's in everything . . . quite phenomenal"*: Andrew Douglas (director), David Sabel (producer), Bill O'Donnell (series producer), David Horn (executive producer), Stephen Sondheim, Marianne Elliott, Katrina Lenk, Patti LuPone, Adrian Lester, Raúl Esparza, and other members of the 1970, 1995, 2006, 2018, and 2021 casts (stars), *Great Performances: Keeping Company with Stephen Sondheim*, PBS, May 27, 2022, https://www.pbs.org/wnet/gperf/keeping-company-with-sondheim-about/13669/.

page 118: *first Black actor . . . to take on the role*: *Variety* Staff, "Color-Blind 'Company,'" *Variety*, December 10, 1995, https://variety.com/1995/legit/news/color-blind-company-99130362/.

page 118: *"It's very tricky . . . bring it out"*: Mark Dundas Wood, "Anyone Can Whistle—Or Can They?," *Backstage*, May 14, 2002.

page 118: *transferred . . . to Broadway's Ethel Barrymore Theatre*: Performance attended by author, November 28, 2006.

page 119: *"It just felt forced"*: Max, "Stephen Sondheim's Lesson."

page 119: *"It feels so relevant . . . in 1969"*: Kyle Turner, "Love Is 'Company': Director Marianne Elliott on Her Revival of Sondheim's Classic Musical," *Interview*, April 27, 2020, https://www.interviewmagazine.com/art/company-marianne-elliott-broadway.

page 120: *A national tour was planned afterward*: Michael Paulson, "Tony-Winning 'Company' Revival Will End Broadway Run July 31," *New York Times*, June 21, 2022, https://www.nytimes.com/2022/06/21/theater/company-broadway-closing.html.

page 120: *how open he was to new opinions*: Greg Evans, "'You'll Need to Be Sitting Down for This One': Emails Between Stephen Sondheim and Marianne Elliott Chronicle the Birth of a 21st Century 'Company,'" *Deadline*, June 8, 2022, https://deadline.com/2022/06/stephen-sondheim-marianne-elliott-new-emails-company-evolution-1235037493/.

page 121: *"This is not . . . I love the idea"*: Turner, "Love Is 'Company.'"

page 121: *Bobby became . . . Katrina Lenk in New York*: Performance attended by author, December 15, 2021.

page 121: *"Boys don't . . . beautiful women"*: Maureen Dowd, "Bravado Softened by Vulnerability," *New York Times*, December 12, 2021, section ST, p. 1.

II.

page 122: *the costliest adaptation of all time*: Anne Thompson, "'Beauty and the Beast': How Bill Condon Built Hollywood's Most Expensive Musical," *IndieWire*, March 14, 2017, https://www.indiewire.com/2017/03/420-disney-beauty-and-the-beast-bill-condon-emma-watson-musical-1201791591/.

page 122: *"Follies was a huge . . . wouldn't want my name on"*: "Master Showman," Academy of Achievement, June 22, 2007, https://achievement.org/achiever/harold-prince/#interview.

page 122: *"I was much influenced . . . to do with time"*: Lipton, "Stephen Sondheim, The Art of the Musical."

page 123: *"they each had . . . to kill whom?"*: McLaughlin, *Sondheim and the Reinvention of the American Musical*, p. 80.

page 123: *"It was extremely well-written . . . and I didn't like it"*: Mel Gussow, "Prince Recalls the Evolution of 'Follies,'" *New York Times*, April 9, 1971, p. 20.

page 123: *He let his option . . . lapse*: Gussow, "Prince Recalls."

page 123: *"I wasn't remotely interested . . . these middle-aged couples"*: Hirsch, *Harold Prince*, p. 93.

page 124: *"a gauzy feeling"*: Gussow, "Prince Recalls."

page 124: *to bring out Mayor Jimmy Walker*: Ben M. Hall, *The Best Remaining Seats: The Story of the Golden Age of the Movie Palace* (New York: Bramhall House, 1961), p.259.

page 124: *the French word for madness (*folie*)*: Prince, *Sense of Occasion*, pp. 159–160.

page 124: *"James and I had limited . . . stage simultaneously"*: "Maestro of Broadway."

page 125: *"In the thirty years . . . the country has"*: Mandelbaum, *"A Chorus Line" and the Musicals of Michael Bennett*, p. 67.

page 125: *"Hal wanted the challenge" of making everything work onstage*: Sondheim, "The Musical Theatre."

page 125: *"with affection . . . What they are is innocent"*: Gussow, "Prince Recalls."

page 125: *"a scrapbook or revue"*: Horowitz, *Sondheim on Music*, p. 206.

page 126: *has been attributed . . . to George Gershwin's "The Man I Love"*: Rick Pender, *The Stephen Sondheim Encyclopedia* (Lanham, MD: Rowman & Littlefield, 2021), p. 299.

page 126: *"referred to it as the character's Helen Morgan song"*: Prince, *Sense of Occasion*, p. 162.

page 126: *"finally woke up . . . at a party"*: McLaughlin, *Sondheim and the Reinvention of the American Musical*, p. 80.

page 127: *lyrics tweaked by Sondheim himself*: David J. Fox, "Rewrite by Sondheim," *Los Angeles Times*, September 9, 1990, https://www.latimes.com/archives/la-xpm-1990-09-09-ca-389-story.html.

page 128: *at Avery Fisher Hall . . . September 6 and 7, 1985*: Performance attended by author, September 6, 1985.

page 128: *"We all know . . . as much as they do"*: Peter Marks, "For Carol Burnett, the Sondheim Award Is Personal," *Washington Post*, May 19, 2022, https://www.washingtonpost.com/theater-dance/2022/05/19/carol-burnett-sondheim/.

page 129: *"Michael Bennett suggested . . . old figures in it"*: "Maestro of Broadway."

page 129: *adding a line here and there*: Ted Chapin, *Everything Was Possible: The Birth of the Musical* Follies (New York: Alfred A. Knopf, 2003), p. 108.

page 129: *ended up looking like a mistake*: Avian, *Dancing Man*, p. 65.

page 129: *"in mirror-laden costumes . . . number's climax"*: Mandelbaum, *"A Chorus Line" and the Musicals of Michael Bennett*, p. 69.

page 130: *"The mirror . . . in my life"*: Mandelbaum, *"A Chorus Line" and the Musicals of Michael Bennett*, p. 69.

page 130: *"Rarely have such . . . expertise"*: Ted E. Kalem, "Seascape with Frieze of Girls," *Time*, April 12, 1971, p. 78.

page 131: *"That could have been written for me"*: John Springer, "'Follies'; A Movie That Wasn't," *New York Times*, April 8, 2001, section 2, p. 4.

page 131: *for a series of tributes*: John Springer, conversation with author, circa 1993.

page 131: *"I would say that's apocryphal"*: Matt Weinstock, "Loveland," *Paris Review*, November 29, 2013, https://www.theparisreview.org/blog/2013/11/29/loveland/.

page 131: *"Let him play it"*: Springer, "'Follies'; A Movie That Wasn't."

page 131: *to find a role for Shelley Winters*: Springer, conversation with author.

page 131: *"I won't work with the bitch again"*: Springer, "'Follies'; A Movie That Wasn't."

page 131: *studio head Daniel Melnick*: Springer, "'Follies'; A Movie That Wasn't."

page 131: *"We had that . . . money to charity"*: Bryer and Davison, *Art of the American Musical*, p. 171.

page 131: *MGM to compile old musical clips . . . instead of* Follies: Chapin, *Everything Was Possible*, p. 310.

page 132: *"The world of the dead . . . turned out not to be"*: Chapin, *Everything Was Possible*, p. 194.

page 132: *"Eighty percent . . . show ever"*: Avian, *Dancing Man*, p. 71.

page 132: *"one of . . . ever written"*: Richard Christiansen, "Flaws and All, 'Follies' Still Vintage Sondheim," *Chicago Tribune*, February 7, 1999, https://www.chicagotribune.com/news/ct-xpm-1999-02-07-9902060057-story.html.

page 133: *"That's four performers . . . deserved reputation"*: Katy Homan (director and producer), Alan Yentob (presenter), Cameron Mackintosh (star), and Stephen Sondheim (guest), *Cameron Mackintosh: The Musical Man*, BBC, September 11, 2017, available on Ian Schelfaut, "Imagine—*Cameron Mackintosh: the Musical Man*," YouTube, September 14, 2018, video, https://youtu.be/a6WIWKjilU4.

page 134: *the exulted Roxy*: Production attended by author, August 8, 1987.

page 134: *"All of us . . . I didn't like it anymore"*: Barbara Rosen, "The Mackintosh 'Follies,'" *Washington Post*, July 8, 1987, https://www.washingtonpost.com/archive/lifestyle/1987/07/08/the-mackintosh-follies/b9c37c98-1637-49e0-8649-6e75929e90c3/.

page 135: *"James Goldman's skillful . . . into a movie"*: Vlessing, "Dominic Cooke Sets Movie Adaptation of Stephen Sondheim's 'Follies.'"

III.

page 136: *"I have a voice . . . keep on note"*: Glynis Johns, comments at the Paley Center for Media in Los Angeles, May 24, 2000.

page 136: *"There was a spot . . . probably unlikely"*: You'reGonnaLoveTomorrow, "Stephen Sondheim Interview—1987," YouTube, January 22, 2020, video, https://youtu.be/M3NuW6rPBAA.

page 136: *"When I'm writing . . . he has some place to go"*: Craig Carnelia, "In Conversation with Stephen Sondheim," *Sondheim Review*, Fall 2008, p. 16.

page 137: *"She had . . . silvery voice"*: "Maestro of Broadway."

page 137: *"That's really . . . musically and lyrically"*: Horowitz, *Sondheim on Music*, p. 48.

page 137: *"That's par for . . . the show"*: Stephen Grover, "Bringing a New Show to the Broadway Stage Is High Drama in Itself," *Wall Street Journal*, February 27, 1973, p. 1.

page 137: *"The very first song . . . occurred to me"*: Mel Gussow, "Prince Revels in 'A Little Night Music,'" *New York Times*, March 27, 1973, p. 54.

page 138: *"Then Hal said . . . 'ad-lib it'"*: Terri Roberts, "Glynis Johns: Still Tearful in 'Clowns,'" *Sondheim Review*, Summer 1998, p. 16.

page 138: *"Hal was . . . writing this song"*: Johns, at Paley Center.

page 138: *"It was never to be . . . So she gives up"*: Stephen Sondheim, comments during intermission of 1990 PBS telecast *Live from Lincoln Center: A Little Night Music*, available on clementj1, "*A Little Night Music* 1990 Restored," YouTube, July 18, 2019, video, https://youtu.be/8nfd98fE9T8.

page 138: *"essentially overnight . . . come to me"*: Sondheim and Guettel, in *The Art of Songwriting*.

page 138: *"I felt . . . seventy-four"*: Grover, "Bringing a New Show to the Broadway Stage."

page 139: *"It read . . . Anouilh play"*: "From Oedipus to 'Me as King Lear,'" *Sondheim Review*, Summer 1998, p. 18.

page 139: *He sat down and played the number*: Roberts, "Glynis Johns."

page 139: *"Well, sing it . . . crying"*: Johns, at Paley Center.

page 140: *"Something that deals . . . with age"*: Grover, "Bringing a New Show to the Broadway Stage."

page 140: *"was about having a hit"*: Gottfried, *Sondheim*, p. 102.

page 140: *paid its investors back 352 percent*: Alisa Solomon, "Six Things You May Not Have Known About 'Fiddler on the Roof,'" *Smithsonian Magazine*, September 19, 2014, https://www.smithsonianmag.com/arts-culture/six-things-you-may-not-have-known-about-fiddler-roof-180952771/.

page 140: *"There are scores . . . going on someplace"*: Mark Stryker, "'I'm Not an Opera Fan': A 2009 *Free Press* Interview with Theater Composer Stephen Sondheim," *Detroit Free Press*, November 26, 2021, https://www.freep.com/story/entertainment/music/2021/11/26/stephen-sondheim-pondered-opera-musicals-2009-free-press-interview/8770543002/.

page 141: *"I still believe . . . be stimulated"*: Anonymous, "Master Showman," Academy of Achievement, YouTube, https://www.youtube.com/watch?v=UJXOWoB3ljo.

SOURCE NOTES

page 141: *"But, like most . . . and watch"*: Stephen Sondheim, TV interview, in You'reGonnaLoveTomorrow, *"A Little Night Music*—1995," YouTube, March 13, 2021, video, https://youtu.be/_dEOH1Tnn44.

page 141: *"and we went to work"*: Prince, *Sense of Occasion*, pp. 171–172.

page 142: *signed to A Little Night Music in early 1972*: Grover, "Bringing a New Show to the Broadway Stage."

page 142: *"The songs that . . . 'knives underneath'"*: Sondheim, in *"A Little Night Music*—1995."

page 142: *based on memories . . .* Blank Signature: Rich with Aronson, *The Theatre Art of Boris Aronson*, pp. 250–252.

page 142: *"I remember standing . . . for a cigarette"*: Stryker, "'I'm Not an Opera Fan.'"

page 143: *standing actors into their chairs*: Grover, "Bringing a New Show to the Broadway Stage."

page 143: *"When Tammy . . . hesitated"*: Bill Evans, conversation with author, February 11, 2022.

page 144: *"The real triumph . . . and enchanting"*: Clive Barnes, "The Theater: 'A Little Night Music,'" *New York Times*, February 26, 1973, https://archive.nytimes.com/www.nytimes.com/books/98/07/19/specials/sondheim-night.html.

page 144: *"This Night Music . . . not as much fun"*: Sondheim, in *"A Little Night Music*—1995."

page 145: *"About forty percent . . . Broadway shows"*: Stryker, "'I'm Not an Opera Fan.'"

page 145: *moved to the larger Majestic Theatre*: Performance attended by author, November 15, 1973.

page 145: *"and they know . . . keeping the faith"*: Hildy Parks (writer), Clark Jones (director), Alexander H. Cohen (producer), Rex Harrison, Celeste Holm, Eddie Albert, Rossano Brazzi, Yul Brynner, Diahann Carroll, Sandy Duncan, Nanette Fabray, Helen Gallagher, Ken Howard, Paula Kelly, Alan King, Cleo Laine, Michelle Lee, Donna McKechnie, Jerry Orbach, Christopher Plummer, Walter Slezak, Alexis Smith, Tommy Steele, Peter Ustinov, and Gwen Verdon (hosts), *The 1973 Tony Awards*, CBS, March 25, 1973, available on MissPoochSmooch, "*1973 Tony Awards~COMPLETE*," YouTube, July 21, 2013, video, https://www.youtube.com/watch?v=s89lQaC_yog.

page 145: *125 percent return on their investment*: Gottfried, *Sondheim*, p. 113.

page 146: *"His orchestration . . . which I grew up on"*: Maureen Lee Lenker, "Remembering That Time Stephen Sondheim Won a Grammy for Song of the Year," *Entertainment Weekly*, April 2, 2022, https://ew.com/awards/grammys/stephen-sondheim-send-in-the-clowns-grammy-song-of-the-year-judy-collins/.

page 146: *"they made it a hit"*: "Maestro of Broadway."

page 146: *"Frank Sinatra said . . . was very proud of that"*: Evans, conversation with author.

page 147: *ten violins . . . along with another horn*: Royal S. Brown, "'A Little Night Music' in the Studio," *High Fidelity*, July 1973, p. 72.

page 147: *"The first person . . . as a composer"*: Stephen Sondheim, in masterworksbwayVEVO, "Stephen Sondheim—on Glynis Johns," YouTube, March 4, 2013, video, https://www.youtube.com/watch?v=oSgyBoyoXnc.

A PUZZLEMENT

page 149: *"'Why don't you' . . . alternate scenes"*: Isenberg, "Sondheim, Songless."

page 149: *clue written in the icing*: Winecoff, *Anthony Perkins*, p. 247.

page 149: *"You'd pull up . . . 'getting married'"*: Dale, interview with author.

page 149: *"One of the guests . . . Tony could play it"*: Isenberg, "Sondheim, Songless."

page 150: *"He was so terrified . . . after Psycho!"*: Winecoff, *Anthony Perkins*, p. 249.

page 150: *"I saw . . . in musical theater"*: Isenberg, "Sondheim, Songless."

page 151: *"There are two . . . who the murderer is"*: Isenberg, "Sondheim, Songless."

page 151: *"The first time . . . 'what you look like'"*: "Show Business: Sweet and Sour Sue," *Time*, March 26, 1973, https://content.time.com/time/subscriber/article/0,33009,907002,00.html.

page 152: *plans for a Last of Sheila remake*: Borys Kit, "New Line to Remake Murder Mystery 'The Last of Sheila' (Exclusive)," *Hollywood Reporter*, June 18, 2012, https://www.hollywoodreporter.com/business/business-news/new-line-remake-last-sheila-murder-mystery-338801/.

page 152: *"so funky . . . and someone dies"*: John Boone, "'Knives Out': Director Rian Johnson Reveals 3 Movies to Watch Ahead of His Whodunit," *Entertainment Tonight*, November 25, 2019, https://www.etonline.com/knives-out-director-rian-johnson-reveals-3-movies-to-watch-ahead-of-his-whodunit-134682.

page 152: *"It's fitting . . . virtually invisible"*: Isenberg, "Sondheim, Songless."

page 152-153: *"the final twenty . . . rearview mirror"*: Stephen Sondheim and Anthony Shaffer, "Theater; Of Mystery, Murder and Other Delights," *New York Times*, March 10, 1996, https://archive.nytimes.com/www.nytimes.com/books/98/07/19/specials/sondheim-shaffer.html.

page 153: *"I was into . . . way out of it"*: Susan King, "Dyan Cannon and Richard Benjamin Fondly Look Back at 'The Last of Sheila,'" *Los Angeles Times*, January 24, 2020, https://www.latimes.com/entertainment-arts/movies/story/2020-01-24/dyan-cannon-and-richard-benjamin-fondly-look-back-at-the-last-of-sheila.

page 153: *"girls getting murdered . . . figure it out"*: Mandelbaum, *"A Chorus Line" and the Musicals of Michael Bennett*, p. 106.

page 153: *"It concerns . . . their psychiatrist"*: Isenberg, "Sondheim, Songless."

page 153: *"Christie's . . . and Anthony Perkins"*: Vincent Canby, "A Most Sinister Gathering of Not-So-Usual Suspects," *New York Times*, March 18, 1996, pp. 38–39.

EAST GREETS WEST

page 154: *"Steve relies very . . . go to work"*: Bryer and Davison, *Art of the American Musical*, p. 267.

page 155: *"Whether or not . . . a commercial setting"*: Clive Hirschhorn, "Will Sondheim Succeed in Being Genuinely Japanese?," *New York Times*, January 4, 1976, section D, p. 1.

page 155: *"At Harvard . . . at Yale"*: Jesse Kornbluth, "Storytelling with Sondheim," *Harvard Magazine*, January–February 2011, https://www.harvardmagazine.com/2011/01/storytelling-with-sondheim#.

page 155-156: *"a fortune in those days"*: Bryer and Davison, *Art of the American Musical*, p. 259.

page 156: *"Potent theatrical storytelling"*: Prince, *Sense of Occasion*, p. 209.

page 156: *"I was coming . . . 'to be a musical'"*: Suzanne Bixby, "Two-Way Street," *Sondheim Review*, Fall 2010, p. 35.

page 156: *"The play was confined . . . to give it size"*: Hirsch, *Harold Prince*, p. 109.

page 156: *"ringmaster . . . bullied . . . the material"*: Bixby, "Two-Way Street."

page 156: *"Steve really thought I was crazy"*: Zadan, *Sondheim & Co.*, p. 210.

page 156: *"At first I thought . . . music would fit"*: Zadan, *Sondheim & Co.*, p. 210.

page 157: *"He twisted . . . and started over"*: Bryer and Davison, *Art of the American Musical*, p. 261.

page 157: *"Often, what appeals . . . in love with it"*: Robert Berkvist, "Stephen Sondheim Takes a Stab at Grand Guignol," *New York Times*, February 25, 1979, https://archive.nytimes.com/www.nytimes.com/books/98/07/19/specials/sondheim-guignol.html.

page 158: *"Give us the tone . . . The King and I"*: Hirschhorn, "Will Sondheim Succeed."

page 158: *"We began to realize . . . as Western as you can get"*: Hirsch, *Harold Prince*, p. 109.

page 158: *"Not that it was . . . and what is now"*: Horowitz, *Sondheim on Music*, p.156.

page 158: *"to echo musically . . . never gets bored"*: Horowitz, *Sondheim on Music*, pp. 157–158.

page 158: *As an opening number*: Los Angeles Civic Light Opera production of Broadway original attended by author, 1976.

page 160: *"I was trying to start . . . of the opening number"*: Bryer and Davison, *Art of the American Musical*, p. 199.

page 160: *"so the idea for . . . the kid in a tree"*: Bryer and Davison, *Art of the American Musical*, p. 267.

page 160: *"The score . . . built on variety"*: Sondheim, "The Musical Theatre," p. 19.

page 161: *"Mr. Doyle's genius . . . possible relief"*: Terry Teachout, "'Pacific Overtures' Review: Shortening Sondheim," *Wall Street Journal*, May 4, 2017, https://www.wsj.com/articles/pacific-overtures-review-shortening-sondheim-1493944200.

page 161: *"documentary vaudeville"*: Rich with Aronson, *The Theatre Art of Boris Aronson*, p. 261.

page 161: *"I expected them . . . to be okay with that"*: Bixby, "Two-Way Street."

page 161: *"Very serious . . . airless as the moon"*: Dan Dietz, *The Complete Book of 1970s Broadway Musicals* (Lanham, MD: Rowman & Littlefield, 2015), p. 283.

page 161: *"it remains one . . . other is* Sweeney Todd*"*: Robert Hofler, "Critical Response," *Variety*, December 12, 2004, https://variety.com/2004/legit/columns/critical-response-1117914841/.

page 161: *"I think . . . proud of the show"*: Berkvist, "Sondheim Takes a Stab at Grand Guignol."

BLOODY HELL

page 162: *"Sweeney Todd . . . is built . . . a lot of it is"*: Sondheim and Guettel, in *The Art of Songwriting*.

page 163: *sinister quality of their filling*: James Malcolm Rymer, *The String of Pearls; or, the Barber of Fleet Street, a Domestic Romance*, edited by Alex Crary and Matthew McAnelly, The James Malcolm Rymer Collection, University of Wisconsin, Green Bay, http://salisburysquare.com/TSOP/content/TSOP.1850.UNC.chap.001.xml. Originally published in 1850.

page 164: *Lansbury's West End debut in* Gypsy: Secrest, *Sondheim: A Life*, p. 288.

page 164: *"I went . . . richer than the others"*: Berkvist, "Sondheim Takes a Stab at Grand Guignol."

page 164: *"You are prisoners . . . of the factory"*: Prince, *Sense of Occasion*, p. 225.

page 165: *"always thought . . . smokestacks of factories"*: Prince, *Sense of Occasion*, p. 223.

page 165: *"I thought it was about scaring people"*: "Remembering Stephen Sondheim."

page 165: *previous New York stage credits . . .* Who's Afraid of Virginia Woolf?: Mervyn Rothstein, "Richard Barr, 71, Stage Producer and Theater League Head, Dies," *New York Times*, January 10, 1989, section B, p. 7.

page 165: *Fryer's other productions . . .* Travels with My Aunt: Don Shirley, "Robert Fryer; Producer, Former Ahmanson Director," *Los Angeles Times*, May 31, 2000, https://www.latimes.com/archives/la-xpm-2000-may-31-me-35862-story.html.

page 166: *only part of the subtext*: Hirsch, *Harold Prince*, p. 120.

SOURCE NOTES

page 166: *"I encouraged . . . nearly all music"*: Citron, *Sondheim & Lloyd-Webber*, p. 245.

page 166: *from beginning to end*: Pender, *Sondheim Encyclopedia*, p. 556.

page 166: *"Smoke . . . half to death"*: Citron, *Sondheim & Lloyd-Webber*, p. 244.

page 167: *"We analyzed a Bach . . . didn't get to my heart"*: Sondheim and Guettel, in *The Art of Songwriting*.

page 167: *"The whole point . . . Tolstoy might disagree"*: masterworksbwayVEVO, "The Story So Far . . . *Sweeney Todd*," YouTube, February 25, 2022, video, https://www.youtube.com/watch?v=jvJ0xXGnTXo.

page 167: *"When I was fifteen . . . murdering people"*: Lipton, "Stephen Sondheim, The Art of the Musical."

page 167: *"The true story . . . to kill!"*: "Hangover Square—Trailer," IMDB.com, https://www.imdb.com/video/vi1459077913/?ref_=tt_vi_i_1.

page 167: *"It had . . . going all the time"*: Lipton, "Stephen Sondheim, The Art of the Musical."

page 167: *only 20 percent dialogue*: Stryker, "'I'm Not an Opera Fan.'"

page 167: *"is one . . . full of menace"*: Lipton, "Stephen Sondheim, The Art of the Musical."

page 168: *"Hal was not looking . . . Prince was looking for"*: Citron, *Sondheim & Lloyd-Webber*, p. 245.

page 168: *paid $25,000 for the structure*: Prince, *Sense of Occasion*, p. 223.

page 168: *cost $100,000 . . . and resurrect*: Rex Reed, "Sweeney Soars," (New York) *Daily News*, March 3, 1979, p. 8.

page 168: *tryout method, and it worked*: Prince, *Sense of Occasion*, p. 225.

page 168: *"British Bee Hive" . . . sat Queen Victoria*: "The British Bee Hive," British Library, https://www.bl.uk/collection-items/the-british-bee-hive.

page 168: *"I suggested . . . torture them"*: Prince, *Sense of Occasion*, p. 225.

page 169: *in the musical,* Nellie: Robert L. Mack, *The Wonderful and Surprising History of Sweeney Todd: The Life and Times of an Urban Legend* (London: Bloomsbury Academic, 2007), p. 307.

page 169: *she met the same fate*: Mark Gribben, "Sweeney Todd—Man or Myth?," Crime Library, truTV, https://web.archive.org/web/20080405180719/http://www.crimelibrary.com/serial_killers/weird/todd/index_1.html.

page 169: *"Not sexy . . . just perfect"*: Gottfried, *Balancing Act*, p. 228.

page 170: *"It's scary . . . Todd after you"*: Gottfried, *Balancing Act*, p. 229.

page 170: *"Hal is . . . going to be all right?"*: Shapiro, *Nothing Like a Dame*, pp. 86-87.

page 171: *"When an actor . . . with actors, right?"*: Jesse Green, "Side by Side: Stephen Sondheim and Angela Lansbury on a Lifetime in Theatre," *New York*, December 21–28, 2009, p. 104.

page 171: *"Do you . . . see this?"*: Angela Lansbury, interview with author, February 19, 1979.

page 171: *"Once the audience . . . went for it"*: Shapiro, *Nothing Like a Dame*, p. 88.

page 172: *coproduction . . . Susan Bullock*: Gregory Barnett, "'Sweeney Todd': Houston Grand Opera," *Opera News*, July 2015, https://www.operanews.com/Opera_News_Magazine/2015/7/Reviews/HOUSTON__Sweeney_Todd.html.

page 172: *"Sweeney . . . opera companies"*: Patricia Rice, "'Sweeney Todd' Was Always Meant to Be an Opera," St. Louis Public Radio, May 21, 2012, https://news.stlpublicradio.org/arts/2012-05-21/sweeney-todd-was-always-meant-to-be-an-opera.

page 174: *"It was three hours . . . unfair"*: Gottfried, *Balancing Act*, p. 243.

page 174: *"They got it"*: masterworksbwayVEVO, "Stephen Sondheim—The Story So Far . . . Finale," YouTube, June 17, 2022, video, https://www.youtube.com/watch?v=wi1Jf8AeAQQ.

page 174: *"I think the most unbelievable . . . is* Sweeney Todd*"*: Zadan, *Sondheim & Co.*, p. 390.

page 174: *"Disgusting enough . . . temperament perfectly"*: Rodgers and Green, *Shy*, p. 185.

page 174: *draw of Lansbury*: Performance attended by author, March 1, 1979.

page 174: *eight Tony awards*: Ceremony attended by author, June 3, 1979.

page 174: *"Sweeney . . . physical stamina"*: Kent Thompson, *Directing Professionally: A Practical Guide to Developing a Successful Career in Today's Theatre* (London: Methuen Drama, 2019), p. 53.

page 175: *cannibalism is a hard sell*: Hal Prince, interview with author, September 1987.

page 175: *"I got home . . . perfectly fine"*: Teeman, "Up Close and Very Personal with the Real Stephen Sondheim."

page 175: *Also stopped . . . exercise regime*: Secrest, *Sondheim: A Life*, pp. 305–306.

page 176: *"I'd never heard . . . 'a great movie score'"*: Jeff Dawson, "Tim Burton Explains Why Musicals Still Cut It," (London) *Sunday Times*, January 6, 2008, https://www.thetimes.co.uk/article/tim-burton-explains-why-musicals-still-cut-it-zjh88x9m0d0.

page 176: *"We had done tests . . . 'dare do this?'"*: Sylviane Gold, "Demon Barber, Meat Pies and All, Sing on Screen," *New York Times*, November 4, 2007, https://www.nytimes.com/2007/11/04/movies/moviesspecial/04gold.html.

page 176: *she was not a singer*: Mark Salisbury, "A Pie-in-the-Sky Dream Come True," *Los Angeles Times*, December 28, 2007, https://www.latimes.com/archives/la-xpm-2007-dec-28-et-helena28-story.html.

page 176: *"The fact that he came . . . was musical"*: Dawson, "Tim Burton Explains."

page 177: *"It would have been . . . lyrics were wonderful"*: Ernio Hernandez, "Cut: Christopher Lee and Ghosts are Nixed from 'Sweeney Todd' Film," *Playbill*, May 22. 2007, https://www.playbill.com/article/cut-christopher-lee-and-ghosts-are-nixed-from-sweeney-todd-film-com-140979.

page 177: *"As the bodies pile . . . keep watching"*: Richard Corliss, "'Sweeney Todd': Horror and Humanity," *Time*, December 21, 2007, http://content.time.com/time/arts/article/0,8599,1697909,00.html.

page 177: *"The Sound of Music—with blood!"*: Dawson, "Tim Burton Explains."

page 178: *minimalist production on Broadway*: Performance attended by author, November 4, 2005.

page 178: *"It opened . . . other than spectacle"*: Patricia Cohen, "'Sweeney Todd' (2005 Revival)," *New York Times*, April 13, 2020, https://www.nytimes.com/interactive/2020/04/13/t-magazine/sweeney-todd-revival.html.

page 178: *"Sometimes, when I think . . . Sondheim's sofa"*: Lyn Gardner, "The Amazing Mr. Musicals," *Guardian*, January 24, 2008, https://www.theguardian.com/stage/2008/jan/24/theatre.musicals.

page 179: *take place all over the world*: Peter Khoury, "Stephen Sondheim and the Australian Connection to His Work," *On Stage*, June 1, 2022, https://theatreheritage.org.au/on-stage-magazine/itemlist/tag/Stephen%20Sondheim.

page 179: *"I have been inspired . . . on any device"*: American Theatre Editors, "Disney+ Announces Plans for 'Sweeney Todd' Animated Series," *American Theatre*, April 1, 2022, https://www.americantheatre.org/2022/04/01/disney-announces-plans-for-sweeney-todd-animated-series/.

page 179: *"The stuff we wrote was confident"*: "Sondheim—The Story So Far . . . Finale."

TIME TRAVELERS

page 180: *"said it was going . . . and hurt"*: Secrest, *Sondheim: A Life*, p. 310.

page 181: *been shooting since 2019*: Galuppo, "Richard Linklater Musical."

page 182: *directed by Maria Friedman*: Greg Evans, "Daniel Radcliffe to Star in Off Broadway Revival of Sondheim's 'Merrily We Roll Along,'" *Deadline*, March 7, 2022, https://deadline.com/2022/03/daniel-radcliffe-off-broadway-stephen-sondheim-merrily-we-roll-along-1234972678/.

page 182: *"He wrote about people's . . . direct"*: Kate Kellaway, "Maria Friedman: 'Sondheim Was a Kind Man, but God, He Could Be Very Direct,'" *Guardian*, February 13, 2022, https://www.theguardian.com/stage/2022/feb/13/maria-friedman-sondheim-was-a-kind-man-but-he-could-be-very-direct-legacy-menier-chocolate-factory-interview.

page 182: *"The songs are all based . . . our friendships do"*: Zadan, *Sondheim & Co.*, p. 270.

page 183: *"We wanted to get in there . . . true collaborator"*: Stuart Emmrich, "For the Cult of Sondheim, 'Merrily We Roll Along,' and on, and on, and . . . ," *Los Angeles Times*, March 4, 2019, https://www.latimes.com/entertainment/arts/la-et-cm-merrily-we-roll-along-20190304-story.html.

page 184: *"He said . . . what a gift he gave us"*: Tim Allis, "What Stephen Sondheim Thinks of the 'Merrily We Roll Along' Doc," *Playbill*, November 16, 2016, https://playbill.com/article/what-stephen-sondheim-thinks-of-the-merrily-we-roll-along-doc.

page 185: *"as if . . . born middle-aged"*: Sondheim, *Finishing the Hat*, p. 382.

page 185: *"As for why I stopped . . . last collaboration"*: Janiga, "Side by Side with Sondheim."

page 185: *"But it flopped . . . creative sessions"*: Prince, *Sense of Occasion*, p. 230.

page 185: *Sondheim shared the same feeling*: Gottfried, *Sondheim*, p. 153.

page 185: *brutal reception on Broadway*: Citron, *Sondheim & Lloyd-Webber*, p. 286.

page 186: *"I had been playing piano for vocal coaches . . . not a weakness, but a superpower"*: Darrell Brown, phone conversation with author, March 19, 2022.

page 188: *"We decided . . . bad idea"*: Prince, *Sense of Occasion*, p. 228.

page 188: *"But the set . . . could do about it"*: Janiga, "Side by Side with Sondheim."

page 188: *"The hatred . . . was that intense"*: Robert Hofler, conversation with author, June 12, 2022.

page 188: *"I went to bed . . . flop sweat"*: Prince, *Sense of Occasion*, p. 229.

page 188: *"that nobody's . . . compromiser"*: Janiga, "Side by Side with Sondheim."

page 189: *"Like Pacific Overtures . . . underlying the relationships"*: Hirsch, *Harold Prince*, p. 134.

page 189: *"Usually . . . 'start with the fragments'"*: Citron, *Sondheim & Lloyd-Webber*, p. 281.

page 189: *"Opening Doors . . . period of my life"*: Sondheim, *Finishing the Hat*, p. 419.

REGENERATION

I.

page 192: *"Britten shows up . . . English music"*: Lipton, "Stephen Sondheim, The Art of the Musical," *Paris Review*.

page 193: *"suggests that . . . present moment"*: McLaughlin, *Sondheim and the Reinvention of the American Musical*, p. 165

page 193: *"if it works . . . Less Is More"*: Sondheim, *Look, I Made a Hat*, p. 52.

page 193: *writing mysteries instead of musicals*: Suzanne Bixby, "Jumping In," *Sondheim Review*, Summer 2010, p. 28.

page 193: *"I really don't . . . very young age"*: Sondheim and Guettel, in *The Art of Songwriting*.

page 193: *Lapine as Sondheim's collaborator*: Bixby, "Jumping In."

page 193: *too similar to* Candide: Lapine, *Putting It Together*, p. 17.

page 194: *"I compare . . . more than the content"*: Guettel, conversation with author.

page 194-195: *"theme and variations . . . hard it is to make art"*: Lipton, "Stephen Sondheim, The Art of the Musical."

page 194: *handed him a joint*: Lapine, *Putting It Together*, p. 16.

page 195: *"My life changed . . . what I'd come from"*: Sondheim and Guettel, in *The Art of Songwriting*.

page 195: *"I found myself . . . story itself"*: Sondheim, *Look, I Made a Hat*, p. 6.

page 195: *"I came from . . . what he did"*: Bixby, "Jumping In."

page 195: *Lapine traced . . . so he could get to know them*: Lapine, *Putting It Together*, p. 31.

page 195: *"I'd always loved . . . right to the present"*: David Richards, "The Lowdown on Sondheim's Partner," *Washington Post*, April 20, 1997, https://www.washingtonpost.com/archive/lifestyle/style/1997/04/20/the-lowdown-on-sondheims-partner/689f219b-c989-475a-8cb0-a451c108b3e5/.

page 195: *"It takes him . . . the wrong song"*: Bixby, "Jumping In."

page 195: *"I guess it comes . . . about the song"*: Lapine, *Putting It Together*, p. 36.

page 195: *"Once you say . . . that tells a story"*: "Maestro of Broadway."

page 197: *"Like very few . . . as I'm concerned"*: Chip Crews, "Broadway's Bernadette Peters: Viva the Diva, Her Fans Say," *Los Angeles Times*, January 12, 1999, https://www.latimes.com/archives/la-xpm-1999-jan-12-ca-62620-story.html.

page 197: *"Even then . . . people like me"*: Lapine, *Putting It Together*, p. 39.

page 197: *playing only the opening chords*: Bixby, "Jumping In."

page 197: *"Steve would start . . . 'talking like this'"*: Bixby, "Jumping In," p. 29.

page 197: *"Point taken . . . stopped making trouble"*: Lapine, *Putting It Together*, pp. 54–55.

page 198: *would be perfect as Georges*: Lapine, *Putting It Together*, pp. 57–58.

page 199: *the character stated in the title*: Lapine, *Putting It Together*, p.58.

page 199: *"He doesn't like . . . a little tutorial"*: Bixby, "Jumping In."

page 199: *"it's pleasanter . . . leads to more work"*: "Maestro of Broadway."

page 199: *"In the same way . . . it's Monday night"*: Lapine, *Putting It Together*, p. 144.

page 199: *"It's a song . . . and she resents it"*: "Maestro of Broadway."

page 199: *"Steve Sondheim comes over . . . delivered nothing"*: Ruthie Fierberg, "Mandy Patinkin Shares the Story Behind Hearing 'Sunday in the Park with George's' 'Finishing the Hat' for the 1st Time," *Playbill*, July 2, 2020, https://playbill.com/article/mandy-patinkin-shares-the-story-behind-hearing-sunday-in-the-park-with-georges-finishing-the-hat-for-the-1st-time.

page 200: *"The definition . . . Sondheim"*: Rachel Syme, "Mandy Patinkin Is Still Singing," *New Yorker*, October 11, 2020, https://www.newyorker.com/culture/the-new-yorker-interview/mandy-patinkin-is-still-singing.

page 200: *"If I give you another . . . second act?"*: Lapine, *Putting It Together*, p. 130.

page 200: *"It's always surprising . . . were writing it"*: Richards, "The Lowdown on Sondheim's Partner."

page 200: *should be within earshot*: Gerald Schoenfeld, conversation with author, Spring 1984.

page 201: *"I met Sondheim . . . past that crisis"*: Errico, email to author.

page 201: *flop called La Strada*: Lapine, *Putting It Together*, pp. 214–215.

page 201: *"he retreated . . . out of his mind"*: Richards, "The Lowdown on Sondheim's Partner."

page 202: Chromoluminarism *. . . into a third color*: Lapine, *Putting It Together*, p. 166.

page 206: *opened May 2, 1984*: Performance attended by author, May 2, 1984.

page 202: *exception of Frank Rich's in the* Times: Frank Rich, "Stage: 'Sunday in the Park with George,'" *New York Times*, May 3, 1984, section C, p. 21.

page 203: *"I must have seen it . . . grow with his shows"*: Lars Linnhoff, conversation with author, February 11, 2022.

page 204: *"Welcome to my world"*: Lapine, *Putting It Together*, p. 253.

page 204: *"That wasn't very gentlemanly, was it?"*: Jack Kroll, conversation with author at Tony Awards, June 3, 1984.

page 204: A Little Night Music *had been revived*: Harvey Fierstein, *I Was Better Last Night: A Memoir* (New York: Alfred A. Knopf, 2022), pp. 259–261.

page 204: *"Six hundred . . . seventy-six trombones and"*: Fierstein, *I Was Better Last Night*, p. 267.

page 204: *"I wish I could say . . . 'that's nice'"*: "Maestro of Broadway."

page 205: *"This is just a note . . . of the celebration"*: George Abud, interview with author, March 22, 2022.

page 205: *"It mirrors . . . the human voice"*: Abud, interview with author.

page 205: *Presentation of the project*: Jeanine Tesori, "A Heart Broken, Also Full: What Sondheim Gave Us," *American Theatre,* December

1, 2021, https://www.americantheatre.org/2021/12/01/a-heart-broken-also-full-what-sondheim-gave-us/.

II.

page 207: *"A lot of it . . . generation to generation"*: Ned Sherrin (host) and Stephen Sondheim (guest), *Newsnight,* BBC, 1990, available on Anthony Keetch, "Sondheim on *Newsnight* 1990," YouTube, August 1, 2014, video, https://youtu.be/k8ayRl1VL9E.

page 207: *"I want to write . . . this one"*: Lapine, *Putting It Together,* p. 121.

page 207: *"I always wanted to do . . . it grew that way"*: Edwin Newman (host), *"Into the Woods*: A Conversation with Stephen Sondheim and James Lapine," PBS, 1991, available on Broadway History, *"Into the Woods*: A Conversation with Sondheim and Lapine—1991 PBS TV," YouTube, August 10, 2020, video, https://youtu.be/9Bjr0LbDKks.

page 207-208: *"like The Wizard of Oz . . . 'What's that story about?'"*: Sherrin and Sondheim, "Sondheim on *Newsnight* 1990"

page 209: *"which is totally . . . invention"*: Newman, *"Into the Woods."*

page 209: *"I wanted to do something . . . at the same time"*: Michiko Kakutani, "Theater; Beyond Happily Ever After," *New York Times,* August 30, 1987, section 6, p. 30.

page 210: *Red Riding Hood, Jack, and Cinderella*: Newman, *"Into the Woods."*

page 210: *"I chose these . . . it was useful"*: Newman, *"Into the Woods."*

page 210: *"a lot of ditty-like . . . a bounce going"*: Kakutani, "Theater; Beyond Happily Ever After."

page 210: *"It's sort of fun . . . that theme crops up"*: Sherrin and Sondheim, "Sondheim on *Newsnight* 1990."

page 211: *"it's really the Baker . . . in the wrong story"*: Joanna Gleason, comments at the Paley Center for Media in Los Angeles, May 24, 2000.

page 211: *as some accusers would have it*: Terry Teachout, "Sondheim at 90," *Commentary,* March 2020, https://www.commentary.org/articles/terry-teachout/broadway-musical-talent-sondheim/.

page 212: *"It means we are . . . 'an island'"*: Sherrin and Sondheim, "Sondheim on *Newsnight* 1990."

page 212: *"You can't just . . . everybody else"*: Kakutani, "Theater; Beyond Happily Ever After."

page 212: *"We had 'Boom'" . . . role was available*: Zadan, *Sondheim & Co.,* p. 346.

page 212: *"I remember being . . . the first time"*: Michael Portantiere, "The Greatest Gift," *Sondheim Review,* Spring 2012, p. 10.

page 212: *"Into the Woods wasn't . . . necks with notes"*: Bixby, "Jumping In," p. 30.

page 213: *"for the courage . . . on any continent"*: Jeffrey Lane (writer and coproducer), Walter C. Miller (director), David J. Goldberg (producer), Don Mischer (executive producer), Angela Lansbury (host), *The 1988 Tony Awards,* CBS, June 5, 1988, available on MissPoochSmooch, *"1988 Tony Awards—*COMPLETE," YouTube, August 13, 2014, video, https://youtu.be/S1TYwKVVH-M.

page 213: *wherever English . . . and Danish*: Pender, *The Stephen Sondheim Encyclopedia,* p. 242.

page 215: *"in New York with my mum . . . He was incredible"*: Jacqui Dankworth, phone conversation with author, May 4, 2022.

page 217: *Rumblings of a movie . . . the Giant*: Scott Foundas, "Film Review: 'Into the Woods,'" *Variety,* December 17, 2014, https://variety.com/2014/film/reviews/film-review-into-the-woods-1201381097/.

page 217: *"When I turned forty . . . 'another way'"*: Seth Abramovitch, "Perverted Wolves, Cheating Wives and a Fired 10-Year-Old: The Dark Path to Disney's 'Into the Woods,'" *Hollywood Reporter,* December 10, 2014, https://www.hollywoodreporter.com/news/general-news/perverted-wolves-cheating-wives-a-755359/.

DEATH AND LOVE

I.

page 218: *"How could one . . . is about"*: Sondheim, *Look, I Made a Hat,* p. 113.

page 219: *"Nowadays . . . everything goes"*: Mervyn Rothstein, "Sondheim's 'Assassins': Insane Realities of History," *New York Times,* January 27, 1991, https://archive.nytimes.com/www.nytimes.com/books/98/07/19/specials/sondheim-assassins.html.

page 219: *about real-life assassins*: Charles Gilbert, "A Tale of Two Assassins," Chas. Gilbert (personal website), 2001, http://www.chasgilbert.com/articles/assassins.html (URL inactive; information based on 2001 printout).

page 219: *"There was something . . . entertaining to me"*: "Charles Gilbert: Full Circle," *Sondheim Review,* Summer 1994, p. 15.

page 219: *"For example . . . most interesting about"*: Rothstein, "Sondheim's 'Assassins.'"

page 220: *"a sort of Sidney . . . politicians' letters"*: "Maestro of Broadway."

page 220: *"the narrative seemed . . . 'had that idea'"*: Rothstein, "Sondheim's 'Assassins.'"

page 220: *"Step right up . . . win a prize!"*: Gilbert, "A Tale of Two Assassins."

SOURCE NOTES

page 220: *"I said . . . 'idea of* Assassins'": "Maestro of Broadway."

page 220: *"I was baffled . . . Weidman in mind"*: "Charles Gilbert: Full Circle."

page 220: *"Steve will admit . . . like trying to write"*: Bryer and Davison, *Art of the American Musical*, p. 277.

page 220: *"Assassins is . . . a lot of trouble"*: Citron, *Sondheim & Lloyd-Webber*, p. 346.

page 221: *"I felt very . . . material required"*: Bryer and Davison, *Art of the American Musical*, p. 277.

page 221: *"We first decided . . . presidential assassins"*: "Maestro of Broadway."

page 221: *"The idea that people . . . parallels and contrasts"*: Rothstein, "Sondheim's 'Assassins.'"

page 221: *"One of the things . . . those lives reveal"*: Rothstein, "Sondheim's 'Assassins.'"

page 221: *"some were . . . more than crazy"*: Rothstein, "Sondheim's 'Assassins.'"

page 222-223: *"We projected . . . in [the assassins'] minds"*: Jerry Floyd, "Sondheim&Signature: Side by Side with Eric D. Schaeffer," Stephen Sondheim Stage, 1998, http://www.sondheim.com/interview/sig.html.

page 223: *"I didn't know . . . he wasn't sure either"*: Zadan, *Sondheim & Co.*, p, 378.

page 223: *"Her phrasing . . . and grace"*: Zadan, *Sondheim & Co.*, p. 380.

page 223: *"I don't very . . . in my films"*: Robert Koehler, "Legend in His Own Time," *Variety*, October 15, 1999, p. A1.

page 223: *"Goodbye for Now"*: Bruce Kimmel, "Reds," Sondheim.com. http://www.sondheim.com/works/reds/.

page 223: *"During my formative . . . view of the world"*: Michael Phillips, "Stephen Sondheim Devoured Cinema. Here's How His Movie Love Fed His Own Work, on Stage and Screen," *Chicago Tribune*, November 29, 2021, https://www.chicagotribune.com/entertainment/movies/michael-phillips/sc-ent-sondheim-movies-phillips-1128-20211129-y22pcegy2fbhxfwrzpidffcdsq-story.html.

page 223: *"The reviews . . . were good"*: Bryer and Davison, *Art of the American Musical*, p. 279.

page 223: *four hundred . . . over the next decade*: Joe Marchese, "'Assassins" Enduring Popularity," *Sondheim Review*, Winter 2015, p. 20.

page 224: *"Assassins is very much . . . the characters"*: Horowitz, *Sondheim on Music*, p. 57.

page 225: *Cerveris . . . for Lighting Design and Orchestrations*: Tonys ceremony attended by author, June 6, 2004.

page 225: *Classic Stage Company version*: Performance attended by author, December 26, 2021.

II.

page 226: *"Kind of a cool . . . what I wrote"*: Shapiro, *Nothing Like a Dame*, pp. 192–193.

page 226: *"Passion is . . . through-composition"*: Secrest, *Sondheim: A Life*, p. 388.

page 227: *"the nature . . . so many things"*: Shapiro, *Nothing Like a Dame*, p. 192.

page 227: *"I asked her . . . something very personal"*: Wayman Wong, "Her 'Passion' Is Acting," *Sondheim Review*, Summer 1994, p. 7.

page 227: *"I wanted to open the show that night"*: Stephen Sondheim and Frank Rich, "A Life in the Theatre," Avery Fisher Hall, Lincoln Center, New York City, January 18, 2009.

page 227: *"I wanted . . . to do it"*: "Sondheim: 'It Was a Hard One to Write,'" *Sondheim Review*, Summer 1994, p. 3.

page 227: *an assessment Sondheim found "fair"*: "Sondheim: 'It Was a Hard One to Write,'" p. 30.

page 228: *"This can't be . . . 'heard.'"*: Lapine, *Putting It Together*, p. 126.

page 228: *"First of all . . . kind of music"*: Anonymous, "Sondheim: 'It Was a Hard One to Write.'"

page 228: *"Passion seemed like . . . books are about appearances"*: Wayman Wong, "Sondheim Speaks About His 'Passion,'" *Sondheim Review*, Summer 1994, p. 6.

page 228-229: *"Donna is a gorgeous . . . how to act ugly"*: Wong, "Her 'Passion' Is Acting."

page 229: *"I thought about . . . 'with Fosca?'"*: Shapiro, *Nothing Like a Dame*, p. 192.

page 229: *Previews proved rocky*: First preview attended by author, March 24, 1994.

page 229: *"I was old enough . . . no thank you"*: Guettel, conversation with author.

page 230: *"Would Andrew be . . . in a Sondheim musical?"*: LuPone with Diehl, *Patti LuPone: A Memoir*.

III.

page 231: *the recital was part of*: Performance attended by author, June 20, 2022.

page 232: *"I think we . . . too long"*: Bryer and Davison, *Art of the American Musical*, p. 201.

page 232: *Wilson's primary gift . . . Bat Masterson*: John Burke, *Rogue's Progress: The Fabulous Adventures of Wilson Mizner* (New York: G. P. Putnam's Sons, 1975), p. 254.

page 233: *"Addison . . . found himself"*: Chris Jones, Sid Smith, and Michael Phillips, "The Team Behind 'Bounce,'" *Chicago Tribune*, June 22, 2003.

page 233: *"Well . . . brother is interesting"*: Bixby, "Two-Way Street," p. 37.

page 233-234: *"in the way . . . to be a musical"*: Jones et al., "The Team Behind 'Bounce.'"

page 234: *"I don't think . . . writing about"*: Bixby, "Two-Way Street," p. 37.

page 234: *"We started with . . . musical comedy"*: Jones et al., "The Team Behind 'Bounce.'"

page 234: *"Hal tried . . . lost in the shuffle"*: Bryer and Davison, *Art of the American Musical*, p. 200.

page 234: *two years later at the Public*: Performance attended by author, November 19, 2008.

page 234: *made it into every production*: Pender, *The Stephen Sondheim Encyclopedia*, p. 449.

page 234: *"These characters . . . all of us"*: Kristin Huffman, "Rich and Rewarding," *Sondheim Review*, Summer 2009, p. 17.

page 235: *"I still can't believe . . . Unforgettable"*: Michael Price (@mikepriceinla), "When he finished playing and singing he asked 'is that it? We done?' I said 'just one more thing. Please play me the entire score to Sweeney Todd.' He frowned . . . and then played those first low rumble notes of the opening number with a big smile on his face. Unforgettable," Twitter, November 27, 2021, 7:02 a.m., https://twitter.com/mikepriceinla/status/1464489697481134085.

IV.

page 236: *"He used irony . . . he is God"*: Kaley McMahon, interview with author, April 1, 2022.

page 237: *Sondheim . . . asked for the recipe*: Marc Peyser, "Send in the Fanatics," *Newsweek*, May 25, 1998, p. 73.

LATER

page 239: *"Sometimes . . . kill myself"*: Matt Wolf, "Stephen Sondheim Turns 80," Stage Whispers, https://www.stagewhispers.com.au/articles/193/stephen-sondheim-turns-80.

page 239: *"As he got older . . . to the bathroom"*: Sam Mendes, "Sam Mendes on Stephen Sondheim: 'He Was Passionate, Utterly Open, and Sharp as a Knife,'" *Guardian*, November 29, 2021, https://www.theguardian.com/stage/2021/nov/29/sam-mendes-stephen-sondheim-passionate-sharp-knife-musicals.

page 239: *"You would think . . . opposite of that"*: Kerry Breen, "Broadway Legend Stephen Sondheim Took Time to Mentor Young Creatives. Here's What It Meant to Them," *Today*, NBC News, December 30, 2021, https://www.today.com/popculture/broadway-legend-stephen-sondheim-took-time-mentor-young-creatives-here-t243972.

page 239: *"I was wearing . . . your face"*: Jama McMahon, interview with author, February 18, 2022.

page 240: *its title,* Square One: Greg Evans, "Stephen Sondheim Writing New Musical 'Square One,' Reveals Plans to Stephen Colbert," *Deadline*, September 12, 2021, https://deadline.com/2021/09/stephen-sondheim-stephen-colbert-new-musical-square-one-1234838060/.

page 244: *"I'm not a retiring . . . happens at the piano"*: Teeman, "Up Close and Very Personal with the Real Stephen Sondheim."

page 244: *"If I had to live . . . a great regret"*: Alan Franks, "Stephen Sondheim: 'My Ideal Collaborator Is Me,'" *Times* (of London), April 25, 2009, https://www.thetimes.co.uk/article/stephen-sondheim-my-ideal-collaborator-is-me-j0ghgwbz072.

page 240: *Sondheim was both encouraging*: Jody Rosen, "The American Revolutionary," *T Magazine*, July 8, 2015, https://www.nytimes.com/interactive/2015/07/08/t-magazine/hamilton-lin-manuel-miranda-roots-sondheim.html.

page 240: *"the opening . . . character speaks"*: W. Anthony Sheppard, "Finishing the Line: Wit, Rhythm, and Rhyme in Sondheim," in *Sondheim in Our Time and His*, edited by W. Anthony Sheppard (New York: Oxford University Press, 2022), pp. 409–410.

page 241: *He was generous with his estate . . . along with other friends*: Priscilla DeGregory, "Stephen Sondheim Left Behind an Estate Worth an Estimated $75 Million," *New York Post*, January 23, 2022, https://nypost.com/2022/01/23/stephen-sondheim-left-behind-an-estate-worth-an-estimated-75-million/.

page 242: *McDonald said there was no greater gift*: Andrew Gans, "Angela Lansbury, Audra McDonald, Bernadette Peters, Norm Lewis, Patti LuPone, More Remember Stephen Sondheim," *Playbill*, March 22, 2022, https://www.playbill.com/article/angela-lansbury-audra-mcdonald-bernadette-peters-norm-lewis-patti-lupone-more-remember-stephen-sondheim.

page 242: *"One of the things . . . as much as possible"*: Wolf, "Stephen Sondheim Turns 80."

page 242: *"The worst thing . . . yourself a service"*: "Maestro of Broadway."

INDEX

Note: Page numbers in *italics* reference photo captions.

INDEX

Feldstein, Beanie, 5–7, 181
Fiasco Theater, 182–183
Fiddler on the Roof, 140
Fierstein, Harvey, 204
Fine, Sylvia, 105
"Finishing the Hat," 199
Finn, Terry, *185*
Finn, William, 195
Finneran, Katie, 118
Firth, David, *225*
Flaherty, Stephen, 239
Follies
    "Ah, Paris!," 125
    Bennett as choreographer, 129, *129*, 132
    "Broadway Baby," 125
    characters, 125
    as a concert, 135
    developmental phase, 126
    film version, 135, *135*
    "I'm Still Here," 126, 131
    Kennedy Center revival of, 135
    look and theme inspiration, *125*
    "Loveland" sequence, 130, *130*
    Mackintosh's version of, 134
    mirror number, 129–130
    movie potential, 131
    "One More Kiss," 125
    Peters' performance in, 135
    plot, 126
    production costs, 122
    "Rain on the Roof," 125
    reviews, 130, 132
    revivals of, 134–135
    score, 125–126
    story development, 123–125
    Tony nominations, 132
    "Who's That Woman," 129–130
Follies in Concert, 128
Fonda, Henry, 131
Fosca (Tarchetti), 227
Fosse, Bob, 37
Foster, Sutton, 92
fourth wall, 111
Franchi, Sergio, *94*
Francis, Arlene, 31
Friedman, Maria, 92, *143*, 182–183, *228*, 230, 242
The Frogs, 82–83
Fryer, Robert, 165
Funny Girl, 63
A Funny Thing Happened on the Way to the Forum
    casting, 76–77
    cast's reception to Robbins, 80–81
    choreography, 80

    clown quartet, *80*
    disparity between score and book, 77–78
    "Invocation," 79
    movie version, 81
    producer shuffle, 74–76
    revival, 84
    Robbins saving, 78–81
    set design, 80
    Sondheim's description of, 73–74
    Tony nominations, 84
Furth, George, 105–107, 153, 185
Fussell, Sam, 228

G

Gabel, Martin, 31
Gaines, Boyd, *71*, 118
Gallagher, Peter, 228
Garber, Victor, 135, 221, *221*, *232*
Garfield, Andrew, 237
Garrison, Mary Catherine, 224
Gay Men's Health Crisis benefit performance, 92
Gelbart, Larry, 29, 73–75, *75*, *78*
Gemignani, Alexander, 234
Gemignani, Paul, 83, 118, 171
Generation X, 3
Generation Y, 3
Generation Z, 3
Gennaro, Peter, *38*
George School, *24*
Germann, Greg, *221*
Gershwin, George, 9
Gets, Malcolm, 183
Getting Away with Murder, 153
Gilbert, Charles, Jr., 219–220
Gilford, Jack, *80*, 81
Gilford, Madeline Lee, 78
Gilfry, Rod, 172
Gill, Ray, *215*
Gilliam, Terry, 213
Gingold, Hermione, *138*, 144
Giovanine, Brad, *225*
The Girls of Summer, 42n
The Girls Upstairs, 107, 123
"The Glamorous Life," 136, 145
Gleason, Joanna, *210*, 211
"God," *236*
Gold, Louise, *225*
Gold, Sylviane, 176
Goldberg, Whoopi, 84
Golden, Annie, 221, *221*
Golden Age of the Broadway Musical, 21, 25, *25*

Goldman, James, 77, 99n, 107, 122–125, *123*, 131, 134
Goldsberry, Renée Elise, 5, *5*
"Goodbye for Now," 223
Goodman, Henry, *225*
Gordon, John Steele, *15*
Gordon, Ruth, 29
Gottfried, Martin, 170
Gottlieb, Jack, 34
Grammer, Kelsey, 199
Grant, Cary, 11
Gray, Dolores, 134
Gray, Kevin, *161*
Green, Adolph, 33, 36n, 63
Green, Johnny, 46
Green Grow the Lilacs (Riggs play), *19*
Greene, Herb, *91*
Greenstreet, Sydney, 220n
Greenwood, Jane, *229*
Griffith, Robert, 42
Griffiths, Bobby, 77
Grimes, Tammy, 143
Groban, Josh, 179
Groff, Jonathan, 182
Gross, Terry, *2*
Grusin, Dave, 223
Guardino, Harry, 91, *91*
Guare, John, 132
Guettel, Adam, 97–98, *97*, 107–108, *194*, 229
Guittard, Laurence, *139*
Gunn, Nathan, 172
Gussow, Mel, 116
Gyllenhaal, Jake, 202n, *202*
Gypsy
    box office earnings, 64
    critics, 67
    "Everything's Coming Up Roses," 58, 66, 68
    film version, 68–70
    Laurents signing on for, 56
    Lee's autobiography as inspiration for, 53–54
    "Little Lamb," 67
    Madame Rose compared to Sondheim's mother, *61*
    Merman's reaction to script, 59–60
    musical score for, 61–62
    rehearsals, *57*
    Robbins recommending Sondheim for, 56–57
    "Small World," 59, 60
    "Some People" sequence, 53, 60
    Sondheim's earnings from, 64

McCartney, Paul, 8
McDonald, Audra, 92, 145, 242
McGillin, Howard, *233*
McGrath, Michael, 135
McKechnie, Donna, 112, 113, 129
McKenzie, Julia, 92, *116*, 133, 134, 242
McMahon, Jama, *238*, 239
McMahon, Kaley, 236
McMartin, John, 107, 125, *126*
McNally, Terrence, 200
McNeill, Robert Duncan, *215*
Meadows, Hazel, *10*
Mendes, Sam, 118, 223, *225*, *232*, 239
Mendez, Lindsay, 181–182
Mengers, Sue, 151–152
Merman, Ethel
    Annie Get Your Gun producers and, *25*
    in *Call Me Madam*, 114
    Church and, *65*
    foul mouth of, 58–59
    guaranteeing her participation in
        Gypsy, 60–61
    on *Gypsy* as a play, 59
    Klugman and, *67*
    Lee and, *62*
    on *The Loretta Young Show*, 58–59
    Robbins and, *58*
    Sondheim and, *59*
Merrick, David, 53, 56, 62, 74, 123
Merrily We Roll Along
    1934 play of, *183*
    1981 development of, 184–188
    audience reaction to, 188, 193
    cast album recording of, 5
    Cincinnati Playhouse in the Park
        production, 183
    deconstructed, intermission-less
        version, 182–183
    Haymarket Theatre production of,
        215
    movie adaptation of, 181
    narrative structure, 181
    New York City Encores! production,
        183
    New York Theatre Workshop
        production, 182
    "Not a Day Goes By," 215
    "Opening Doors," 189
    posters for, *188*
    previews, 188
    revivals of, 182–183, 204
    score, 181, 189
    Tunick on, *180*
Mescal, Paul, 5–7, 181
Meyers, Seth, 5

Midler, Bette, 69, 70, 152
"The Miller's Son," 142
minimalist culture, 158
Minnelli, Vincente, 16
Miranda, Lin-Manuel, 8, 183, 237, *240*
Mirisch, Walter, 44–45
Mitchell, Ruth, 145
Miyamoto, Amon, 161
Mizner, Addison and Wilson, 231, *233*
Mizzy, Robert, *56*
Monk, Debra, 221, *221*
Montevecchi, Liliane, *128*
Moreno, Rita, 49–50
Morrison, Ann, *182*, 185, *185*
Morrison, Rob, *225*
Morton, Euan, 236
Mostel, Zero
    as blacklisted, 78
    Forum casting, 77
    Gelbart and, *78*
    as Pseudolus, *80*, *84*
    reprising *Forum* role, 81
    Robbins and, 80–81, 81n
"Move On," 193
Mulaney, John, 5, *5*
Murphy, Donna, 92, *92*, 135, 226
Muscle (Fussell), 228
Myers, Pamela, 109, *116*

N

Nelson, Gene, 125, *126*
Nelson, Richard, 204
New York City Encores!, 183
New York Military Academy at Cornwall,
    15
New York State Council on the Arts, 197
New York Theatre Workshop, 182
Newsweek, 236
"Next," 160
Nicholaw, Casey, 92, 135
Nixon, Marni, 45
No, No, Nanette, 117
Nolen, Timothy, 172
nonconformity of Sondheim, 1–3
"Not a Day Goes By," 215
"Not While I'm Around," *175*
"Now," 142
Nunn, Trevor, 144, *144*

O

Obama, Barack, *9*
O'Connor, Caroline, *143*
Oh, Soon-Tek, *158*

O'Hare, Denis, 224
Oklahoma!, 19–24, *20*
Old Friends, 242
Olivier, Laurence, 150
On a Clear Day You Can See Forever
    (film), 107
On the Town, 33
On Your Toes, 22
"One More Kiss," 125
"Opening Doors," 189
Operation Desert Storm, 222
Opie, Iona and Peter, 209
Oppenheimer, George, 28–29, 91
"Order out of chaos" theme, *2*
Original Cast Album: Company, 4, 112
Original Cast Album: Co-Op, 5
Ostrow, Stuart, 123
Ovenden, Julian, *143*, 242

P

Pacific Overtures
    awakening Sondheim to Japanese
        culture, 158
    costume design, *157*, 161
    as documentary vaudeville, 161
    opening night, 239
    opening number, 158
    plot, 155, 157–158
    premiere, 157
    restaging, 161
    scenic design, 161
    score, 160
    set design, *156*
    setting as a musical, 156–157
    songs for, 158–160
    timeframe, 155
    Tony nominations, *158*, 161
Padrón, Jacob, 51
Paice, Jill, 118
Paige, Elaine, 135
Pal Joey, 54
Parry, William, *221*
Pasquale, Steven, 225
Passion, 1, 226–230
Patinkin, Mandy
    Follies in Concert performance, 128,
        128
    as Georges Seurat, 198–199, *198*
    Oscar & Steve album, 21, *21*
    presenting Tony to Sondheim, 213
    on Sondheim's genius, 199–200
Patrick, Lee, 11n
Pauk, Michelle, *232*
Pell, Paula, 5

ILLUSTRATION CREDITS

20th Century Studios/Photofest: © 20th Century Studios: 48, 50 (top), 51

Adam Scull/PHOTOlink.net: 196

The Al Hirschfeld Foundation: © The Al Hirschfeld Foundation. www.AlHirschfeldFoundation.org: 6

Alamy: 9, 121, 240, 245

Atlantis Theatrical: 172 (bottom)

Atlas Media: 184 (top)

Author's private collection: 13 (both), 14 (all), 15, 16, 26, 33 (bottom), 36, 37, 43, 47, 50 (bottom), 60, 62, 63, 69, 82, 83, 86, 88, 91, 92, 99, 101, 103 (both), 108, 120, 122, 125 (right), 128, 134, 140, 148, 150, 152, 154, 164 (both), 166, 184 (bottom), 188, 222, 227, 228, 237

The Barnstormers: 172 (top)

Bernard Gotfryd Photograph Collection/Library of Congress: 3

Bibliothèque Nationale de France: 30

Billy Rose Theatre Division, The New York Public Library: © The New York Public Library: 57

The British Broadcasting Corporation (BBC): 143, 245

British Library/Alamy: 169

Broadwaypins.com: 85 (all)

Bros Theatre Company: 191

CBS/Photofest: © CBS: 12

Classic Stage Company: 160 (bottom), 224

Clint Spaulding/PMC: © Patrick McMullan: 241

Donald Cooper/Photofest: 133

Donald Cooper/Alamy: 224

Donna Murphy: 231

Dramatists Guild Foundation: 97

DreamWorks LLC and Warner Bros. Entertainment/Photofest: © DreamWorks LLC and Warner Bros. Entertainment: 176 (photographer: Leah Gallo), 177, 179

Elektra/Photofest: 146

Eliot Elisofon/*Life*: 125

Eric Gray/Masheter Movie Archive/Alamy: 10

Ezio Petersen/Alamy: 178

Fox Broadcasting/Photofest © Fox Broadcasting: 235

Fred Palumbo/ Library of Congress Prints and Photographs Division. New York World-Telegram and the Sun Newspaper Photograph Collection: 55

Fred R. Conrad/New York Times Co./Getty Images: Front cover

George Abud: 205

George School: 18 (right)

Goodman Theatre: 237 (top)

Jacqui Dankworth: 214

Jama McMahon: 238

Jerry Jackson/HBO: 2

Joan Marcus: 182

John Stillwell/Alamy: 8

Lars Linnhoff: 203

The Long Center for the Performing Arts: 173 (top)

Melissa Errico: 201

National Theatre: 135

New York City Center: 187, 232 (bottom)

Nonesuch: 21, 118

Northwestern University: 190

Photofest: x, 4, 7, 17, 20, 23, 25, 30, 32, 33 (top), 34, 38, 39, 40, 49, 52, 54, 56, 58, 64, 65, 67, 68, 70, 72, 74, 75, 76, 79, 80, 86, 90, 93, 94, 95, 104, 106, 111, 112, 113, 115, 116, 119 (top right), 119 (bottom left), 123, 124, 126, 127, 129, 130 (both), 132, 136, 137, 138, 139, 145, 156, 157 (both), 158, 159, 162, 170, 171, 174, 175, 180, 183, 192, 197, 194, 198, 199, 202, 207, 208 (photographer: Marc Bryan-Brown), 209, 210, 212-213, 215, 218, 220, 221, 226, 233

PS Classics: 236 (top), 236

RGR Collection/Alamy: 151

Rhys Thomas/IFC: 6

Ryan Brenizer: 229

Santander Theater: 173 (bottom)

Snap/Shutterstock: 8

Temple University: 189

Theatre Magazine Company/Vandamm Studio: 19

Tiffany Babb: 110

Time: 134

Tommaso Boddi/Getty Images for ASCAP: 187

United Artists/Photofest: © United Artists: 45, 46, 78, 84

UPI/Alamy: 71

The Walt Disney Company: 216

WENN/Alamy: 119 (top left), 144

Wikimedia Commons: 28, 61

Williams College: 18 (left), 24

York Theatre: 160 (top)